FIELD GUIDE TO THE
BATTLEFIELDS
OF SOUTH AFRICA

FIELD GUIDE TO THE
BATTLEFIELDS
OF SOUTH AFRICA

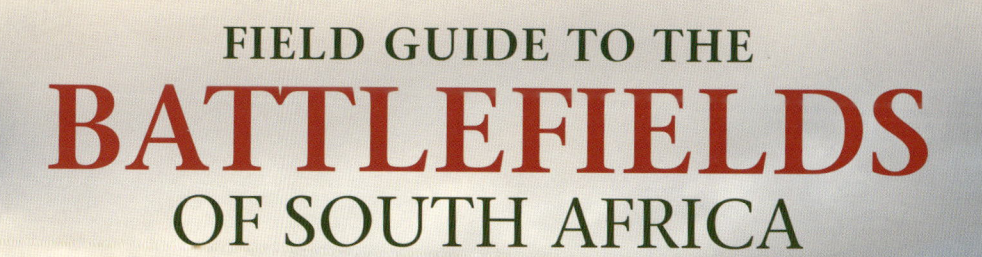

NICKI VON DER HEYDE

First published in 2013 by Struik Travel & Heritage
(an imprint of Random House Struik (Pty) Ltd)
Company Reg. No. 1966/003153/07
Wembley Square, First Floor, Solan Road, Gardens, Cape Town 8001
PO Box 1144, Cape Town 8000, South Africa

www.randomstruik.co.za

Copyright © in published edition: Random House Struik 2013
Copyright © in text: Nicki von der Heyde 2013
Copyright © in maps: MapStudio (road maps); Random House Struik (battle maps) 2013
Copyright © in photographs: See credits on page 338

PUBLISHER: Pippa Parker
MANAGING EDITOR: Roelien Theron
EDITOR: Claudia Dos Santos
CONCEPT DESIGNER: Janice Evans
DESIGNER: Sean Robertson
CARTOGRAPHER (BATTLE MAPS): Liezel Bohdanowicz
PROJECT ASSISTANT: Alana Bolligelo
PICTURE RESEARCHER: Colette Stott
PROOFREADER: Lesley Hay-Whitton
INDEXER: Michel Cozien

Reproduction by Hirt & Carter Cape (Pty) Ltd
Printing and binding: 1010 Printing International Ltd, China

ISBN (Print) 978 1 43170 100 1
ISBN (ePub) 978 1 92054 575 8
ISBN (PDF) 978 1 92054 576 5

10 9 8 7 6 5 4 3 2 1

All rights reserved. No part of this publication may be reproduced,
stored in a retrieval system or transmitted, in any form or by any means,
electronic, mechanical, photocopying, recording or otherwise, without the prior written
permission of the publishers and the copyright holder(s).

While every effort has been made to ensure that the information in this book
was correct at the time of going to press, some details might since have changed.
The authors and publishers accept no responsibility for any consequences, loss,
injury, damage or inconvenience sustained by any person using this book.
Please email any comments or updates to: battlefields_fieldguide@randomstruik.co.za

Get monthly updates and news by subscribing to our newsletter at
www.randomstruik.co.za

Front cover (clockwise from top): Zulu king Cetshwayo; British troops marching to Johannesburg, Gauteng, 1900; Victoria Cross medal; Mauser rifle; Graves at the Isandlwana battle site near Nqutu, KwaZulu-Natal; Battle of Groenkop monument near Kestell, Free State. **Half-title page**: British troops at Fort Nolela the day before the Battle of Ulundi, 1879. **Title page**: Boer monument on the summit of Spioenkop Mountain near Ladysmith, KwaZulu-Natal. **Back cover (clockwise from top)**: Queen's South Africa medal; General Koos de la Rey; General Sir Redvers Buller; Bloemfontein concentration camp.

Preface

In my early twenties I represented Western Province in the equestrian sports of eventing and show jumping. In an old seven-ton lorry, converted into a six-berth horse carrier, I would trundle between Cape Town, Johannesburg, Durban, Port Elizabeth and even Windhoek to compete. During many long hours spent rumbling along quiet roads, my curiosity was aroused by the ubiquitous and sometimes mysterious brown tourism signs found beside country roads throughout South Africa that pointed to battlefields or monuments. However, when I got around to visiting some of these sites with the recommended guide, I often found the account of the action so detailed and localised that the bigger picture remained blurred and largely unintelligible to a layperson like me. I wanted to know more about the background and the context, and perhaps less about the military detail.

Later, I became a guide myself and took delight in making the battles come alive for others. I found that women can be enthralled by tales of battle if the human aspects are brought to the fore. They want to hear who the soldiers were, how they lived and died, their tragedy and elation, the acts of bravery, heroism and, sometimes, betrayal. Male visitors are responsive to this approach as well – after all, what is a battle except the individual actions of each man acting in obedience (or, occasionally, disobedience) to his orders?

I hope this book will help readers piece together the jigsaw puzzle of South African military history – the power-play between black and white, Boer and Briton, Zulu and other African peoples, as well as the roles played by missionaries and traders. I write for the mainstream reader, not just the battlefield enthusiast or military historian, and do not profess to offer many new insights into the battles described in this book. Where original source material was not readily available, I drew on other writers' descriptions.

The scope of the work has made it impossible to cover every battle, or any one event in great depth, and readers are encouraged to read more detailed accounts *after* visiting the sites. One thing I have learnt is that detailed reports, even by those who participated, vary greatly. Consequently, some of what I have written may be contentious and I look forward to the comments and assertions of candid readers.

I hope to encourage people to delve a little deeper into the past and to emerge from their exploration with greater tolerance towards those of different race groups or political persuasions, whose many previous conflicts and clashes have forged South Africa's unique 'rainbow nation'. If we do not understand the past, how can we make sense of the present, or ponder the future? We live in a beautiful land whose rich soil has soaked in too much blood. Let us look forward to a more peaceful place, where battlefields are a curiosity and not the norm of human existence.

Nicki von der Heyde
Underberg, 2013

Contents

Acknowledgements 9
Foreword 10
About this book 12
Introduction: Battle categories 14
Map 22

KWAZULU-NATAL 24

**PIETERMARITZBURG
& DURBAN REGION** 26
Battle of **Zaailaager** 28
Battle of **Durban** 31
Battle of **Mome Gorge** 34

ULUNDI REGION 38
Battle of **Ndondakasuka** 40
Battle of **Gingingdlovu** 43
Battle of **Italeni** 48

*TOP: British troops ride into a Boer ambush in the Transvaal during the 2nd Anglo-Boer War.
LEFT: Matabele (Ndebele) warrior illustrated by Charles Bell*

Battle of **Gqokli Hill**	51
Battle of **Ulundi**	53
Battle of **Tshaneni**	56
LADYSMITH REGION	**58**
Battle of **Willowgrange**	60
Armoured train disaster and Churchill's capture	66
Battle of **Colenso**	69
Battle of **Spioenkop**	80
Battle of **Vaalkrans**	92
Battle of **Tugela Heights**	98
Battle of **Platrand**	106
Battle of **Ladysmith**	112
Battle of **Rietfontein**	118
Battle of **Elandslaagte**	120
Battle of **Surrender Hill**	126
Battle of **Groenkop**	129

DUNDEE REGION	**132**
Battle of **Isandlwana**	134
Battle of **Rorke's Drift**	144
Death of the Prince Imperial of France	150
Battle of **Talana Hill**	153
Battle of **Blood River**	162
Battle of **Blood River Poort**	165
Battle of **Scheeper's Nek**	167
Battle of **Hlobane**	169
Battle of **Khambula**	173
Battle of **Holkrans**	178
NEWCASTLE REGION	**180**
Battle of **Ingogo**	182
Battle of **Botha's Pass**	185
Battle of **Laing's Nek**	187
Battle of **Majuba Hill**	189
Battle of **Alleman Nek**	196

GAUTENG & SURROUNDS — 200

PRETORIA, JOHANNESBURG & SURROUNDING REGIONS — 202

Battle of **Bergendal**	205
Battle of **Bakenlaagte**	208
Battle of **Rhenosterkop**	210
Battle of **Bronkhorstspruit**	212
Battle of **Diamond Hill**	215
Battle of **Doornkop**	220
Battle of **Roodewal**	223
Battle of **Doornkraal**	226
Battle of **Rooiwal**	228
Battle of **Vegkop**	231

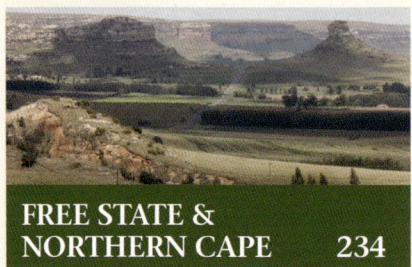

FREE STATE & NORTHERN CAPE — 234

BLOEMFONTEIN & KIMBERLEY REGIONS — 236

Battle of **Biddulphsberg**	240
Battle of **Berea**	242
Battle of **Sannaspos**	245
Battle of **Driefontein**	249
Battle of **Poplar Grove**	251
Battle of **Paardeberg**	254
Battle of **Boshof**	258
Battle of **Magersfontein**	260
Battle of **Modder River**	268
Battle of **Koedoesberg Drift**	274
Battle of **Graspan**	277
Battle of **Belmont**	280
Battle of **Fabersput**	282
Battle of **Lattakoo**	284

COLESBERG REGION — 286

Battle of **Boomplaats**	288
Battle of **Swartkoppies**	291
Battle of **Pink Hill**	296
Battle of **West Australia Hill**	298
Battle of **Stormberg**	301
Battle of **Labuschagne's Nek**	305

EASTERN CAPE — 312

GRAHAMSTOWN REGION — 314

Slagtersnek Rebellion	317
Battle of **Grahamstown**	319

WESTERN CAPE — 322

CAPE TOWN REGION — 324

Battle of **Muizenberg**	326
Battle of **Blaauwberg**	330

Chronology of battles and checklist	334
Glossary	337
Bibliography	338
Picture credits	341
Index	344

Acknowledgements

My special thanks go to author and historian Professor Donal McCracken, for his keen enthusiasm and help with this project, and to Patricia McCracken, who introduced me to Claudia Dos Santos at Random House Struik, an enthusiastic participant in what turned out to be a mammoth project.

Thank you, Peter Jarvis, my photographer and companion during the extensive field trips, who was a steady and unfailing support in every circumstance. Together we travelled over 6,000km in a Land Rover and another 4,000km in the car or on motorbikes in the quest for photographs and information. Some of the roads were not signposted and we learned that our bossy Garmin lady is not always right.

I owe a debt of thanks to the late Professor Barnard, who shared with me with his passion for Anglo-Boer War history and whose maps (which first appeared in his book *Generaal Botha op die Natalse Front*) inspired some of those that are included in this book. Thank you, Liezel Bohdanowicz, for your skill and thoroughness in producing all the battle maps as they now appear in the book.

Thank you to Charles Aikenhead for providing me with some of the historic pictures in the book, many of which have not been published before, and to Ken Gillings for giving me directions to some of the more obscure sites in KwaZulu-Natal. Ken is always generous with his knowledge, and much of the information for the Battle of Tshaneni was gleaned from a talk he gave to the Military History Society in October 2010.

Ron Lock, well-known author of books about the battlefields, started me on my guiding career and has remained a good friend. Historian Robin Smith gave me information on a battlefield that I had never heard of and proved a rich and willing source of detailed knowledge. Chris Moore helped me with research and Chris Schoeman provided input to the battle accounts in the book. The inhabitants of the Marais Farm at Groenkop were generous with their time, directing us to the trail leading up the hill and allowing us access to their farmlands. The account of the Battle of Groenkop is drawn largely from information in a booklet available from them, which was written and researched by J. A. J. and J. Lourens, whose grandfather was killed in the battle. Mrs Elaine Faber owns the farm Moja, where the Battle of Fabersput was fought. Thank you for allowing us access to your land.

Thank you to Delia and John Francis who had me to stay in their lovely Hillcrest home each time I travelled to Durban to visit libraries, museums or archives.

Roelien Theron of Random House Struik has been a tireless and meticulous managing editor of the book. She combined her great inspiration with amazing attention to detail, eventually pulling all the threads together to produce an integrated and attractive whole.

Lastly, I thank my children, Luke and Stephanie, who without demur saw me take a year off work to live on a farm near Underberg and write this book, a project they selflessly encouraged and supported.

Foreword

There are two major types of battlefield terrain in South Africa: first the open plains, the areas of scrub bush, savannah lands of acacia trees and of occasional flat-topped koppies, a land where cavalry rules supreme. Here the horse was less prone to sickness and the ox-wagon could trundle along at the leisurely pace of a human being – but for longer. The second type of battle terrain is the thorn bush, especially of the Eastern Cape. This allowed for a mixture of warfare engagements, but skirmishing was generally the order of the day rather than set-piece battles. Then in what is now KwaZulu-Natal, the two terrains merge to create the country's most dramatic battlefield landscape. Here were the March lands of South Africa, where the fates of colony, republic and kingdom were decided. The gracefully winding Tugela River runs through what is, in effect, one of the largest military graveyards in the world.

In the Eastern Cape and KwaZulu-Natal, the British found military movement difficult, having to depend too much on the lumbering ox-wagon. It is said that the pace of the 1879 Anglo-Zulu War was dictated by the speed of British military wagons. The British military commander, Lord Chelmsford, drily observed: 'Ox-wagon transport is enough to destroy the reputation of a number of commanders.' This was in stark difference to the relatively rapid advance of Lord Roberts a generation later when the primary modes of transport of military ordnance were rail and horse-drawn wagons.

South Africa's most all-encompassing war prior to the 1980s Border War was the 2nd Anglo-Boer War (1899–1902). Hundreds of thousands of men fought in the conflict, which inevitably also pulled in large numbers of Africans, who served in a variety of roles, including armed combatants. In that conflict, the British authorities used over half a million mules and horses. While railways played an important part in the conflict, not least in frequently dictating the line of battle, this was one of the last great horse wars. This is reflected in the fact that 400,000 or 60 per cent of military horses and mules died during the campaign.

The Anglo-Boer War was certainly the last great cavalry war of the modern era, especially with the advent of the mounted commando guerrilla phase of the war. But, as in the Anglo-Zulu War, ox- or mule-drawn wagons were still an important part of the conflict. As an ox-wagon team was usually 16 animals, this meant the supply of some 35,000 'salted' oxen for the conflict. This was military-transport logistics on a gigantic scale, not to be equalled until World War I.

This volume by Nicki von der Heyde is ground-breaking in that it is the first on-the-ground practical guide for the whole of the country. For that she is to be commended. It is a useful tool for the professional and enthusiastic amateur military historian and discerning heritage tourist. Of course, candid friends will inevitably point out that such-and-such an engagement is not included. What constitutes a battle and what a skirmish is a moot point.

Nicki von der Heyde is a woman in a man's world. Or is she? Women are an integral part of warfare, if in the past not frontline troops. Their roles were usually behind the scenes and more subtle than violent, although there are a few exceptions. There were female nurses and war correspondents as well as the countless women, be they on the Boer side or African refugees, huddled into insanitary concentration camps. So there is nothing incongruous in a woman writing on war and battles, especially one whose professional career is built on battlefield guiding.

The heritage potential for South Africa's battlefields is tremendous, but the reality is that very little has been done to unleash that potential. This is in part because, in the post-revolutionary era in which we live, battles and wars of dispossession are inevitably a sensitive subject. South Africa's heritage industry has to bite the bullet and come to terms with the reality that colonial battlefields attract foreign tourists. They are often likely to be tourists whose ancestors were in colonial armies who fought against indigenous peoples. These are not latter-day, erstwhile, new-age imperialists, though, but more often than not highly educated modern denizens of the world.

On the ground, the scarcity of good signage means that it is all too often practically impossible for a visitor, whether local or foreign, to come away from a battle site with a comprehensive idea of what happened and where. Isolated interpretation centres solve the problem only partially. Kimberley, Mafikeng and Ladysmith need to establish a triumvirate to attract siege tourists; and showpiece historical action needs to become the order of the day. The topography of the Battle of Waterloo has long since been destroyed, that of Isandlwana has not. South Africa has a headstart over a multitude of foreign battlefield sites.

Visiting a battlefield is an act of imagination. Before one lies a maize field or a bend in a slow-moving, muddy-grey river. And yet it was here that for a few hours long ago the sound of musketry resounded across the valley where regimental discipline was pitted against raw courage; modern armament against tradition; and might against tenacity. The 'playing field' was seldom even. When the rest of the world was outlawing soft-nosed or dum-dum bullets in the 1890s, British Military Intelligence was decreeing their use when 'we have to deal with savages or with an enemy who is himself using an expanded bullet'. The civilised rules of warfare tended to be ignored on these African battlefields.

Battlefields determine the future, but they also unfold and expose the human condition. They place humans in extraordinary and often terrifying situations. They foster the primitive and curb enlightened thought. And yet they also create the stoic cynicism of the timeless soldier. As the fusilier remarked when his decimated regiment slowly pulled out of that charnel field – the river loop at Colenso: 'Sure, this beats Athlone on a Saturday night.'

Donal P. McCracken,
D.Phil., F.R.Hist.S.
Senior Professor of History, University of KwaZulu-Natal

About this book

This book presents a fresh look at South African history – from the perspective of conflict and war. It discusses 71 battles, which encompass three major wars and a series of conflicts, ranging from the colonial clashes of the 18th and 19th centuries to the 2nd Anglo-Boer War of 1899–1902. Accounts of the engagements are informative and lively, and special attention is given to historical background, action and outcomes.

The book is structured geographically (with the traveller in mind) according to five main provincial sections: KwaZulu-Natal; Gauteng and surrounds (including Mpumalanga and North West); Free State and Northern Cape; Eastern Cape; and Western Cape. These sections are further divided into 10 regions and individual battles are discussed within each region.

As far as possible, battle discussions are grouped to align with current provincial boundaries. However, exceptions are made where a nearby battle site falls just outside a provincial boundary but is in close proximity to other sites under discussion in the given province.

Battle accounts follow a logical geographical order, again with the traveller in mind and to allow for an overall understanding of the diverse engagements that took place in a given region over time. Proposed routes are clearly indicated on the maps at the start of each of the 10 regional chapters. For a list of battles in *chronological order*, consult pages 334–336.

COLOUR GUIDE

The battles are divided into six categories. They are colour-coded as a quick visual aid to the type of battle under discussion (or cross-referenced elsewhere in the book).

- ■ Colonial and frontier conflicts
- ■ Indigenous conflicts
- ■ Voortrekker battles
- ■ Anglo-Zulu War
- ■ 1st Anglo-Boer War
- ■ 2nd Anglo-Boer War

The six battle categories are explained in detail on pages 14–21.

Battle accounts typically feature five elements: directions to the battle site; context; action; aftermath; and a list of main combatants. Timelines accompanying the battle accounts may include references to other battles, biographical details of protagonists or historical events. In addition, some of the major engagements are illustrated with customised maps and annotations describing the events on the day of the battle.

It is recommended that you use a road map in conjunction with the directions to the battlefields provided in this book. GPS co-ordinates are given for some sites that are not clearly signposted or are relatively inaccessible. Consider visiting the more difficult-to-reach sites with a registered South African Tourism (SATOUR) battlefields guide. In most centres, the local tourism offices will be able to supply a list of guides who specialise in battlefield tours.

The **opener** provides a brief account of the terrain and history of the region under discussion.

A **map** indicates the main cities and towns as well as the locations of the battle sites discussed in the given region.

A **locator map** shows the region in relation to the province and the country.

The battle sites are listed in **geographical order**. The battle accounts follow the same sequence.

The **international timeline** contrasts local battles with global events to provide a snapshot of the political environment at the time.

Colour coding helps to identify the category to which each battle belongs.

Detailed **directions** to battle sites are given at the beginning of each battle account.

Fact files highlight topics of general and human interest.

Features explore specific war- or battle-related themes.

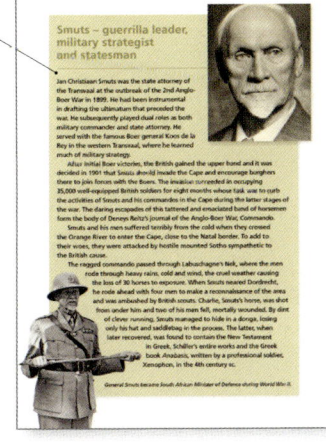

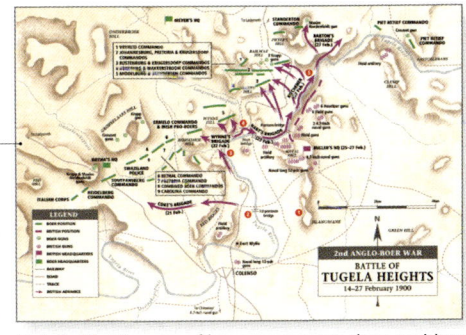

The **timeline** contains information preceding and following the battle and may also highlight significant events or profiles of major military figures.

The historical context, the progress of the battle and its outcomes, and a list of key combatants are given in each **battle account**.

Detailed **battle maps** of key engagements show positions and troop movements.

ABOUT THIS BOOK **13**

Introduction: Battle categories

This book focuses on 71 battles that were fought in South Africa between 1795 and 1906. These cover three wars – the Anglo-Zulu War and the 1st and 2nd Anglo-Boer wars – as well as a range of conflicts that arose from colonisation by the Dutch and the British, and clashes between different African societies over resources and territory.

In December 1850, Xhosa chief Sandile's attack on the British in the Boomah Pass in the Amatole Mountains led to the Eighth Frontier War.

To distinguish between them, the battles have been clustered into six general categories. Whereas the battles associated with a particular war are easily defined, there is a range of other significant engagements that are broadly described here as 'colonial and frontier conflicts', 'indigenous conflicts' and 'Voortrekker battles'. Each category is explained below, and includes a description of the origins of the various conflicts. The categories are colour coded throughout the book (see p. 12) so as to aid identification of the specific type of battle under discussion and to enable the reader to find other, related engagements in the same category that may appear in different sections of the book.

■ Colonial and frontier conflicts (1795–1906)

The Cape, at the southern tip of Africa, was strategically placed on the shipping route between Europe and the Far East, making it a desirable acquisition for European naval powers. The Dutch East India Company had established a refreshment station there in 1652, but Britain, for political reasons, soon contested the harbour.

Trade with the East brought sailing ships – and European settlers – to the Cape.

The first British occupation of the Cape in 1795, following the Battle of Muizenberg, put the small port in British hands until 1802, when the Treaty of Amiens returned it to the Batavian Republic, as Holland was then known. In 1806, however, fear of French influence in Holland at a time when Napoleon's empire was expanding caused Britain once again to take possession of the Cape. Presaged by the Battle of Blaauwberg, the second occupation was to put South Africa under British rule for more than a century.

As European settlers in the Cape extended their farms inland, they inevitably came into conflict with other stock farmers, including the indigenous Khoikhoi and Xhosa. A series of raids and counter-raids ensued. The hostilities, known collectively as the frontier wars, spanned almost 100 years. By the time the ninth, and final, frontier war ended, in 1878, Xhosa resistance to colonial expansion was crushed, and a modicum of peace settled on the eastern front.

At the end of the year, the British army moved from the eastern Cape to Natal, where they embarked, in 1879, on the Anglo-Zulu War. British influence in Port Natal had begun as early as 1822, with the arrival of traders of British origin in Durban Bay. Later, in 1842, the immigrants came into conflict with farmers of Dutch, German and French descent (known as Voortrekkers), who had left the Cape to escape British rule. This clash, known as the Battle of Durban (Congella), was to lead to the colonisation of Natal under Great Britain in 1845.

There was trouble in other frontier regions too. Incursions by the Voortrekkers into the territory north of the Orange River led to clashes with indigenous groups, such as the Ndebele and the Griqua, who had already settled in the area. Unrest developed into open conflict at the battles of Swartkoppies and Boomplaats in 1845 and 1848, respectively. There were also conflicts with the Sotho in southern Transorangia (Free State), and a retaliatory raid by the British against Moshoeshoe was the cause of the Battle of Berea.

■ Indigenous conflicts (1823–84)

The battles in this category are not part of one war, as are those, for example, that make up the Anglo-Zulu War. However, a common thread links them: they are characterised by conflict between the indigenous peoples in southern Africa and invariably arose from competition for supremacy as well as resources such as grazing land for cattle.

Competition for resources caused conflict between indigenous peoples during the 18th and 19th centuries.

INTRODUCTION: BATTLE CATEGORIES   15

Two Zulu factions clashed at Tshaneni Mountain near Mkuze in northern KwaZulu-Natal in 1884.

The warfare that spread through the interior and south-eastern coastal regions of South Africa during the later 18th and mid-19th centuries is referred to by historians as the Mfecane or Difaqane. In these battles for power and territory, the vanquished would either join the victorious, or be displaced and forced to find other land for settlement and grazing.

Indigenous conflicts detailed in this guide include those fought in the Northern Cape, at Lattakoo (near present-day Dithakong), and in KwaZulu-Natal, at Gqokli Hill and Tshaneni.

■ Voortrekker battles (1836–48)

In the early 1830s, white settler farmers living along the north-eastern frontier of the Cape Colony suffered under continuous raids from the Xhosa east of the border. The farmers looked to the British government in the Cape Colony for support and were dissatisfied when no decisive action was taken to protect them. There was further discontent about the amount of compensation paid by the government for their emancipated slaves, as well as with the Cape government's policy of equality between black and white. There was increasing talk among the settlers of leaving the Cape to seek greater peace and security further north. Early in the year 1836, the first families left the Cape to venture into the interior. This was the beginning of a movement called the Great Trek.

The Voortrekkers travelled north in separate groups, each led by a man who was fiercely independent and who did not co-operate easily with other Voortrekker leaders. Each group travelled independently, its long train of ox-wagons containing the Trekkers' only worldly

Voortrekkers bound northwards beat off Ndebele warriors at Vegkop near present-day Heilbron in the Free State.

possessions. These people would, in time, form the independent Boer republics of the Orange Free State and the Transvaal.

As they made their way slowly northwards, they encountered new adversaries: indigenous African societies that were already established in large regions of the interior. When a group of Voortrekkers, led by Hendrik Potgieter, came across the Ndebele (Matabele) in what is today the Free State, conflicts arose over grazing land needed for the Voortrekkers' vast herds of livestock. Tensions reached a head at the Battle of Vegkop. The Ndebele fought the Voortrekkers several times after this and were eventually driven north, where they settled in what is today Zimbabwe.

One small group of Voortrekkers reached the Soutpansberg, north of Pretoria, and travelled from there towards the east coast. Nothing was ever seen of them again and it was rumoured that they had all been killed by a party of raiding Shangaan. Another small group succeeded in reaching Portuguese Lourenço Marques (Maputo) in 1838.

Voortrekker leader Piet Retief

One Voortrekker leader, Piet Retief, turned eastward with his followers, to enter Natal over the Drakensberg escarpment. There the group came up against the Zulu nation and a number of bloody encounters resulted, culminating in the Battle of Blood River in 1838.

■ Anglo-Zulu War (1879)

When Cetshwayo became leader of the Zulu nation in 1856, he was determined to regain for his people some of the power and prestige they had enjoyed during Shaka's reign between 1818 and 1828. He reintroduced the law that no young man be allowed to marry until he had 'washed his spear in blood' and trained up a 40,000-strong army that was both efficient and warlike.

A severe drought in 1878 caused increasing tensions between farmers in the Transvaal (which was at the time a British colony) and the Zulu on the southern border of the colony. A boundary commission set up in 1878 found that the Boers had no rights to land east of the Blood (Ncome) River, which had long been inhabited by the Zulu. This decision caused great dissatisfaction among the already truculent Transvaal Boers, who believed Britain consistently sided against them. Britain wished to keep the peace and had to find a way to appease them.

Here, on the banks of the Tugela River, the British presented an ultimatum to the Zulu nation in December 1878, presaging the Anglo-Zulu War of 1879.

These circumstances played into the hands of Lord Carnarvon, the colonial secretary in London, who had plans for a British confederation of southern African states. However, as long as there was a militant and independent Zulu kingdom on the Natal and Transvaal

These Zulu men, citizens of the British colony of Natal, formed part of the British army that invaded Zululand in 1879.

borders, a peaceful confederation could not be achieved, and the best solution seemed to be to provoke, and win, a war with the Zulu. The Boers could then be appeased with land awards in Zululand, and expansionist plans for the confederation could go ahead.

Britain had an army in South Africa at the time, fighting the Xhosa in the eastern Cape Colony, and this made implementation of the plan simpler. Various pretexts were cobbled together to devise an ultimatum, which was presented to Cetshwayo in December 1878. The Zulu king prevaricated, trying to avoid confrontation, but his attempts at conciliation were rebuffed. When the terms of the ultimatum were not met, a British army invaded Zululand in January 1879.

The British suffered a terrible defeat at the Battle of Isandlwana and were forced to withdraw from Zululand to wait for reinforcements from England before launching a second invasion later in the year, in June. This time the British were successful; after the final batttle of the war, the Battle of Ulundi, in July, the independence and power of the Zulu nation were completely destroyed.

■ 1st Anglo-Boer War (1880–81)

In 1877 the independent Boer republic of the Transvaal was annexed by Britain as part of a larger plan to confederate the southern African states. The annexation was promulgated with little protest from the Volksraad, whose members were well aware of the fact that the arid and landlocked republic was impoverished. There was not enough money to pay government officials, let alone support an army, and yet there were serious threats from hostile groups on and within the borders. The tensions were exacerbated by frequent droughts that caused competition with the neighbouring Zulu for the rich grazing grounds that separated them.

Not all the Boers in the Transvaal were in favour of annexation, however. Deputy president Paul Kruger went to Europe to raise support for his objections, but to no avail. During the next two years circumstances changed for the Boers in the Transvaal. The Anglo-Zulu War had resulted

As a result of the 1st Anglo-Boer War, the Transvaal regained its independence, with Paul Kruger as president.

in the demise of the Zulu kingdom and greatly lessened the threat from Zululand. The war had, paradoxically, also shown the Boers that the British could be beaten: at the Battle of Isandlwana in January 1879 Zulu warriors armed mostly with assegais and shields had inflicted a humiliating defeat on a British army well equipped with the latest weaponry.

The British administrator in the Transvaal, Colonel Sir Owen Lanyon, was an arrogant, tactless man whose policies caused much resentment among the locals, and slowly Boer resistance grew. In December 1880, the burghers decreed the restoration of the republic. Shots were first exchanged in Potchefstroom, where the Boers, intent on using the town's printing press to publish the new decree, clashed with the British garrison. A column of British soldiers despatched from the east to reinforce the Pretoria garrison was ambushed by Boers and shot to pieces at the Battle of Bronkhorstspruit. Lanyon was forced to request help from the armed forces in the British colony of Natal and the passage of these troops was bitterly contested at the Battle of Laing's Nek. Two more battles were fought before Britain, where the political climate had changed from one of expansionism to one less acquisitive, granted the Transvaal its independence.

Colonel Sir Owen Lanyon, unpopular administrator of the Transvaal

■ 2nd Anglo-Boer War (1899–1902)

By the year 1854, both the Transvaal and the Orange Free State had been recognised as independent Boer republics. This meant that South Africa was divided between Britain, which governed the Cape and Natal, and the Boers, who presided in the Transvaal and the Orange Free State. However, peace prevailed between Boer and Briton in South Africa

The Boer army was a citizen force containing many fighters of different circumstances, backgrounds and experience.

INTRODUCTION: BATTLE CATEGORIES   19

General Louis Botha (centre left, seated) and Lord Kitchener (centre right, seated) with senior Boer commanders and staff officers during the peace negotiations that brought the 2nd Anglo-Boer War to an end in 1902

and might have continued, had it not been for the discovery, in 1886, of enormous quantities of gold under the Witwatersrand (where Johannesburg now stands). There was seven times more gold under the ground there than in all the other known gold reserves in the world at that time.

This resulted in the sudden arrival in the Transvaal of gold diggers, fortune seekers, gamblers and swindlers, most of them British citizens. President Paul Kruger, fearing for the hard-won independence of the Boers, opposed the influence of these Uitlanders. He taxed them unmercifully, while at the same time refusing to give them the franchise. Grievances accumulated and culminated in the abortive Jameson Raid of 1896 – an attempt to invade the Transvaal using mainly armed police, and to instigate a pro-uitlander rebellion. Sponsored by Cecil John Rhodes, the raiders got within a few kilometres of Johannesburg before they were ambushed by the Boers and shot or taken prisoner.

Famous Boer generals (left to right): Christiaan de Wet, Koos de la Rey and Louis Botha

20   FIELD GUIDE TO THE BATTLEFIELDS OF SOUTH AFRICA

The raid convinced Kruger that Britain was intent on war; he sent emissaries overseas to purchase the latest guns and rifles to equip his citizen force. In 1899, he issued an ultimatum to Britain, which made war inevitable. Britain believed the war would soon be over, as the dominant view was that an army made up of untrained Boer farmers would not be able to withstand a properly trained and disciplined army. The Boers, well equipped with modern weaponry, scored some notable victories in the early stages of the war and hoped that these successes would result in an easy capitulation by Britain. But Britain poured reinforcements into the country and carried on fighting. By February 1900 the tide of the war had turned and the Boers were on the defensive. However, they were not willing to surrender and changed

By March 1900 British troops fighting in the 2nd Anglo-Boer War had occupied nearly all the Orange Free State towns. Here the Union Jack is hoisted in Ficksburg.

their tactics, engaging in a form of guerrilla warfare that the British found very difficult to counter. There were striking Boer victories at Groenkop in December 1901, and at Ysterspruit and Tweebosch in 1902, before peace was eventually negotiated in May 1902. The war had lasted almost three years.

The peace treaty that ended the 2nd Anglo-Boer War was signed at Melrose House in Pretoria.

MAP OF SOUTH AFRICA

The siege of Mafeking, November 1899-February 1900

1. Western Cape
2. Northern Cape
3. Eastern Cape
4. Free State
5. North West
6. Gauteng
7. Limpopo
8. Mpumalanga
9. KwaZulu-Natal

BOTSWANA

NAMIBIA

Nossob

Kuruman

N14

Upington
Keimoes
Campbell

Vioolsdrif
Orange
Pofadder
Kenhardt
N10
Prieska

Port Nolloth
N7
N14
Springbok

ATLANTIC OCEAN

NORTHERN CAPE

Brandvlei
Carnarvon
N12
Victoria West
Loxton
N1

Vredendal
Calvinia
Fish
Vanrhynsdorp
GREAT KAROO
Fraserburg
Lambert's Bay
Clanwilliam
Sutherland
Beaufort West

St Helena Bay
Paternoster
Vredenburg
WESTERN CAPE
Langebaan
N1
Prince Albert
N9
Yzerfontein
Ceres
Touws River
N12
Malmesbury
Ladismith
Oudtshoorn
Bloubergstrand
N7
Paarl
Worcester
LITTLE KAROO
George
Table Bay
Stellenbosch
Robertson
CAPE TOWN
Muizenberg
N2
Swellendam
Riversdale
N2
Mossel Bay
Knysna
Simon's Town
False Bay
Caledon
Vlees Bay
Hermanus
Bredasdorp
St Sebastian Bay
Walker Bay
Gansbaai
Arniston
L'Agulhas

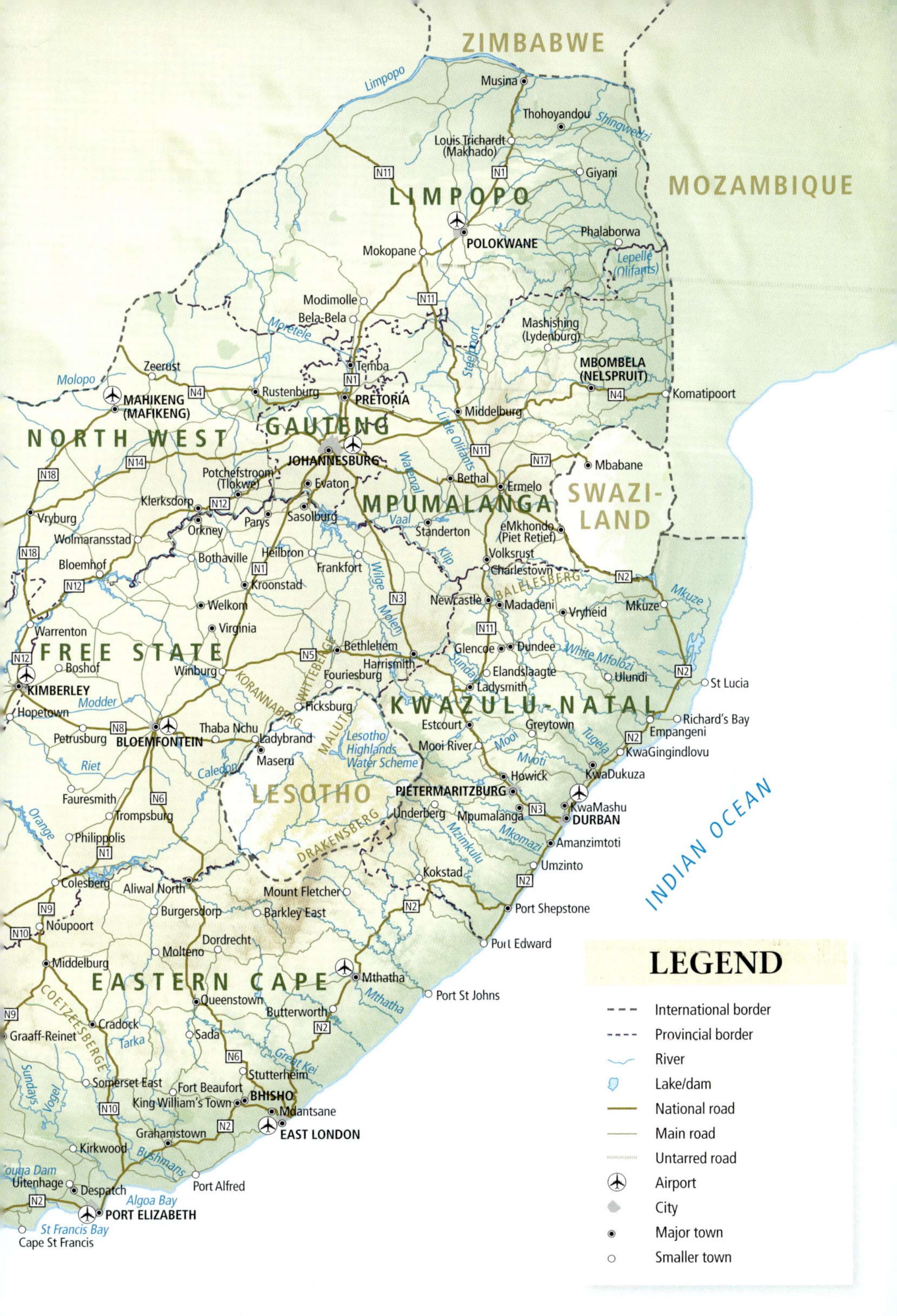
ZIMBABWE
Limpopo
Musina
Thohoyandou
Shingwedzi
Louis Trichardt (Makhado)
N11
N1
Giyani
MOZAMBIQUE
LIMPOPO
POLOKWANE
Phalaborwa
Mokopane
Lepelle (Olifants)
Modimolle
N11
Bela-Bela
Mogalakwena
Mashishing (Lydenburg)
Steelpoort
Temba
MBOMBELA (NELSPRUIT)
Zeerust
N1
Molopo
Rustenburg
N4
PRETORIA
N4
Komatipoort
MAHIKENG (MAFIKENG)
Middelburg
GAUTENG
Little Olifants
NORTH WEST
JOHANNESBURG
N11
N14
N17
Mbabane
N18
Potchefstroom (Tlokwe)
Evaton
Waterval
Bethal
Ermelo
SWAZI-LAND
Klerksdorp
N12
Sasolburg
MPUMALANGA
Vryburg
Parys
Vaal
Standerton
Orkney
eMkhondo (Piet Retief)
Wolmaransstad
N18
Bothaville
Heilbron
Frankfort
Klip
Volksrust
Bloemhof
N1
Wilge
Charlestown
N12
Kroonstad
BALELESBERG
N2
Welkom
N3
Newcastle
Madadeni
Vryheid
Mkuze
Mkuze
Molen
Virginia
N11
Warrenton
FREE STATE
WITTEBERGE
Bethlehem
Glencoe
Dundee
White Mfolozi
N12
N5
Harrismith
Boshof
Winburg
Sundays
Elandslaagte
N2
Ulundi
St Lucia
Fouriesburg
Ladysmith
KIMBERLEY
KORANNABERG
Modder
Ficksburg
KWAZULU-NATAL
Hopetown
MALUTI
Estcourt
Greytown
Richard's Bay
N8
Thaba Nchu
Lesotho Highlands Water Scheme
Tugela
Empangeni
Petrusburg
BLOEMFONTEIN
Ladybrand
Mooi River
Mooi
N2
KwaGingindlovu
Maseru
Mvoti
Riet
Caledon
Howick
KwaDukuza
LESOTHO
PIETERMARITZBURG
Fauresmith
N6
Orange
Trompsburg
Underberg
Mpumalanga
N3
KwaMashu
DURBAN
DRAKENSBERG
Mzimkulu
Mkomazi
Philippolis
Amanzimtoti
INDIAN OCEAN
N1
Umzinto
Colesberg
Kokstad
Aliwal North
Mount Fletcher
N2
N9
Burgersdorp
Barkley East
N2
Port Shepstone
Noupoort
N10
Dordrecht
Molteno
Port Edward
Middelburg
EASTERN CAPE
Mthatha
COETZEESBERGE
Mthatha
Port St Johns
Queenstown
N9
Butterworth
Cradock
Graaff-Reinet
N2
Tarka
Sada
N6
Great Kei
Sundays
Stutterheim
Somerset East
Vogel
Fort Beaufort
BHISHO
King William's Town
N10
Mdantsane
Grahamstown
N2
EAST LONDON
Kirkwood
Bushmans
Kouga Dam
Uitenhage
Port Alfred
Despatch
N2
Algoa Bay
PORT ELIZABETH
St Francis Bay
Cape St Francis
LEGEND
International border
Provincial border
River
Lake/dam
National road
Main road
Untarred road
Airport
City
Major town
Smaller town

Helpmakaar
LADYSMITH
Colenso
Tugela R.
WEENEN
Estcourt
N A T A L
GREYTOWN
Mooi R
FOR VALOUR

KwaZulu-Natal

Drakensberg Mountains

Pietermaritzburg & Durban region

This area was a melting pot where Zulu, British and Boer fought and merged to create the colourful history of KwaZulu-Natal. The first indigenous people to live here, the San, were displaced and driven into the mountains by the Nguni people, who first settled in latter-day South Africa around 1700 years ago. From around 1810 most of the Nguni clans in the Natal region were integrated into the powerful Zulu kingdom, ruled by King Shaka between 1818 and 1828.

The British army camp in Durban, 1842, now the site of the Old Fort

The first white people to inhabit Durban and explore inland were British traders and hunters who sailed up the coast from the Cape in the early 1820s. The wagon track between Durban and the interior crossed the Msunduzi River at the site of what was to become Pietermaritzburg. British settlers established cordial relations with King Shaka, but were to clash with the Voortrekkers, who arrived in the area after 1836. However, after the Bloukrans Massacre (see p. 29) in 1838, the British settlers sided with the Voortrekkers against the Zulu.

Regional battles

	1838	1842
	Zaailaager	Durban

World events

1832	1837	1844	1846
The Great Reform Bill is passed in Great Britain; it gives the lower classes greater representation in the British parliament.	Queen Victoria is crowned less than a month after turning 18. Young and popular, she inspires loyalty in her subjects.	The French are engaged in a series of conflicts in Morocco.	The Corn Laws, which protected agriculture in Britain by imposing high duties on imported grain, are repealed.

26   PIETERMARITZBURG & DURBAN REGION

Pietermaritzburg City Hall

Battlefields

● Zaailaager 1838
● Durban 1842
● Mome Gorge 1906

The Voortrekkers founded the town of Pietermaritzburg in 1839, intending it to be the capital of the independent Republic of Natalia. The new settlement was named after two Great Trek leaders, Piet Retief and Gert Maritz. The Church of the Vow was built near the town centre to commemorate the famous Voortrekker victory over the Zulu at Blood River (see p. 162) in 1838.

British settlers in Port Natal (Durban) were unhappy under Voortrekker rule and sent for troops from the Cape to restore British supremacy. The Battle of Durban (Congella) (see p. 31) in 1842 initially resulted in a siege, but the arrival of British reinforcements eventually forced the Voortrekkers to capitulate. The following year, in 1843, Natal was annexed to the Cape and a British garrison was installed at Fort Napier, a newly built stronghold overlooking Pietermaritzburg. In 1845 the first British governor arrived and Pietermaritzburg became the capital of the British colony of Natal.

Anglo-Zulu War memorial in Pietermaritzburg

1906
Mome Gorge

1900
The Boxer Rebellion in China (against foreign interests and Christians) is quashed when troops sent by an alliance of eight nations, including Britain, defeats the Imperial army.

1901
Queen Victoria dies and is succeeded by her son, Edward VII.

1910
The Union of South Africa is founded as a dominion of the British Empire.

Battle of Zaailaager
Also known as *Battle of Saailaager*
17 February 1838

HOW TO GET THERE
The Zaailaager battlefield is near the present town of Estcourt, close to where the Bushmans River makes a horseshoe bend. Drive from the south on the R103 through Estcourt. Turn right into Connor Street (before you reach the town centre) and continue to Alfred Street, where you turn right. Drive for 700m, then cross the Little Bushmans River at its confluence with the Bushmans. Here you turn right at the 25km/h sign; drive for 400m and then bear right to reach a private farm. Drive through the gates, with the farmer's permission, to view two interpretation panels, several cairns that cover the original cattle stakes and a monument to Gert Maritz.

Zaailaager panels: 29°00'51.9" S 29°53'31.3" E
Gert Maritz Monument: 29°00'48.9" S 29°53'26.8" E

Context
King Dingane feared the mounted Voortrekkers with their guns and the threat they posed to the security of his order. The Trekkers, under Piet Retief, were hoping to negotiate a treaty that would grant them land in Natal; however, negotiations ended badly and, on 5 February 1838, Retief and his retinue were killed on Dingane's orders. The Zulu king then instructed 10,000 warriors to penetrate Natal south of the Tugela River and drive out all the settlers.

Action
The Voortrekkers in Natal believed they had nothing to fear from Dingane. After returning stolen cattle to the Zulu king, Piet Retief was given reason to believe that his request for permission to settle south of the Tugela River would be granted. In November 1837, leaving the rest of the party at the top of the Drakensberg, the Retief deputation rode towards Zululand to sign an agreement with Dingane. Those left behind made their way down to the foothills and set up widely separated camps along the Bushmans and Bloukrans rivers, all the way to Colenso and from there south as far as present-day Willowgrange.

Meanwhile, Piet Retief and his party had been treated to feasting and celebration at the royal homestead, but this was the prelude to their demise – Dingane had ordered that they all be killed. After the execution, the Zulu impi crossed into Natal in the vicinity of Rorke's Drift and made their way over the Helpmekaar ridge and south to the Tugela River. They were not aware of the encampments as far west as the foothills of the Drakensberg, and those Voortrekkers who had settled west of the present N3 escaped the ensuing onslaught.

First to be attacked were the camps near Weenen (the name, meaning 'weeping', recalls the tragedy). The impi had waited for the moon to wane before they attacked at 01h00 on the morning of 17 February. The laagers near present-day Estcourt were forewarned by the firing and had a little time to prepare their defences.

Zaailaager was the name of the farm being established by Great Trek leader Gert Maritz. It was home to a big camp and a number of men were present. Dingane believed that all of the men had been with Retief, and his warriors were surprised at the resistance they met. Maritz and his men had time to set up a small cannon and were further helped by the fact that the Zulu forces had to attack across the swollen Bushmans River. The warriors formed a human chain in their attempt to cross and the defenders repeatedly shot those in the middle, killing many Zulu in the river and preventing others from getting across.

Once the initial surprise had died down, the Voortrekkers defended themselves ferociously. The Zulu were driven off and Maritz and 30 men pursued them on horseback. Many were killed and the remainder fled back into Zululand, taking about 25,000 head of cattle with them. Other defensive actions were fought at Weenen, Van Rensburgspruit, Doornkop and Bloukrans.

Aftermath

The Battle of Zaailaager was one of many such battles fought on the day; collectively they have come to be known as the Great Murder or Bloukrans Massacre. During the course of this massacre 41 men,

Battle of Tugela

After the killing of Piet Retief in February 1838, the Zulu impi had been instructed by Dingane to clear Natal of all white men. The Boer settlers along the banks of the Bloukrans and Bushmans rivers were the first to be attacked, followed by the early British settlers in Durban. The Battle of Tugela, fought in April 1838, arose from the ill-conceived effort by the Durban settlers to take revenge on the Zulu. The motley band of settlers was soundly defeated by the Zulu warriors and many of them were killed on the north bank of the Tugela River near present-day Mandini.

Timeline

1836
Voortrekker leader Hendrik Potgieter makes a successful stance at Vegkop against the cattle-raiding Ndebele, who are eventually displaced north.

1837
Queen Victoria inherits the British throne at the age of 18.

1838
In February Dingane's warriors attack Voortrekkers at Zaailaager, during the Bloukrans Massacre. The Battle of Italeni, in April, sees an unsuccessful Voortrekker attempt to avenge themselves on the Zulu; victory at Blood River in December delivers a longed-for ideal and spells the end of Dingane's reign.

1842
British settlers are alarmed at the Boer presence in Natal, but the intended attack on the British camp at Congella leads, instead, to a siege of the British fort. When the siege is eventually relieved, Britain annexes Natal.

1845
When Voortrekkers push into the Free State and clash with the Griqua, British forces come to the aid of Griqua chief Adam Kok III, and a battle ensues at Swartkoppies. The annexation of Transorangia (the area between the Orange and Vaal rivers) fuels strong, nationalistic feelings among the Voortrekkers.

56 women, 185 children and more than 200 servants were killed. However, the Zulu had fallen far short of their order to kill all the settlers in Natal. Perhaps as significant as the skirmishes was the bitterness the perceived betrayal of Retief and his large entourage caused – the Voortrekkers swore revenge on Dingane and took it, 10 months later, at the Battle of Blood River (see p. 162).

The Bloukrans Massacre

Principal combatants
Voortrekkers: Families in the laager of Great Trek leader Gert Maritz.
Zulu: Warriors under Dingane.

Brave Martinus

When the Zulu attacked the camp at Zaailaager on the morning of 17 February 1838, young Martinus Oosthuizen realised that his beloved pony, Swartjie, was not in the laager and went out to find him. As he came across the pony and vaulted onto his back, he saw that the Van Rensburg family was under attack by forerunners of the Zulu army. The family had not had time to laager their wagons and had fled, instead, to the flat-topped summit of a small hill. From here they fired into the approaching impi to keep them at bay, but they were running low on ammunition. They signalled frantically to Martinus to bring more powder and shot, and the boy galloped away to a wagon at the base of the hill. Stuffing the lead into his pockets, he was about to leave when he noticed a young girl cowering under a sailcloth. He swept her up behind him on Swartjie's back and together they galloped towards the top of the hill. They were through the encircling Zulu impi when disaster struck. Swartjie leapt over a donga, unseating the girl. She fell into a flurry of assegais and was instantly killed. Martinus managed to gain the top of the hill, where he delivered the ammunition. The Zulu were repulsed and the entire family was saved, but the lone grave of the young girl may still be seen in the hills near Estcourt.

Powder horn

30   PIETERMARITZBURG & DURBAN REGION

Battle of Durban
Also known as *Battle of Congella*
23–24 May 1842

> **HOW TO GET THERE**
> Congella lies between the Durban Bay sugar terminals and the University of KwaZulu-Natal. The British camp site is now known as the Old Fort and is on the Old Fort Road, now K. E. Masinga Road, in Durban. As you drive east down K. E. Masinga Road (towards the sea), it is on the left between Old Fort Place (now Archie Gumede Place) and N. M. R. Avenue (now Masabalala Yengwa Avenue).
>
> The Boer camp site is marked by a monument in the park between Umbilo Road and Gale Street (now Magwaza Maphalala Street). Drive south down Penzance Road until you reach Umbilo Road. As you turn left into Umbilo Road, the park is on your right-hand side. There is also an obelisk commemorating the Voortrekker dead behind the Congella station on the bayside.

Context

British settlers in Port Natal were disturbed when the Voortrekkers, encouraged by their victory over the Zulu on 16 December 1838 at Blood River (see p. 162), proclaimed the Republic of Natalia in March 1839. Although the British government was not willing to annex Natal, there was concern over the treatment of black people living in the new republic, and how the new territory might affect the boundaries of the Cape Colony. A garrison consisting of 236 men, as well as women and children, was sent to Durban from the Umngazi River mouth (near Port St Johns) to restore British supremacy. When a small group of British soldiers set off to attack the Voortrekker camp at Congella, they were ambushed and pursued back to their entrenched fort, which was besieged for nearly a month.

Action

Major Thomas Carlton Smith, commanding a force of mostly Inniskilling Fusiliers, marched into Port Natal on 3 May 1842. The journey from the Umngazi River mouth had been gruelling – one man had died and two children were born on the way. They established their camp (later named the Old Fort) on flat ground near the foot of Berea ridge and Smith subsequently met Voortrekker leader Andries Pretorius, who was mustering his men in a camp at Congella.

Attempts at negotiation failed. The Voortrekkers made it clear that they would not accept anything less than complete independence from Britain. Andries Pretorius, emboldened by what later transpired to be a false promise of protection from Holland by a Dutch trader, intentionally provoked Smith by taking all the livestock that was grazing

Timeline

1822
The first British settlers arrive in Durban Bay from the Cape.

1828
King Shaka is assassinated and his half brother, Dingane, becomes the new Zulu king.

1837–1838
The first Voortrekkers arrive in Natal. They send a deputation to negotiate a land settlement with Dingane. After an initial, seemingly positive, reception, 70 men of the retinue are killed and the Zulu impi rampage into Natal, killing Voortrekkers in the Midlands and burning the little settlement of Durban to the ground. In April, the settlers retaliate at the Battle of Tugela and the Voortrekkers at the Battle of Italeni; both are defeated by the Zulu.

1839
The Voortrekkers proclaim the Republic of Natalia. British settlers living in Durban request, in vain, British protection against possible foreign domination in Natal.

1842
A small British garrison from the eastern Cape marches up the coast to establish a post in Durban. The Battle of Durban is fought and British troops are besieged for a month. When the siege is relieved the Voortrekkers depart, many leaving Natal altogether.

1843
Natal is annexed to the Cape and, two years later, to Great Britain.

1850
Many Brits arrive to settle and establish farms in Natal.

1856
Cetshwayo, the new leader of the Zulu nation, builds his army into a fighting force that is perceived as a threat to settlers in Natal.

1879
The Anglo-Zulu War begins.

The secret of eternal youth

Henry Francis Fynn was one of the early British pioneers to settle on the shores of Durban Bay in 1822, as King Shaka was forging the mighty Zulu nation further north. When Fynn met King Shaka he gave him, among other gifts, a bottle of Macassar oil which turns white hair black. Shaka, who was greying prematurely, apparently believed he had been given the secret to eternal youth.

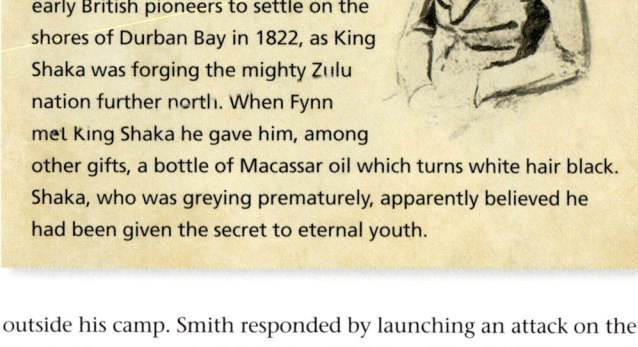

outside his camp. Smith responded by launching an attack on the Voortrekker camp at midnight on 23 May with only 138 men and two howitzers on ox-drawn carriages. Another gun was placed in a small boat, to be rowed parallel to the riflemen as they advanced along the beach. It was a moonlit night – the red coats and shining buttons of the soldiers showed up well against the white sand and the Trekkers were soon alerted to the impending attack. They waited, concealed in the mangrove trees, as the British neared their camp. The boat with the gun had become stuck on a sandbank and was far behind the men. When the Voortrekkers opened fire, the Inniskillings could not see the enemy. The oxen drawing the guns stampeded, 49 men were killed or wounded and the rest turned and fled, leaving the two precious guns behind. Pretorius had his men surround the British camp, hoping to starve the enemy into surrender on his terms.

A British wagon driver and hunter called Dick King was to save his countrymen this indignity. With his servant, Ndongeni, he rowed a small boat across Durban Bay at night, leading two horses behind him. When they reached the Bluff headland at the southern end of the bay, they mounted their horses and rode an epic 977km (crossing 122 rivers on the way) to reach Grahamstown in only 10 days. British authorities there responded to King's desperate request for help by sending a warship up the coast. The *Southampton* reached Port Natal on 25 June and fired its cannon at the Voortrekkers on the shore. A longboat full of armed soldiers was sent ashore. The attackers, realising they were outgunned and outmanned, left for Pietermaritzburg, their capital.

There followed a long period of negotiation and eventually, in May 1843, Natal was annexed to the Cape.

Aftermath

Although this was a small skirmish, the results were far-reaching. Once more Britain had deprived the Voortrekkers of their independence. The Voortrekkers felt extremely aggrieved, considering they had shed so much blood at the hands of the Zulu and then beaten them at the Battle of Blood River (see p. 162). The seeds of resentment were to grow and flower into wars against Britain in 1880 and again in 1899.

British settlers flooded into Natal from the date of annexation – James Rorke of Rorke's Drift (see p. 144) was one of them – and gave Natal a British character that is evident to this day.

Principal combatants
Voortrekkers: Trekkers led by Andries Pretorius.
British: 27th Regiment (Inniskilling Fusiliers); Cape Corps; Royal Artillery.

Dick King statue, Durban

A feisty woman

When Britain annexed Natal in 1843, it heralded the end of the short-lived Republic of Natalia. Leaders of the Volksraad got together in the capital, Pietermaritzburg, to discuss whether the Trekkers should remain in Natal. Susanna Smit, a fiery young woman, stood up and spoke. This was unheard of at the time, as women were not usually allowed in these meetings and were certainly not welcome to speak; but Susanna felt so strongly about the issue that no-one could silence her. She stated that she would rather walk barefoot over the Drakensberg Mountains than remain in Natal to be ruled by the British. Her passion was so great that it inspired most Voortrekkers to leave. A bronze statue at the top of Oliviershoek Pass commemorates her – a barefoot Voortrekker woman wearing a bonnet and a dress appears to be marching resolutely over the rocks, her face to the Orange Free State and her back firmly to Natal.

BATTLE OF DURBAN

Battle of Mome Gorge
Part of the *Bambatha Rebellion*
10 June 1906

HOW TO GET THERE
Mome Gorge lies north-west of Eshowe, in the vicinity of former Zulu king Cetshwayo's grave. Drive towards Nkandla from Eshowe; Mome Gorge is about 20km on the left before you reach Nkandla. *Guide recommended*

Context
The imposition of a poll tax on every adult male over the age of 18 years in January 1906 caused widespread discontent among the Zulu living in Natal. Following two separate incidents, where first a white farmer and then some policemen were killed, colonial troops were deployed to seek out the suspected rebels. The rebel leader, Chief Bambatha, was forced into hiding and the battle resulted when the Natal field force flushed him and his followers out of Mome Gorge, killing many, to end the rebellion.

Action
The new poll tax hit young Zulu men particularly hard. Previously covered by the hut tax paid by their parents, the young adults were now obliged to pay an individual poll tax of £1 per annum. This punitive measure followed in the wake of a devastating hailstorm the

Fortifications were constructed to defend roads near Richmond.

Colonial troops used the heliograph to communicate during their search for the rebels.

previous year that wiped out crops, and an outbreak of East Coast fever that killed many head of cattle, plunging Zulu families into poverty.

Matters came to a head with the murder of a white farmer in Umlaas Road, which was followed by an incident in February 1906 when 14 Natal Mounted Police were sent to arrest a Zulu man who refused to pay his tax. The policemen were surrounded by protesters and two of them were killed. Martial law was proclaimed and a large number of police, army members and volunteer horsemen were called up to counter the rebels.

Bambatha was a chief in the district between Greytown and Keate's Drift. When one of his headmen refused to pay the tax, Bambatha was called to Greytown to answer for him. When he failed to arrive, a force was sent to arrest him. Bambatha escaped to Zululand where he took refuge with the deposed Zulu king, Dinuzulu. It appears that Dinuzulu encouraged Bambatha to continue his protest, as shortly thereafter a policeman was attacked in Bambatha's chiefdom. The police officer took refuge in the hotel near Keate's Drift and had to be rescued by a force of 151 Natal Mounted Police. They also evacuated three women and a child who were staying at the hotel at the time. On their way back to Greytown, four of the policemen were ambushed and killed. One of the bodies was badly mutilated.

Bambatha's homestead was bombarded by the Natal Field Artillery, but Bambatha himself remained at large, gleaning support from one of the king's sons and from Sigananda, a venerable chief who lived in the Mome Gorge.

The Natal militia, commanded by Colonel Duncan McKenzie, made sweeps through Nkandla forest in search of the rebels. The militia established an army camp near Cetshwayo's grave, further inciting the Zulu, who believed the site was being desecrated.

To play for time, the rebels sent a message offering Sigananda's surrender, but McKenzie received intelligence that Bambatha was on his way to the Mome Gorge with 1,000 men. They group was approaching from Qudeni, and McKenzie deployed troops so as to trap the rebels between two columns, one at each end of the gorge. In the south was

Timeline

1845
Natal is annexed to Great Britain. In subsequent years many British emigrants set up farms in the Greytown area.

1879
The Anglo-Zulu War is fought and lost by the Zulu. Their king is relegated to the position of a minor chief, together with others with the same status.

1884
Civil war among the Zulu sees the ascendancy of Dinuzulu, a direct descendant of King Shaka.

1893
Mohandas Karamchand Gandhi is evicted from a 'whites only' train carriage in Pietermaritzburg.

1905
Devastating hailstorms and East Coast fever impoverish farmers, especially Zulu cattle owners, in Natal. A new poll tax introduced by the British gives rise to several incidents of violence; Bambatha emerges as rebel leader.

1906
Two police officers, sent to collect taxes, are killed. Widespread unrest culminates in a fierce battle in Mome Gorge, where Bambatha is beheaded so that his head may be displayed to his followers.

1910
The Union of South Africa is proclaimed with Louis Botha as Prime Minister.

BATTLE OF MOME GORGE   35

Resistance in Richmond

On 7 February 1906 members of the Natal Mounted Police tried unsuccessfully to collect outstanding poll taxes from the Zulu in the area south of Edendale. The men refused to pay and the police were forced to return empty-handed. The following day, armed officers confronted the offenders at the farm Trewirgie, where they resided. Two police officers were killed in the fracas.

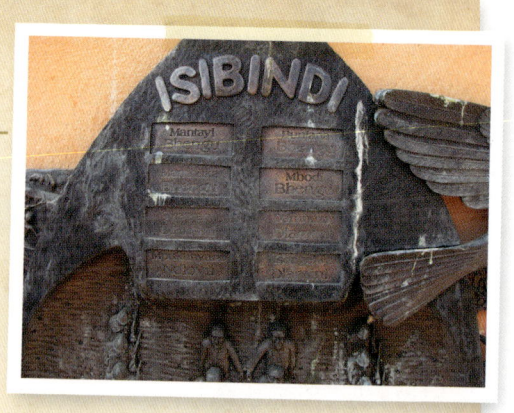

Memorial to the executed Zulu rebels

Martial law was proclaimed and a number of men were eventually found and arrested. Out of these, 12 were executed by firing squad in Richmond. Their mass grave is marked with a monument that carries their names.

Lieutenant Colonel W. F. Barker, who placed his field artillery on a hill near the confluence of the Nsuze and Mome rivers, west of the gorge mouth. He had men with weapons (a Colt and a Maxim gun) on both sides of the river. North-west, further up the gorge, was Colonel McKenzie with his troops and guns, looking down towards Sigananda's homestead.

The rebels were sighted at first light on 10 June in a loop in the river upstream of Barker and his men. Barker's artillery opened fire, hoping to force the rebels up to McKenzie, whose guns also began to bombard the position. The rebels fled, pursued by Barker's troops, and many of them climbed trees, or pretended to be dead to escape their pursuers.

The first shots had been fired at 07h00, and by 16h30 most of the forest north-west of the river loop was clear. About 100 rebels got away and Bambatha was supposedly killed as he attempted to escape. A body was discovered three days after the battle and its head cut off for identification.

Dinuzulu and his legal counsel at his trial in Greytown, 1907

36   PIETERMARITZBURG & DURBAN REGION

Families and farm workers at Helpmekaar protect themselves during the rebellion.

However, it had already begun to decompose and some doubt remains whether it was really Bambatha. Some believe he escaped to Lourenço Marques (Maputo).

Aftermath

The rebellion had been quelled with zealous ferocity; the scale of the action left a legacy of hatred that lasts to this day among some families. The dead rebels numbered 575, but there were doubtlessly many more casualties, their bodies never found. The Natal militia lost three men.

Dinuzulu was tried for high treason and found guilty of complicity in 1907. He was stripped of his chieftainship and sentenced to four years in prison; the sentence was later commuted. The rebellion had cost Natal dearly in terms of money, manpower and goodwill between black and white.

Bambatha Rebellion medal

Principal combatants

Zulu: Warriors commanded by chiefs Bambatha and Sigananda Shezi.
British: African levies; Border Mounted Rifles; Durban Light Infantry; Natal Carbineers; Natal Field Artillery; Natal Mounted Police; Natal Police; Natal Rangers; Natal Royal Regiment; Nongqai Police; Northern Districts Mounted Rifles; Royston's Horse; Transkei Mounted Rifles; Umvoti Mounted Rifles; Zululand Mounted Rifles.

Ulundi region

The town of Ulundi is close to the heart of Zululand. The Valley of the Kings – where the ancestors of Shaka and subsequent rulers were buried – lies north and west of the town, making the area a sacred and important place for the Zulu to this day. Shaka was based not far from the site of the present town when he moulded the Zulu nation out of scattered and disparate clans in the early 1800s. He established a second capital at KwaDukuza (Stanger) in order to increase his influence to the south and it was here that he was stabbed by his half brother Dingane, who succeeded him in 1828.

Partial reconstruction of Dingane's homestead at umGungundlovu

Dingane established his royal homestead, umGungungdlovu, south of Ulundi and it is now the site of an impressive museum and a partial reconstruction of his palace. The Mtonjaneni stream, about 5km away, is said to be where Dingane sent his maidens to draw pure water for his private use. When Dingane fled the area, after the Battle of Blood River in 1838, his royal homestead was burnt to the ground. But the intense heat of the fire baked and preserved the

Regional battles	1818 Gqokli Hill	1838 Italeni	1856 Ndondakasuka
World events	1815 Napoleon Bonaparte is defeated in the Battle of Waterloo, ending Britain's fears of a possible French invasion of Britain.	1833 Slavery is abolished throughout the British Empire.	1852 Napoleon III is proclaimed ruler of the Second French Empire. Two years later the Crimean War breaks out in Russia.

An artist's impression of the Battle of Ulundi

clay floors of many huts comprising his homestead, leaving behind an imprint of its magnitude.

Mpande, who succeeded Dingane, lived at Nodwengu, now part of Ulundi town centre. When Mpande died, his son Cetshwayo built a new capital a few kilometres further east, naming it Ondini (The Heights). It covered almost 60ha and resembled umGungungdlovu in size and magnificence. When the British defeated Cetshwayo's army during the Anglo-Zulu War, Ondini was burnt to the ground. It is now the site of a museum.

The White Mfolozi River runs south of the town, which lies on a gently sloping plain in the direction of Swaziland in the north. East lies the Hluhluwe-iMfolozi Park; a tarred road leads from the town to Cengeni gate in the west of the reserve.

Battlefields

1. Ndondakasuka 1856
2. Gingindlovu 1879
3. Italeni 1838
4. Gqokli Hill 1818
5. Ulundi 1879
6. Tshaneni 1884

Statue of King Cetshwayo at Ondini heritage site outside Ulundi

---

1879 Gingindlovu Ulundi

1884 Tshaneni

1868 Benjamin Disraeli becomes Prime Minister in Britain and passes a bill (the Second Reform Act) that almost doubles the electorate. The pace of reform speeds up.

1879 Thomas Alva Edison's electric light becomes available for use.

1880 The 1st Anglo-Boer War starts, following tensions between the British and the Voortrekkers over Britain's annexation of the Transvaal in 1877.

1891 Automobiles are, for the first time, produced commercially.

ULUNDI REGION 39

Battle of Ndondakasuka

Also known as *Battle of the Princes*

2 December 1856

HOW TO GET THERE
Drive from KwaDukuza (Stanger) towards KwaGingindlovu on the R102. Continue northwards until you reach the Tugela River where the R102 crosses the river on the old John Ross Bridge. If you look upstream from the bridge, about 2km further a small stream enters the river. This marks the eastern side of the action, which was fought on the hill north of the Tugela River between the present town of Mandini and the R102.

John Ross Bridge: 29°10'17.2" S 31°26'22.5" E

Context

There was conflict among the Zulu princes – Cetshwayo, Mbuyazi and Mthonga – regarding succession, as King Mpande had not named a chief wife. According to Zulu custom, the chief wife was not the first wife (who was usually a commoner) but the second, for whom more lobola would have been paid. Mpande's first wife had been part of King Shaka's harem and was given to Mpande as a gift from the king. Her son Mbuyazi was deemed to be Shaka's son. Mpande's second wife was a princess and the mother of Cetshwayo. However, Mpande had married a third woman, who was his favourite wife; she was the mother of Mthonga. Mbuyazi, Cetshwayo and Mthonga all had claims to succession. The battle took place when Cetshwayo's faction attacked Mbuyazi's faction.

Action

King Mpande favoured Mbuyazi over Cetshwayo, but enjoyed their rivalry and encouraged it by presenting both with war shields. Cetshwayo was popular and had a following of 20,000 warriors known as the uSuthu. Mbuyazi had only 7,000 isiGqoza, a bodyguard presented to him by his father.

Mpande gave Mbuyazi land along the north bank of the Tugela River, hoping that his son would garner support from the white settlers in Natal, or flee to safety should the isiGqoza be defeated. In November 1856 there were 20,000 of Mbuyazi's dependants settled close to the river, while his warriors assembled a little further north. Mbuyazi

King Mpande

John Dunn escaped across the Tugela River during the Battle of Ndondakasuka.

himself crossed the river to visit border agent Captain Joshua Walmsley and ask for his help. Walmsley declined to offer Natal government support, but sent John Dunn, a Zulu-speaking trader whom he had paid to act as his interpreter and police officer, to cross the river with guns and a small force in support of Mbuyazi.

Cetshwayo's warriors arrived from the north on the evening of 1 December. A few shots were fired but it was soon dark. The next day Cetshwayo deployed his men in the horns-of-the-buffalo formation (see p. 139) to surround the enemy. Before the battle began, a gust of wind dislodged a feather from Mbuyazi's headrest and sent it fluttering to the ground. This was perceived by his followers to be a bad omen and, after this, they had little stomach for the fight.

Captain Walmsley's daughter

After the Battle of Ndondakasuka, Captain Joshua Walmsley was walking along the north bank of the Tugela River when he heard a child crying. Going to investigate, he found a black girl, about three years old, clinging to her dead mother. Walmsley took the child home to his French wife. They took her in and brought her up as their own. She was educated, taught to converse in French and to play musical instruments. When she was 17, she met a young Zulu man and fell in love, although he had no education and spoke only Zulu. She informed her parents that she wished to marry him and reintegrate herself with her own people. Although her adoptive parents were heartbroken, they let her go, demanding only that the man's family pay a big lobola as this would ensure her status in the community. She was sent away with fine furniture and linen, and never came back to live with the Walmsleys. They later sent the cattle paid as lobola to her as a gift.

Timeline

1838
Dingane is defeated at the Battle of Blood River.

1840
Mpande becomes the new Zulu king.

1852–1854
The Sand River and Bloemfontein conventions grant independence to Voortrekkers in the Transvaal and Orange Free State.

1856
Mpande fails to nominate a successor and two of the princes do battle for supremacy. Cetshwayo attacks Mbuyazi and is victorious. He becomes leader of the Zulu, although he is crowned only some years later.

1879
The Anglo-Zulu War is fought between the Zulu and the British. On 4 July the Zulu are defeated at the Battle of Ulundi.

1882
Cetshwayo is sent to England to plead for his return to Zululand. Queen Victoria supports his request to be allowed back into Zululand, where he is granted a chiefdom.

John Dunn saw that the battle was hopeless and used his horses and guns to force a path through one of the encircling uSuthu horns to reach the river bank and escape the carnage. The left horn of Cetshwayo's army completely overwhelmed the right flank of the isiGqoza, and the left flank fled into the mass of women and children cowering on the river bank. The uSuthu pursued them, killing everyone in their path. The little stream that enters the river was the site of a brutal slaughter and is known to this day as Mathambo (Place of Bones).

John Dunn had ridden his horse into the river, but so many fleeing warriors, women and children clung to it, hoping to be towed to safety, that the beast could not swim. Dunn plunged off its back and swam to safety. The horse was able to kick free and follow him across the river.

Thousands of isiGqoza were slaughtered or drowned; bloated bodies washed up on beaches near Durban for weeks afterwards. In the battle no fewer than six of Mpande's sons were killed, Mbuyazi among them.

John Dunn

John Dunn was born in England. His family emigrated to Natal and settled near Durban in 1836. His father was trampled by an elephant when John was 13 years old and his mother passed away four years later, leaving him to fend for himself.

After being cheated by an employer who refused to pay him for his work as transport rider, John worked for himself as hunter and trader. He later acted as interpreter and bodyguard for Captain Walmsley, the border agent near the lower Tugela Drift. After the Battle of Ndondakasuka in 1856, Dunn successfully retrieved cattle abandoned in Zululand by Natal traders who had fled at the outbreak of hostilities.

He also met with Cetshwayo, who, in spite of the fact that Dunn had supported Mbuyazi in the battle, was cordial. The Zulu king believed that it would be useful to have a European ally to act as interpreter and mediator with the Natal government. He offered Dunn a chieftainship and a tract of land along the north bank of the Tugela River. Dunn accepted and built a homestead where he settled happily with his 'coloured' wife, Catherine Pearce. He took many Zulu wives as well and is reputed to have had a total of 49 wives and 117 children.

Aftermath

From the time of this battle Cetshwayo effectively governed Zululand, but his rule was not recognised by the Natal authorities until some 20 years later. He moulded the nation into a strong military force along the lines of the one Shaka had formed between 1818 and 1828.

Principal combatants

Cetshwayo's army: Zulu warriors of the uSuthu faction; Natal Zulu police led by John Dunn.
Mbuyazi's army: Zulu warriors of the isiGqoza faction.

Battle of Gingindlovu
2 April 1879

HOW TO GET THERE
The battle site is situated between KwaGingindlovu and Eshowe, along the R66. Drive north from KwaDukuza (Stanger) along the N2, then take the turn-off marked 'Eshowe R66'. Follow the R66 to the turn-off to KwaGingindlovu. Do not take this turn, but continue for a short distance on the R66 until you see a sign on your left indicating 'Battle of Gingindlovu'. The monument to those who died in the battle is near the roadside. If you follow the track to the left of the monument into the cane field, you will reach the cemetery where some of the casualties were buried. The British fighting square, a defensive formation used during the battle, was formed close to this spot.

Monument: 29°00'41.57" S 31°34'44.97" E
Cemetery: 29°00'35.90" S 31°34'37.26" E

Context
British troops invaded Zululand at the start of the Anglo-Zulu War in January 1879 in three separate columns. The middle column suffered a disastrous defeat at Isandlwana (see p. 134) and the coastal column was besieged in a makeshift fort in Eshowe. Lord Chelmsford withdrew his forces to Natal, where he waited for reinforcements. In March he set forth with fresh troops, strengthened by the Naval Brigade, to relieve the siege of Eshowe. The Battle of Gingindlovu occurred when the Zulu attempted to halt his advance.

Action
Cetshwayo was aware that British soldiers were approaching Eshowe and had sent close to 11,000 warriors to stop them. Lord Chelmsford, in overall command and accompanying the column of 5,500 men, knew that the Zulu army was approaching from the north as he neared KwaGingindlovu.

On 1 April his force crossed the Amatikulu River and advanced to within 2km of the Nyezane River. John Dunn, who accompanied the column as interpreter and adviser, chose a knoll on which to prepare the defensive fighting square. At 117m², this square was big enough to accommodate 2,000 oxen,

King Cetshwayo

Timeline

1856
Cetshwayo builds a homestead for himself at umGungungdlovu after his victory at the Battle of Ndondakasuka. The name umGungungdlovu means 'swallower of elephants'.

1873
Cetshwayo is crowned king of the Zulu by Theophilus Shepstone in Natal.

1877
Shepstone (above) rides into the Transvaal and persuades President Burgers to accept the annexation of his impoverished republic to Great Britain.

1878
An ultimatum is presented to the Zulu under the Ultimatum Tree, not far from the present-day village of KwaGingindlovu. This leads to the outbreak of war between Zululand and Great Britain.

1879
Zululand is invaded and the British are defeated. In April Lord Chelmsford leads a British force back into Zululand to relieve the siege of Eshowe. His army is attacked by Zulu warriors at KwaGingindlovu, but the British soldiers emerge victorious. Three months later the Zulu are conclusively defeated by the British at the Battle of Ulundi.

1880–1881
Boers in the Transvaal fight for their independence, which is granted them by the British after the Battle of Majuba Hill in February 1881.

Battle of Nyezane

At Nyezane, south of Eshowe, Colonel Charles Pearson's coastal column came up against the Zulu army. Pearson's column narrowly avoided defeat on 22 January 1879, the same day as that when the fateful Battle of Isandlwana was fought.

Memorial to the British who died at Nyezane

300 horses and 2,280 black troops. The 125 wagons were secured around the perimeter with gaps in the corners for the placement of the nine-pounder field guns, the Naval Brigade's rocket tubes and Gatling guns. Trenches were dug around the outside, 13.5m away from the wagons, to shelter the 3,390 British troops. Riflemen were allocated to stand on some of the wagons and fire at individual targets, and the other troops were to concentrate their fire in ordered volleys.

The Zulu were gathered in the Nyezane River valley, to the north, and on the slopes of Misi Hill, west of the fighting square. They consisted of Irregulars and elements of most of the Zulu regiments, some of whom had arrived from Ondini only the night before.

At 04h00 on 2 April the men in the square stood to arms. Two hours later, at 06h00, they could see the Zulu approaching from the north and the west in two lines, the warriors dividing themselves into small groups and advancing in skirmishing order, making good use of whatever cover they could find. Most carried firearms of some kind or another, but very few had modern rifles – ancient muzzle-loaders and unreliable flintlocks predominated. Though they fired as they advanced, most of the projectiles went safely over the heads of the men defending the square.

The Zulu attack came in the usual horns-of-the-buffalo formation (see p. 139) as the 11,000 warriors attempted to envelop the square before pushing home their attack. The left horn approached first; it got within 20m of the British on the north-eastern side of the square and was met with a barrage of lead. The Gatling guns opened fire at 1,000m and were to fire 1,200 rounds during the battle. The nine-pounder dropped shells into the approaching ranks and the rocket tubes caused much consternation as their noisy projectiles landed among the enemy. The British infantry, many of the men young and inexperienced, mostly fired poorly and needed to be steadied by their officers. The Zulu right horn came up against the western and south-western sections of the laager.

The final onslaught took place against the southern face at 07h00, led by Dabulamanzi, half brother to the king. He believed it to be less strongly defended than the others because he mistakenly thought the defenders were solely troops of the Natal Native Contingent. When this attack, too, had been repulsed, the British mounted troops were sent out of the square to pursue and kill. Their follow-up was merciless and all fleeing or wounded Zulu fighters were killed.

Aftermath

Only 13 British soldiers were killed and 48 wounded, but the Zulu suffered badly: an estimated 1,200 men, more than a tenth of the force, were killed.

Principal combatants

Zulu: Warriors under Cetshwayo; Tonga Irregulars.
British: 3rd Regiment (Buffs); 57th Regiment; 60th Rifles; 91st Highlanders; 99th Regiment (Duke of Edinburgh); Mounted infantry; Natal Native Contingent; Natal Volunteer Guides; Naval Brigade; Royal Artillery.

Siege of Eshowe

KwaMondi, the deserted mission station in Eshowe, was chosen as the stores depot for the British column advancing towards Ulundi. The site was chosen for its healthy position in the hills, its supply of fresh water, the distance from Fort Pearson and the buildings, which could be used as storehouses. The area that was fortified can still be seen a short distance east of the town centre. The trench around the rectangular entrenchment was studded with sharpened stakes, some of them still visible today.

After the British central column had suffered its crippling defeat at Isandlwana in January 1879 (see p. 134), the soldiers of the coastal column at KwaMondi were ordered to advance no further, but to defend themselves as best they could against a Zulu attack. They were besieged in their fort until the beginning of April 1879.

KwaMondi today, with the remains of the trench (top)

British supply column camped at the coastal drift on the Tugela River

The ultimatum that led to war in Zululand

At the outbreak of the Anglo-Zulu War in 1879, the coastal column of the British army crossed the Tugela River at the drift close to its confluence with the Indian Ocean. This popular crossing point into Zululand was used by traders, hunters and missionaries. There was a hotel on the Natal side of the river, where John Dunn is reputed to have sat, taking shots at crocodiles and hippos while enjoying the spectacle of Zulu maidens dancing for a hotel audience.

Close to the river grew a large Natal fig tree and it was under this tree that the British ultimatum to the Zulu king was presented in December 1878.

The British had used various pretexts to cobble together the ultimatum, which was intended to make war with the Zulu inevitable. Among other strictures, King Cetshwayo had to allow a British Resident to oversee his governance, dismantle his army, allow the free activity of missionaries, give up one of his chiefs for trial and pay large fines in cattle.

The event was attended by many Natal dignitaries, but not by the Zulu king, who sent representatives on his behalf. A large tarpaulin was strung over the spreading branches of the tree to give shade. A photographer with a box camera and a blanket over his head was there to record the occasion. First on the agenda was a report on the findings of the boundary commission, which had examined the rights of ownership of the land in the north, between Zululand and the Transvaal, an area that had become known as the disputed territories. The result was favourable to the Zulu and this welcome announcement was followed by lunch.

However, after lunch, the ultimatum, which was to lead to war, was read to Cetshwayo's headmen, who were not literate and had to memorise the entire document in order to deliver it to their king. The terms were so stringent that they feared Cetshwayo's reaction to their recital and delayed their return to him as long as they could. When the message was finally delivered, Cetshwayo prevaricated, trying to avoid confrontation, but his attempts at conciliation were rebuffed.

In January 1879, soon after the ultimatum had expired, the British army invaded Zululand, and Cetshwayo immediately despatched his warriors to drive them out. The war had begun. Had Cetshwayo complied with the British demands, he would have compromised the independence of Zululand and relinquished control over his people.

The Natal fig tree, where the British delivered an ultimatum to representatives of the Zulu king Cetshwayo

When Lord Chelmsford planned his invasion, he initially divided his army into five main columns, later reduced to three because of a lack of troops. The columns were to cross the border into Zululand at different places to reduce the risk of having the Zulu armies outflank his force and invade Natal behind him. The northern column was to enter Zululand from Utrecht, the central column across Rorke's Drift, and the coastal column would cross the Tugela close to the Ultimatum Tree. Engineers built a pontoon bridge to carry the 4,500 men with all their livestock, equipment and ox-wagons across the water.

A rudimentary stronghold, known as Fort Pearson, was built on the cliffs overlooking the river from the south to protect the pontoon bridge, while Fort Tenedos rose on the opposite bank for the same purpose. Today, little remains of Fort Tenedos apart from a plaque amid a sea of sugar cane, but the entrenchments at Fort Pearson are still clearly visible on the cliffs above the river. Also at the Fort Pearson site is a display about the Battle of Tugela (see p. 29).

The Ultimatum Tree and Fort Pearson can be accessed from the R102 between Darnall and the Tugela River. The turn-off is marked about 7km north of Darnall.

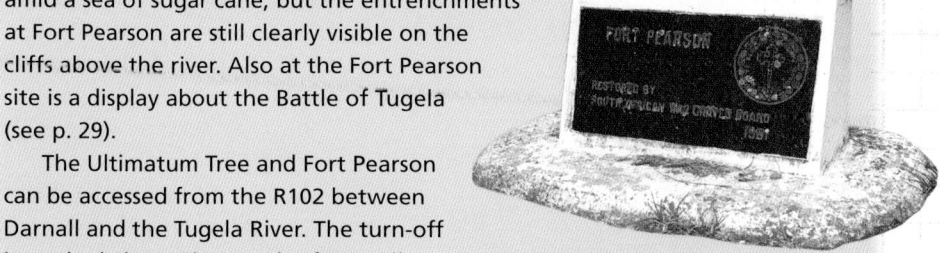

Plaque at Fort Pearson cemetery

Battle of Italeni
Also known as *Battle of Vlug Kommando*
10 April 1838

> **HOW TO GET THERE**
> The battlefield is situated south-west of umGungungdlovu (Dingaanstad), the site of Dingane's royal homestead, south of present-day Babanango in northern KwaZulu-Natal. The actual site is difficult to access, and controversial, as the battle was fought over a distance of more than 20km. According to Ian Uys (*Rearguard – The Life and Times of Piet Uys*), the initial confrontation between the Zulu and Voortrekkers took place approximately 4.8km south-west of umGungundlovu, where the road to the royal homestead passed between two hills. *Guide recommended*

Context

After the murder of Piet Retief and the Bloukrans Massacre (see p. 29) of February 1838, the Voortrekkers were in a precarious position. Despite being weakened by the loss of men and livestock, and being vulnerable to further Zulu attacks, they were determined to stay in Natal, and sent messages requesting help from their compatriots in the Orange Free State. Piet Uys and his commando came to their aid. Hendrik Potgieter and his commando came as well, although not as eagerly. The Battle of Italeni was the unsuccessful attempt by Uys and Potgieter to reach Dingane's homestead and defeat the Zulu army.

Action

The two leaders of the planned foray into Zululand, Pieter Uys and Hendrik Potgieter, did not co-operate with each other. Neither was willing to allow the other to lead all the men, and so it was agreed that each would retain leadership of his own men while at the same time loosely co-operating with each other. This strategy proved to be disastrous and the 347-strong force that set off from below the Drakensberg west of present-day Estcourt later became known as the Vlug Kommando (Flight Commando).

The horsemen were armed with muzzle-loading guns and accompanied by a number of packhorses carrying spare powder

An illustration of King Dingane by Captain Allen Francis Gardiner, 1836

The Spirit of the Nation monument in the Valley of the Kings near Ulundi

and lead. Piet Uys's 15-year-old son, Dirkie, accompanied the column as it crossed first the Tugela River and then the Buffalo River in the vicinity of Rorke's Drift to enter Zululand. From there the men rode towards the Babanango ridge to reach the Umhlatuzi River. They then headed east towards umGungundlovu.

King Dingane was aware of their approach and had sent about 7,000 impi to oppose them. The Zulu commander had chosen his position carefully, placing his men on both sides of the road to umGungundlovu where it ran between two hills.

Uys and Potgieter spotted the Zulu, and Potgieter chose to attack those on the left of the road and in the valley, while Uys engaged the warriors on the hill to the right. Forty men were left with the packhorses. Uys approached to within close range of the enemy and opened fire. One of his men, known for his accurate shooting, killed the Zulu commander. Controlled volley fire from Uys's other men cut swathes through the Zulu, who soon turned and fled. Meanwhile, Potgieter had made a very feeble attempt to engage the enemy and soon turned to withdraw, leaving behind 16 of his men who had become separated in the mêlée.

As Uys and his men pursued the fleeing Zulu, Uys shouted to Potgieter to cover his rear, since he intended going forward towards umGungungdlovu. At that moment Uys noticed that two members of his commando, the Malan brothers, were riding into an ambush. Taking 15 volunteers with him, Uys rode forward to save them. As the group retreated, with the Malans racing ahead of them, Uys was hit in the small of his back by an assegai. He pulled it out, but was bleeding profusely. The wound was to prove fatal.

Timeline

1836–1837
Voortrekkers leave the eastern Cape to escape British rule. Piet Retief brings his family and followers over the Drakensberg Mountains to enter Natal near present-day Estcourt.

1838
In February, after an unsuccessful attempt by the Voortrekkers to get a land grant south of the Tugela River, Dingane's warriors attack the Boers at Zaailaager.

In April the Battle of Italeni sees an unsuccessful Voortrekker attempt to avenge themselves on the Zulu.

In December, the Voortrekkers defeat the Zulu at the Battle of Blood River, spelling the end of Dingane's reign.

1839
The Boers proclaim the Republic of Natalia, much to the consternation of British settlers in Durban.

1842
A battle is fought in Durban between Voortrekkers and a British garrison from Port St Johns. The British prevail and many Voortrekkers leave Natal.

1845
Natal becomes a British colony.

BATTLE OF ITALENI **49**

The death of Dirkie Uys is depicted in this section of a large frieze at the Voortrekker Monument in Pretoria.

The Zulu pursuit of the stricken Boers took them over a distance of more than 20km, during which time Uys fainted and fell from his horse repeatedly. Each time he was helped back on and supported by his men as they rode on. Both the Malans were killed during this retreat.

At one point the party became separated by a ridge. Piet Uys knew he could not go on and begged the others to leave him and save themselves. Dirkie Uys was riding with the other party and, separated from his father, it seems unlikely that he was present when Piet died. However, a well-known account states that he was galloping away with the others when he turned and saw his father lift his head to look at the approaching Zulu. This caused him to wrench his horse around and charge back at the warriors, shooting three of them dead before he was pulled from his horse and stabbed to death near his father. Yet another version is presented in Ian Uys's book *Rearguard – The Life and Times of Piet Uys*. He writes that a Zulu reported years later that Dirkie was taken alive and presented to Dingane, who was so impressed by the boy's bravery that he ordered him cut into pieces and made into a soup that all of his men drank, so that they, too, would be brave. However, apart from this single report, there is no evidence to substantiate this story.

Aftermath

The Boers lost 10 men. They learned two powerful lessons: that the Zulu should be engaged only from an entrenched position and that an attacking force should take care never to become separated. They used these lessons to good effect at Blood River (see p. 162) in December of the same year.

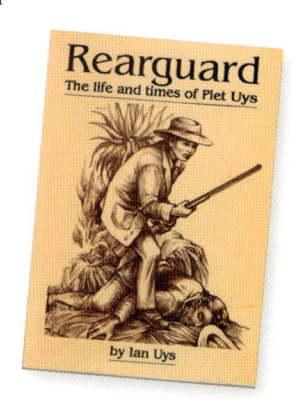

Rearguard – The Life and Times of Piet Uys is a valuable piece of Africana.

Principal combatants

Voortrekkers: Led by Pieter Uys and Hendrik Potgieter.
Zulu: Warriors from umGungundlovu. Sources differ as to whether they were commanded by Ndlela or Dambusa (Nzoba kaSobadli).

Battle of Gqokli Hill
April 1818

HOW TO GET THERE
Driving from the south towards Ulundi on the R66, you will notice Gqokli Hill on the left-hand side of the road before you reach the White Mfolozi River. It is signposted.

Gqokli Hill: *28°22'52.2" S 31°21'41.1" E*

Context
Shaka, the illegitimate son of Zulu chief Senzangakhona, was brought up by his mother under the protection of the Mthethwa, led by Dingiswayo. Shaka showed great fighting prowess and helped the Mthethwa in their battle against their arch-enemies, the Ndwandwe, under Zwide. Like many chiefdoms across the western Highveld and the south-eastern coastal region of South Africa in the late 18th century, the Ndwandwe and Mthethwa had been in combat over territorial expansion. Animosity between the two chiefdoms came to a head in 1818, and, when Dingiswayo died in a campaign against the Ndwandwe, Shaka amalgamated the Zulu and Mthethwa to form a strong fighting force more than able to defeat its rivals. The Battle at Gqokli Hill was Shaka's triumphant defence against a Ndwandwe attack.

Action
Accounts of what took place on Gqokli Hill are difficult to verify, as there are scant records of the event. The description below has been drawn from available records, some of which are likely to be conjecture.

Shaka knew that he would be outnumbered by the approaching Ndwandwe army of 12,000, commanded by Nomahlanjana, Zwide's heir. In order to give his 5,000 men the advantage, Shaka had positioned 500 warriors on the summit of Gqokli Hill. Another 4,000 sat in five concentric circles around the hill, one behind the other, giving the impression that there were far fewer men than there really were. In addition, a decoy of 500 warriors was sent off to draw the Ndwandwe on and deplete their ranks. If the pursuing

King Shaka

BATTLE OF GQOKLI HILL   51

Timeline

After 1795
Trade through Delagoa Bay leads to conflict between the Mthethwa and Ndwandwe.

About 1799
Dingiswayo succeeds Jobe, chief of the Mthethwa. He develops a military system that drafts all young men into age-differentiated regiments. Mthethwa society increases in power.

1809
Shaka is conscripted into Dingiswayo's army and becomes renowned for his fighting and leadership skills.

1816
Shaka (below) takes control of the Zulu when his father, Senzangakhona, dies. He introduces the Mthethwa military system.

1818
Shaka defeats the rival Ndwandwe at Gqokli Hill.

1822
The first white settlers arrive in Durban and strike camp in the vicinity of the present-day city hall.

1828
Shaka is assassinated and succeeded by his half brother, Dingane.

Ndwandwe should turn back to rejoin the main force, the Zulu warriors were instructed to warn Shaka with smoke signals. Shaka also stored water and food on the flat summit to take advantage of the enemy's lack of water, as there was none in close proximity.

Nomahlanjana, who was about Shaka's age, launched his first attack at 09h00. A line of impi approached the northern base of the hill, bunching together as they did so. When the men began their ascent, the space became even more crowded and the warriors found it difficult to wield their spears. The waiting Zulu came down to attack, wreaking havoc among the enemy and forcing them to withdraw. The second attack saw the Zulu rush forward, fighting hand to hand with their thick-bladed stabbing spears. The carnage was dreadful and the Ndwandwe had to retreat once more. The third attack came at midday when many of Nomahlanjana's men had gone in search of water and the force was depleted. The Zulu pre-empted the attack and charged into the enemy. Finally the Ndwandwe changed their tactics. Men from the southern perimeter of the hill came round to join the best warriors on the northern face.

At about this time, smoke signals showed Shaka that the Ndwandwe warriors who had gone after the cattle were returning, leaving him little time to strike at the weakened enemy. He sent two attacking forces from the reserve troops that had been waiting on the summit down each side of the ascending enemy column. The enemy was enveloped and totally defeated.

Replicas of Zulu weapons, showing (left to right): battle axes, a broad-bladed stabbing spear and two throwing spears

Aftermath

The Zulu lost almost 2,000 men, but the Ndwandwe suffered far worse, with 7,500 warriors lying dead around the hill. Shaka defeated his major enemy and was now able to conquer the surrounding chiefdoms. A series of campaigns was to follow, which saw him consolidate his power in the area north of the Tugela River.

Principal combatants

Ndwandwe army: Warriors commanded by Nomahlanjana.
Zulu (including the Mthethwa) army: Warriors commanded by Shaka.

IN MEMORY OF THE BRAVE WARRIORS WHO FELL HERE IN 1879 IN DEFENCE OF THE OLD ZULU ORDER

Battle of Ulundi
4 July 1879

HOW TO GET THERE
As you approach Ulundi on the R66 (travelling north), you cross the White Mfolozi River. Here, on the slopes of the hill overlooking the river, on the left-hand side is Fort Nolela, the point of departure for the British army. Continue over the river into the town and take the turn-off to the airport (Prince Mangosuthu Buthelezi Airport) and Hluhluwe-iMfolozi Park. You are now on the Mhlabatini Plain and the route is roughly the same as that taken by the 'fighting square'. The battlefield is on your left (visible shortly after you pass the airport on your right) and is distinguished by a monument with a domed arch in the centre of a rectangle fenced with aloe bushes. This marks part of the area covered by the British formation. As you enter the gate and walk towards the dome, Ondini lies in front of you. The site is now surrounded by small houses; at the time of the battle there were no trees or other cover and the Zulu attacks against the British square would have been made over open ground.

Monument: 28°18'39.3" S 31°25'32.2" E

Context
This, the final battle of the Anglo-Zulu War, took place almost six months after a spectacular Zulu victory at Isandlwana (see p. 134). The reinforced British troops, approximately 5,500 men, were convinced that they were, at last, to deal the death blow to the Zulu army and avenge the 1,329 British soldiers killed at Isandlwana. They reached Fort Nolela on 1 July, an entrenched position on the slopes of a hill overlooking the White Mfolozi River. Lord Chelmsford was determined to rescue his reputation with a solid victory and intended to attack the Zulu on the open plain, close to King Cetshwayo's dwellings at Ondini.

British troops at Fort Nolela the day before the battle

BATTLE OF ULUNDI   53

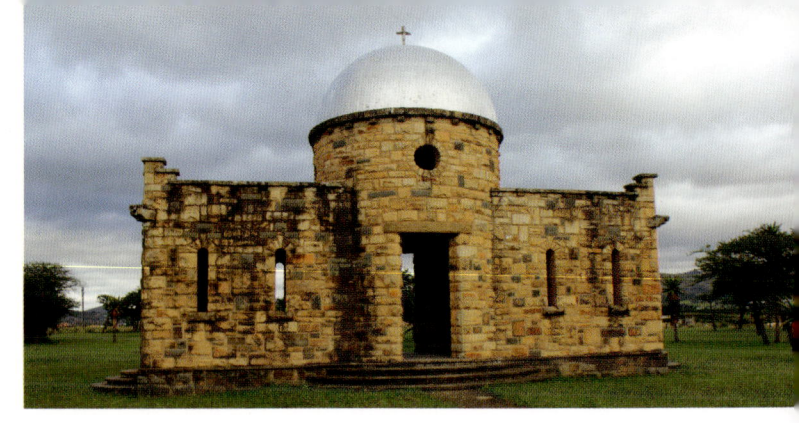

This monument marks the centre of the British fighting square at Ulundi.

Timeline

1856
King Cetshwayo fights and wins the Battle of Ndondakasuka to become overall leader of the Zulu. He raises a formidable army.

1877
The Transvaal, on the borders of Zululand, is annexed to Great Britain. There are frequent grazing land disputes on the borders between northern Natal, the Transvaal and Zululand.

1878
Britain presents the Zulu king with an ultimatum, which leads to the Anglo-Zulu War.

1879
In January Lord Chelmsford invades Zululand at three different places. The central column is defeated at the Battle of Isandlwana and the coastal column is besieged in Eshowe.

In June Chelmsford invades Natal again. The Prince Imperial of France is killed by a scouting party of Zulu, marking the end of the Napoleonic dynasty.

In July the Zulu are soundly defeated by the British at the Battle of Ulundi. Cetshwayo flees, but is later captured and imprisoned in the Castle in Cape Town.

1880–1881
The Transvaal Boers fight for, and win, their independence.

1884
Cetshwayo dies near Eshowe.

1887
Zululand is finally annexed to Great Britain, to be handed over to Natal 10 years later.

Action

The day before the battle, mounted men led by Lieutenant Colonel Redvers Buller splashed across the river and scouted the route for the advance on the Zulu capital. The party narrowly escaped ambush and three men were killed. The rest got back to Fort Nolela by nightfall, but the sound of Zulu chanting and singing floated eerily across the river.

About 25,000 Zulu were located in various fighting camps around Ondini, but only 15,000 men took part in the battle. The nearest of the camps was Nodwengu, which was north-east of where the British were to cross the river. Cetshwayo himself was in a camp at a safe distance from Ondini and had posted lookouts to watch and report on the battle. The warriors, encouraged by the ambush of mounted men the day before and buoyed by muti, were keen to encounter the British in the open. Lord Chelmsford was intent on giving them the battle they wanted.

The British left Fort Nolela and crossed the White Mfolozi shortly after sunrise on 4 July to form themselves into what was known as a fighting square. This was a rectangle of which the borders were made up of five companies on the front face, eight companies on each side and four on the rear face. Each company comprised about 130 men. Ammunition wagons and carts were marched alongside, but were pulled into the protective formation when it halted. The fighting square covered an area almost 3.5ha in extent (135m x 240m). When the square needed to change direction, the order was given to wheel to the left or right. This was easily done by the men on foot, but the wagons had to be manhandled around.

The formation reached the high point of the Mhlabatini Plain, overlooking Ondini, at about 08h30. The British had been ordered not to fire unless attacked and had to watch while the Zulu deployed around them into their famous horns-of-the-buffalo attack formation (see p. 139). The centre of the horns was to the rear of the square, to cut off any retreat, while the right and left horns advanced, with skirmishers to cover them, against the right and left faces of the British square.

As the Zulu neared, the mounted men, who were drawing them on to attack, were ordered to retire into the protection of the square. Then the nine-pounder artillery guns opened fire. The Zulu advanced with enormous bravery, some of them almost gaining entry at the rear right of the square. They were beaten back, but the British were taking casualties as the Zulu attack developed on all sides of the square. British Gatling guns, capable of firing between 250 and 300 rounds per minute, were plagued with stoppages, and Zulu bullets were flying – too high – over the British in the square. By 09h00 controlled volley fire by the British was keeping the Zulu at bay.

As the attacks wavered, Chelmsford seized the opportunity; he opened a corner of the square and sent his mounted men out to charge and kill the fleeing Zulu warriors. There were few prisoners taken that day, as the deaths of the British officers and soldiers at Isandlwana and at subsequent engagements were brutally avenged.

A rider of note

An excellent horseman, Lord William Leslie de la Poer Beresford was attached to Lieutenant Colonel Buller's Frontier Light Horse. During the reconnaissance the day before the Battle of Ulundi he rescued a wounded man and was recommended for the Victoria Cross. The rescue was aided by Sergeant O'Toole, and Beresford refused to accept the award unless O'Toole received it too. This was done. Beresford was the first British man to enter Ondini after the battle, leaping his horse over the thorn palisade and earning himself the nickname Ulundi Beresford.

Aftermath

All the Zulu fighting camps were torched. The Zulu lost at least 1,500 men, whereas the British suffered 12 dead and 90 wounded. Chelmsford's reputation was safe and his disaster at Isandlwana was forgotten in this victory, the final Anglo-Zulu clash at Ulundi.

Cetshwayo evaded capture for nearly two months, but was eventually tracked down and sent to Cape Town, where he was imprisoned. He was advised that he would be freed if he refrained from entering Zululand, which the British had divided into 13 chiefdoms. He refused, and was sent to Britain in July 1882 to state his case. There he met Queen Victoria, who was much taken by him. Upon his return to Zululand in January 1883, Cetshwayo was given one of the chiefdoms to rule. However, there was civil war among the Zulu and Cetshwayo was soon forced to flee, taking refuge in the Nkandla forest near Eshowe. When he died in February 1884, it was suspected that he had been poisoned. The Zulu defeat at Ulundi marked the end of independent Zululand.

Principal combatants

Zulu: All Zulu regiments (excluding the two that were guarding Cetshwayo).
British: 17th Lancers; 13th and 90th Light Infantry; 21st, 58th, 80th and 94th Regiments; Colonial mounted infantry; King's Dragoon Guards; Natal Native Contingent; Natal Native Horse; Natal Native Pioneers; Royal Artillery; Wood's Irregulars.

Battle of Tshaneni
Also known as *Battle of Ghost Mountain*
5 June 1884

HOW TO GET THERE
From the N2 northbound, take the turn-off to Mkuze village. Follow the road as it runs east, through the town of Mkuze, and continue on the same road as it bears south. To your left you will see the twin peaks of Gaza and Tshaneni. The co-ordinates below were taken on the road where it runs close to the base of these twin peaks.

Base of Gaza and Tshaneni peaks: 27°37'58" S 32°04'18.2" E

Context
At the conclusion of the Anglo-Zulu War in July 1879, the victorious British divided Zululand into 13 separate chiefdoms, each ruled by a different chief. Dinuzulu, King Cetshwayo's son, was one of them, as was Zibhebhu, a relation of the king and chief of the Mandlakazi. The Battle of Tshaneni was a fight for supremacy between Dinuzulu and Zibhebhu and their respective allies.

Action
When King Cetshwayo returned from exile in Cape Town and built a new home near his old one at Ondini, Zibhebhu feared that Dinuzulu would succeed him to become the most powerful chief in Zululand. Hoping to prevent this, he attacked Ondini in July, causing Cetshwayo to flee to Eshowe where he later died.

Dinuzulu was afraid of Zibhebhu and his growing support base, and he approached the Boers in the Vryheid district for help. They agreed to assist – in exchange for land on which they hoped to establish an independent republic in Natal, where they would be free of British rule. Some 100 Boers and a few Germans, led by Lucas Meyer and Louis Botha, accompanied the 1,000 uSuthu (young Zulu warriors under Dinuzulu) to confront the Mandlakazi (followers of Zibhebhu). Zibhebhu, known for his tactical skills in battle, had set up an ambush close to the Mkuze River in the Lebombo mountain range. He concealed his warriors in the thick bush between Tshaneni Mountain and the river and hid his cattle, women and children in a gorge north of the river. Non-combatants were concealed on the southern slopes of the mountain.

The uSuthu approached along the Mkuze River and reached Tshaneni on the morning of 5 June 1884. Fortunately for them, one of the Mandlakazi fired a shot prematurely, thus warning the mounted Boers who had kept a safe distance away from the gun-wielding Mandlakazi in the thick bush.

The uSuthu deployed in their usual horns-of-the-buffalo formation (see p. 139), but the right horn was confronted immediately by the full force of the Mandlakazi warriors, while the river and gorge prevented the left horn from encircling the enemy. The enemy on the right was overwhelmed and fled, only to be met by the Boers, who used their guns to force them back into the fray. The uSuthu then turned again to pursue the Mandlakazi up the slopes of the mountain.

Meanwhile, a contingent of abaQulusi warriors, allies of the uSuthu, had discovered the women, children and cattle on the north bank of the river. They killed a number of them and made off with the cattle. Zibhebhu, mounted on a horse, saw his wealth disappearing and his warriors being killed or drowned in the river as they tried to flee. He too fled, taking refuge near Eshowe. Six of his brothers were killed in the battle, which lasted only about an hour.

Aftermath

The Boers were given large tracts of land and were able to found what they called the New Republic. It was very short-lived, however, and Lucas Meyer became its first and only president.

The civil war was to continue until 1888, when Dinuzulu was exiled to St Helena. When he returned 10 years later, he was appointed chief of the uSuthu.

Principal combatants

Dinuzulu's army: uSuthu warriors; abaQulusi warriors; 100 Boers from the Vryheid district and some Germans, commanded by Lucas Meyer and Louis Botha.

Zibhebhu's army: Mandlakazi warriors.

Ghost Mountain

Long ago, Tshaneni Mountain was occupied by the Ndwandwe. When Shaka forged the mighty Zulu nation, beginning in 1818, he defeated the Ndwandwe, forcing the head of the ruling Gaza family, Chief Soshangane, to flee to Mozambique. Here, the Gaza became founder members of the Shangaan. However, they continued to view Tshaneni as their spiritual home and their dead chiefs were buried in a cave high on the slopes of the mountain. Some believe it to be haunted – there have been reports of strange lights and sounds at night.

Timeline

1879
The Zulu lose the Anglo-Zulu War and the Zulu king is relegated to the position of a minor chief, together with other chiefs.

1880–1881
The Boers in the Transvaal fight for, and win, their independence from Britain.

1884
Civil war among the Zulu, culminating in the Battle of Tshaneni, sees the ascendancy of Dinuzulu, a direct descendant of King Shaka. Cetshwayo dies amid suspicions that he was poisoned.

1887
Zululand is annexed to Great Britain.

1888
Dinuzulu, suspected of fomenting rebellion against the government in Natal and convicted of crimes against the state, is exiled to St Helena.

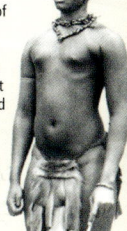

1898
Dinuzulu is returned to Zululand and appointed local headman over a portion of the Nongoma district.

1903–1904
Zululand is demarcated into different areas for black and white settlement.

1906
Dinuzulu is suspected of supporting Bambatha in his rebellion against the Natal government. The rebels are defeated in the Mome Gorge near Greytown and many are killed.

1913
Dinuzulu dies in banishment in the Transvaal.

BATTLE OF TSHANENI

Ladysmith region

The battles in this region are all related, directly or indirectly, to the siege of Ladysmith that lasted 118 days, from 2 November 1899 until 27 February 1900. The town was the northern post of the British garrison in Natal, chosen for its strategic position on the Klip River and at the junction of the railway lines from Durban to both Kimberley and Johannesburg, providing vital communications between the harbour and the interior.

View from Ladysmith showing Spioenkop and Twin Peaks on the distant skyline

The region was first populated by the San people who were displaced by Nguni herders from the north around 1,600 years ago. Much later, Voortrekkers from the Cape settled on the banks of the Klip River and proclaimed the Klip River Republic in 1847. However, the territory was part of the British colony of Natal (annexed in 1843) and the republic was short-lived. British farmers and traders settled in the area and, in 1850, the town of Ladysmith was proclaimed. It was named after the Spanish wife of the Governor of the Cape, Sir Harry Smith. It was an important staging post between the coast and the interior.

Regional battles						1899	
						Elandslaagte Rietfontein Ladysmith	Churchill's capture Willowgrange Colenso
World events	1896 Sudan is conquered.		1898 Marie and Pierre Curie discover radium.	1898 International steel production increases to 10 million tons a year, with the US producing more steel than Great Britain and Germany combined.		1898 Americans intervene in the ongoing Cuban War of Independence, resulting in a conflict in Cuba between Spain and the United States.	

58   LADYSMITH REGION

This is an area of diverse terrain, ranging from good farmland on the banks of rivers and tributaries flowing from their source in the Drakensberg to parched thornveld in the rain shadow regions, where little vegetation survives apart from succulents and thorn bush. The high ground dominating the north bank of the Tugela River rises from the river bed in a series of rock-strewn, grassy ridges to hills towering 500m above its course. The tallest of these are Spioenkop and Doringkop, both of which lie between Bergville and Colenso.

The Drakensberg peaks form a dramatic backdrop to rolling grass plains that glow verdant green during the wet season, but fade to brown and yellow in the dry winter months. Although the area is cleft by many rivers, it is not a high-rainfall region and is subject to breathlessly hot summers and harsh, dry winters with cruel frosts.

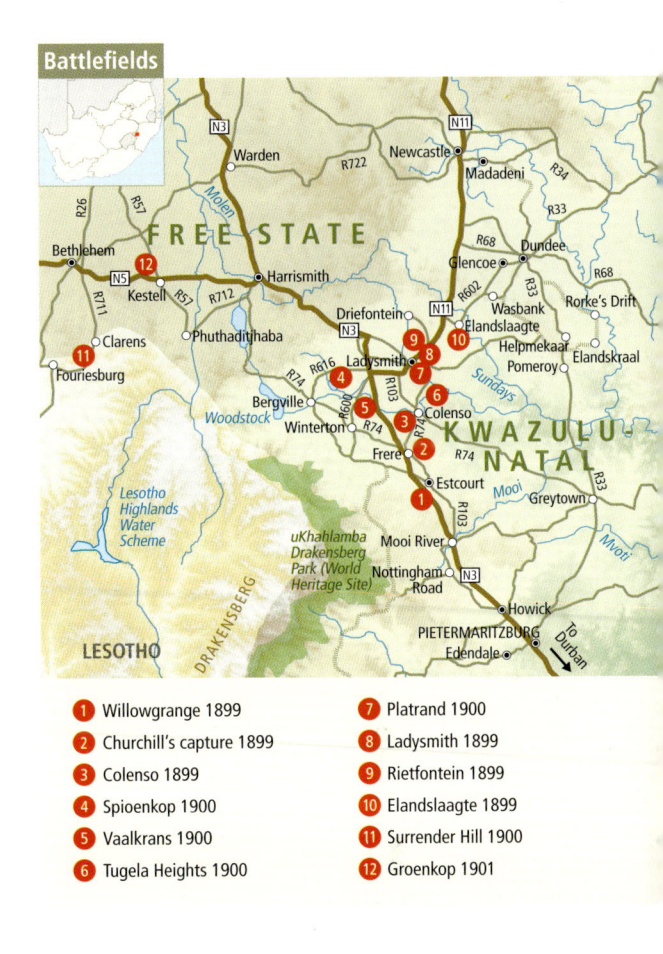

Battlefields

1. Willowgrange 1899
2. Churchill's capture 1899
3. Colenso 1899
4. Spioenkop 1900
5. Vaalkrans 1900
6. Tugela Heights 1900
7. Platrand 1900
8. Ladysmith 1899
9. Rietfontein 1899
10. Elandslaagte 1899
11. Surrender Hill 1900
12. Groenkop 1901

The boulders and rocks scattered across the hills make the passage of wheeled animal-drawn transport impossible in the absence of roads. Even horses would have found it difficult to travel at speed in these parts. The terrain lent itself to the guerrilla-type warfare favoured by the Boers, whereas the British were hampered by their huge supply trains.

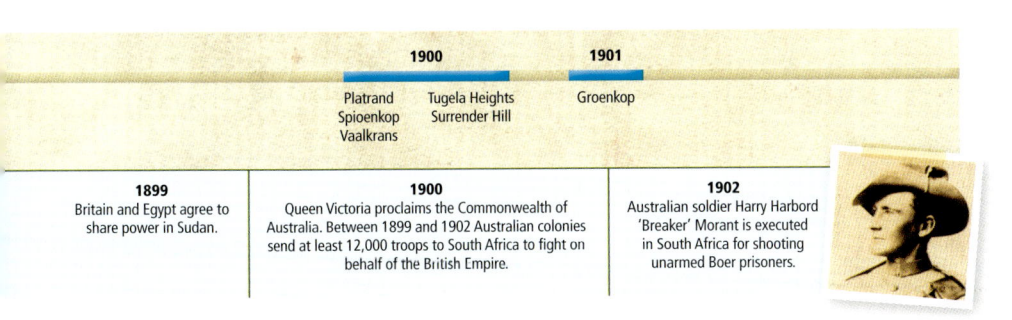

1900
Platrand
Spioenkop
Vaalkrans
Tugela Heights
Surrender Hill

1901
Groenkop

1899
Britain and Egypt agree to share power in Sudan.

1900
Queen Victoria proclaims the Commonwealth of Australia. Between 1899 and 1902 Australian colonies send at least 12,000 troops to South Africa to fight on behalf of the British Empire.

1902
Australian soldier Harry Harbord 'Breaker' Morant is executed in South Africa for shooting unarmed Boer prisoners.

LADYSMITH REGION

Battle of Willowgrange
23 November 1899

HOW TO GET THERE

The Willowgrange battlefield is situated between Mooi River and Estcourt in the KwaZulu-Natal Midlands. From Mooi River, take the R103 north in the direction of Estcourt. Pass the Willowgrange Hotel on your right and shortly afterwards turn left onto a dirt road signposted 'Battlefields and Lowlands'. Continue on this road over the N3 highway and up the hill. On the brow you will see a small cemetery on your left. As you stand in the graveyard with your back to the road, the steep hill in front and to your right is Harris Hill (then called Brynbella Hill). Turn around and look across the valley to your right; the big hill on the skyline just left (west) of the N3 highway is Beacon Hill. Look towards the left of its summit along the ridge to find the second, southern summit and pick out the line of the stone wall that marked the British advance. The wall stretches from this summit down to the road on which you are parked and up to the top of Harris Hill. Estcourt is visible in the north-east.

Cemetery: 29°05'54.4" S 29°55'18.8" E

Context

Ladysmith had been besieged by the Boers since 2 November 1899. The Boers subsequently captured a British armoured train at Chieveley, north of Estcourt (see p. 66). Buoyed by their successes and encouraged by their brilliant young commander, Louis Botha, who promised that they would soon be eating fish in Durban, two Boer commandos moved south of the Tugela River, passing one on either side of the British garrison at Estcourt, to reach the hills overlooking Mooi River. There the two commandos joined forces and cut the telegraph lines and railway line. They mounted their Creusot gun on the high ground and fired a few shells into the Mooi River garrison before pulling the gun up onto Harris Hill. Commanded by Major General H. J. T. Hildyard, the British garrison in Estcourt was 5,200 men strong, while Major General Barton's garrison in Mooi River consisted of 5,400 men. Hildyard saw the need to restore communications with Mooi River and launched an attack on the Boer position with the objective of capturing the Creusot gun on Harris Hill.

Major General Hildyard

Action

Hildyard planned to attack the Boer position at night. On 22 November the naval long 12-pounder gun was hauled out of Estcourt and heaved up the steep north-eastern slopes of

60   LADYSMITH REGION

British troops advanced up the hill on both sides of this stone wall at Willowgrange.

Beacon Hill. There were violent storms between 17h00 and about 03h00 the next morning – men on both sides, as well as six of the Boers' horses, were killed by lightning. Nonetheless, the Boers fired on the British soldiers visible on Beacon Hill and, when the big 12-pounder answered, they realised that an attack was imminent and prudently withdrew their gun from Harris Hill.

The British advance began at nightfall in thick mist and rain. A local farmer guided the troops from the slopes of Beacon Hill to its southern summit. From there, a stone wall led to the top of Harris Hill. Men of the

Fateful deaths

Trooper George J. Fitzpatrick, the brother of Sir Percy Fitzpatrick who wrote *Jock of the Bushveld*, was a member of the Imperial Light Horse. During the Battle of Willowgrange, these mounted men were moved up the valley to assist with the withdrawal of the West Yorks from the summit of Harris Hill. Trooper Fitzpatrick was killed when he stopped to help a wounded man. He lies buried in Estcourt.

Local farmer Frick Chapman guided the British during their night attack on Harris Hill. He was accidentally shot the next morning by a trigger-happy British soldier who saw his slouch hat and mistook him for a Boer. Chapman fell dead as he sat on a rock between Misty Kop and the foot of Harris Hill. He, too, is buried in Estcourt.

Timeline

1845
Natal becomes a British colony.

1852
The Sand River Convention grants independence to the Transvaal. The independence of the Orange Free State follows soon afterwards.

1877
The extreme poverty of the Transvaal Republic persuades President Thomas Burgers (right) to accept British sovereignty. Vice President Paul Kruger travels overseas to object to the annexation, but to no avail.

1879
The end of the Anglo-Zulu War sees the demise of the Zulu kingdom.

1880–1881
The 1st Anglo-Boer War is fought and won by the Boers, who regain the Transvaal.

1886
Gold is discovered in on the Witwatersrand.

1896
The Jameson Raid persuades President Kruger that war with Britain is inevitable and he begins to purchase state-of-the-art weaponry from abroad.

1899
War breaks out in South Africa and the Boers invade the British colonies of the Cape and Natal. In Natal, the British are defeated in Dundee and the garrison town of Ladysmith is besieged. The Boers embark on a raid towards the coast to blockade the port of Durban. The battle at Willowgrange, however, fought on 23 November, persuades them against the idea and they move back to defensive positions at the Tugela River.

BATTLE OF WILLOWGRANGE

Doctors operating in the field during the battle

East Surrey Regiment and West Yorkshire Regiment were told to advance on both sides of the wall. In the pitch darkness 300 men got completely lost – tragically those men behind mistook those ahead for Boers and shot at them. One drummer was killed before order could be restored.

At 03h00 the attackers reached the crest and their bayonet charge drove the Boers off the summit, but the Creusot gun was gone. All the British found were some ponies and a few blankets. When dawn broke, the British on the summit of Harris Hill found themselves under shell and rifle fire from the Boers below as they advanced through dead ground, threatening to reclaim the position. Hildyard ordered a withdrawal, supported by the gun on Beacon Hill and men on its slopes. However, the gun was not able to fire to its range because the trail was not well secured in the steep ground. The Boers, again on Harris Hill, fired into the retreating British.

The Mauser rifle

The Mauser rifle used by the Boers during the 2nd Anglo-Boer War proved to be a humane weapon. As one British naval surgeon wrote: 'The wounds produced by Mauser bullets are all that could be desired. The entrance and exit are practically of the same size and very minute. Most of the patients make an uninterrupted recovery. It is a much more humane bullet than our own Lee-Metford, for two reasons: its calibre is less and its velocity is considerably higher.'

There are records of men who recovered well from the following injuries:
- a bullet entering between the eyes, passing through the palate and mouth and coming out at the root of the neck;
- a bullet through the forehead and passing through the head;
- a shot in the middle of the neck, the bullet passing through the mouth and touching the spine;
- a bullet through the left armpit, through the lung and emerging just below the heart;
- a bullet through the abdomen and exiting on the left side of the heart.

LADYSMITH REGION

The cemetery at Willowgrange is unusual in that it includes graves of both Boers and Brits.

Aftermath

The British lost 22 men. Although the Boers had scored a tactical victory, they were demoralised by the number of British troops they had seen both north and south of Willowgrange. Soon, they feared, they would be cut off and surrounded. The decision was made to retreat and take up a defensive position at the Tugela, but the Boers were encumbered by a number of wagons filled with loot from deserted farms, as well as herds of stolen livestock. Had the British attacked them as they left Estcourt through a narrow valley, they might have been completely wiped out.

This engagement is important in that it marks a significant change in Boer tactics – from attack to defence. It was after this battle that they ceased their advance on Durban and retreated to hold the Tugela line. The farms around Nottingham Road mark the limit of the Boers' southward foray.

Principal combatants

British: Border Regiment; Durban Light Infantry; East Surrey Regiment; Imperial Light Horse; Natal Carbineers; Naval Brigade; Queen's Regiment; Royal Field Artillery; West Yorkshire Regiment.

Boers: Johannesburg Police; detachments from the Boksburg, Carolina, Ermelo, Frankfort, Heidelberg, Krugersdorp, Middelburg, Senekal, Standerton, Utrecht, Vrede and Vryheid commandos.

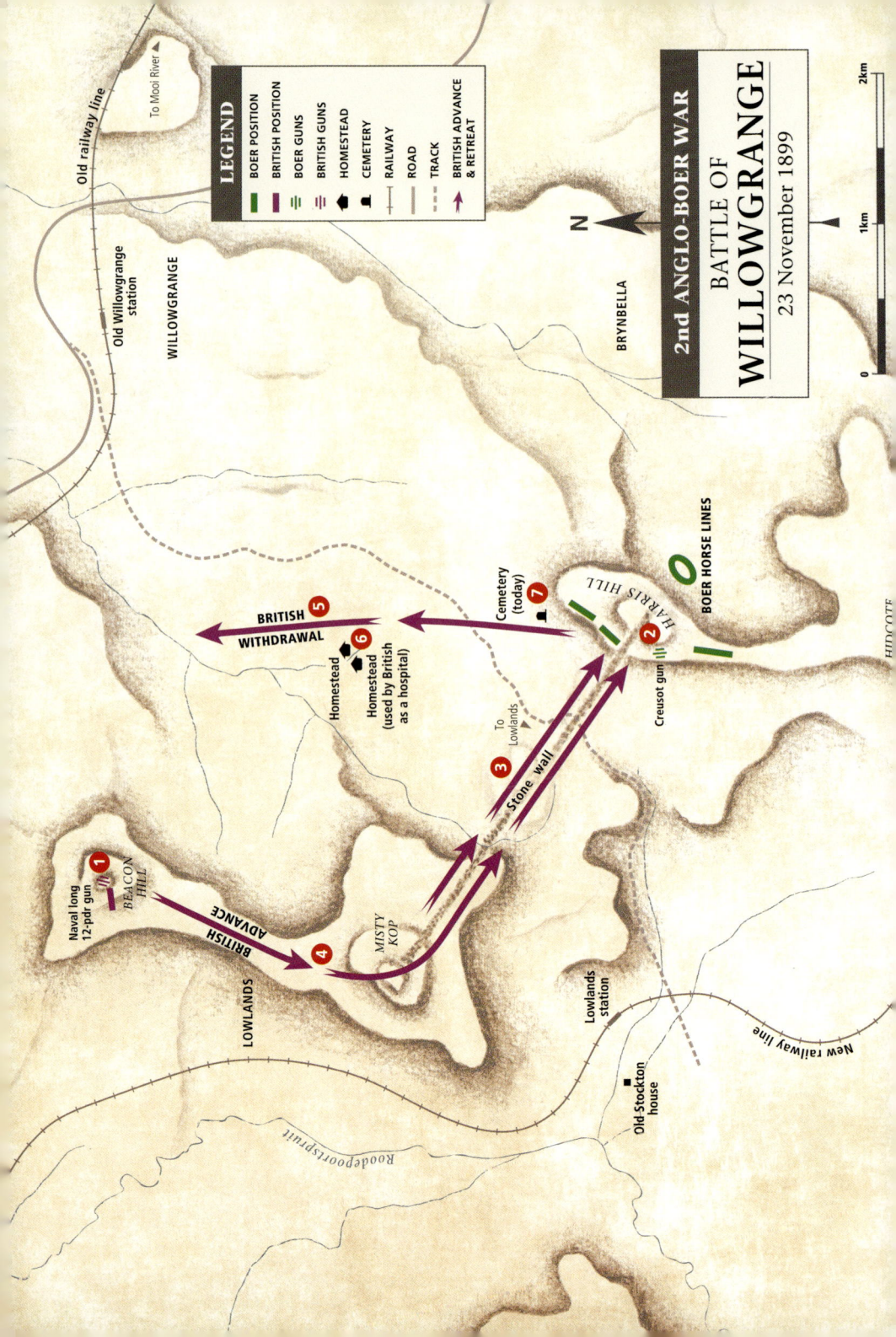

2nd ANGLO-BOER WAR
BATTLE OF WILLOWGRANGE
23 November 1899

① On the night of 22 November 1899 the British manhandled a naval long 12-pounder up the steep slopes of Beacon Hill. This alerted the Boers that an attack was imminent and allowed them to remove their gun from its vulnerable position on Harris Hill.

② The Boer Creusot gun was positioned here until nightfall on 22 November, when it was removed to the safety of the slopes below.

③ This was the stone wall along which the British advanced. It was a misty night and some of the troops got separated during the climb, with tragic consequences.

④ These arrows mark the path of the British advance from the slopes of Beacon Hill via Misty Kop to their objective, Harris Hill.

⑤ These arrows mark the direction of the British withdrawal under fire from the Boers on the slopes below. The Boers subsequently retook Harris Hill.

⑥ Trooper G. J. Fitzpatrick was killed here. He was the younger brother of Percy Fitzpatrick, the author of the famous book *Jock of the Bushveld*.

⑦ The present-day cemetery contains the graves of Boer and British combatants.

The straight line of vegetation up Harris Hill marks the stone wall along which the British advanced, hoping to capture the Boers' Creusot gun. However, the gun had been removed the day before and the Boers withdrew without detriment.

Armoured train disaster and Churchill's capture
15 November 1899

HOW TO GET THERE
Drive from Durban past Pietermaritzburg and Mooi River on the N3. Take exit number 194, marked Bergville/Colenso/R74, onto the R74. At the end of the off-ramp, turn right towards Colenso. At the first major turn-off, turn right onto the R103 towards Estcourt. Turn immediately left onto a byroad and drive towards the railway track. Park when you see a plaque on your right and walk to the tracks. A mass grave is visible on the other side of the railway line, about 50m south of the plaque. The small settlement with red-roofed houses that straddles the railway line south of the grave site is Frere. Colenso lies on the line in the other direction (north). Chieveley lies between the Estcourt and Colenso.

Context
During October and November 1899 British troops arrived by ship in Durban harbour and were sent to the Natal war front by train. There were British garrisons in Mooi River and Estcourt; further up the line were the small settlements of Frere and Chieveley. Beyond Chieveley lay the Tugela River and the village of Colenso, where road and railway bridges spanned the water.

The Boers had encircled Ladysmith by 2 November and were making tentative movements south. They had also occupied Colenso and the British troops stationed there had been withdrawn to Estcourt. It was essential for the British to know where the Boers were heading and as part of their reconnaissance they sent an armoured train up the line from Estcourt to Colenso. Also on board on the day was a young reporter for the *Morning Post*, Winston Churchill, who was always on the lookout for adventure and glory.

Action
The armoured train had traversed this route uneventfully many times before, but precautions were taken nonetheless to protect it against a possible attack. The steam engine was clad with tresses of thick rope that hung to the ground and trembled as the train moved, leading to its nickname Hairy Mary. The armoured trucks before and after the engine were no more than open cattle trucks that had been reinforced with steel and loopholed for the barrels of Lee-Metford rifles. A flat-bed truck on which was mounted a ship's cannon preceded the train. The last truck, too, was a flat-bed; it carried plate-layers and tools, in case repairs to the line were needed.

The train left Estcourt at dawn on 15 November with Captain Aylmer Haldane in command. The train progressed as far as Chieveley when Boers were observed through

Chieveley station, where the armoured train in which Churchill was travelling began its return trip to Estcourt

the mist on both sides of the line. It was early morning and visibility was poor, but the train was nonetheless ordered back to Estcourt.

A scouting party of General Louis Botha's Boer force had seen the train steaming north. The men waited until it was over the rise, knowing it would have to come back the same way, and then placed rocks on the tracks at the bottom of the steep slope. When the train returned, they opened fire to speed its progress into the trap. The trucks were now in reverse order from how they had left that morning, the first one being the plate-layers' truck and the last the flat-bed with the ship's cannon. In-between were the engine and five armoured trucks manned by 120 men of the Dublin Fusiliers and the Durban Light Infantry.

The train hurtled down the slope to escape the gunfire and hit the obstruction with a tremendous crash. The initial impact was enough to lift the first truck off the line and overturn it, scattering plate-layers over the surrounding veld. The next two trucks, containing a part of the 120-strong escort, were also derailed and one of them lodged firmly across the tracks, effectively blocking the line.

The attacking Boer horsemen drew closer, firing their Mauser rifles into the stricken convoy. They also had a Maxim Nordenfeldt gun that fired small shells at the rate of 60 per minute. These had sufficient impact to tear through the armour plating of the open trucks.

Haldane and Churchill conferred hastily and agreed that the captain should arrange the defence, while Churchill attempted to clear the line by persuading the driver to use the engine as a battering ram. The civilian driver, nursing a deep cut to his head and bleeding profusely, required a lot

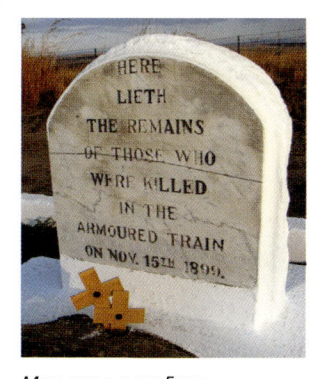

Mass grave near Frere

Timeline

1874
Jennie Jerome, the daughter of an American millionaire, marries Lord Randolph Churchill. Her elder son, Winston, is born in London later that year.

1895
Young Winston Churchill graduates from Sandhurst Military College and is commissioned into the 4th Hussars. After only nine months' service, he takes leave to travel to Cuba, where he marches with the Spanish army to quell a rebellion.

1898
Churchill takes part in the famous British cavalry charge at Omdurman.

1899
War is declared between Britain and South Africa. On 2 November 13,000 British troops and 5,000 civilians are besieged in Ladysmith.

On 15 November the young war reporter Churchill is captured when the Boers ambush the armoured train on which he is travelling from Chieveley.

On 15 December the British army is defeated by the Boers at the Battle of Colenso. Churchill escapes from the prisoner-of-war camp in Pretoria and arrives, via Lourenço Marques (Maputo), back in Durban. Soon he is back at the war front.

1900
The Battle of Spioenkop is fought and lost by the British. During the armistice, Churchill is on Spioenkop Mountain with Louis Botha, future Prime Minister of the Union of South Africa, and Mahatma Gandhi, later famed for his passive resistance campaign.

ARMOURED TRAIN DISASTER AND CHURCHILL'S CAPTURE 67

Churchill's search for adventure

Labelled a dunce at school, Winston Churchill enrolled at Sandhurst where he excelled, ranking eighth in his class when he graduated in 1895. He was commissioned to the 4th Hussars and, while on leave, he visited Cuba where Spain was putting down a rebellion.

He fought so bravely for Spain that he was awarded a medal. He then went to India with his regiment in 1896, where he rode and fought with Sir Bindon Blood. When he heard of the pending war in the Sudan, he took leave from his regiment and used his connections to join the 21st Lancers who were stationed there. He fought in the Battle of Omdurman and took part in the famous charge of the Dervishes. When the war in South Africa broke out in 1899, he secured a job as journalist with the *Morning Post*, which paid his passage. Aged only 24, he arrived in Durban on the same ship, the *Dunnottar Castle*, as General Sir Redvers Buller.

---

of persuasion, but Churchill assured him that no-one was ever hit twice on the same day. He also promised him an award for bravery. (Many years later, when he was British Home Secretary, he saw to it that the driver received it.)

When the line was eventually cleared, 40 minutes later and under heavy fire, the injured were loaded onto the engine and the uninjured were told to use its cover as they retreated. They escaped, but Churchill (who made his way back to the overturned trucks) and a number of the Dublin Fusiliers were captured and became prisoners of war.

Aftermath

Although regarded as a minor skirmish, the event had enormous repercussions for Churchill, as he used it as a springboard to launch his political career. He made a dramatic escape from Pretoria, where he was held, and reached Durban by way of Lourenço Marques (now Maputo), where he picked up a southbound steamer. In Durban he gave a triumphant speech on the steps of the Town Hall (now the post office) and was soon on his way to the war front once more. Churchill used his heroic role in the action to bully General Sir Redvers Buller into giving him an honorary commission in the South African Light Horse, which gave him a front-row seat in the battles fought in Natal.

Buried near the Churchill capture site are four Dublin Fusiliers, killed during the ambush.

Principal combatants
British: Durban Light Infantry; Naval Brigade; Royal Dublin Fusiliers.
Boers: Commandos from Boksburg, Krugersdorp and Wakkerstroom.

Battle of Colenso
15 December 1899

HOW TO GET THERE

Start at the Clouston Field of Remembrance on the R74/R103 south of Colenso and continue to the Colenso Gun Site, leaving Ambleside Military Cemetery until last.

Clouston Field of Remembrance: After leaving the N3, take exit 194, then turn right towards Colenso. Drive past the site of Churchill's capture, then continue for approximately 15km until you see a brown sign on your left indicating 'Clouston Field of Remembrance'. At the turn-off, drive a short distance up a dirt track to the cemetery. Walk up the path to the concrete plinth placed behind the tallest monument on the hill.

At this point, the Tugela River is in front of you as you look over the fence towards the hills rising in the north. The river, invisible in the low ground, is indicated by the trees that line its banks. The loop where the Irish were trapped is slightly to your right. Follow the river line further to your right to see the cooling towers of a disused power station in the little town of Colenso. This marks the place where the road and rail bridges cross the river. It was about 800m south of the towers that Colonel C. J. Long lost his guns. The big, humpbacked hill rising behind and to the east of the town is Hlangwane. The Ladysmith road, going through the hills behind the town in a north-westerly direction, is visible through a pair of binoculars.

Colenso Gun Site: From the Clouston Field of Remembrance site, continue along the R74 towards Colenso. Near the town, take the off-ramp to your left, marked 'Colenso'. At the stop street at the top of the ramp turn right over the bridge. From there, follow the signs to Colenso and the gun site. You will cross the railway line over a high road bridge. Shortly after this bridge, look down and to your left for the white markers lying low on the ground; these show the gun positions.

Ambleside Military Cemetery: Return to the bridge over the road. Continue over the bridge towards Winterton; after a short distance, cross a narrow bridge over a stream. Look out for signs on your right saying 'Ambleside Graves'. Turn off onto a dirt track; the graveyard will be on your left. Park next to the track and go through a turnstile to visit the cemetery.

Field of Remembrance: 28°46'44.3" S 29°48'37" E

Grave of Captain Hughes

BATTLE OF COLENSO 69

Timeline

1839
Redvers Buller is born in Devon. He attends Eton, where he is considered a dullard.

1858
Buller joins the army and proves his ability and bravery early in his military career.

1879
Buller serves in the Anglo-Zulu War and is awarded a VC for his actions at Hlobane.

1886
Gold is discovered in vast quantities on the Witwatersrand. There is seven times more gold here than in all other known gold reserves in the world. General Buller revamps the British Army Service Corps.

1899
The 2nd Anglo-Boer War begins and the Boers invade Natal and besiege Ladysmith. The Boers attempt to reach Durban, but are discouraged by British troops already stationed as far north as Estcourt. They choose to withdraw to the Tugela River where they make their defensive line. Buller is appointed commander-in-chief of the army in South Africa. On 15 December Buller is defeated at the Battle of Colenso. He is replaced as commander-in-chief by Lord Roberts, whose son was killed at Colenso. Buller remains in command of the British forces in Natal.

1900
The siege of Ladysmith is relieved and Buller moves his army north into the Transvaal.

1901
Buller returns to England and is put in command at Aldershot. He is relieved of this command in October and retires to his Devon estate.

Context

The town of Ladysmith had been surrounded and besieged by the Boers since 2 November 1899. The Boers had stationed about 10,000 men around the town to prevent the 13,000-strong garrison from breaking out. They had also entrenched themselves on the north bank of the Tugela River and in the hills above it, hoping to keep the British from advancing on Ladysmith from the south.

The Battle of Colenso was British General Sir Redvers Buller's first attempt to break the Boer defensive line along the north bank of the river. It was the most obvious route to Ladysmith, as Colenso is situated on the Tugela River where road and railway line span the water. Buller and his 15,000 troops were dependent on the railway for transport of equipment and food supplies.

On viewing the terrain, which gave the Boers strong positions in high and broken ground north of the river, Buller decided that it would be better to make a flanking attack to the west and get around the right of the Boer line near Spioenkop.

Meanwhile, other divisions of the British army had suffered two defeats in the Cape, one at the Stormberg railway junction on 10 December 1899 (see p. 301) and the other at the Battle of Magersfontein a day later (see p. 260). It was these reverses that changed Buller's mind again. In his capacity as overall commander of the British army in South Africa, he decided that a quick and decisive victory at Colenso was needed, both to restore morale and to free him up to go to the Cape. It would take too long to outflank the Boers on their right because this route was away from the railway line and transport would be slow and difficult. He resolved to push straight through the Boer line at Colenso, following the railway line to Ladysmith. The Battle of Colenso was his failed attempt to do so.

British officers observing the Battle of Colenso

Memorials and graves in the Clouston Field of Remembrance near Colenso

Action

Buller brought his troops up from Durban harbour by rail to Chieveley, just south of Colenso, where they set up camp. On 12 December 1899 he ordered the naval guns to open a bombardment on likely Boer positions in the hills on the north bank of the Tugela River.

The Boers, under the command of General Louis Botha, had entrenched themselves strongly in the low ground close to the north bank of the river. They had trenches and dummy gun emplacements on the hills overlooking the river, but the main trenches were dug along the river bank and manned by marksmen with Mauser rifles. Botha planned to lure the British across the river and then attack, using artillery and rifle fire, as the British advanced, with the river at their rear preventing their retreat.

General Louis Botha

Buller put together a three-pronged attack. The left-hand column, consisting of Major General Fitzroy Hart's 5th Irish Brigade, would advance west of the town, cross the river and move to the right in support of the centre column, made up of the 2nd Brigade commanded by Major General Hildyard. The 2nd Brigade was instructed to enter the village, cross the iron bridge and take the low hills immediately north of the bridge. Finally, the Mounted Brigade under the Earl of Dundonald would advance east of the town towards a large Boer-occupied hill called Hlangwane, situated on the south bank of the river, where the river looped sharply to the north. If this hill were in British hands, Boer trenches on the north bank could be enfiladed and their occupants forced to evacuate. The 6th Brigade (Barton's) would support the 2nd and the Mounted Brigades. The 4th Brigade (Lyttelton's) would support the 5th (Irish) and the 2nd brigades.

BATTLE OF COLENSO

Cross dedicated to the Natal Carbineers at the Clouston Field of Remembrance

Hart's 5th Brigade mistook the route they should have taken due to a faulty map. At 07h30 the men entered a big loop in the river west of the town. The crossing point should have been west of this loop, but the local guide they recruited led them to a minor drift in the toe of the loop. Here the brigade was in a deadly trap, surrounded on three sides by Boers in trenches along the river banks. They were also under shell fire from Boer guns in the high ground north of the river. In spite of their exceptional bravery (a few of the Irish managed to cross the river), they were unable to continue. By 08h00 the impossibility of advancing further was clear and by 10h00 the order came to withdraw. Although Lyttelton's 4th Brigade provided covering fire, there were heavy casualties.

Meanwhile, Hildyard's central brigade gained the town and took cover among the buildings. However, their supporting artillery, commanded by Colonel C. J. Long, took up position too close to the river. Long was later to blame the early morning light for his confused sense of distance.

It was the close proximity of the 12 field guns to the Boer trenches that caused the Boers to open fire prematurely and spoil Botha's original plan. However, the two enemy gun batteries did not stand a chance – under fire at close range most of the gunners were killed within minutes. The remainder continued to fire with great tenacity until their ammunition was exhausted. Since replacement ammunition limbers were unable to approach, the surviving men took shelter in a nearby donga. Long had been badly wounded and lay there with them.

From his vantage point further back and close to the big naval guns, Buller could not see anyone standing to the guns and, believing all his gunners to be wounded or dead, ordered a general withdrawal, a decision that was later severely criticised. But he had been badly bruised by a shell fragment, and his personal physician and friend, the surgeon M. L. Hughes, had been killed close to him. Hart's Irish Brigade, badly mauled in the loop, was retiring and Hildyard could go no further without artillery support.

British soldiers fire at an invisible enemy at Colenso.

All these factors affected Buller's judgement when he called for volunteers to retrieve the guns under fire, though they could have been defended by Barton's and Lyttelton's brigades and retrieved after dark. Several volunteers attempted what proved to be an impossible task and only two guns were recovered. It was here that the gallant Lieutenant Freddy Roberts, son of Field Marshal Roberts, fell. Victoria Crosses were awarded to seven of the volunteers, Roberts included.

This road bridge across the Tugela River at Colenso was destroyed by Boers.

Dundonald's Mounted Brigade had gained the lower slopes of Hlangwane. Leaving their horses under the cover of a stream bed and continuing up the hill on foot, they were unable to progress further. He requested support from Barton's brigade, but this officer, aware of what was happening elsewhere on the battlefield, did not respond. There was a general withdrawal of all troops back to Chieveley.

Aftermath

The British suffered almost 1,450 casualties. Boer casualties amounted to only 38. The effects were far-reaching, for, not only was Buller demoralised, but he was now also forced to await reinforcements before he could make another attempt at getting to Ladysmith. When the reinforcements did arrive, under command of General Sir Charles Warren, the lack of co-operation between the two generals boded ill for the second British attempt to break through the Boers' defence at Spioenkop in January 1900 (see p. 80).

Buller's Colenso defeat persuaded the War Office in London that he should be superseded by Roberts as overall commander in South Africa. Buller was, thenceforth, commander of operations in Natal only.

Principal combatants

British: 13th Hussars; Bethune's Mounted Infantry; Border Regiment; Composite Regiment; Connaught Rangers; Devonshire Regiment; Dublin Fusiliers; Durham Light Infantry; East Surrey Regiment; Inniskilling Fusiliers; Irish Fusiliers; King's Royal Rifle Corps; Natal Carbineers; Naval Brigade; Rifle Brigade; Royal Dragoons; Royal Field Artillery; Royal Fusiliers; Royal Scots Fusiliers; Scottish Rifles; South African Light Horse; Thorneycroft's Mounted Infantry; Welsh Fusiliers; West Surrey Regiment; West Yorkshire Regiment.
Boers: Commandos from Boksburg, Ermelo, Heidelberg, Johannesburg, Krugersdorp, Middelburg, Soutpansberg, Standerton, Vryheid and Wakkerstroom; Irish pro-Boers; Johannesburg Police; Swaziland Police.

Memorial to the 66th Battery Royal Field Artillery at the Clouston Garden of Remembrance

Key British figures at the Battle of Colenso

General Sir Redvers Buller

During the opening stages of the Anglo-Boer War General Sir Redvers Buller commanded the British army in South Africa. He was reputed to have a liking for good champagne, and, on his arrival in Durban harbour, crates labelled 'Castor Oil' were offloaded, concealing bottles of his favourite tipple. The story goes that his hapless commissary officer, unable to locate the crates in the newly established camp, rustled up all of the bottles of castor oil he could find and had them delivered to Buller's tent.

Buller's insistence on providing good fare, not only for himself but also for his troops, made him popular with the men. But it also prevented him from moving his army anywhere quickly. 'It is surely poor economy to feed your men well for four days at the expense of having them killed on the fifth' was a comment made about Buller at the time. He would never send his men into battle without feeding them a hot meal first, and would not engage the enemy unless a field hospital was in place close to the front line. He would not eat until he knew his men had had food. However, he was also pompous and vain and became a figure of mockery when he failed to break through the Boer line, gaining himself nicknames like 'Sir Reverse Buller' and the 'Ferryman of the Tugela River'.

General Sir Redvers Buller

Buller is said to have had a total disregard for shell and rifle fire. Though badly bruised by a shell fragment during the Battle of Colenso, he was seen encouraging his horse to drink from a small stream, all the while under heavy fire from Boer marksmen. The fragment that bruised Buller's ribs was part of the shell that killed his personal friend and surgeon, Captain M. L. Hughes of the Royal Army Medical Corps. Hughes was a leader in the field of bacteriology and was working on a vaccine against typhoid, a disease that was to kill thousands of soldiers and civilians during the 2nd Anglo-Boer War.

During the Battle of Colenso, Buller made his headquarters on the hill that is now the Clouston Field of Remembrance. The remains of many of the men killed during the battle were exhumed and buried here. There are also monuments to some of those who remain buried elsewhere.

Memorial stone tablet at Clouston

Lieutenant Freddy Roberts

Freddy Roberts, son of Lord Roberts, died a few days after the Battle of Colenso as a result of his brave attempt to save the British guns. At the time there was

This image of Freddy Roberts forms part of a series of embossed paintings portraying British soldiers' deeds of valour that earned a Victoria Cross.

KEY BRITISH FIGURES AT THE BATTLE OF COLENSO   75

This cairn, erected on the spot where Freddy Roberts fell, was relocated to Clouston from the original site.

no provision for granting posthumous awards for acts of bravery in the British armed services. However, Queen Victoria approved a request to award Roberts a Victoria Cross after his death and his was the first of many such posthumous decorations, including those made to lieutenants Melvill and Coghill, who died saving the Queen's Colour at Fugitives' Drift in 1879 (see p. 140). Their families received the medals in 1902.

The grave of Freddy Roberts can be found in the little graveyard at Chieveley. His original gravestone is next to the old toll house on the bridge over the Tugela River in Colenso.

The Irish regiments

The Irish regiments fought exceptionally well at Colenso, but suffered many casualties when they were unwittingly misled into a loop of the Tugela River and came under Boer fire from three sides.

The 1st and 2nd battalions of the Royal Dublin Fusiliers were part of the brigade commanded by General Fitzroy Hart, who made them stand to arms before dawn each day and inspected them for cleanliness. Being a stickler for discipline, he made the men advance into battle in close order as if on the parade ground, which resulted in more casualties than necessary.

The Royal Dublin Fusiliers formed the vanguard of the advance into the loop of the river. When the order came to retire, many in the centre and on the right did not get the message. As a result they were the last to retire and suffered the worst. One Dublin Fusilier was heard by his officer to remark to a comrade, 'This beats Athlone on a Saturday night.'

Four companies of the Royal Inniskilling Fusiliers were in the loop on the river bank when the Boers began firing at 06h00. At 10h30 they received the order to retire. One or two small parties of men were engaged at the very head of the loop at close quarters with some Boers, as they either did not receive the order or disregarded it. They fought

General Fitzroy Hart

Royal Dublin Fusiliers fought for the British, but there were also Irishmen, members of Colonel John Blake's Irish pro-Boer Brigade, who fought on the side of the Boers.

on until they were surrounded and taken prisoner. But commanding officer Lieutenant Colonel Thackeray used his wit to escape. 'Why should I surrender?' he quipped. 'If you don't like it, go back to where you came from and we'll begin the fight over again.' The Boer commandant was highly amused at the suggestion and allowed Thackeray to lead his men away, which he did, after inviting his would-be captors to dine with him when he had taken Pretoria.

Some members of the Irish pro-Boer Brigade fought with the Boers against the British at the Battle of Colenso. They sent a messenger to the Royal Dublin Fusiliers on the other side of the river, stating that they were keen to meet the Dublin Boys and wipe them off the face of the earth.
A polite note was sent in reply, remarking that the Dublin Boys were equally eager for this meeting and that they would go through the Irish pro-Boers 'as the devil went through Athlone'.

John Francis Dunne

Among the Royal Dublin Fusiliers was a young bugler, John Francis Dunne, whose father was colour sergeant with the brigade. During the confusion in the loop of the Tugela River, the boy suddenly found himself in the front line of troops advancing towards the river. He was so caught up in the action that he sounded the advance and accompanied the bayonet charge into the river. Dunne was wounded twice during the charge, but he ran on until he reached the river, where he lost his bugle. After recovering in hospital he was sent back to England where Queen Victoria presented him with a shining new bugle 'to replace the bugle lost by him on the field of battle at Colenso on 15 December 1899, when he was wounded'.

2nd ANGLO-BOER WAR
BATTLE OF
COLENSO
15 December 1899
LEGEND
BOER POSITION
BRITISH POSITION
BOER GUNS
BRITISH GUNS
BRITISH HEADQUARTERS
BRITISH CAMP
RAILWAY
ROAD
TRACK
BRITISH ADVANCE
N
0
2km
4km
To Ladysmith
To Ladysmith
To Springfield
GROBBELAARS HILL
Onderbroekspruit
KANONKOPPIE
Creusot gun
5
SOUTPANSBERG COMMANDO
SWAZILAND POLICE
ORANGE FREE STATE COMMANDOS
ERMELO COMMANDO
MIDDELBURG COMMANDO
Farm
JOHANNESBURG COMMANDO
6
Drift
2
Drift
Wagon drift
Tugela River
Drift (footpath)
Drift
RED HILLS
VRYHEID COMMANDO
Krupp guns
JOHANNESBURG POLICE
Maxim Nordenfeldt gun
Fort Wylie
KRUGERSDORP COMMANDO
HEIDELBERG COMMANDO
COLENSO
Tugela River
HLANGWANE
4
Gombaspruit
DUNDONALD'S MOUNTED BRIGADE
3
Long's artillery
Field artillery
Naval guns
Field artillery
ROYAL DRAGOONS
GENERAL HART'S BRIGADE
GENERAL LYTTELTON'S BRIGADE
4.7-inch & naval long 12-pdr guns
NAVAL GUN HILL
BULLER'S HQ
SHOOTER'S HILL
1
Naval long 12-pdr guns
GENERAL HILDYARD'S BRIGADE
GENERAL BARTON'S BRIGADE
Doringkopspruit

*FAR LEFT: The Clouston Field of Remembrance
ABOVE: The British camp at Frere
LEFT: Boer trenches at Colenso*

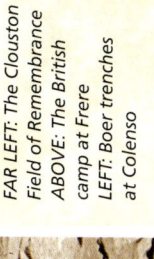

① This is the hill on which the British long-ranging naval guns were placed during the initial bombardment of the hills north of the river. The area close under the north-eastern slopes is now the Clouston Field of Remembrance.

② The loop in the river was a trap for Major General Hart's Irish Brigade. The guide led the men towards the drift in the toe of the loop where the soldiers were exposed to Boer rifle fire on two sides, as well as shells from Boer guns on the hills above.

③ This is the position where Colonel Long placed his two batteries of field guns. He admitted later that the early morning light had confused his sense of distance and that the guns were too close to the Boers, who were just north of the river and had the batteries well within range of their Mauser rifles and their artillery pieces.

④ This humpbacked ridge, Hlangwane, was an important feature, vital for the Boers to hold. Although it is on the south bank of the river, its position would have made it possible for the British, had they taken it, to enfilade Boer trenches on the north bank of the river.

⑤ These hills were strongly held by the Boers who placed both dummy emplacements and real guns there. However, the British bombardment, which began on 12 December, concentrated on these hills while the Boers mostly lay safely below them in concealed trenches close to the river.

⑥ Remnants of these trenches may still be seen on the north bank of the river, close to the loop.

Battle of Spioenkop
24 January 1900

HOW TO GET THERE

From Durban take the N3 to Johannesburg. Take exit number 230, which will take you onto the R616. At the end of the off-ramp turn left towards Bergville and after 4km turn left onto a gravel road signposted 'Spioenkop Battlefield'. Follow the road until you reach the boom and entry gate to the battlefield. You are now on the 'Boer side' of the mountain; the high ground on your left is Conical Hill, which the Boers held throughout the battle. When you reach the top of the concrete road, look behind you and to your left to see the top of Conical Hill. Continue up the track to the summit and the car park. The stretch of water ahead and below is the Spioenkop Dam on the Tugela River. If you walk ahead in the same direction your vehicle was facing when you reached the summit, you will arrive at the south-western crest of Spioenkop. Looking down to your left you will see the shoulder up which the British made their famous night ascent.

Return to the car park and walk up the concrete path to the main monument. As you approach it, look to your left to see the Boer monument about 130m away on the north-eastern crest. At the main British monument, follow the line of the mass grave down the hill; this was the main trench of the British. The detached knoll on your left is Aloe Knoll, which was held by the Boers during the battle. The double peaks to the east and behind are Twin Peaks, taken by the Rifle Brigade. From the lowest end of the main trench, look across the Tugela River valley to the dark-green ridge in the middle distance. Its highest point, east of the tarred road that crosses the river, is Mount Alice, where General Sir Redvers Buller had his headquarters. On a clear day, and with a good pair of binoculars, you may pick out the great silver cross that marks the spot.

Entry gate: 28°38'53.4" S 29°31'00.3" E

This cross, erected at the site of the main trench at Spioenkop, marks the spot where Major General Edward Woodgate fell during the battle.

Context

The Boer forces invaded the British colony of Natal in October 1899 and successfully besieged the garrison town of Ladysmith, an important railway junction between the Transvaal, Natal and Orange Free State. After an unsuccessful attempt by the British army to break through the Boer defences at Colenso (see p. 69), General Sir Redvers Buller realised that the approach to Ladysmith along the railway line was too well defended by the Boers. He decided to outflank them on their right by taking his army west and crossing the Tugela via Springfield (near

View of Spioenkop from the side of the British position

present-day Winterton). The battle fought on Spioenkop was the climax of almost a week's fighting on the north bank of the river, during which the British were unable to break through the Boer line.

Action

At the Battle of Colenso on 15 December, Buller's army had suffered 1,450 casualties, and he thus preferred to wait for reinforcements before commencing operations against the right flank of the Boer line near Spioenkop. This delay gave the Boers ample time to improve defences on this thinly held sector of their defensive line. British reinforcements in the form of the 10th Division duly arrived under the command of General Sir Charles Warren. About the same age, the two men could not have been more different. The friction between them resulted in a series of tactical errors that played into the Boers' hands.

Putting supply before strategy

Whereas Boer commandos carried little other than their greatcoats, some coffee and biltong, the British were so well equipped and provisioned that their supply column consisted of more than 1,000 wagons. This detracted greatly from their mobility and caused a member of General Buller's staff to say that Buller put supply before strategy. Apparently he even insisted that the officers' mess piano accompany the column.

Timeline

1869
Mohandas Gandhi is born in Porbandar in India. He qualifies in London as a barrister in 1891.

1893
Gandhi arrives in South Africa to practise law and is deeply affected when he is forced to vacate a first-class train compartment because he is not white.

1894
Gandhi founds the Natal Indian Congress.

1896
Escalating grievances among the Uitlanders in Transvaal gold-mining areas culminate in the Jameson Raid, aimed at overthrowing the Boer government. Three years later war breaks out between the Boers and the British.

1899
At the outbreak of the 2nd Anglo-Boer War, Gandhi offers to raise an Indian regiment to serve with the British. When the offer is refused, he raises the Indian Ambulance Corps of 1,100 men.

1900
The Battle of Spioenkop is fought in January. Louis Botha leads the Boers to an unlikely victory. The stretcher bearers trained by Gandhi perform valuable service to both sides.

1902
The Treaty of Vereeniging marks the end of war in South Africa.

1907
Botha becomes Prime Minister of the Transvaal and, three years later, is chosen as the first premier of the Union of South Africa.

BATTLE OF SPIOENKOP   81

A man of few words

The British military hospital (now the site of a military cemetery) lay under the southern slopes of Mount Alice, General Sir Redvers Buller's vantage point during the Battle of Spioenkop. The surgeon in charge, Sir Frederick Treves, later wrote *Tale of a Field Hospital* in which he recounted his experiences. In the book he tells of a young casualty who arrived in an ambulance wagon after the Battle of Spioenkop, half of his face shot away by a shell fragment. He had lain in the sun for nearly 48 hours, insisting that the stretcher bearers take the more seriously injured men before him. He was barely conscious when he arrived at the hospital in the evening of the day after the battle. As he could not speak, he signalled that he wanted to write something. Thinking he wanted to compose a final message to his loved ones, someone gave him a pencil and paper. He wrote just three words: 'Did we win?'

Buller planned a two-pronged assault: a feint attack over Potgieter's Drift (a river crossing close to Mount Alice), led by Major General Neville G. Lyttelton, and the real attack across Trichardt's Drift, further west, under the command of Warren.

The dual advance began on 16 January 1900. Lyttelton's crossing was virtually uncontested and the men took up position in some small hills north of the river, where they sheltered from shells fired by well-entrenched Boers on the Brakfontein ridges.

Early the same morning, Warren began his flanking movement towards the west. The attack was intended to take the Boers by surprise, but, by the time Warren's force – including 15,000 infantry, 1,200 cavalry and all the supply wagons – had reached Trichardt's Drift, the Boers were well aware of his intentions and had already moved men across to the west to reinforce their right flank. It took Warren a full 37 hours to move all his men, oxen and supplies across the river.

While Warren was organising the river crossing on two pontoon bridges, the dashing Earl of Dundonald had taken his cavalry west along the north bank of the river to find the extreme right of the Boer line. He came to the Acton Homes road that led eastward into Ladysmith and there spotted an approaching and unsuspecting Boer commando. Dundonald and his men waited for them to enter a narrow defile and then opened fire. The Boers fled, but some were killed and others taken prisoner. The road to Ladysmith was open. However, when Dundonald sent word back to Warren asking for reinforcements, the general ordered the cavalry back immediately, as the horses, he said, were needed to guard the oxen.

General Louis Botha

The British 4.7-inch (120mm) naval gun, which had the range to combat the Boer Long Tom

Boer general Louis Botha was later to say that, if the British had forced their way through that evening, the Boers would have been very hard-pressed to stop them. As it was, Botha had ample time to reinforce his defence before the main British offensive began. When it did, Warren found he was unable to progress. As the British troops advanced against the ridges of the Tabanyama range, they came up against an invisible enemy in head-high, slit trenches that could neither be dislodged by shellfire nor reached by bayonet-wielding soldiers. Warren's men fell in increasing numbers, shot by an enemy they never saw.

A series of similar disastrous engagements was fought over a period of four days. Eventually Buller became impatient at the lack of progress and mounting casualties and threatened to withdraw Warren's command if he did not do something decisive. Warren countered by saying that he would attempt to force his way through by another road, close under Spioenkop, but in order to do so he would have to take the hill. Buller retorted that he should do so quickly.

Colonel Alexander Thorneycroft volunteered to find a way up the almost-sheer south-facing slopes of Spioenkop and spent the day before the battle planning a route up the shoulder of the mountain, the only practical line from the south. At nightfall, a 1,700-strong assault force of men from the Lancashire Regiment, South Lancashires, Royal Lancasters, Thorneycroft's Mounted Infantry and a half-company of Royal Engineers marched from their headquarters on Three Tree Hill across the valley below to the base of the

Memorials on the mass grave at Spioenkop

BATTLE OF SPIOENKOP   83

This British memorial was erected on the site of the main trench.

shoulder that Thorneycroft had chosen for the ascent. It was an honour to be included in the assault force, but the attack seemed doomed from the outset: the men had insufficient water with them; the sandbags, which could be filled with soil dug from a trench and used as a parapet, were left behind; only 50 entrenching tools were carried to the summit, hardly sufficient to entrench 200 men, let alone 1,700; the mountain gun that could have been dismantled and carried to the top could not be found; and, finally, the telephone cable needed for communications with headquarters was left, fully wound on its drum, at the bottom of the hill.

The men were nonetheless in good spirits and walked in silence up the steep slope. Smoking and talking were not allowed and the only sound was the swish of their trousers through the long, wet grass. We are told that a big dog joined them halfway up and, when no-one was willing to kill it, a bugler led it back down the hill, using a rifle pull-through as a lead. The boy was fortunate not to be on the mountain the following morning.

At 03h00 the British assault force reached the summit. The Boers were not in force on the summit, although they had begun preparing a position for a gun that had not yet been installed. The only defence they had on the mountain was a small group of sentries, two of whom were on outpost duty in a forward position near the top of the shoulder by which the British ascended. The sentries, little more than boys, were asleep and wakened only when

The Indian stretcher bearers

At the time of the 2nd Anglo-Boer War, Mahatma Gandhi was a practising lawyer in Durban. He organised more than 1,000 Indians into a stretcher-bearing corps to carry wounded soldiers off the battlefield. The stretchers mostly consisted of canvas pieces slung between two bamboo poles. The stretcher bearers were trained to run with a strange, shambling gait in order to minimise jolting. They were trained by an English doctor named L. P. Booth.

LADYSMITH REGION

the British dropped some entrenching tools on the rocky ground. They leaped to their feet, shouting a challenge and firing blindly into the darkness. The British had been ordered to lie flat in the event of a challenge, and then, when the bolt-action rifles of the Boers were being reloaded, to rush forwards, bayonets fixed, and charge. This they did and one of the sentries, who paused too long to put on his boots, was 'tossed into the air like a shook of corn' on the bayonet of a burly British soldier. The Battle of Spioenkop had begun.

The only means of informing Warren that they had taken Spioenkop was to give three cheers in the direction of his headquarters. The British soldiers then made their way in the dark to reach the highest point and began to entrench themselves against the counterattack that was bound to come the next morning. However, the ground was hard and rocky and there were no sandbags and only 50 entrenching tools, making the entrenchment less than adequate to protect the 1,700 men spread so vulnerably across the summit.

Meanwhile, General Louis Botha, the young Boer commander, had been informed that the 'khakis' had taken Spioenkop. His response was calm. 'Well,' he said, 'then we will have to take it back.' He spent the remaining hours of darkness on the back of his grey pony, visiting the gunners manning each of the seven guns he had below the hill and instructing them to train their weapons on the summit. He then positioned a young schoolmaster, Bothma, in a place where he could signal to all seven gunners and receive signals from Botha. He also instructed his best men, members of the Carolina Commando, to climb the northeast face of the mountain and conceal themselves just below the crest.

The sun was smothered in thick cloud and the hill enshrouded in damp mist until about 08h00 on 24 January. When the sun suddenly broke through, a young lieutenant sitting in the shallow trench and eating a Gentleman's Relish sandwich was hit between the eyes by a bullet from a Boer rifle scarcely 20m away. Major General Edward Woodgate, in command on the summit, realised that his trench was too far from the crest of the hill and that he

Messages between British forces at Ladysmith and Mount Alice were exchanged by heliograph.

BATTLE OF SPIOENKOP 85

would have to prize the Boers from the sheltered firing positions from where they were firing into his men at almost point-blank range. As the mist cleared, he ordered a bayonet charge over the open ground in front of the trench and the Boers were driven off the crest and down the hill. Tragically, Warren, who had heard that the Boers had occupied the crest, ordered his artillery to fire into them, resulting in some of his own men being killed by friendly fire before the British gunners were ordered to stop firing.

Botha, meanwhile, had told his heliograph signaller to instruct all seven guns to shell the summit. As Boer shells rained onto the rocky ground, billows of dust and lethal splinters of rock flew into the men cowering in their shallow trench. Woodgate took a rock splinter in the brain and was carried from the summit shouting, 'Leave me alone!' (He died two months later and was buried at Mooi River.) This was very demoralising for his men and the question of command on the summit now became a problem. The next in seniority was Colonel Malby Crofton, but the message he sent to Warren was garbled (the British heliograph had been smashed by a shell): 'Reinforce at once or all is lost. General dead.'

When Buller read this he thought Crofton should be replaced by someone stronger and recommended Thorneycroft. The message was sent to Thorneycroft that he was now in command, but none of the other officers, all of them senior in rank to Thorneycroft, was aware of his promotion. Throughout the long day, the men had no idea whether they should be obeying Crofton, Hill, Cooke, Coke or Thorneycroft.

Towards midday, a thick, dirty cloud covered the summit. As more shells fell on rocky ground, packed with an ever-increasing number of reinforcements, casualties rose. Those men in the right-hand end of the main trench suffered grievously. Without water and surrounded by the horribly mutilated remains of their comrades, they also had to endure the flies and

The main trench on Spioenkop was used to bury the dead, most of them British soldiers.

These memorials honour British soldiers who were killed. A memorial to Boer fighters stands on the north-eastern crest of the hill.

the stifling heat. The enemy was nowhere to be seen and yet exploding shells and Mauser bullets winging into the end of the trench were taking their deadly toll. These came from the rifles of Boer marksmen moving up through the dead ground between Aloe Knoll, a feature adjoining the main summit and held throughout by the Boers, and the right-hand end of the main trench. These Boers were almost successful in working their way around this end of the trench and behind the British position. It was only when reinforcements arrived up the steep southern slopes that the Boers were repulsed. There was hand-to-hand fighting as the Boers were forced back towards Aloe Knoll.

Botha recommenced the shelling of the summit and eventually the British at the extreme right of the main trench could take it no more and a white handkerchief was raised by one of the young privates. The Boer commander, his rifle at the trail, came to take prisoners. One hundred and twenty men were led off the hill before Thorneycroft caught sight of the unofficial surrender. He rushed down the hill, hobbling on a stick, as he had sprained his ankle on the uneven ground. He grabbed the Boer commandant by the shoulder and shouted, 'There is no surrender. These are my men. Get your men back to hell, sir!' He ordered the remaining bugler to sound a charge and a wave of bayonet-wielding men surged down the slope to drive the Boers back to their positions below the crest.

The shells then continued to rain on the summit, wreaking their terrible destruction. It was at this stage, we are told, that a black man was seen wandering about on the summit searching for his young Boer master. Men on both sides pleaded with him to take cover, but he was unheeding and fell, before long, to join the other dead on the hillside.

Meanwhile, General Lyttelton, in command of the feint attack at Potgieter's Drift, had been watching the damage that was being inflicted on the British by the Boer guns on Twin Peaks. He decided that a diversion was desperately needed to relieve the situation on the summit and that the

General Sir Charles Warren commanded the British during the battle.

Aloe Knoll is to the left and Twin Peaks lies beyond.

best move would be to attack the Boer guns. He sent the King's Royal Rifle Corps scrambling in half-companies up the almost sheer, grassy hillsides of both peaks, each half-company covering the other as it climbed. This was the first time the fire-and-manoeuvre technique was used successfully. These brave men succeeded in reaching the dead ground below the Boer guns and, as they rose to charge the position with their bayonets, the Boers fled, taking their guns with them. The King's Royal Rifles had taken Twin Peaks.

It was at this point that the entire course of the battle could have changed, as from Twin Peaks the British would have been able to clear Aloe Knoll and the north-eastern slopes of Spioenkop of Boers and to relieve the pressure on the main trench. However, Buller ordered the King's Royal Rifles to abandon their position and withdraw, afraid that they would be isolated, surrounded and defeated. This was his personal regiment and he could not bear to have them so vulnerable. It was also unfortunate that the commander of the Rifles, Lieutenant Colonel Buchanan-Riddell, was killed by a Boer sharpshooter as evening fell, leaving his second in command no option but to lead the troops down the slopes.

Boer commando on the slopes of Spioenkop

88   LADYSMITH REGION

Meanwhile, Boer general Schalk Burger, who had been driven from Twin Peaks, realised how key the position was that he had lost to the British and had started withdrawing his men towards Ladysmith. When Thorneycroft, on the bloody summit of the mountain, observed the Rifles' withdrawal he concluded that the Boers would be up there again the next morning and that there was, therefore, no point in holding the summit any longer. He gave orders for a withdrawal towards the south-west. And so elements of both armies began to withdraw, thinking that the other side had won. However, General Botha was convinced that the battle had been won by the Boers and persuaded most of his men to stay.

Football and war

To this day, one end of Anfield Football pitch in Liverpool, England, is known as The Kop, in memory of the Lancashire men who lost their lives during the Battle of Spioenkop. The assault force that took the hill was chosen from men of the Lancashire Fusiliers, the Royal Lancaster Regiment and the South Lancashire Regiment.

Aftermath

The British failed in their second attempt to break the Boer defensive line and Ladysmith was to remain besieged for another month. Both sides suffered heavy casualties. Between 16 and 24 January, British casualties amounted to almost 1,500 men (deaths as well as prisoners and wounded), while the Boers lost about 50 killed and 140 wounded, most of them on Spioenkop itself. The next day was declared an armistice so that the dead and wounded could be collected.

Principal combatants
(on the day of the battle and during the preceding week)
British: 13th Hussars; Bethune's Mounted Infantry; Border Regiment; Connaught Rangers; Devonshire Regiment; Dorsetshire Regiment; Dublin Fusiliers; East Surrey Regiment; Imperial Light Horse; Imperial Mounted Infantry; King's Royal Rifle Corps; Lancashire Fusiliers; Middlesex Regiment; Natal Carbineers; Natal Police; Naval Brigade; Royal Dragoons; Royal Field Artillery; Royal Inniskilling Fusiliers; Royal Lancaster Regiment; Scottish Rifles; Somersetshire Light Infantry; South African Light Horse; South Lancashire Regiment; Thorneycroft's Mounted Infantry; West Surrey Regiment; West Yorkshire Regiment.
Boers: Commandos from Bethal, Boksburg, Carolina, Ermelo, Heidelberg, Heilbron, Johannesburg, Krugersdorp, Middelburg, Piet Retief, Pretoria, Soutpansberg, Utrecht, Vryheid, Wakkerstroom and Winburg; German Corps; Staatsartillerie.

2nd ANGLO-BOER WAR
BATTLE OF
SPIOENKOP
24 January 1900
N
0
1km
2km
To Ladysmith
To Acton Homes
TABANYAMA
2 Creusot guns
Krupp & Maxim Nordenfeldt guns
BOTHA'S HQ
Krupp gun
BASTION HILL
GREEN HILL
Field guns
PIQUET HILL
CONICAL HILL
Maxim Nordenfeldt gun
CAROLINA COMMANDO
BRAKFONTEIN RIDGES
Krupp gun
THREE TREE HILL
SPIOENKOP
ALOE KNOLL
TWIN PEAKS
Ventersspruit
Field guns
Fairview Farm
WARREN'S HQ
GENERAL WOODGATE'S ASSAULT FORCE
KING'S ROYAL RIFLE CORPS
SCOTTISH RIFLES
Tugela River
VAALKRANS
Field guns
Kaffir Drift
GENERAL LYTTELTON'S BRIGADE
ROOIKOPPIES
Field guns
Trichardt's Drift
Pontoon bridges
Munger's Drift
Potgieter's Drift
SCOTTISH RIFLES
KING'S ROYAL RIFLE CORPS
4.7-inch naval gun
MOUNT ALICE
BULLER'S HQ
SWARTKOP
LEGEND
BOER POSITION
BRITISH POSITION
BOER GUNS
BRITISH GUNS
BRITISH HEADQUARTERS
BOER HEADQUARTERS
BOER CAMP
TRACK
BOER ADVANCE
BRITISH ADVANCE

The mass grave on the summit of Spioenkop

① Tabanyama ridge was the scene of fighting from 20 to 23 January, where the British suffered over 400 casualties. The Boers had two lines of defence on these ridges and, when forced back to the second, had a clear field of fire from their well-concealed trenches. They also used their artillery here to good effect, especially the 75mm Creusot guns, ably manned by members of the well-trained Staatsartillerie.

② British field guns positioned here were outranged by the Boer guns and were ineffective during the battle.

③ Warren's position on Three Tree Hill meant that he could not see that the Boers had occupied Aloe Knoll.

④ The path taken by the British assault force was the only practical way to the top from the British position under Three Tree Hill.

⑤ The British 4.7-inch (120mm) naval gun positioned near Mount Alice began to shell Aloe Knoll, but was ordered by Warren to stop since he believed Aloe Knoll was held by the British.

⑥ Buller was positioned on Mount Alice. Although he had given command to Warren, he frequently interfered and it was he who forced Warren into a premature assault on the hill, before proper reconnaissance could be completed. It was also Buller who recommended the appointment of Thorneycroft as commanding officer when General Woodgate had been mortally wounded. This led to confusion as there were other, higher ranking officers present.

⑦ The British trench was taped out in the darkness and, although on the highest point of the hill, it did not command the crest.

⑧ A schoolmaster by the name of Bothma manned a heliograph in this position and was able to direct all seven Boer gunners when and where to fire their shells. When one of the tripod legs was blown off, he propped the instrument on a boulder and continued to signal to the gunners.

⑨ Seven Boer guns caused devastation among the closely packed men in the British trenches.

⑩ Bravely led by Lieutenant Colonel Buchanan-Riddell, the men of the King's Royal Rifle Corps used the fire-and-manoeuvre technique to reach the summits of Twin Peaks and cause the withdrawal of the Boers and the one gun they had there. This could have been the turning point of the battle and resulted in a British victory. However, Buller, fearing for the safety of the men, ordered them to withdraw down the slopes to safety. They incurred casualties as they did so.

Battle of Vaalkrans
5–7 February 1900

HOW TO GET THERE
This battlefield is best visited with a knowledgeable guide who is familiar with the terrain and can identify the salient features of the battle across the entire site.

From the Spioenkop battlefield (see p. 80), retrace your route on the R616, travelling towards Ladysmith. You will then cross over the N3, the main highway to Johannesburg. At the first T-junction, turn right (south) onto the R103 towards Colenso and proceed until you reach a gravel turn-off to the right signposted 'Skietdrift and Vaalkrans'.

Continue on the gravel road until it crosses over the N3. Shortly thereafter you will see a series of monuments on your right. The small hill above these monuments is Vaalkrans. (If you reach the Tugela River you would have missed the monuments and gone too far.) It is along this track that leads to the river that you will get the best view of the area of operations.

As you near the distinctive, flat-topped Swartkop Mountain on the right, turn around and look back (north) towards Vaalkrans. On your extreme left (west), Spioenkop is visible in the distance. To its right (east) are the Twin Peaks and east of them are the low Brakfontein ridges, ending in the double-humped Vaalkrans in front of you. The N3 highway runs to your right. On the opposite side of the N3, as it passes Vaalkrans, lies Green Hill. The very high mountain on your right (east) is Doringkop. Ladysmith lies to your north-east. *Guide recommended*

Context

This battle was the third attempt by General Sir Redvers Buller to break through the Boer line and relieve the siege of Ladysmith (see p. 112). He had suffered a reverse on 24 January at Spioenkop where his attempt to outflank the Boers had failed. He blamed the failure on General Sir Charles Warren to whom he had delegated responsibility. Buller was now ready to try again at a place that he had defined as 'the key to Ladysmith'.

It is said that he reached this conclusion through information gleaned from a farmer of British descent who had been supplying the Boers on the Colenso–Spioenkop line with eggs and milk. The man, Thornley, offered the intelligence because he felt aggrieved at having been taken prisoner by the Boers when he was found reading an English newspaper. He promised to show Buller a gap in the hills that would make an easy access route for his troops into Ladysmith. Buller was impressed by the gap in the line of jagged hills east of Spioenkop that Thornley pointed out him and was convinced that it would, indeed, be the best place to break the Boer defences.

The way through the hills is now traversed by the N3, the main highway between Johannesburg and Durban.

Six naval long 12-pounders were hauled onto Swartkop prior to the battle.

Action

Buller planned to attack the Boers on Vaalkrans, a low double-humped hill just west of the present-day highway. At the same time he would force the Boers off Green Hill, the high ground on the opposite side of the road. Buller had planned the attack from his viewpoint on Swartkop, the tall, flat-topped mountain commanding Vaalkrans from the south side of the river where he planned to place his artillery and bombard the Boers before sending his infantry up to take the hill.

While the engineers pondered how to build a road up the almost-sheer slopes under the summit, the Naval Brigade took matters into their own hands: 14 guns (including six naval long 12-pounders) were hauled up under cover of darkness with the help of pulleys and steel hawsers. This was no mean feat and was due to the skill and muscle power of the Blue Jackets and their escort of Royal Scots Fusiliers.

The Boers were thinly stretched at this point. There were only about 3,600 of them between Spioenkop and Colenso, a distance of over 40km. General Louis Botha, believing the British would wait at least two weeks after their disastrous reverse at Spioenkop before entering the fray again, had gone to Pretoria on leave. General Schalk Burger was left to command the western flank and General Tobias Smuts was in charge of the

General Schalk Burger

Timeline

1868
Ben Viljoen is born in the Cape, but grows up in the Transkei. He marries and moves to Johannesburg, where he serves as a policeman in Krugersdorp.

1886
Viljoen serves on the Volksraad and works as a journalist. He raises a volunteer corps of soldiers. Gold is discovered in the Witwatersrand, attracting foreign miners and adventurers to Johannesburg.

1896
Dr Leander Starr Jameson leads a party of raiders to Johannesburg to overthrow the Boer government. Viljoen takes part in the fight against them.

1897
President Paul Kruger of the Transvaal sends emissaries overseas to buy long-ranging artillery pieces and modern magazine rifles.

1899
The outbreak of the 2nd Anglo-Boer War sees Viljoen as commandant of the Johannesburg Commando. He fights at the Battle of Elandslaagte under General J. H. M. Kock. General Sir Redvers Buller realises after the Battle of Talana that the British field artillery is outranged by the Boer guns.

1900
At the Battle of Vaalkrans in February, the naval guns are used to great effect by the British. Viljoen and his commando hold a key position which they are forced to vacate. A lyddite shell knocks Viljoen unconscious, but not before he has saved the Boer gun. In August, at the Battle of Bergendal, a recovered Viljoen again holds a key position.

1902
Viljoen is captured and exiled to St Helena. The war ends in May with the Peace of Vereeniging. Viljoen writes his memoirs entitled *My Reminiscences of the Anglo-Boer War*. He returns to South Africa but soon emigrates to the USA to settle in New Mexico.

1912–1913
Viljoen serves in the Mexican army and helps to overthrow the dictator.

BATTLE OF VAALKRANS   93

eastern flank, with Commandant Ben Viljoen of the Johannesburg Commando manning the trenches on Vaalkrans. Noting the massing of infantry and guns under Mount Alice, Viljoen was well aware that the British were planning to attack and called for reinforcements and more guns. A message was sent to Botha to return.

The battle began with a feint attack against the Brakfontein ridges on the morning of 5 February. This well-entrenched line of low hills was strongly held by the Boers in deep trenches. They did not respond to the bombardment, content to wait until the British were within range of their rifles.

At midday the British guns and infantry lining the flat land facing the Brakfontein ridges were withdrawn and crossed a pontoon bridge over the river to take up positions further east, under Vaalkrans. Unfortunately, the element of surprise was lost when the river crossing was delayed, allowing the Boers ample time to regroup and defend the new area of attack.

The naval guns on Swartkop opened a murderous fire on Vaalkrans and, under its cover, the Infantry Brigade advanced. The foot soldiers approached through a deep donga that afforded some cover. As the attackers swarmed up the rocky hillside, the Boers abandoned their trenches and fled, taking their Maxim Nordenfeldt gun with them. Viljoen was badly wounded by an exploding shell, but made a dramatic recovery and was fighting again by May.

The British stormed and gained the southern summit of Vaalkrans, but the troops were unable to place artillery there or to progress further. Buller had not carried out the second part of his plan, which was to take Green Hill, believing it would cost too many lives. Furthermore, the Boers still held the northern summit of Vaalkrans, from where they harassed the British on the southern summit, forcing them to keep under cover as best they could.

In the meanwhile, Botha had arrived and taken command. He saw to the placing of a Long Tom (155mm Creusot gun) on Doringkop, the high ground that dominated Vaalkrans from the east.

An illustration showing ammunition being carried up the steep slopes of Swartkop Mountain

On 6 February the British troops, exposed on the rocky summit of Vaalkrans, came under terrific shell bombardment all day. They were relieved under cover of darkness by a brigade of fresh men. However, the following day, 7 February, was no different and culminated in a massive artillery duel between the big guns of both sides. The men on the summit suffered terribly and were eventually led off the hill that night, crossing the fast-flowing river by means of a pontoon bridge hastily constructed in close proximity to the southern slope. There was a general withdrawal after that, all troops being recalled to Chieveley.

> ### The agterryers
>
> The Boers rode to battle with loyal black or 'coloured' servants to assist them. Called agterryers (after riders), they cared for the horses, foraged for food, carried spare guns and ammunition, and generally supported their employers. Although the agterryers carried rifles, it was unusual for them to take part in the fighting. However, among the dead Boers on Vaalkrans was an agterryer who had been fighting with the burghers led by Commandant Ben Viljoen.

Aftermath

Buller had failed, once again, to break the Boer line in spite of expending more artillery shells than in any other single engagement in the war – there were 72 British guns firing into the Boer positions during the battle. Casualties on both sides were heavy and the damage to British morale was severe. Despite these setbacks, Buller was learning to use the artillery to drop shells just ahead of advancing infantry to keep the enemy heads down. This technique was used to excellent effect in his final, successful attempt at breaking the Boer line at the Battle of Tugela Heights (see p. 98).

Principal combatants

British: Border Regiment; Connaught Rangers; Devonshire Regiment; Durham Light Infantry; East Surrey Regiment; King's Royal Rifle Corps; Lancaster Regiment; Middlesex Regiment; Naval Brigade; Rifle Brigade; Royal Dragoons; Royal Dublin Fusiliers; Royal Field Artillery; Royal Scots Fusiliers; Royal West Surrey Regiment; Scottish Rifles; South Lancashire Regiment; West Yorkshire Regiment; York and Lancaster Regiment.
Boers: Commandos from Bethal, Heidelberg, Heilbron, Johannesburg, Krugersdorp, Piet Retief, Senekal, Soutpansberg, Standerton, Vrede and Winburg; Staatsartillerie.

Commandant Ben Viljoen saved the Boer gun on Vaalkrans.

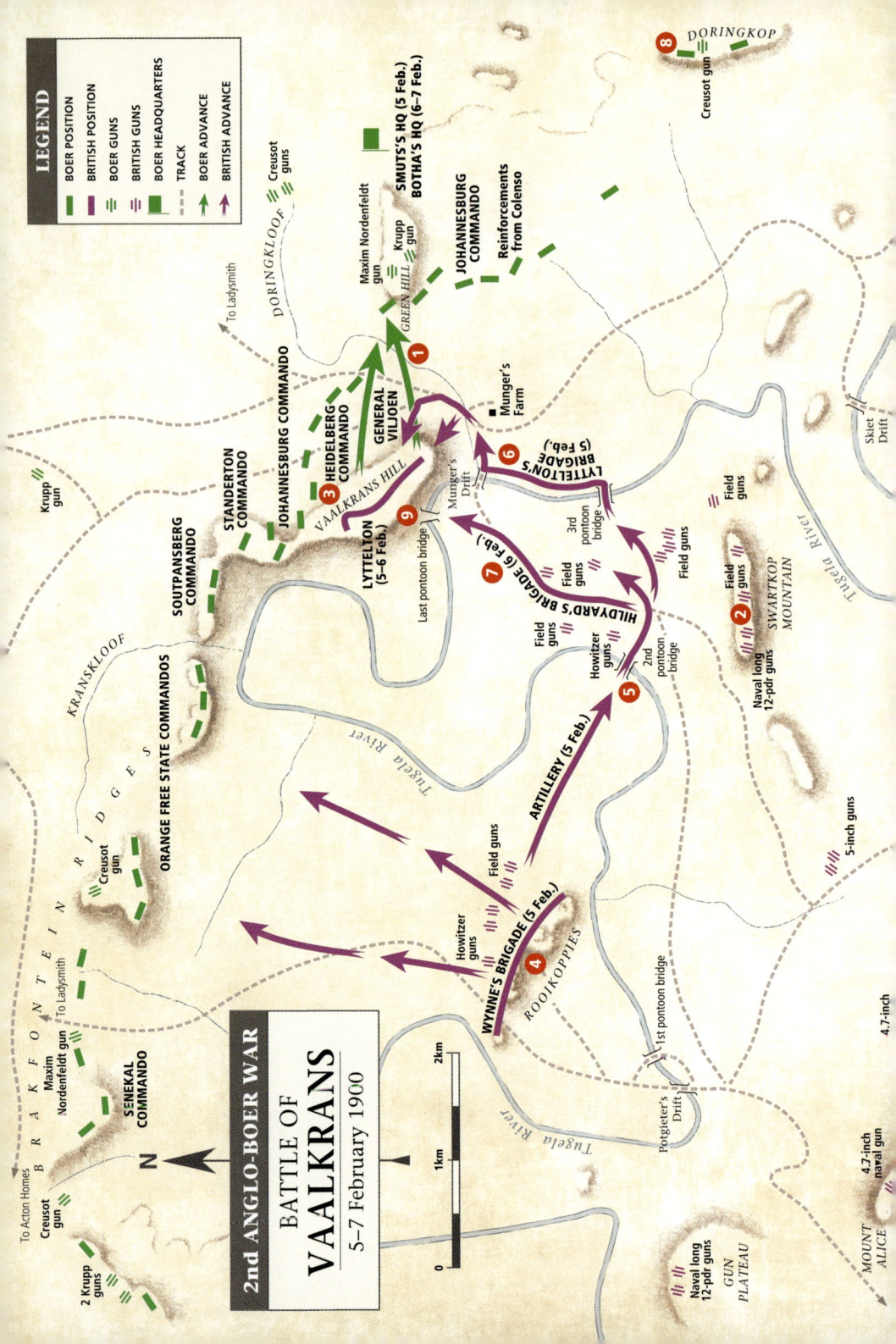

2nd ANGLO-BOER WAR
BATTLE OF VAALKRANS
5–7 February 1900

LEGEND
- BOER POSITION
- BRITISH POSITION
- BOER GUNS
- BRITISH GUNS
- BOER HEADQUARTERS
- TRACK
- BOER ADVANCE
- BRITISH ADVANCE
- Creusot guns

Boer positions and units:
- Creusot gun — Doringkop (8)
- Maxim Nordenfeldt gun
- Krupp gun — Green Hill
- Smuts's HQ (5 Feb.)
- Botha's HQ (6–7 Feb.)
- Johannesburg Commando — Reinforcements from Colenso
- General Viljoen
- Heidelberg Commando
- Johannesburg Commando
- Standerton Commando
- Soutpansberg Commando
- Orange Free State Commandos — Kranskloof
- Krupp gun
- Creusot gun — Brakfontein Ridges
- Senekal Commando
- Maxim Nordenfeldt gun
- Creusot gun — To Acton Homes
- 2 Krupp guns

British positions and movements:
- (1) Vaalkrans Hill
- (3) Vaalkrans Hill
- (9) Lyttelton (5–6 Feb.) — Last pontoon bridge, Munger's Drift
- (6) Lyttelton's Brigade (5 Feb.) — Munger's Farm
- (7) Hildyard's Brigade (6 Feb.) — 3rd pontoon bridge, Field guns
- (2) Swartkop Mountain — Field guns, Naval long 12-pdr guns
- (5) Artillery (5 Feb.) — 2nd pontoon bridge, Howitzer guns, Field guns
- 5-inch guns
- (4) Wynne's Brigade (5 Feb.) — Rooikoppies, Howitzer guns, Field guns
- 1st pontoon bridge, Potgieter's Drift
- 4.7-inch
- Naval long 12-pdr guns, Gun Plateau
- 4.7-inch naval gun, Mount Alice
- Skiet Drift
- Tugela River
- To Ladysmith

Scale: 0 – 1km – 2km

N

Lord Dundonald and men of his mounted brigade in their camp near Swartkop

1 This was the gap in the hills (between the Tugela River and Ladysmith) that General Redvers Buller saw as 'the key to Ladysmith'.

2 Swartkop is the flat-topped, steep-sided mountain on the south bank of the river that General Buller viewed as the best platform for his long-ranging naval guns to bombard Vaalkrans. The guns were manhandled up the almost sheer slopes by the Naval Brigade.

3 The Boer line was thinly held at this point and, when it became clear that an attack on Vaalkrans was imminent, urgent messages were sent requesting reinforcements.

4 On 5 February the British launched an artillery bombardment against the Brakfontein ridges and followed with a feint attack by the infantry, thereby hoping to draw the Boers away from the site of the real attack on Vaalkrans.

5 The artillery was withdrawn over this pontoon bridge to support the infantry assault on Vaalkrans. Due to a delay in getting the guns across the river, the Boers had ample time to move men east to Vaalkrans from Brakfontein to support those holding the double-humped summit.

6 This was the line of the first British assault. The men advanced under cover of a donga at the base of the hill.

7 Lyttelton's 4th Brigade was relieved under cover of darkness by Hildyard's brigade, which was subjected to severe shellfire the whole of the next day.

8 The Boer 155mm Creusot gun was manhandled to this position, where it was used to shell the British on the summit of Vaalkrans.

9 The British were all withdrawn over this pontoon bridge, constructed at night under the steep slope of the hill.

Battle of Tugela Heights
14–27 February 1900

HOW TO GET THERE
Start at Wynne Hill just off the R103 north of Colenso and continue to Hart's Hill, the Pom-Pom Bridge and, finally, Pieter's Hill.

Wynne Hill: Take the R103 from Colenso towards Ladysmith. Shortly after crossing the Tugela River, take the first major, tarred road to the right marked 'Newcastle and Ezakheni'. Continue until you see a fenced cemetery on your left. Further on you will see a monument on your right. Wynne Hill is the high ground on your left. There is a path to the top of the hill that leads past a homestead on the slope.

Hart's Hill: Continue along the tarred road past Wynne Hill, until you see a sign to the right saying 'Hart's Hill'. Turn off onto a dirt track that runs parallel to the railway; you will now be going in the direction from which you came. On your left you will see an Anglo-Boer War monument. This monument marks the bottom of Railway Hill. Continue past the monument on the dirt track, driving over a cattle grid and down a hill until you see a faint track going up the hill on your right. Turn right onto this track (you will need a 4x4 vehicle because the tracks are badly eroded) and drive up Hart's Hill to the monument.

Pom-Pom Bridge: From Hart's Hill, continue along the track until you come across a series of mass graves on the left-hand side of the road. Many of these are dedicated to the Irish regiments that fought at the Battle of Tugela Heights. Continue on this track (very eroded at the time of writing) until you can go no further. Park your car and walk down to the Langverwachtspruit on the left-hand side of the road to find the remains of the Pom-Pom Bridge.

Pieter's Hill: From the Pom-Pom Bridge, go back the way you came, following the dirt track until you reach the tarred road, where you turn right. Continue on this road until you cross the railway line over a bridge. Soon you will come to a T-junction. At this junction, turn right towards Ezakheni and follow the tarred road between two small hills. The monument is visible on the hill to the left of the road. The track that leads up to the monument is accessible only on foot or with a 4x4 vehicle. There are other monuments and cemeteries north and east of the main structure. *Guide recommended*

Cemetery (Wynne Hill): *28°42'03.6" S 29°49'26.5" E*
Anglo-Boer War monument (Railway Hill): *28°40'28.9" S 29°50'24.6" E*
Monument (Hart's Hill): *28°41'09.7" S 29°50'29.9" E*

Context

General Sir Redvers Buller had already made three unsuccessful attempts to relieve the siege of Ladysmith (see p. 112). Despite commanding a superior army, he had failed to break through the Boer line at Colenso, Spioenkop and Vaalkrans. The series of battles, collectively known as the Battle of Tugela Heights, represented his fourth assault on the Boers in an effort to relieve Ladysmith.

At the Battle of Tugela Heights, Buller commanded a force of about 26,000 men with 78 artillery pieces and 22 machine guns, whereas the Boers had only about 3,000 men and 12 guns. Greatly outnumbered by their enemy, the Boers, under the command of General Louis Botha, were running on empty. Morale was low, especially after they had been forced out of their trenches on Hlangwane Hill on 19 February, a key position south of the river and close to Colenso village.

The British struggle to haul a 4.7-inch (120mm) naval gun across the Tugela River.

Action

By 20 February 1900 the British forces under Buller and General Sir Charles Warren had occupied all the ground east of Colenso and south of the Tugela River, where it loops to the north.

The following day the 11th Brigade crossed the Tugela River by means of a pontoon bridge and attempted to advance in a north-westerly direction to gain the open road that led to Ladysmith. However, the Boers were strongly entrenched in the hills above the road. Buller found it impossible to advance this way and was forced to take an alternative route along the railway line and river. He aimed to roll up the Boer positions from south to north by progressively taking the Boer-held hills along the line of his advance. The men in the Boer trenches west of the Langverwachtspruit were commanded by General Louis Botha and those to the east of this tributary by General Lucas Meyer.

Timeline

1899
In December the British are defeated at the Battle of Colenso. General Sir Redvers Buller loses 10 field guns and incurs 1,450 casualties. Reinforcements are brought in by ship from India and Britain.

1900
In January the reinforcing division arrives, commanded by General Sir Charles Warren. In charge of the British forces at Spioenkop, Buller and Warren do not see eye to eye and the battle is another British reverse.

In February, at the Battle of Vaalkrans, General Warren's initiates drop artillery shells just ahead of the advancing infantry, enabling the British to take Vaalkrans. The British are, nonetheless, defeated. Between 14 and 27 February, by dint of using the rolling artillery barrage, the British take most of the hills north of Colenso. This series of battles is known as the Battle of Tugela Heights. On 28 February Ladysmith is relieved, 13 days after the relief of Kimberley.

On 16 May the siege of Mafeking ends.

In September the Transvaal is annexed and guerrilla warfare replaces set-piece battles such as those fought on the Tugela line.

1908
Robert Baden-Powell, commander of Mafeking, founds the Boy Scout movement, which is said to have originated in Baden-Powell's use of schoolboys as messengers during the siege.

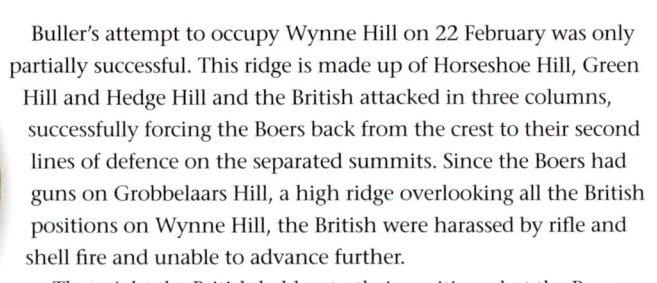

General Redvers Buller, whose force defeated the Boers at Tugela Heights

Buller's attempt to occupy Wynne Hill on 22 February was only partially successful. This ridge is made up of Horseshoe Hill, Green Hill and Hedge Hill and the British attacked in three columns, successfully forcing the Boers back from the crest to their second lines of defence on the separated summits. Since the Boers had guns on Grobbelaars Hill, a high ridge overlooking all the British positions on Wynne Hill, the British were harassed by rifle and shell fire and unable to advance further.

That night the British held onto their positions, but the Boers kept up their Mauser rifle fire until midnight, as they moved from their well-entrenched sangars towards the British line. The next morning firing resumed with the British trying to extricate themselves. Both Warren and Buller were under the impression that Wynne Hill had been taken and had launched the next phase of their advance along the river

It took the Irish Brigade under Major General Fitzroy Hart four hours to scramble through the mud along the left bank of the river towards Hart's Hill (also sometimes known as Terrace Hill or Inniskilling Hill). The soldiers crossed the Langverwachtspruit on an iron bridge (Pom-Pom Bridge) under a hail of Maxim Nordenfeldt (Pom-Pom) shells and Mauser bullets. Many fell, wounded or dead, as they carried their ammunition across by hand, the mules steadfastly refusing to mount the bridge.

Memorials to officers of the Gordon Highlanders, Royal Dublin Fusiliers and Inniskillings, who are buried below Hart's Hill

While the British troops advanced, the Boers in trenches on Hart's Hill were subjected to a fearsome bombardment from the British guns across the river. Hart's Brigade arrived in a sheltered hollow under the hill and close to the river at about 17h00. Hart was eager to take the hill before dark and hurried the men forward to attack before they had all arrived in the hollow.

They left the shelter of their position and climbed the hill under a hail of Boer bullets. Hart's bugler repeatedly sounded the regimental calls of the Inniskillings and the Rangers, followed by the Advance, Double and Charge, but the Boers were standing above them pouring fire into their ranks. The Irish stormed the trenches bravely, but as they charged over the line of the false crest they were met with a roar of musketry. By this time it was too dark for the British artillery to give supporting fire, and the Boers fired into the advancing men with impunity. The British soldiers were exposed to fire from the left, front and right.

Boers behind these fortifications fired into the attacking Irish, killing and wounding many.

Some curious facts

- On 26 February the Boers at Tugela Heights were subjected to an artillery bombardment from 78 guns. This was the largest number of guns used in a single action in the war thus far.
- Boxes of chocolate were found on many of the dead men. These had been sent by Queen Victoria to all troops then serving in South Africa.
- For their heroism, the Dublin Fusiliers were put in the van of the procession into Ladysmith. Many of the soldiers who lined the streets and saw the five officers and small clump of men – the remains of what had been a strong battalion – realised what their relief had cost in terms of human suffering, and sobbed like children.
- According to the regimental diary of the Dublin Fusiliers, the courage of the Irish greatly impressed the Boers, who actually allowed a few of the Irishmen to leap unharmed into their trenches, and then seized and disarmed them before they could use their bayonets.
- Lieutenant Lane of the Dublin Fusiliers was shot clean through the head, from one side to the other. Astonishingly, he made a marvellous recovery.

Queen Victoria sent boxes of chocolate to troops in South Africa.

BATTLE OF TUGELA HEIGHTS

The survivors crawled backwards on their stomachs to the shelter of the false crest, but 72 per cent of the Inniskillings officers who had gone into action on 23 February had fallen. During this time no-one knew the whereabouts of Hart, nor had anyone received any orders, which added to the soldiers' state of demoralisation. They held this position through the night, but the next morning the Boers attacked again from the south-west. A retirement was ordered at 08h00 when the men were moved back to the railway, where they lay throughout the day. At 17h30 they were moved to a hollow about half a kilometre below the railway.

An armistice was declared on 25 February. British and Boer soldiers exchanged tobacco and shared whisky while the dead and wounded were carried off the battlefields. The British had lost about 1,170 officers and men, the Irish having suffered most heavily. Boer casualties were estimated at 102 men.

The next day, after reconnaissance by Warren and Buller, a combined attack on Pieter's Hill, the Boers' left flank, and Railway and Harts hills was planned. Now hopelessly outnumbered, the Boers were subjected to a devastating artillery bombardment. A day later Barton's Brigade crossed the Tugela on a pontoon bridge and moved downstream (north), to advance up the steep slope below Pieter's Hill. The Irish Fusiliers forced their way across the base of the koppies to occupy the one furthest south, coming under fire from Boers on Railway Hill, while Royal Scots Fusiliers occupied the central koppies. Further advance was prevented by the Boer defence. Three companies of the Irish Fusiliers, ordered to move forward in support, came up at about 17h30 and rushed to the left of the position, while three companies of the Dublin Fusiliers led by Captain Venour assaulted the right. The Irish Fusiliers lost almost a third of their men, and all their officers were either killed or wounded. However, by midnight the Boers had abandoned their positions, partly because they had heard about General Piet Cronjé's surrender at Paardeberg (see p. 254) and were feeling extremely dejected.

Early in the morning of 28 February there was a general Boer withdrawal and soon the men were in full retreat. The vanguard of the British was in Ladysmith that evening.

British cavalry crossing the Tugela River on a pontoon bridge

The Connaught Rangers monument at Tugela Heights. The cooling towers mark the town of Colenso.

Aftermath

Both sides suffered heavy casualties. In the 13 days from 14 to 27 February, 426 British soldiers were killed and 1,743 wounded, although reports of the number of dead and injured vary. The Boers lost 48 men while 135 were wounded, although this may well be a conservative estimate.

This series of engagements was the first during the Natal campaign where the British had used all their troops combined. They had also made use of a creeping artillery barrage to enable them to approach and storm the Boer trenches. This meant that the British artillery was instructed to fire immediately ahead of the advancing foot soldiers, even at the risk of hitting them. These tactics proved so successful that they were used during World War I.

Principal combatants

British: Connaught Rangers; Devonshire Regiment; Dorsetshire Regiment; Durham Light Infantry; East Surrey Regiment; Imperial Light Infantry; King's Royal Rifle Corps; Middlesex Regiment; Naval Brigade; Rifle Brigade; Royal Dublin Fusiliers; Royal Field Artillery; Royal Inniskilling Fusiliers; Royal Irish Fusiliers; Royal Lancaster Regiment; Royal Scots Fusiliers; Royal Welsh Fusiliers Regiment; Scottish Rifles; Somerset Light Infantry Regiment; South Lancashire Regiment; West Surrey Regiment; West York Regiment; York and Lancaster Regiment.

Boers: Commandos from Bethal, Boksburg, Carolina, Ermelo, Heidelberg, Johannesburg, Krugersdorp, Middelburg, Piet Retief, Pretoria, Rustenburg, Soutpansberg, Standerton, Vryheid and Wakkerstroom; Irish pro-Boers; Italian Corps; Staatsartillerie; Swaziland Police.

The uniform of a private in the Royal Irish Fusiliers

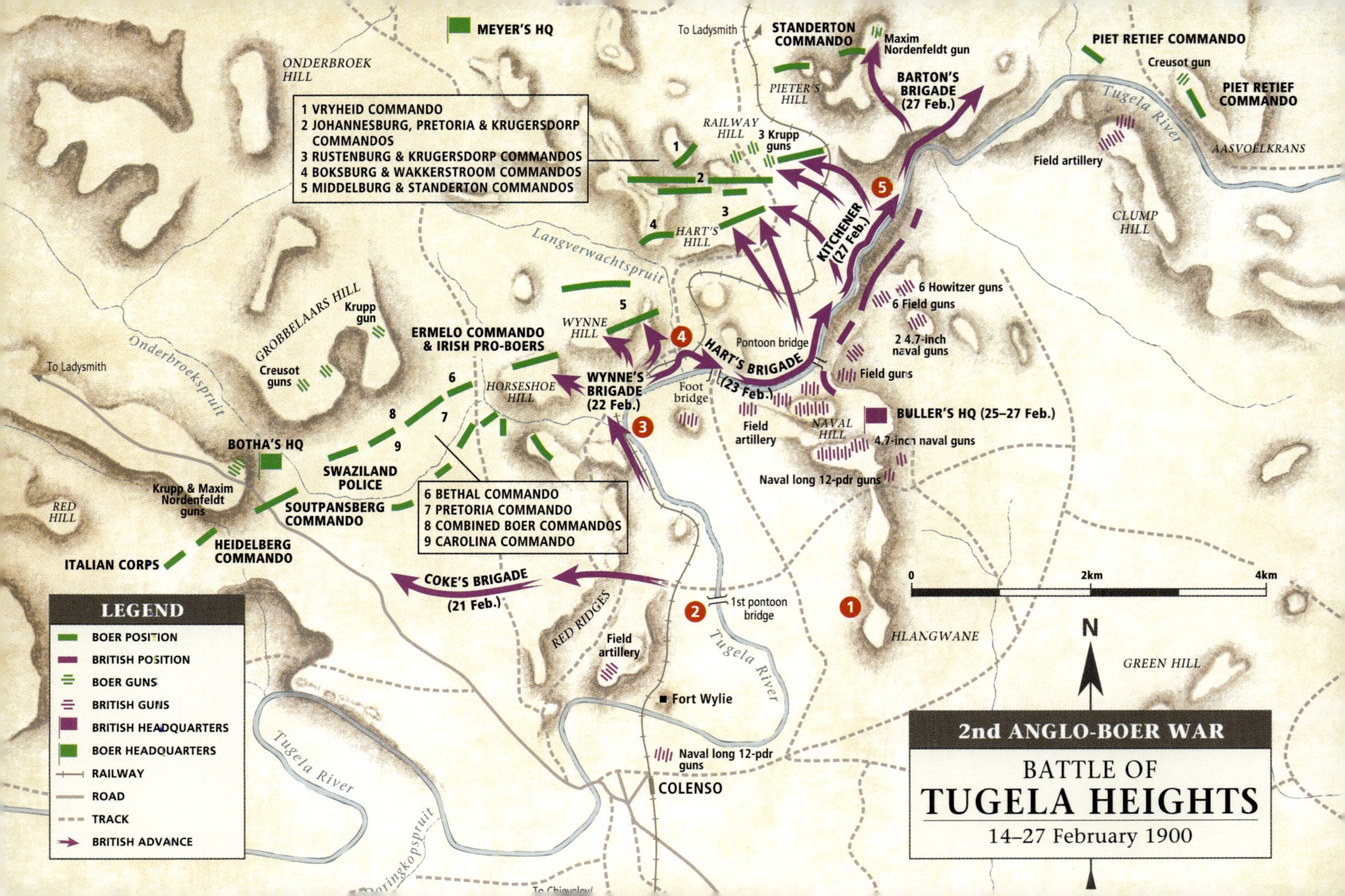
2nd ANGLO-BOER WAR
BATTLE OF
TUGELA HEIGHTS
14–27 February 1900
LEGEND
BOER POSITION
BRITISH POSITION
BOER GUNS
BRITISH GUNS
BRITISH HEADQUARTERS
BOER HEADQUARTERS
RAILWAY
ROAD
TRACK
BRITISH ADVANCE
1 VRYHEID COMMANDO
2 JOHANNESBURG, PRETORIA & KRUGERSDORP COMMANDOS
3 RUSTENBURG & KRUGERSDORP COMMANDOS
4 BOKSBURG & WAKKERSTROOM COMMANDOS
5 MIDDELBURG & STANDERTON COMMANDOS
6 BETHAL COMMANDO
7 PRETORIA COMMANDO
8 COMBINED BOER COMMANDOS
9 CAROLINA COMMANDO
MEYER'S HQ
ONDERBROEK HILL
To Ladysmith
STANDERTON COMMANDO
Maxim Nordenfeldt gun
PIET RETIEF COMMANDO
Creusot gun
PIET RETIEF COMMANDO
BARTON'S BRIGADE (27 Feb.)
PIETER'S HILL
RAILWAY HILL
3 Krupp guns
Tugela River
AASVOËLKRANS
Field artillery
CLUMP HILL
HART'S HILL
Langverwachtspruit
KITCHENER (27 Feb.)
6 Howitzer guns
6 Field guns
2 4.7-inch naval guns
Field guns
GROBBELAARS HILL
Krupp gun
Creusot guns
Onderbroekspruit
To Ladysmith
ERMELO COMMANDO & IRISH PRO-BOERS
WYNNE HILL
HORSESHOE HILL
WYNNE'S BRIGADE (22 Feb.)
Pontoon bridge
HART'S BRIGADE (23 Feb.)
Foot bridge
Field artillery
NAVAL HILL
BULLER'S HQ (25–27 Feb.)
4.7-inch naval guns
Naval long 12-pdr guns
BOTHA'S HQ
Krupp & Maxim Nordenfeldt guns
RED HILL
SWAZILAND POLICE
SOUTPANSBERG COMMANDO
HEIDELBERG COMMANDO
ITALIAN CORPS
COKE'S BRIGADE (21 Feb.)
1st pontoon bridge
HLANGWANE
RED RIDGES
Field artillery
Tugela River
Fort Wylie
Naval long 12-pdr guns
COLENSO
GREEN HILL
N
0
2km
4km
Tugela River
Doringkopspruit
To Chieveley

LEFT: The cemetery below Wynne's Hill
RIGHT: Connaught Rangers Memorial, honouring the soldiers in the Irish Brigade who fell at the battles of Colenso and Tugela Heights

❶ Hlangwane was a key position south of the Tugela River, as it commanded Boer positions on the northern bank. It was held by the Boers until 19 February, when they were forced out of their trenches by the British.

❷ The British first crossed the river here and attempted to gain the main road to Ladysmith. However, the Boers were well entrenched in the surrounding hills and forced them back.

❸ The second attempt by the British was the assault on the triple summit of Wynne Hill. They gained the summit but were pinned down there and unable to progress further.

❹ This is the iron bridge across the Langverwachtspruit, where General Hart's Irish Brigade came under fire from the Boers' Maxim Nordenfeldt gun. The bridge was subsequently known as Pom-Pom Bridge. The brigade, once across, assembled in Hart's Hollow close to the river, from where they stormed Hart's Hill.

❺ This combined attack on Railway and Pieter's hills on 27 February eventually caused the Boers to flee.

Battle of Platrand

Also known as *Battle of Caesar's Camp*
and *Battle of Wagon Hill*

6 January 1900

HOW TO GET THERE

Drive from Colenso on the R103 towards Ladysmith. When you reach the outskirts of the town, look on your right for the sign to Platrand Lodge. Turn right and drive along the dirt road towards the lodge. Continue past the hotel and up the hill until you reach a gate and a crossroad on the nek. Turn either east (right) to reach Caesar's Camp or west (left) to reach Wagon Hill – both are signposted.

Wagon Hill: On Wagon Hill, leave your vehicle close to the prominent Devonshire Regiment monument and walk towards the southern crest. Look down the steep slope to the flat ground below over which the Boers approached in the dark. To your right is Wagon Point. Walk to the nek between Wagon Hill and Wagon Point. This is where the Boers were first heard as they climbed the slope. The gun emplacements on Wagon Point are easily found as you walk towards the western end of the hill.

Caesar's Camp: The tarred road on Caesar's Camp affords spectacular views over the valley to the south through which the Boers approached. On your left are the ruins of some of the stone forts that lined the northern crest. The ruins of the Boers killed in Natal during the war are buried in the crypt of the huge monument on your left. Further along on the same road, note the gun emplacements on the right and visit the monuments to the Rifle Brigade, the Manchesters and others on the eastern crest of the hill in the direction of the wireless mast. The sangar held by Private James Pitts and Private Robert Scott was not far from this point.

Platrand monument (Caesar's Camp): 28°35'16.5" S 29°46'21.2" E

Context

About 10,000 Boers had surrounded Ladysmith since 2 November 1899. The British army corps had meanwhile arrived and General Sir Redvers Buller had made his first unsuccessful attempt to get his army across the Tugela River. General Piet Joubert, advised by Louis Botha and with the backing of President Paul Kruger, decided to launch a direct attack on the town. He needed the Boers, who were encircling the town, to defend the Tugela line and prevent Buller from getting through. Joubert had correctly defined the big flat-topped hill south of the town as the key to Ladysmith. This battle was the Boers' attempt to take the hill.

The memorial to 781 Boers killed in Natal during the 2nd Anglo-Boer War depicts seven stylised hands reaching upwards. Each represents a battle; on each 'wrist' are the names of the men who fell fighting.

Action

General Sir George White, who commanded the Ladysmith garrison, had also recognised the strategic importance of the double-humped hill and designated General Ian Hamilton to its defence. With only 1,000 men at his disposal, it was impossible to man a continuous line along the roughly 4km-long southern crest. Hamilton had, therefore, arranged the construction of seven stone forts along the northern crest. South of each fort were gun emplacements and in front of those, close to the southern crest, were stone sangars that gave shelter to pickets – the forward line of defence.

Boer general Piet Joubert and his commandants had decided that their attack on the hill should take place on the night of 5 January. By strange coincidence, White's orders for the same night were that gun emplacements for three naval guns should be completed on the western end of Wagon Hill and that a 4.7-inch (120mm) naval gun should be hauled up and installed. These guns were intended to aid Buller's hoped-for appearance in the west and preparations were to be completed in the dark, out of sight of the Boers in the surrounding hills.

The Boer advance began at 22h00, when about 4,000 men approached Platrand from the south. The Transvaal commandos were to attack Caesar's Camp in the east, and the Orange Free State commandos were to take Wagon Hill in the west. They gathered below the hill, but discipline was poor and it is unlikely that more than 1,000 men actually took part in the attack.

At 02h30 a British sentry on the nek between Wagon Hill and Wagon Point heard the sound of approaching men on the steep slopes below. He reported the news and then returned to shout a challenge. When this produced no result he fired into the darkness and was answered by a barrage of Mauser bullets. There was point-blank firing in the darkness

Timeline

1899
In October the Boers invade Natal and occupy Dundee. They ride south to besiege the town of Ladysmith containing the British garrison.

In November the Battle of Willowgrange persuades the Boers to abandon their attacking strategy. They withdraw to the Tugela River and position men and guns in defensive positions on the north bank. In addition, they have about 10,000 men in the hills surrounding Ladysmith.

In December the Battle of Colenso sees the British forced back, south of the Tugela River.

1900
In January British reinforcements arrive in large numbers. General Piet Joubert realises that he needs the men surrounding Ladysmith to strengthen the Tugela line against the increasing number of soldiers advancing from the south. An attack is planned on Platrand.

The British succeed in holding Platrand; the hill is essential for the defence of Ladysmith. The Boers fail to take the town and release those men surrounding it.

In February the siege of Ladysmith is relieved.

In May the British forces push through into the Transvaal to join Lord Roberts's army. Johannesburg and Pretoria both fall to the British.

BATTLE OF PLATRAND   107

until a British Hotchkiss gun in the nek was brought into operation and the Boers had to pause their advance. However, they then used the cover of rocks and scrub to get very close to the Imperial Light Horse fort and were forced back only when British reinforcements arrived.

As the morning drew on, a stalemate arose with neither side managing to drive the other out of its position. At midday, when the heat was terrible and many had gone down the hill to get water, the Boers launched a flanking attack up the steep western slope of Wagon Point and almost succeeded in driving the British out of the gun emplacements there. However, the heroic actions of Royal Engineer Lieutenant Digby-Jones and others forced them back again. Late afternoon saw the Boers sheltering in the rocks on Wagon Hill, unable to progress.

The Devonshire Regiment had arrived from the far end of town to support the troops, who had been fighting all day, and Hamilton requested the fresh men to dislodge the Boers with a bayonet charge. Colonel C. W. Park, commanding officer of the Devons, agreed to try. At about 16h00 a ferocious thunderstorm broke over Ladysmith. In lightning, thunder and driving rain, they made their charge across open ground under heavy fire. Many fell, but the Boers retreated to take up positions a little further down the hill. Later, realising that the Transvalers were not coming to reinforce them, they retired under cover of darkness.

Meanwhile, the eastern section of the hill had seen heavy fighting all day. The Transvaal commandos had managed, in the early hours of the morning, to gain the south-eastern crest and take many of the forward British sangars, manned mainly by men of the Manchester Regiment. Those remaining held on bravely.

The British artillery, on an open plain below, opened fire on the south-eastern slopes of the hill and thus prevented Boer reinforcements from reaching the summit by this route. The Boer gun on Bulwana Mountain had caused more harm than good by shelling the south-eastern crest and wounding some of the Boers.

British reinforcements arrived throughout the day and there was ferocious fighting all along the north-eastern crest, but when the storm broke in the late afternoon the Boers took the opportunity to withdraw. They were anxious that the heavy rain would raise the level of the swollen stream below the hill and hamper their retreat.

Aftermath

The British had held the hill, but at the cost of 183 men killed and 249 wounded. The Boers also suffered severely: 68 men were killed and 135 wounded. This marked the last attempt by the Boers to take Ladysmith by force. They resigned themselves to a prolonged siege, a mode of war unsuited to the temperament of a citizen force branded as 'hunters' and 'undisciplined fighters'. Ladysmith was eventually relieved by Buller's troops on 27 February 1900.

British soldiers in Ladysmith watch the battle rage on Platrand

High honours

A young man from Blackburn in Manchester won the greatest reward for bravery for his actions during the battle on Caesar's Camp. James Pitts, one of 16 children, was born in February 1877. He joined the Manchester Regiment when he turned 19 and was sent to Gibraltar on garrison duty until embarking for South Africa at the start of the Anglo-Boer War in 1899. Only 22, he was a popular, friendly fellow with a passion for football and a strong sense of duty.

Pitts was involved in the fighting at Elandslaagte and then besieged in Ladysmith, where he was stationed with the Manchester Regiment, manning the stone forts and the picket line on flat-topped Caesar's Camp. Young Pitts was in one of these sangars with his friend Robert Scott and 14 others when, at 03h00 on 6 January 1900, the Boers climbed up the southern slopes and attacked. There was point-blank firing in the pitch darkness until dawn broke, when the area became a killing field as the Boers occupied some of the British sangars and were able to enfilade the others.

By mid-morning only Pitts and Scott were still alive in their sangar, but they held on doggedly, enduring 15 hours without food or water. Had they abandoned their position, the Boers would have broken the British line and taken the entire hill, which could have led to the fall of Ladysmith, with enormous implications.

To the left rear and within 20m of Pitts and Scott were Boer marksmen, whom Pitts was able to pick off when Scott moved slightly to provoke them into showing themselves. Pitts replenished his ammunition from the supplies of his dead comrades, and the two men played their cat-and-mouse game until darkness fell.

For their courage and stoicism in the face of incredible odds, both young men were recommended for Victoria Crosses, but Pitts was deployed to Singapore at the end of the Anglo-Boer War. When he returned home after an absence of eight years, he was at last given a civic reception, along with his award and a purse of £50, as a mark of public appreciation.

Pitts became a labourer in Blackburn and was sometimes out of work, but even when he was poverty-stricken he steadfastly refused to sell his medal. He died at the age of 78 at the Royal Infirmary in Blackburn.

Principal combatants

British: Border Mounted Rifles; Devonshire Regiment; Gordon Highlanders; Imperial Light Horse; King's Royal Rifle Corps; Manchester Regiment; Natal Hotchkiss Contingent; Natal Volunteers; Rifle Brigade; Royal Engineers; Royal Field Artillery.
Boers: Commandos from Harrismith, Heidelberg, Heilbron, Kroonstad, Krugersdorp, Utrecht, Vryheid, Wakkerstroom and Winburg.

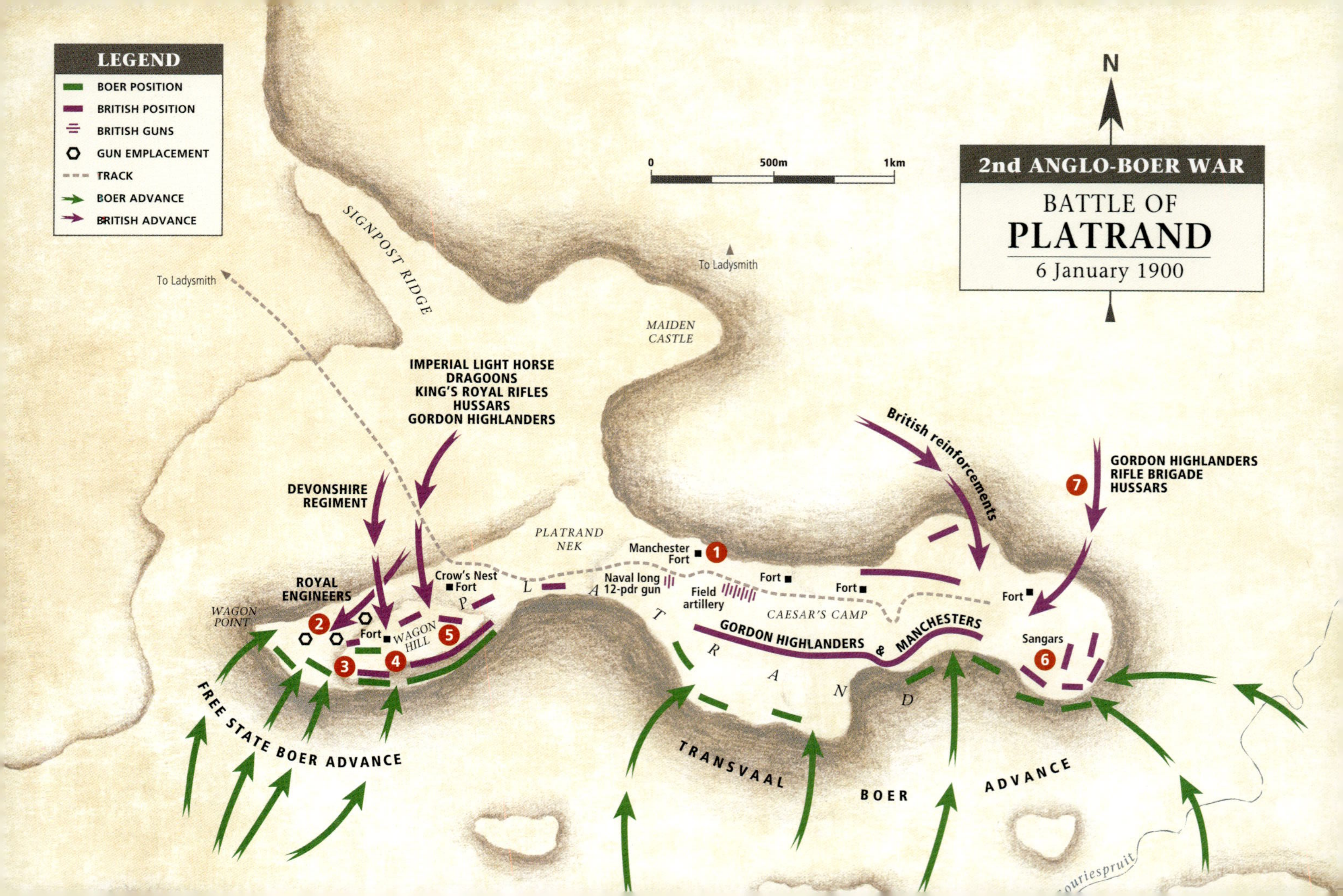
LEGEND
BOER POSITION
BRITISH POSITION
BRITISH GUNS
GUN EMPLACEMENT
TRACK
BOER ADVANCE
BRITISH ADVANCE
2nd ANGLO-BOER WAR
BATTLE OF
PLATRAND
6 January 1900
N
0
500m
1km
To Ladysmith
To Ladysmith
SIGNPOST RIDGE
MAIDEN CASTLE
IMPERIAL LIGHT HORSE
DRAGOONS
KING'S ROYAL RIFLES
HUSSARS
GORDON HIGHLANDERS
DEVONSHIRE REGIMENT
ROYAL ENGINEERS
WAGON POINT
Crow's Nest Fort
Fort
WAGON HILL
PLATRAND NEK
Manchester Fort
Naval long 12-pdr gun
Field artillery
Fort
Fort
Fort
CAESAR'S CAMP
GORDON HIGHLANDERS & MANCHESTERS
British reinforcements
GORDON HIGHLANDERS
RIFLE BRIGADE
HUSSARS
Sangars
P L A T R A N D
FREE STATE BOER ADVANCE
TRANSVAAL BOER ADVANCE
Fouriespruit
1
2
3
4
5
6
7

The Manchester Regiment on their arrival in South Africa

1 A series of stone forts was built up by the British along the northern crest of the hill. In front of them were batteries of field guns and in front of these outlying pickets, who could warn of an approaching enemy. In this way, General Ian Hamilton managed to protect a 4km front with only 1,000 men.

2 The gun emplacements for two naval long 12-pounders were being prepared here by the British, as well as one for the big naval 4.7-inch (120mm) gun. These long-ranging guns were supposed to aid General Buller's hoped-for appearance from the south-west. However, Buller did not succeed in getting through the Boer defensive line at Spioenkop, which made the emplacements superfluous.

3 This is the nek between Wagon Hill and Wagon Point, where fighting began before first light on the morning of 6 January 1900.

4 The Boers used the cover of rocks and low scrub to get very close to the Imperial Light Horse fort, which stood at this point. However, they were unable to progress further and were eventually forced back to take cover on the slopes of Wagon Hill.

5 The Devonshire Regiment made a brave bayonet charge over this bare ground in an attempt to get the Boers out of their positions on Wagon Hill. The charge took place in a torrential thunderstorm.

6 The brave endurance of two young men in the Manchester Regiment earned them a Victoria Cross. Privates Scott and Pitts held out in a sangar when all their companions had been killed. They continued to snipe at the Boers all day, without food or water, refusing to retire until they were eventually relieved late in the afternoon.

7 Artillery shells from the Boer Creusot gun on Bulwana fell among the British reinforcements approaching from the north-east.

Battle of Ladysmith
30 October 1899

HOW TO GET THERE

Trenchgula (Tchrengula) Hill: In Ladysmith, follow signs to Trenchgula Guest Lodge from Cochrane Road. At the sign to the lodge in Cochrane Road, turn right into Fairclough Road, then cross the railway line before turning left into Hyde Road (D343). It is a further 3km to the entrance gate of the lodge. There is a trail leading up the eastern face of the mountain; it follows the British ascent route. The flat-topped summit has memorials to the men of the Royal Irish Fusiliers and the Gloucestershire Regiment who are buried there. Look to the north, where Nicholson's Nek is visible as the road disappears between two hills. At the time of writing the battlefield was accessible only by prior arrangement with the lodge owners, and the use of a guide is recommended.

Long Hill and Lombard's Kop: To see where Colonel Geoffrey Grimwood's column was engaged, drive north out of Ladysmith on the N11. At the first set of traffic lights after the railway bridge, turn right towards Ekuvukeni and Helpmekaar. After about 2km, you will see Lombard's Kop to the left and, beyond it, the low rise of Long Hill where Grimwood launched his attack.

Pepworth Hill: To see Pepworth Hill, where the Irish pro-Boer Brigade manned the Creusot gun, drive north out of Ladysmith on the N11 towards Newcastle. After about 8km, the hill will be clearly visible on your left. The Irish pro-Boers had set up camp close to the stream under Pepworth Hill, 12km out of Ladysmith. The site where their camp was placed is across the road from the turn-off to present-day Nambiti Private Game Reserve. *Guide recommended*

Context

This battle was General Sir George White's last, desperate attempt to prevent the approaching Boer commandos from surrounding and investing Ladysmith. There were two separate engagements to this battle: the Battle of Modderspruit and the Battle of Nicholson's Nek. But they were part of one plan: to dislodge the Boers from their positions around Pepworth Hill north-east of Ladysmith, and to drive them into the arms of a second British column waiting in Nicholson's Nek, a road leading out of Ladysmith between hills to the north. This would also prevent the Boers from the Orange Free State from joining up with the Transvaal commandos near Pepworth.

Action

The Boers, encouraged by their successful occupation of Dundee, were approaching Ladysmith in increasing numbers and had made their headquarters near Pepworth Hill. They also held positions on Long Hill, on the other side of the railway line from Pepworth.

They had seven guns at their disposal, one of them a 155mm Creusot, or Long Tom, with a range of 10,000m, which was hauled to the summit of Pepworth Hill. The Boer line was a semicircle with its open side towards Ladysmith, stretching from a point just north-west of Pepworth to the ridges east of Long Hill.

Battle of Modderspruit

White sent two infantry brigades out of town to the north-east, both supported by cavalry and artillery. The first, commanded by Colonel Geoffrey Grimwood, left before first light and prepared to take Long Hill by means of an artillery bombardment followed by an infantry attack, with the cavalry poised to pursue the fleeing Boers. The other brigade, commanded by Colonel Ian Hamilton, was to take Pepworth Hill.

General Piet Joubert, suspecting that the British would launch an attack on Long Hill, had ensured the removal of guns and men from the hill and deployed them further east. That command fell to the brilliant young Boer general, Louis Botha.

As expected, Grimwood launched his attack on Long Hill and found the enemy gone. Instead, Botha was threatening his flanks, making it so uncomfortable that Grimwood had to withdraw or suffer considerable casualties. The British cavalry helped to extricate them as they retreated. Meanwhile, the column under Hamilton had engaged the Boer Long Tom gun on Pepworth Hill and was threatening Joubert's position when orders were received from White to withdraw – they were in danger of being outflanked now that Grimwood's column was in retreat.

The Boer Long Tom, no longer under attack, was now free to bombard the retreating column. The casualties would have been much heavier had it not been for the timely arrival of a naval long 12-pounder gun on the train from Durban. It was swiftly brought into range and kept the Boers' heads down, enabling Hamilton and his men to get back into town. By then, it was mid-morning, and White sent orders to the column he had despatched north (to occupy Nicholson's Nek) to withdraw to Ladysmith as soon as possible. However, the men were already in terrible trouble.

Replica of a Long Tom in Ladysmith

Timeline

1879
Major Sir George White wins a Victoria Cross at Charasiah, during the Afghan War.

1898
Transvaal President Paul Kruger is returned to office with twice as many votes as his two competitors combined (Schalk Burger and Piet Joubert).

1899
On 7 October, the day the British army is ordered to mobilise, Sir George White lands in Durban to lead the British forces in South Africa. He goes to Ladysmith where he commands a garrison of 9,000 men. After the Battle of Talana on 20 October the British garrison in Dundee withdraws to Ladysmith to swell the number of soldiers there to over 13,000. White telegrams Simon's Town requesting naval personnel and guns, which entrain in Durban, to arrive in Ladysmith nine days later. On 30 October the British combined garrisons take on the Boers in the Battle of Ladysmith, but fail to rid the areas north and west of the town of the encroaching enemy.

By November Ladysmith is surrounded and besieged. British troops outside Ladysmith withdraw south of the Tugela River.

In December the Battle of Colenso is fought and lost by the British. There are also reverses at Magersfontein and Stormberg.

1900
Despite the British troops' failed attempt to reach Ladysmith via Vaalkrans in February, the siege is relieved at the end of that month

Battle of Nicholson's Nek

The 1,100 men chosen for the night march to Nicholson's Nek were commanded by Lieutenant Colonel F. R. C. Carleton of the Irish Fusiliers. The men were taken from the Gloucestershire Regiment (recently arrived from India), who had lost their commanding officer a few days before at the Battle of Rietfontein (see p. 118), and from the Irish Fusiliers, who had endured a four-day forced march from Dundee a few days earlier. They were all exhausted, having slept only one night in the previous eight days.

The Gloucesters paraded at 20h30 on the night of 29 October, but it was not until 22h30 that the march got under way, because the Royal Irish Fusiliers arrived late. They had paraded with dum-dum bullets, but, as this type of bullet had recently been outlawed, the Fusiliers had to change them for hard-nosed bullets before they could proceed. The column was accompanied by a mountain battery and reserve ammunition on mule-drawn carts. A local farmer guided the column northwards, close to Bellspruit. However, the late start made it impossible to reach their objective before daybreak. When Carleton realised this, he took up a defensive position on the high ground to his left, on a flat-topped, steep-sided hill known as Trenchgula.

The Orange Free State Boers, under the leadership of Christiaan de Wet, were already encamped in the hills to the east. A sentry posted on Trenchgula Hill took fright at the British approach, fired into the night and then dashed down the hill. As a result, the mules stampeded, trampling their handlers and taking parts of the mountain gun and most of the spare ammunition with them. It was pandemonium until the officers were able to restore order and the climb could resume.

On the summit, the British got to work on protective sangars facing the high ridge in the north, from where attack seemed likely, as well as around the eastern and western rims of the southern summit. A rocky knoll on the northern edge of the southern summit offered a good field of fire to the north, but proved vulnerable when the Boers were able to outflank and enfilade this position. The Gloucesters were stationed on the western rim, and the Royal Irish Fusiliers on the east, overlooking the road to Nicholson's Nek.

At dawn the Boers, about 900-strong, encircled the mountain. De Wet's men approached from the north and by 11h00 the British had been forced to withdraw from their most extended fortifications. Many of the Boers had Martini-Henry rifles and these big-calibre, single-shot weapons were used to break down the protective stone breastworks. When Hamilton's column withdrew from the attack on Pepworth Hill, Transvaal Boers from these positions were sent to support the Orange Free Staters, who by then had surrounded Carleton's force. Soon the British were forced towards the southern summit, but, even there, Boers sheltering in the rocks lining the western crest enfiladed their line, and the number of casualties mounted. Worse still, the British

A Boer in action during the battle

defenders were running low on ammunition, the reserve having been lost with the fleeing mules. Those soldiers forward of the rocky knoll were outflanked and, when they thought themselves surrounded, they raised a white flag. Colonel Carleton, having received the message from General White that he and his force should retire to Ladysmith, realised that he could not rely on support from the two brigades at Modderspruit and that he had no alternative but to surrender.

The Irish were furious, although some of them were so tired that they had been dropping off to sleep even under fire. A large white sheet was raised on the end of a sword and the Boers approached to take prisoners. British wounded were treated with respect and kindness by the Boers, many of whom were sickened by the killing.

Carleton replied to White's message by means of mounted messengers and one of these riders, John Norwood, won the Victoria Cross for rescuing a man who was shot through the throat during the ride.

Aftermath

The Gloucesters lost 32 members and the Royal Irish Fusiliers 10. Of Carleton's initial force of 1,100 soldiers, 917 were taken prisoner. The Boers lost 16 men. The defeat was a crushing blow to the British, who incurred 1,200 casualties (killed, wounded and taken prisoner) in the two engagements. It was the biggest disaster for the British in South Africa since Majuba, almost 20 years earlier. Two days later, the railway line south of Ladysmith was cut and the town was encircled by the Boers. Ladysmith was to remain under siege for 118 days.

Ladysmith Town Hall

During the siege of Ladysmith, Boer artillery on the surrounding hills shelled positions around the town where British troops were stationed. Shells also fell in the town, one of them damaging the clock tower of the Town Hall that was being used as a hospital.

The townsfolk at times spent the daylight hours sheltering in hollows dug in the banks of the Klip River, returning to their homes at night, after the Boer guns had fallen silent.

Principal combatants

British: 5th Dragoon Guards; 18th Hussars; Devonshire Regiment; Gloucestershire Regiment; Gordon Highlanders; Imperial Light Horse; King's Royal Rifle Corps; Leicestershire Regiment; Manchester Regiment; Natal Carbineers; Natal Cavalry; Natal Field Artillery; Naval Brigade; Royal Field Artillery; Royal Irish Fusiliers.
Boers: Commandos from Harrismith, Heilbron, Kroonstad, Krugersdorp, Middelburg, Piet Retief, Standerton, Swaziland, Wakkerstroom and Winburg; German Corps; Irish pro-Boers; Johannesburg Police.

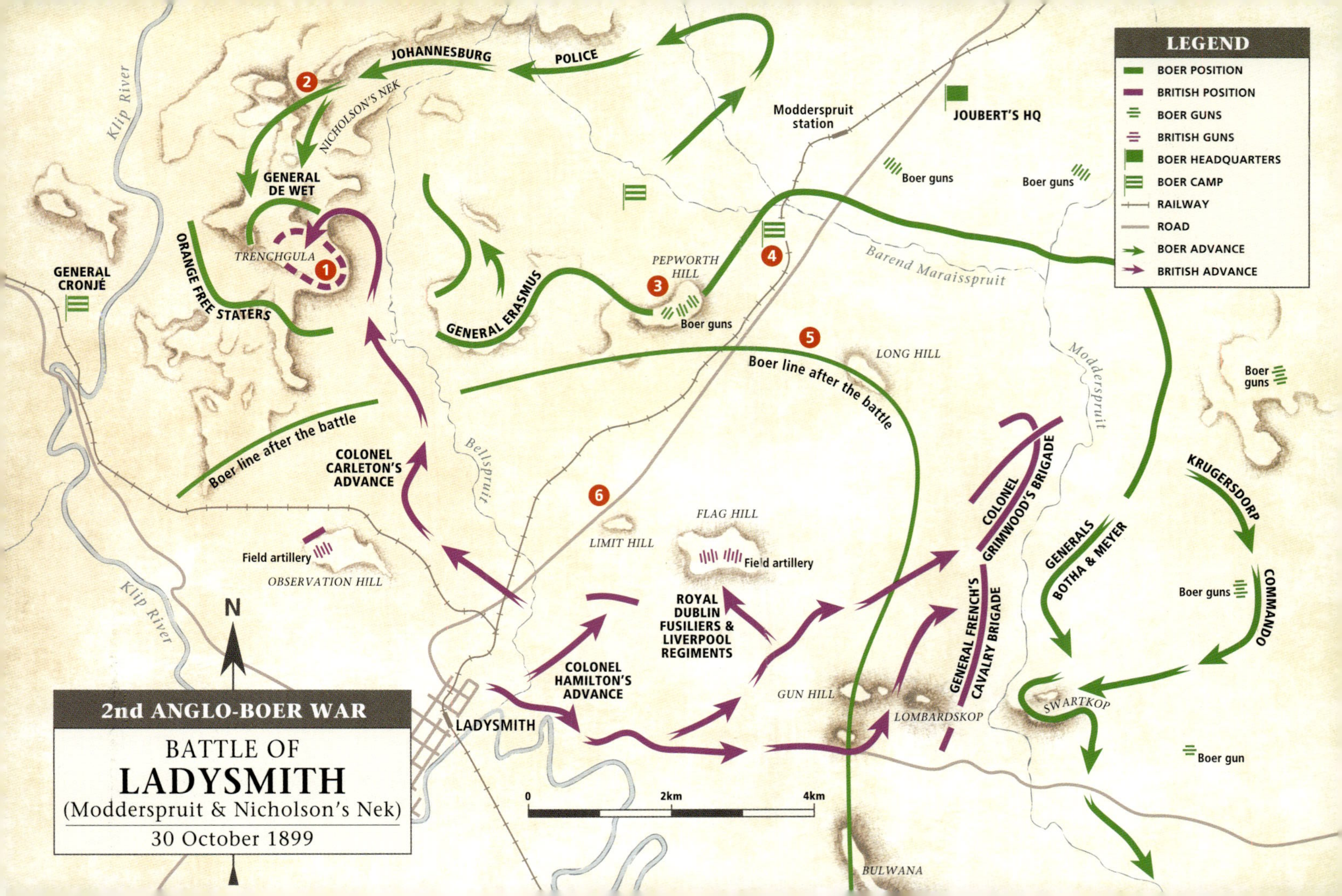
2nd ANGLO-BOER WAR
BATTLE OF
LADYSMITH
(Modderspruit & Nicholson's Nek)
30 October 1899
LEGEND
BOER POSITION
BRITISH POSITION
BOER GUNS
BRITISH GUNS
BOER HEADQUARTERS
BOER CAMP
RAILWAY
ROAD
BOER ADVANCE
BRITISH ADVANCE
JOHANNESBURG
POLICE
NICHOLSON'S NEK
GENERAL DE WET
TRENCHGULA
ORANGE FREE STATERS
GENERAL CRONJÉ
Klip River
GENERAL ERASMUS
PEPWORTH HILL
Boer guns
Modderspruit station
JOUBERT'S HQ
Boer guns
Boer guns
Barend Maraisspruit
Boer line after the battle
LONG HILL
Modderspruit
Boer guns
Boer line after the battle
COLONEL CARLETON'S ADVANCE
Bellspruit
FLAG HILL
LIMIT HILL
Field artillery
Field artillery
OBSERVATION HILL
ROYAL DUBLIN FUSILIERS & LIVERPOOL REGIMENTS
COLONEL HAMILTON'S ADVANCE
LADYSMITH
GUN HILL
LOMBARDSKOP
BULWANA
COLONEL GRIMWOOD'S BRIGADE
GENERAL FRENCH'S CAVALRY BRIGADE
GENERALS BOTHA & MEYER
KRUGERSDORP
COMMANDO
Boer guns
SWARTKOP
Boer gun
N
0
2km
4km
1
2
3
4
5
6

The tranquillity of the landscape in the Ladysmith region belies the turmoil of the battles fought here more than a century ago.

1 This flat-topped hill was known to the Boers as Kainguba, to the British as Trenchgula (Tchrengula) Hill. When the British found themselves unable to reach their objective (the hills overlooking Nicholson's Nek) before dawn, they took up a position on this hill instead.

2 The road north from Ladysmith went through a gap in the hills here, known as Nicholson's Nek. General White wanted to block it to prevent Boers escaping this way.

3 Pepworth Hill lay just south of Boer general Piet Joubert's headquarters and was the site of the long-ranging 155 mm Creusot gun supported by the Irish pro-Boer Brigade. At least eight men of the Irish pro-Boers were wounded during the battle, one of them being their leader, Colonel Blake, leaving Major John MacBride to take over command until Blake's recovery.

4 The camp site of the Irish pro-Boers was completely destroyed during the battle.

5 This marks the Boer line after the Boers had forced the British to withdraw to Ladysmith, where they were to be fully surrounded and besieged two days later.

6 British casualties would have been much greater had it not been for the timely arrival of the long-ranging naval gun from Durban. The gun was unlimbered and fired from here, engaging the Boer Creusot on Pepworth Hill and putting it out of action.

Battle of Rietfontein

Also known as *Battle of Tinta Nyoni*

24 October 1899

> **HOW TO GET THERE**
> Drive out of Ladysmith on the N11 towards Newcastle and continue until you see a sign to Driefontein and Watersmeet on the left. Turn left onto this road, cross the railway line and drive for a short distance before turning right into a driveway lined with tall bluegum trees to arrive at a farmhouse. The battle was fought in the high ground behind and above the farm. The battle site is on private land and permission to visit it should be obtained from the farm owner. *Guide recommended*

Context

After the first major battle of the 2nd Anglo-Boer War at Talana on 20 October (see p. 153), the 4,000-strong Dundee garrison was forced to withdraw to Ladysmith. Commander of the Ladysmith garrison, General Sir George White sent troops out on the Newcastle road to protect the Dundee column, led by Colonel James Yule, as it approached the town.

Action

Early on the morning of 24 October, General Sir George White marched 5,300 British troops out of Ladysmith, following the road and the railway line in a north-easterly direction. Meanwhile, General Piet Joubert, in overall command of the Boers, had made his headquarters at the farm Rietfontein, north of Ladysmith.

About 1,000 Boers from the Orange Free State had arrived the day before to take up positions about 10km from the town on the high ground west of the road and the railway line. They were heading towards Elandslaagte and had with them a 75mm Krupp gun, which had a range of over 7,000m. Christiaan de Wet (who was later to become a Boer general) was with the force. For now, the Boers' commander was 66-year-old General Andries Cronjé.

The British cavalry was ahead of the artillery and infantry when they came under dropping fire from Boer riflemen on the ridge overlooking the road and railway line. The 5th Lancers pushed ahead to engage the parties of Boers advancing from the heights and managed to keep them back until the infantry arrived.

The Boer Krupp gun came into action from the eastern summit of Tinta Nyoni Mountain, firing a shell that landed at the head of the British column close to White and his staff. Two batteries

Memorial to Colonel E. P Wilford and the men of the Gloucestershire Regiment who fell at Rietfontein

118   LADYSMITH REGION

of British field guns wheeled to the left, crossed the railway line at the level crossing and proceeded to fire at the Krupp from a range of about 4,500m. When the Krupp was hit and withdrawn to safety, the British infantry scrambled up to the crest of a low ridge, separated from the Boer positions only by a valley some 800m wide.

Once the infantrymen had gained the crest of the ridge, they lay flat, exchanging fire with the invisible enemy. White had gained his objective in keeping the Boers away from Yule's Dundee column, which had been approaching Ladysmith from the northeast, and casualties were low. However, at about 11h00, Colonel E. P. Wilford, commanding the Gloucestershire Regiment, led an inexplicable charge forward over the crest. The men were exposed to a hail of bullets and the Maxim detachment that went with them was cut down immediately. Six were killed, Wilford included, and many more wounded. The men were withdrawn under fire, incurring yet more casualties.

The Boers to the left of the British then came forward from Ndwatshana Hill and threatened to outflank the British line, but there was a screen of cavalry on both British flanks and it was the Natal Mounted Infantry that galloped forward to stop the movement. Once they had done so, they held their position and fired into the men of the Kroonstad Commando on the higher ridge, causing them to move back and take cover. However, White's objective had been achieved and there was no point in risking further casualties. At 15h00 the men were given the order for general retirement.

Mrs Hendrina Joubert, who was with her husband, Piet, in the Boer camp at Rietfontein

Aftermath

Casualties on both sides were comparatively low, with 11 dead on the Boer side (some reports say nine or 13) and six on the British (some reports claim 11 or 13). Over 100 men were wounded. Both sides claimed victory, the Boers believing that the British had tried and failed to take the high ridges they occupied, and the British satisfied that Colonel Yule and his 4,000 men were able to reach Ladysmith unchallenged by the Boers.

Principal combatants

British: 5th Lancers; 19th Hussars; Border Mounted Rifles; Devonshire Regiment; Gloucestershire Regiment; Imperial Light Horse; King's Royal Rifle Corps; Liverpool Regiment; Natal Carbineers; Natal Field Artillery.
Boers: Commandos from Harrismith, Kroonstad and Winburg.

Timeline

1879
Captain William Penn Symons visits Dundee with the 24th Regiment during the Anglo-Zulu War.

1899
In September Penn Symons, now a major general, is posted to Dundee to take precautionary measures against the Boers on the northern frontiers of Natal.

In October the Battle of Talana results in the death of Penn Symons and the withdrawal of the entire Dundee garrison to Ladysmith. On 24 October the Ladysmith garrison demonstrates against the Boers north and west of the farm Rietfontein to allow the Dundee garrison to enter Ladysmith unmolested.

On 2 November Ladysmith is surrounded and besieged for 118 days. The battles of Belmont, Graspan and Modder River are fought in the west.

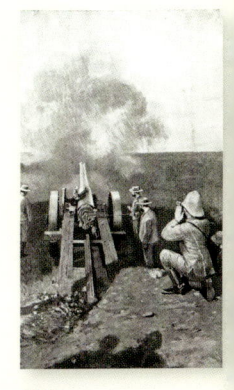

1900
In February the battles of Vaalkrans and Tugela Heights are fought north of Colenso. Ladysmith is relieved.

In May Dundee is reoccupied by the British. The war moves north into the Transvaal.

BATTLE OF RIETFONTEIN   119

Battle of Elandslaagte
21 October 1899

HOW TO GET THERE
Take the N11 out of Ladysmith towards Newcastle; after 20km turn right onto the R602 towards Dundee. After a short distance turn right at the sign to Elandslaagte. Follow the road over the railway line and then turn left at the first junction. There is a sign to the battlefield to your right. Drive along this gravel road until you are in the nek between the ridge on your right and the detached hill on the left. There is a place to park close to the Hollander monument on the detached hill. Climb the steps to the monument and look north-west towards the railway line until you have located the station buildings.

The Boer gun position was on the rocky ridge behind you, on the other side of the road along which you came. The Devonshire Regiment advanced against this ridge and the hill on which you stand. The flanking attack took place along the top of the ridge on the other side of the road. There is a path leading up the ridge that takes you to various British monuments. Continue along the road through the nek to reach the British graveyard.

Hollander monument: 28°25'25.8" S 29°58'44.6" E

The Imperial Light Horse monument at Elandslaagte

Context
In October 1899, when the Boer ultimatum to the British to withdraw their troops from the Transvaal and Orange Free State expired, the Boers invaded Natal in three columns. The right-hand (western) column, led by General Johannes Kock, commander of the Hollander Corps, approached the railway line between Dundee and Ladysmith from the Biggarsberg Mountains. They took Elandslaagte station, effectively cutting communications between Ladysmith and Dundee. The Battle of Elandslaagte ensued when the British sent troops up the line from Ladysmith to oust the Boers and restore communications.

120 LADYSMITH REGION

General Johannes Kock (seated, right) and members of the Hollander Corps

Action

The approaching Boers saw a train nearing the station of Elandslaagte and some of them galloped ahead to intercept it. The train managed to pull away in time, but the Boers took the station master, mine manager and other civilians prisoner. Another train arrived, loaded with supplies – among which was a carriage-load of whisky – for the troops in Dundee. There was joyful offloading, followed by a merry party that night that saw a British prisoner play the piano while the 'Volkslied' (national anthem) of the Transvaal and 'God Save the Queen' were sung. But dawn brought the reality of war.

Stationed in Ladysmith, General Sir George White had received a telegram informing him of the attack on the station. A reconnaissance force sent out at first light the next morning, 20 October, confirmed that the Boers were at Elandslaagte in force. Meanwhile, Colonel Adolph Schiel of the German Corps had arrived at the station and ordered the whisky bottles to be smashed. The British prisoners had been tried and sentenced in a cordial way and then the Boers, with two 75mm guns, took up a defensive position on the rocky ridge that curves away towards Ladysmith, south of the station buildings.

Early the following morning, troops under the command of General John French arrived on the train from Ladysmith. The Natal Field Artillery opened fire on the station and this was immediately returned by the Boer guns on the ridge. The British field guns were hopelessly outranged, and French realised that he would need a stronger force if he were to dislodge the Boers from their position. The real battle was to begin only when the reinforcements arrived at noon.

Timeline

October 1899
10 Oct. The ultimatum issued by President Paul Kruger (right) is received in London, and war with Britain is inevitable. The Orange Free State's President Steyn agrees to back the Transvaal.

12 Oct. Boers invade Natal over Botha's Pass, moving south towards Dundee.

14 Oct. General Buller and Winston Churchill board the *Dunnottar Castle* in Southampton, bound for Cape Town. Meanwhile, the Boers cut the railway line at Modder River and engage Robert Baden-Powell in Mafeking.

15 Oct. Martial law is proclaimed in Natal.

16 Oct. Kimberley and Mafeking are besieged.

19 Oct. Two Boer columns reach Dundee, while a third cuts communications between Ladysmith and Dundee at Elandslaagte.

20 Oct. The Battle of Talana is fought in Dundee. Major General William Penn Symons is mortally wounded. The Boers at Elandslaagte take up positions on the ridge south of the station.

21 Oct. The Battle of Elandslaagte is fought.

24 Oct. The Boers occupy Dundee. The Battle of Rietfontein is fought outside Ladysmith.

30 Oct. The Battle of Ladysmith results in the investment of Ladysmith.

BATTLE OF ELANDSLAAGTE   121

A memorial to the Boers and Dutch volunteers who fell at Elandslaagte is at the top of this hill.

General French soon had 3,500 men at his disposal; they were of the Imperial Light Horse, the Gordon Highlanders, the Manchester Regiment and the Devonshire Regiment. There were also squadrons of the 5th Dragoon Guards and the 5th Lancers, as well as batteries of artillery. The force was up against about 1,000 Boers. The infantry was commanded by Colonel Ian Hamilton who had been wounded by the Boers at Majuba in 1881 and had a score to settle.

French first ordered an artillery bombardment of the ridge. Then the Devons were to advance in open order against the hill. Meanwhile, the Manchesters, Imperial Light Horse and Gordon Highlanders would work their way around the long, curving ridge from the south and attack the flank of the Boer-held position on the north end of the ridge.

The Devons got to within 800m of the Boer rifles and then took cover behind termite mounds. The flanking attack took place from the south and the soldiers came up against a barbed-wire fence, where they incurred heavy casualties from the Boers' Mausers. At this stage, a heavy storm burst over the battlefield – men dashed forward in the teeming rain, bayonets fixed. After a sharp engagement, where many fell on both sides, the Boer position was taken. A counterattack led by Colonel Schiel from the eastern slope of the ridge was beaten off and the Boers fled as fast as they could towards the north. Here the 5th Lancers and 5th Dragoon Guards were waiting and a terrifying cavalry

A perfect example

Elandslaagte, one of the first engagements of the Anglo-Boer War, was later adopted by the Imperial German army as the best example of a typical set-piece battle of that era, exemplified by artillery 'softening' the defensive position, followed by an infantry advance culminating in a bayonet charge, and concluding with a 'mopping-up' of the fleeing enemy by the cavalry.

The train captured by Boers at Elandslaagte station, two days before the battle

charge was unleashed. Boers pleading for mercy were speared through with lances and no quarter was given as the great chargers thundered through the fleeing men. When night came, the battlefield was littered with dead and dying men lying in the rain and cold. Many who might have survived died from exposure.

Aftermath

The British did not follow up their victory because White feared an attack from the Orange Free State Boers and recalled his men to Ladysmith that evening. Casualties on both sides were high. General Kock was badly wounded and died a few days later in Ladysmith as a prisoner of war. Colonel Schiel was wounded and captured. The battle had been of little avail because Ladysmith was soon besieged and would remain that way until relieved by General Redvers Buller's advance in February the following year. This battle saw the end of the original Hollander Corps as a unit: eight of its members died in the attack and 46 were captured.

The British Naval Cemetery at Elandslaagte

Principal combatants

British: 5th Dragoon Guards; 5th Lancers; Devonshire Regiment; Gordon Highlanders; Imperial Light Horse; Manchester Regiment; Natal Field Artillery; Natal Mounted Rifles; Royal Field Artillery.
Boers: German Corps; Hollander Corps; Johannesburg Commando; Vrede Commando.

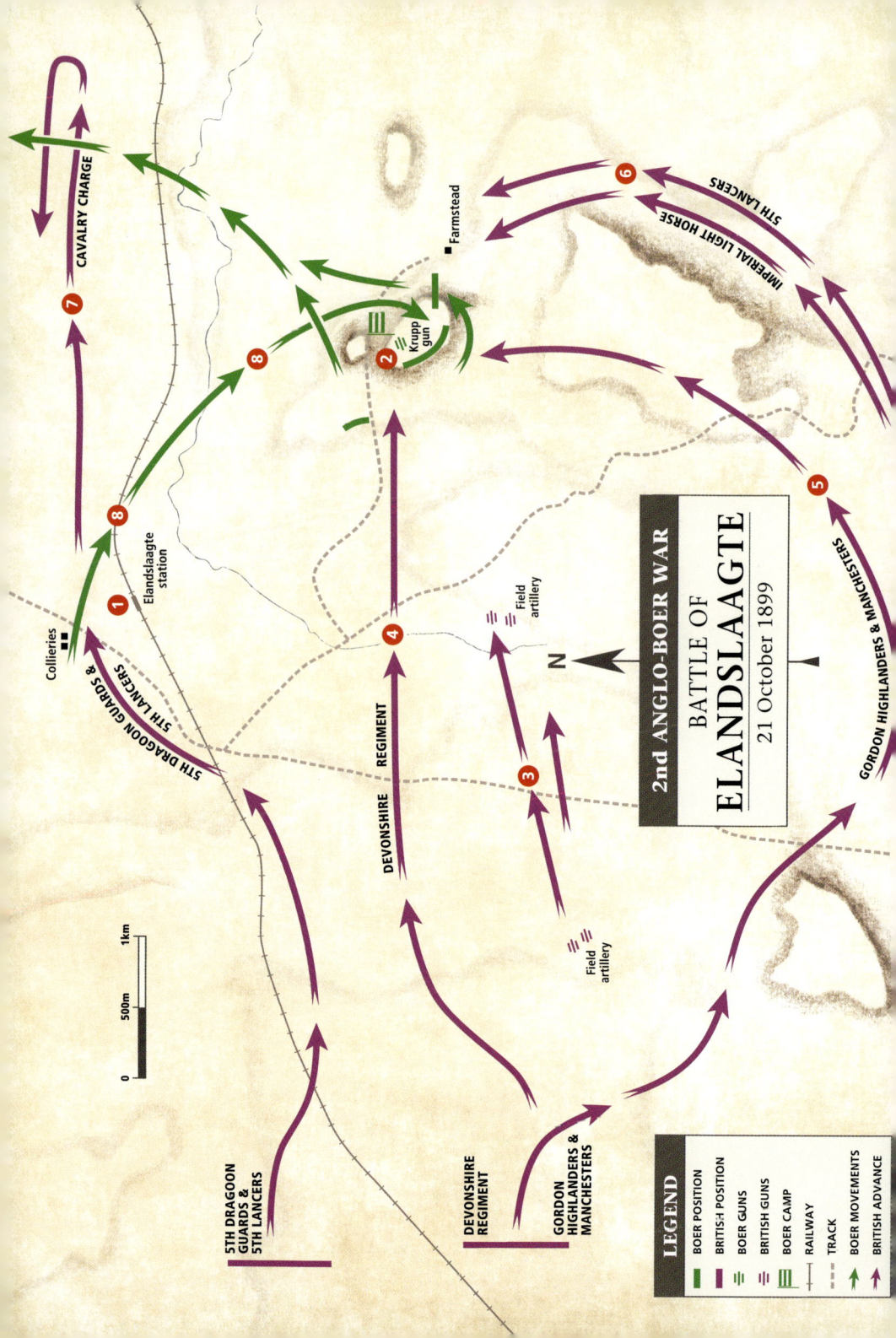

2nd Anglo-Boer War
BATTLE OF ELANDSLAAGTE
21 October 1899

LEGEND
- Boer Position
- British Position
- Boer Guns
- British Guns
- Boer Camp
- Railway
- Track
- Boer Movements
- British Advance

Cavalry Charge

Farmstead

Krupp gun

Elandslaagte station

Collieries

Field artillery

5TH DRAGOON GUARDS & 5TH LANCERS

DEVONSHIRE REGIMENT

GORDON HIGHLANDERS & MANCHESTERS

IMPERIAL LIGHT HORSE

5TH LANCERS

FAR LEFT: View northwards from the battlefield
LEFT: A wounded man in the advance on Elandslaagte

1. The Travellers' Rest Hotel was near Elandslaagte station and it was here that the Boers and their British prisoners, as well as the station master, enjoyed a convivial evening together shortly before the battle.

2. The Boers chose to defend their position from these small hills. There were Boer riflemen on the small detached koppie, and a Krupp gun was placed on the higher ridge south-east of the nek.

3. The British artillery opened fire on the ridge, moving progressively closer to the main Boer position as the infantry advanced.

4. The Devonshire Regiment advanced along this line.

5. The Gordon Highlanders and the Manchester Regiment advanced against the left of the Boer position. They remained undetected by the Boers until they reached the sloping ground leading up to the ridge. Here they came under fire from Boers on the high ground. They were soon up against a farm fence, but Colonel Ian Hamilton rode over to urge them forward. When the fence was cut, the advance became unstoppable.

6. The Imperial Light Horse and some of the 5th Lancers attacked the Boer position from the south-east, joining the Gordon Highlanders and the Manchesters in their final charge.

7. The cavalry charge took place here. The 5th Dragoon Guards and the other 5th Lancers waited west of the railway line to attack any Boers withdrawing northwards. Their cavalry charge through the fleeing horsemen gave rise to much bitterness on the part of the Boers. This was the last time a cavalry charge was used in battle by the British army.

8. This was the scene of the counterattack launched by Colonel Schiel from the north-east after a white flag had been shown by the Boers.

Battle of Surrender Hill
Also known as *Battle of Slaapkranz*
28–30 July 1900

HOW TO GET THERE
Although the Surrender Hill battle site is situated in present-day Free State, it is within easy driving distance from Ladysmith (between 2½ and 3 hours).

Drive from Harrismith towards Bethlehem on the N5. After 45km, you will pass through Kestell. A further 30km will bring you to the turn-off to Clarens (R711). Continue on the R711 past Clarens and drive a further 18km towards Fouriesburg. Surrender Hill is situated beside the R711, on your right, about 17km east of Fouriesburg. It is on one of the passes out of the Brandwater Basin. There is a sign indicating the hill where the surrender took place and a monument next to the road.

Surrender Hill: 28°36'33.2" S 28°23'10.1" E

Context
The British had gained the upper hand in the Orange Free State and General Christiaan de Wet had narrowly avoided being surrounded in the Brandwater Basin, formed by the Wittebergen, Roodebergen and Drakensberg mountain ranges, on the eastern border of the Free State. He had escaped to the northern Orange Free State with President Jan Brand just in time. But more than 4,000 Boers remained in the Basin and the British were rapidly closing all passes leading out of it. After a sharp engagement on 28 July, General Marthinus Prinsloo sent a message offering the unconditional surrender of all the Boers in the Brandwater Basin. The handing over of their guns, rifles, ammunition, livestock and horses took place on the farm Slaapkranz, now called Surrender Hill.

Action
There was much infighting among the Boer leaders in the Orange Free State. Marthinus Prinsloo claimed to be chief commandant, though the title had been conferred on Christiaan de Wet. Prinsloo had resigned in anger at the beginning of July, claiming ill health, but subsequently took back the title with no right to do so. He had the support of some of the commandants in the Brandwater Basin; the popular Boer leader Paul Roux was supported by others. Morale was low among the men as British troops massed at all the exit passes out of the Basin.

General Marthinus Prinsloo

The official surrender of the Boers under General Prinsloo in the Brandwater Basin

The commandos moved to the farm Slaapkranz in an attempt to keep an escape route open. On 28 July the British attacked the main position with a heavy artillery bombardment followed by a cavalry charge. The Boers abandoned Slaapkranz Nek and Prinsloo was unnerved. On 29 July Prinsloo sent a message to Lieutenant General Archibald Hunter requesting a four-day armistice. Not surprisingly, Hunter refused. Prinsloo offered the surrender of all the commandos in the Basin the very next day. This caused anger among Boer fighters loyal to De Wet and Roux and 1,500 of them managed to escape with guns and horses.

De Wet received news of the surrender from Prinsloo's secretary, Albert Grobler, who had taken the message to General Charles Knox in Kroonstad. Knox sent the message on to De Wet, who agreed to offer safe passage to Grobler. De Wet and President Steyn met him away from their laager so as not to give away its location. It seems that De Wet was more annoyed at the fact that Prinsloo considered himself chief commandant, than at the news of the surrender.

It took until 9 August for all the Boers remaining in the Brandwater Basin to surrender. The British took over 4,300 prisoners, three guns, two million rounds of ammunition and over 6,000 horses and mules.

Aftermath

This all but destroyed Boer resistance in the Orange Free State. Bare patches of ground on the slopes of Surrender Hill, where grass will not grow to this day, are said to be the places where the Boer ammunition was blown up. Harrismith was occupied by the British on 4 August and

Timeline

1900
In February the sieges of Ladysmith and Kimberley are relieved. General Piet Cronjé surrenders his forces at Paardeberg. Lord Roberts and his huge army push towards Johannesburg.

In March General Christiaan de Wet ambushes a British convoy at Sannaspos east of Bloemfontein.

In April, at the Battle of Boshof, Comte De Villebois-Mareuil and his men are overcome by the British. De Villebois-Mareuil is killed.

In May De Wet succeeds Lucas Meyer (above, centre) as commander-in-chief of the Boer forces. A Boer deputation is sent to the USA to garner support and is enthusiastically received, but does not gain significant aid. At the end of May Johannesburg falls to the British and Britain annexes the Orange Free State.

In June Pretoria falls and General Sir Redvers Buller's army enters the Transvaal from Natal via Botha's Pass and Alleman Nek.

In July, following the Battle of Surrender Hill, a number of Boers concede defeat and relinquish their arms and ammunition.

In August, despite the brave stand made by the Johannesburg Police at the Battle of Bergendal, the Boers have to withdraw.

In November President Steyn narrowly escapes capture at the Battle of Doornkraal, south of Bothaville. De Wet subsequently regroups his scattered forces and they continue the guerrilla war.

BATTLE OF SURRENDER HILL

A colourful reminder

During the 2nd Anglo-Boer War, British cavalry horses had to be fed with imported fodder, as there was insufficient cut fodder available in South Africa. Unlike the Boer ponies, the imported horses could not survive on the veld grass. In the imported bales of hay came seeds of various exotic flowers, one of them the cosmos – the white, pink and purple blossoms are to be found along the routes travelled by the British army during their three-year campaign.

this opened the railway to Durban for them, making supply of materiel much easier for Lord Roberts and his army, which was advancing on Pretoria. He could now use the Durban line instead of the Cape railway – a big advantage, as his massive army had been suffering a lack of supplies due to the long distances goods had to travel.

Principal combatants

British: 16th Lancers; Bedfordshire Regiment; Black Watch; Cameron Highlanders; Gordon Highlanders; Grenadier Guards; Highland Light Infantry; Leinster Regiment; Life Guards; Manchester Regiment; Munster Fusiliers; Naval Brigade; Royal Field Artillery; Royal Horse Guards; Royal Irish Regiment; Royal Sussex Regiment; Scots Guards; Seaforth Highlanders; South Staffordshire Regiment; South African and other colonial units; West Kent Regiment; Wiltshire Regiment; Worcestershire Regiment; Yorkshire Light Infantry.
Boers: Commandos that served in the Brandwater Basin (not all were on Surrender Hill): Bethlehem, Bloemfontein, Boshof, Fauresmith, Ficksburg, Harrismith, Heilbron, Jacobsdal, Kroonstad, Ladybrand, Potchefstroom, Rouxville, Senekal, Smithfield, Thaba Nchu, Vrede, Vredefort and Winburg.

Battle of Groenkop

Also known as *Battle of Christmas Kop, Battle of Tweefontein* and *Battle of Krismiskop*

24–25 December 1901

HOW TO GET THERE

The Groenkop battle site is located in the Free State, but is easily accessible from the towns in northern KwaZulu-Natal. Situated between Harrismith and Bethlehem, it can be reached from the N5 or the R57 between Reitz and Kestell, where the turn-off to the farm Groenkop is 13km from Kestell on the R57. The owners will arrange access to the battlefield. They also have copies of an information leaflet about the battle, which was produced by a descendant of one of the men who fought there.

Groenkop farmhouse: *28°14'10.2" S 28°40'15.5" E*
Monuments: *28°14'11.2" S 28°39'30.0" E*

This monument at the Groenkop battle site is dedicated to the Boers.

Context

Lord Kitchener had taken over operations in South Africa in November 1900, replacing Lord Roberts as commander-in-chief of the British forces. Boer morale was at an all-time low due to the scorched-earth policy, initiated by Roberts but zealously executed by Kitchener, that saw the systematic destruction of the Boers' farmsteads, crops and livestock, and the proliferation of concentration camps for women and children from the second half of 1900 onwards. Aware of the commandos' flagging spirit, General De Wet decided that renewed attacks on the British in the Orange Free State were needed to restore confidence. He made his move at Groenkop on Christmas day 1901, surprising and defeating a British column that was protecting the construction of a line of blockhouses between Harrismith and Bethlehem.

BATTLE OF GROENKOP   129

Timeline

1901

In September Jan Smuts and his commando invade the Cape, hoping to foment rebellion among the Afrikaners living under British rule. General Louis Botha invades Natal, engaging British forces in Zululand at Fort Itala and Fort Prospect.

In October, the Boers, under generals Sarel Grobler and Botha, attack and overcome a British column at the Battle of Bakenlaagte near Bethal in the Transvaal.

In December, in an attempt to raise flagging Boer morale, General Christiaan de Wet launches a night attack on the British column at Groenkop, capturing guns, ammunition, food and drink.

1902

In January Sir Michael Campbell-Bannerman, leader of the opposition in England, launches an attack on the British government for its conduct during the 2nd Anglo-Boer War. There is a skirmish at Bankkop (Onverwacht) near Ermelo.

In March the Battle of Tweebosch, during which General Lord Methuen is wounded and captured, is a victory for General Koos de la Rey.

In April the last battle of the war, the Battle of Roodewal, is fought. It results in the death of Boer commandant Hendrik Potgieter.

In May Boers are massacred by a Zulu force at Holkrans. The war ends.

This 5-inch Armstrong fortress gun captured by Boer fighters at the Groenkop battle is on display at the Anglo-Boer War Museum in Bloemfontein.

Action

Groenkop was a stopover for convoys taking supplies to the British who were building a line of blockhouses between Harrismith and Bethlehem. The British soldiers were aware that De Wet was in the area, as there had been a skirmish at Tierkloof on 18 December. But, when De Wet pretended to have left the area, Major George Williams was persuaded to take 600 men away from their well-protected camp at Elands River and set them up at Groenkop. Lieutenant General Leslie Rundle, in charge of blockhouse construction, ordered 150 of the men at Groenkop to travel 8km north-east to help with building work there.

De Wet reconnoitred the British position carefully, climbing a hill south of Groenkop from where he was able to observe all British movements. He even sent two horsemen north-west past Groenkop to draw fire from their guns so that he knew where the artillery was placed.

British intelligence reports indicated to Major Williams that an attack from the north was unlikely, while the south was clear of Boers. The British camp was spread on the eastern slope of the hill, which descends gently, whereas the western, southern and northern slopes are steep. Williams ordered the construction of sangars facing the expected line of attack (east) and the placement of an Armstrong and some Maxim guns on the summit.

On Christmas Eve De Wet gathered about 600 horsemen on a farm 7km north-west of Groenkop. Leaving 100 men behind with the packhorses, the rest rode to a point 250m from the base of the steep north-western slopes of Groenkop. The horses were left with 50 men, while the remaining 450 men, in stockinged feet, scrambled up the boulder-strewn slopes in the dark.

British pickets heard them when they were over halfway to the top. The alarm was sounded and many of the British soldiers fled in panic. However, the gunners and most of the Imperial Yeomanry made their way bravely upwards to their posts. The gunners managed to fire only two shots with the Armstrong 5-inch (127mm) gun. The Boers charged forward, firing from the hip, to form a line along the northern crest. Some of the British, coming up from the south, fired at Boers who were lit against the skyline by a full moon. The battle lasted about 20 minutes, during which time the British suffered heavy casualties – 67 British and 25 black soldiers died.

The Boers had lost 16 men, but, when the fighting was over, they were able to claim 20 wagons laden with food and drink designed to spoil the British troops for Christmas. They also gained over 500 horses and mules and took 240 prisoners.

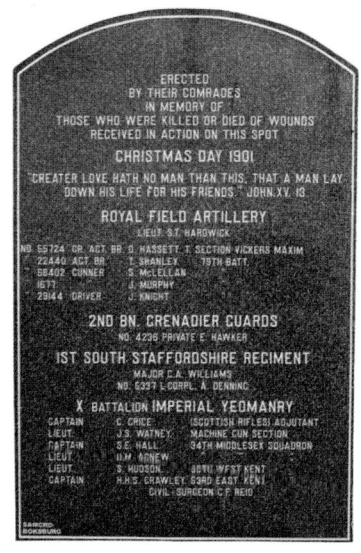

Memorial to the British soldiers who died at Groenkop

Rundle, in the hills 7km away, heard the firing and sent 60 men to investigate. Only on their return did he attempt to send a telegram to Elands River asking for help. However, the telegram operator was asleep at the time and a messenger had to be sent instead. By the time the mounted infantry arrived at Groenkop, De Wet and his men were long gone. There was no pursuit.

Aftermath

News of De Wet's victory instilled new hope in the Boers. The British lost valuable supplies and equipment, some of which were auctioned at Reitz a few days later. The Armstrong gun is now in the Anglo-Boer War Museum in Bloemfontein.

The British had learned the folly of dividing their force into small, vulnerable groups.

General Christiaan de Wet

Principal combatants

British: Imperial Yeomanry; Support units.
Boers: About 450 men led by General Christiaan de Wet.

BATTLE OF GROENKOP **131**

Dundee region

The small town of Dundee was settled on the slopes of the Biggarsberg in north-western KwaZulu-Natal in 1882 on a farm owned by Peter Smith, a settler of British descent. It is in this region, amid the undulating hills that form a natural barrier between Dundee and Ladysmith, that Boer, Zulu and Brit battled it out for supremacy over a period of more than 60 years during the 1800s.

A working coal mine near Dundee, 1898. The town was once a thriving coal-mining centre.

Early Voortrekkers, making their way through Natal in the 1830s, discovered that the Dundee area was rich in surface deposits of coal. However, 20 years were to pass before the local mining industry took off. In 1850, Smith uncovered outcrops rich in coal on his newly laid-out farm on the slopes of Talana Hill. By 1862, he was able to send wagonloads of the combustible black rock to Pietermaritzburg, earning so much money that he was able to give up farming altogether. Others soon followed, staking their claims in the resource-rich district. Many of the new settlers came from Scotland, which accounts for the profusion of Scottish names given to the towns and farms in this picturesque region of KwaZulu-Natal.

Regional battles	1838			1879
	Blood River			Isandlwana / Rorke's Drift / Death of the Prince Imperial of France / Hlobane / Khambula

World events	1827	1851	1871
	During the Battle of Navarino, the Ottoman fleet is destroyed through superior firepower and gunnery by an allied force of British, French and Russian vessels. This is the last sea battle fought entirely with sailing ships.	The Great Exhibition attracts over six million visitors to the Crystal Palace in London, where 100,000 objects from all over the world are displayed.	The Royal Albert Hall, named in memory of Prince Albert, Queen Victoria's beloved husband, is opened in London.

During the Anglo-Zulu War of 1879, officers in the British army found friendly hospitality from British settlers in the town of Dundee. One of these officers was young Captain William Penn Symons who, 20 years later, found himself back in South Africa to fight the Boers. His concern for the inhabitants of the town persuaded him to keep his 4,000-strong garrison in Dundee at the outbreak of the 2nd Anglo-Boer War, against the advice of his commander, General Sir George White, who wanted him to withdraw south to Ladysmith.

Dundee was also the scene of the first major set-piece battle of the 2nd Anglo-Boer War, the Battle of Talana Hill, which took place here on 20 October 1899. The history of the area and this battle is well portrayed in the excellent Talana Museum, 3km east of the town centre on the R33 to Vryheid.

Dundee is situated only 40 minutes' drive from Zululand and is a convenient centre from which to visit battlefields relating to the Voortrekkers, the Anglo-Zulu War, and the 1st and 2nd Anglo-Boer wars.

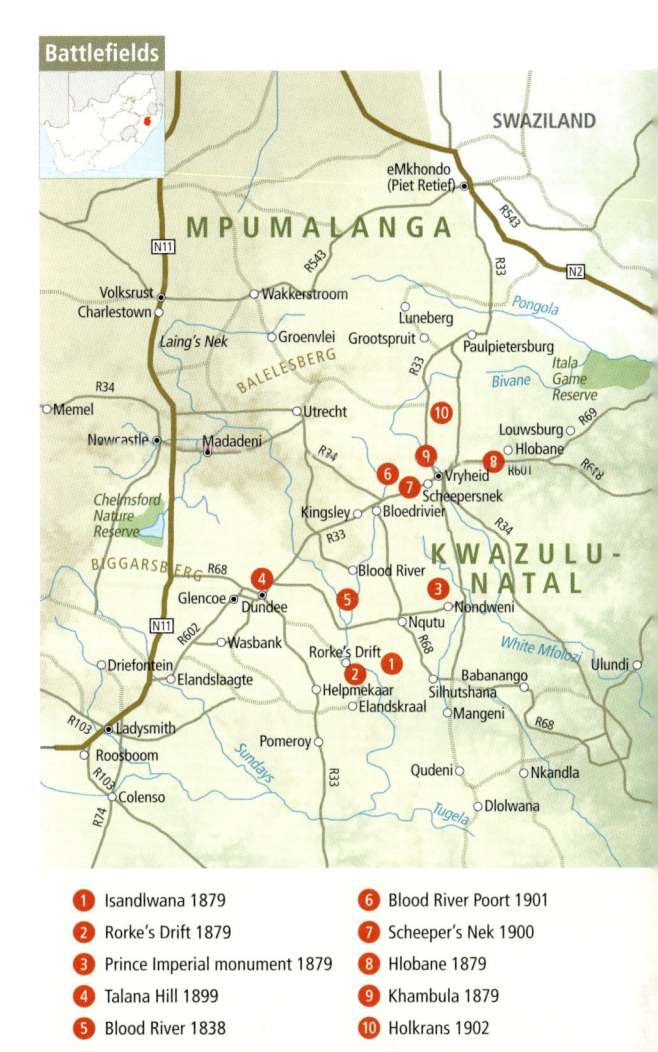

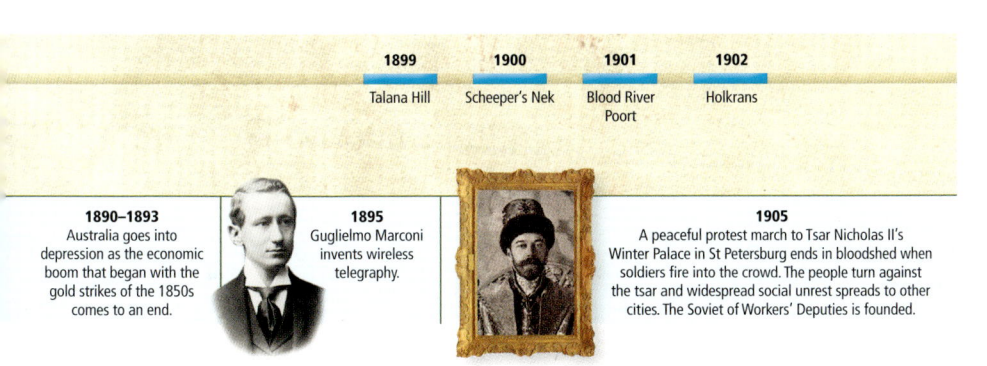

Battlefields

1. Isandlwana 1879
2. Rorke's Drift 1879
3. Prince Imperial monument 1879
4. Talana Hill 1899
5. Blood River 1838
6. Blood River Poort 1901
7. Scheeper's Nek 1900
8. Hlobane 1879
9. Khambula 1879
10. Holkrans 1902

1899 Talana Hill
1900 Scheeper's Nek
1901 Blood River Poort
1902 Holkrans

1890–1893 Australia goes into depression as the economic boom that began with the gold strikes of the 1850s comes to an end.

1895 Guglielmo Marconi invents wireless telegraphy.

1905 A peaceful protest march to Tsar Nicholas II's Winter Palace in St Petersburg ends in bloodshed when soldiers fire into the crowd. The people turn against the tsar and widespread social unrest spreads to other cities. The Soviet of Workers' Deputies is founded.

DUNDEE REGION   133

Battle of Isandlwana
22 January 1879

HOW TO GET THERE
Isandlwana is situated south-east of Dundee in northern KwaZulu-Natal. If you drive from Dundee to Vryheid on the R33, turn right onto the R68 to Nqutu. When you reach Nqutu, turn right at the four-way stop in the town centre, then continue on the R68 towards Melmoth. The turn-off to Isandlwana is on your right, 14km out of Nqutu. Follow signs to the Isandlwana Interpretive Centre.

On the battlefield, stand in the car park with your back to the sphinx-shaped Isandlwana Mountain. In front of you is a stony hill known as Black's Koppie. To your right, about 14km across the valley, is a distinctive hill shaped a bit like a pyramid, with a rocky outcrop on the summit. This feature marks the location of Rorke's Drift and the Buffalo River. Then turn around so that you face Isandlwana. Beyond the hill is the flat-topped Nqutu plateau. The main Zulu attack came from here. To your right is Conical Hill. The donga in which Colonel Anthony Durnford took up his position against the left horn of the Zulu army runs from the base of Conical Hill to the red-roofed clinic buildings that you can see almost behind you. The distant hills on the skyline to your right are where Lord Chelmsford went to look for Zulu fighters who were not there.

Context

The British army under Lord Chelmsford had moved from the eastern Cape border to the Zululand border during 1878. When the British ultimatum to the Zulu king, Cetshwayo, expired in January 1879 (see p. 46), the British invaded Zululand in three separate columns. The Battle of Isandlwana ensued when the central column came into contact with the Zulu army and was defeated.

More has perhaps been written about this battle than any other single engagement in the history of South Africa. One of the reasons for this is that the true story will never be known; all the British soldiers who stayed until the end were killed. Zulu reports suffer from inaccurate translation and from the time lapse between the battle and their recording. British reports often attempt to make excuses for the defeat.

Action

The central column of the invading British army consisted of about 4,500 men, accompanied by Lord Chelmsford himself. Almost half of the column consisted of Zulu members of the Natal Native Contingent; they were poorly trained and there was only one rifle for every 10 men. The easy successes that Chelmsford had enjoyed against the Xhosa in the eastern Cape Colony made him over-confident.

An artist's depiction of Isandlwana after the battle

The force crossed the Buffalo River at Rorke's Drift, on the border between Natal and Zululand, on 10 January. It took them a week to progress about 12km into Zululand, in the direction of Ulundi, the seat of the Zulu king, because roads had to be built for the wagons. There were 220 wagons, transporting supplies of food, equipment, arms and ammunition.

During this time, Chelmsford received intelligence from a border agent that Chief Matshana intended to let him go a little way into Zululand before attacking his flanks and rear. As a result, Chelmsford decided to make camp at Isandlwana and pause his infantry there while his mounted men brought Matshana to bay. He would then be free to progress towards Ulundi unmolested.

The main Zulu army, meanwhile, had left Ulundi with an order from King Cetshwayo to rid his land of the invaders. The strongest regiments, numbering about 22,000 warriors, were sent towards Rorke's Drift to engage the central British column. They were led by chiefs Mavumengwana and Tshingwayo, both gifted strategists.

On 20 January the Zulu warriors were at Isipesi Hill, close to Isandlwana, from where they watched the British set up their numerous canvas tents. Spies were sent forward to gauge enemy strength, and the Zulu commanders were overjoyed when they saw mounted men leave the camp and ride towards Matshana's stronghold. They immediately sent warriors to reinforce Matshana and to encourage Chelmsford to send more of his men out of camp. Their aim was to take the main camp, which was rich in supplies, arms, oxen and wagons.

Timeline

1845
Natal becomes a British colony.

1856
Cetshwayo (left) defeats his half brother Mbuyazi at the Battle of Ndondakasuka, and assumes leadership of the Zulu nation.

1873
Cetshwayo is crowned king of the Zulu.

1877
The Transvaal is annexed to Great Britain. There are border disputes between Boer and Zulu in the territory between the Blood and Buffalo rivers.

1878
The British present an ultimatum to the Zulu king, which makes war inevitable.

1879
Early in the year the British invade Zululand. They are victorious at the Battle of Nyezane but suffer a devastating defeat at Isandlwana on 22 January. Eshowe is besieged a few days later.

In March there is a British reverse at Hlobane and a victory at Khambula.

In June, during the second invasion of Zululand, the Prince Imperial of France is killed when he accompanies a scouting expedition.

In July the British defeat the Zulu army at the Battle of Ulundi.

1880–1881
The 1st Anglo-Boer War is fought and won by the Boers. The Transvaal is once more an independent Boer republic.

1886
Gold is discovered on the Witwatersrand.

1899
The 2nd Anglo Boer-War breaks out.

The British mounted men under Major John Dartnell reached the slopes below Matshana's stronghold in the afternoon and were alarmed to see Zulu warriors appearing and disappearing in the hills all around them. When night fell, the area was alive with camp fires, leading Dartnell to believe, incorrectly, that the main force of the Zulu army was close by. He sent a message back to Chelmsford asking for reinforcements so that they could attack the next morning. Meanwhile, the Zulu commanders, their mission accomplished, withdrew their men to the well-watered Ngwebini valley north of the British camp.

Early on the morning of 22 January, Chelmsford himself and most of his men left the camp in Dartnell's direction. Chelmsford's force consisted of the 2nd Battalion of the 24th Regiment, 1,000 members of the Natal Native Contingent and all the mounted men except those out on patrol duty. He also took four of six artillery guns with him. The Zulu, noting this with satisfaction, moved their men up out of the valley to deploy, in the formation of the horns of the buffalo (see p. 139), towards the main camp.

The main camp had been left under the command of Brevet Colonel Henry Pulleine, an excellent administrator, but inexperienced in action. A message had been sent to Rorke's Drift ordering that Colonel Durnford and his 250 mounted troops should come up in support. He duly arrived in the Isandlwana camp site at about 10h00 and found that Pulleine had

A tragic figure

Anthony Durnford had lived in South Africa for seven years prior to the outbreak of the Anglo-Zulu War. He was based with the garrison in Pietermaritzburg where his wife was reputed to have had a series of affairs with fellow officers, as a result of which Durnford sent her back to England.

He liked the Zulu people and raised up a mounted unit of about 250 well-trained and loyal Zulu soldiers in Pietermaritzburg. They were all uniformed and armed with the latest Martini-Henry carbines. Known as the Natal Native Horse, they remained devoted to Durnford even after his death.

Durnford shared his love of the Zulu people with Bishop Colenso, a controversial man who spoke fluent Zulu and championed their cause. The two men became close friends, which made Durnford unpopular with the inhabitants of Pietermaritzburg, who already disliked him. In his loneliness (someone even poisoned his dog), Durnford developed a very close friendship with Bishop Colenso's daughter, Fanny, but nothing came of it because he was still married.

Durnford was killed at the Battle of Isandlwana, along with 1,300 other British soldiers. Lord Chelmsford tried to blame the disaster on him, but Fanny left no stone unturned in her efforts to clear his name and reputation. With the help of Durnford's brother, she eventually found evidence that exonerated him.

This memorial at Isandlwana is dedicated to the Zulu fighters who lost their lives during the battle. It portrays the necklace awarded to warriors who demonstrated exceptional valour.

put out a firing line of men beyond the tents, on the report that Zulu had been sighted to the east. Unbeknown to him, these were young warriors who had been ordered to get the mounted picket off the hills to the east from whence they might have noticed the main army approaching over the Nqutu plateau. Durnford suggested that the men should breakfast while he scouted in the direction of the sighting and would then proceed towards Matshana's stronghold in support of Chelmsford.

There had also been reports of Zulu spotted on the Nqutu plateau 'retiring' towards the west. With hindsight, we know that these were elements of the right horn, running to take up positions west and south of the camp. The left horn, having less distance to travel, was already in position behind Tusi, the highest point on the plateau.

As Durnford, with a mule cart carrying a rocket battery, approached on the track below them, the young warriors of the left horn were unable to resist the temptation to attack this vulnerable target. They fell upon the unfortunate battery, hacking it to extinction. Durnford and his men, who had ridden ahead, came back to take up defensive positions in a great donga below Conical Hill from where it was easy to keep the attacking left horn of the Zulu army at bay.

Meanwhile, one of Durnford's mounted officers had stumbled on the middle section of the Zulu attack formation on a great sweep of low-lying ground scarcely 5km north of the British camp. The men were squatting on their shields and waiting while the horns got into

BATTLE OF ISANDLWANA 137

The Isandlwana battlefield today

position. He galloped back to report the news. Pulleine, instead of pulling his men back, inexplicably sent another company up onto a spur of the plateau. The firing line was put out again, in two sections, one facing north and the other east. It was a thin line, as the companies were all below strength. It was also a long way from the centre of the camp, due to the spread of the tents and the dead ground to the left front of the position. In the knuckle between the lines of men were the two artillery pieces and, close by, 1,000 members of the Natal Native Contingent.

By this time it was around midday and Durnford's men were running short of ammunition. He was forced to leave his position to take up another, closer to the camp. As he did so, the left horn came forward to occupy the donga he vacated. The right horn was almost in position and, as the Zulu fighters rushed the camp through the wagon park in the rear, so the main army swirled down off the plateau to fall on the thin firing line. It wasn't long before the soldiers of the Natal Native Contingent fled, leaving a gap for the Zulu, who swarmed in among the tents.

The retreat was sounded and men tried to save themselves as best they could. All the soldiers in the firing line were killed. The last to die was a company of men that had fought a fighting retreat up onto the shoulder of the mountain. When the men ran out ammunition, the Zulu surged forward. Some of the mounted men managed to flee between the two horns of the Zulu army. In a nightmarish scramble, they made their way down what is now known as Fugitives' Trail to get to the Buffalo River, which was then in flood. Only 55 white men escaped this way. Many more were killed as they fled.

Aftermath

This was an expensive victory for the Zulu, as more than 1,000 warriors were killed. But it was a disastrous defeat for Britain and could have

Dabulamanzi (centre) led the uThulwana Regiment.

138   DUNDEE REGION

led to insurrections in her other southern African colonies. All in all, 1,329 men, including African auxiliaries, died for Britain on this battlefield. To deflect attention from the defeat at Isandlwana, much was made of the successful defence of Rorke's Drift the same afternoon.

Lord Chelmsford had to wait for reinforcements before invading Zululand for the second time in June of the same year.

Principal combatants

Zulu: Regiments commanded by chiefs Mavumengwana and Tshingwayo: inDluyengwa, inGobamakhosi, isaNgqu, mBonambi, umCijo, umHlanga, uDloko, uDlondlo, uDududu, uNdi, uThulwana and uVe.

British: 1st and 2nd Battalions, 24th Regiment; Buffalo Border Guard; Mounted infantry; Natal Carbineers; Natal Mounted Police; Natal Native Contingent; Natal Native Horse; Newcastle Mounted Rifles; Rocket Battery; Royal Artillery.

The horns-of-the-buffalo formation

The attack strategy employed by the Zulu at the Battle of Isandlwana, known as the 'horns of the buffalo', was designed by Shaka, a formidable military strategist. The method, whereby the enemy is surrounded and then engaged in close combat, was more advanced than that of any of the Zulu king's opponents.

In the horn formation, the younger warriors, members of age-related regiments, were placed on either end of an attacking line, while the more experienced fighters remained in the middle. The younger men were fleeter of foot and better able to run around the foe, whereas the veterans waited in the centre until the encirclement was complete before attacking. Once everyone was in place, the entire formation would move forward to crush the enemy.

The warriors were trained to fight at close quarters with a short, thick-bladed stabbing spear (*iklwa*) that replaced the older throwing spear as their main weapon.

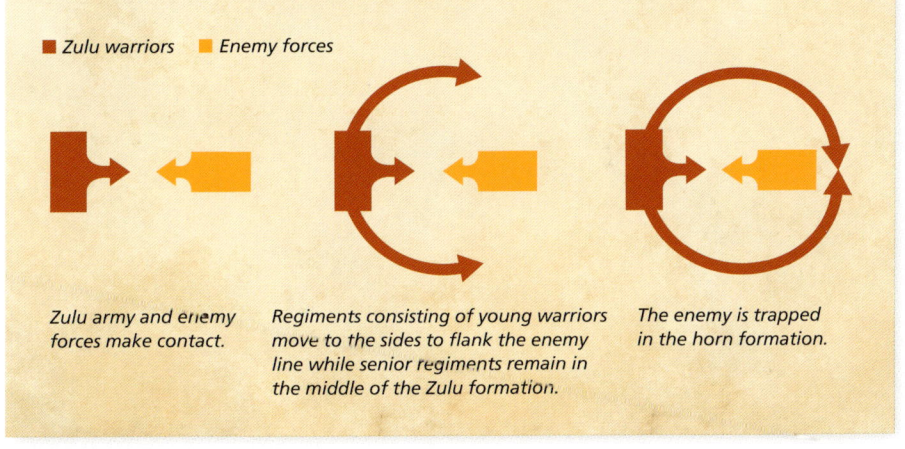

■ *Zulu warriors*   ■ *Enemy forces*

| Zulu army and enemy forces make contact. | Regiments consisting of young warriors move to the sides to flank the enemy line while senior regiments remain in the middle of the Zulu formation. | The enemy is trapped in the horn formation. |

The Buffalo River at Fugitives' Drift

Saving the Queen's Colour

Lieutenant Melvill

At the close of the Battle of Isandlwana, when the Zulu were in the British camp and there could be no hope of saving the situation, Lieutenant Teignmouth Melvill, an adjutant of the 1st Battalion, 24th Regiment, took the Queen's Colour (the flag that carried the name of the regiment and the Union Jack and to which all regimental honour is attached) with the intention of keeping it from enemy hands, or perhaps to rally the troops.

The road back to the safety of the Natal border at Rorke's Drift, on the Buffalo River, was blocked by warriors and the only escape was the rough country south, between the battlefield and the river. As it was impossible to outrun the Zulu, the only escape was on horseback and Melvill forced his mount through ravines, over boulders, up steep scree-covered slopes and down precipitous crags towards the river.

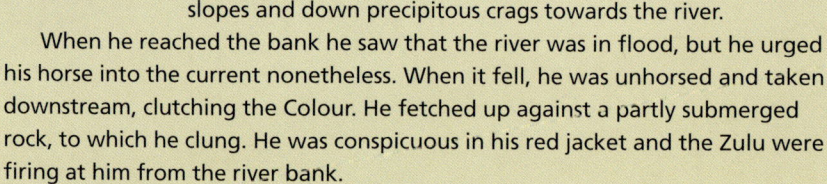

When he reached the bank he saw that the river was in flood, but he urged his horse into the current nonetheless. When it fell, he was unhorsed and taken downstream, clutching the Colour. He fetched up against a partly submerged rock, to which he clung. He was conspicuous in his red jacket and the Zulu were firing at him from the river bank.

140   DUNDEE REGION

Meanwhile, his friend Lieutenant Neville Coghill had reached the bank on the Natal side on his horse. He had been wearing his blue patrol jacket that day and had had a slightly easier ride from Isandlwana. (Cetshwayo had instructed his warriors not to kill civilians and had told them that they would know the soldiers by their red coats.) Coghill was about to ride to safety when he saw his friend in the water. Without a thought for his own safety, he spurred his horse back into the torrent. The animal was shot between the eyes as it entered the river and Coghill was pitched into the water. A strong swimmer, he swam to Melvill and helped him through the churning water, but the current ripped the Colour from their clutch and it disappeared downstream.

Lieutenant Coghill

They reached the river bank on the Natal side, helped by the covering fire of some of the men of the Natal Native Horse. Here they attempted to climb the steep, boulder-strewn south bank. Coghill had an injured knee and had to be half-carried up the slope. When they were almost at the top, Melvill could go no further. They sank down against a boulder to rest, but Zulu approached, possibly from the Natal side, and both men were killed.

The graves of Melvill and Coghill at Fugitives' Drift

The Colour was found embedded in the mud of the river a few days later. It was returned to the regiment at Rorke's Drift amid great rejoicing.

More than two decades later, in 1902, the bravery of the two men was rewarded when an application to grant them posthumous Victoria Crosses was approved. The decorations were presented to their respective families.

The graves of Melvill and Coghill are marked by white stones on a steep slope above the Buffalo River at Fugitives' Drift. They are on private land but may be accessed through the gates at Fugitives' Drift Lodge.

Graves of Melvill and Coghill: *28°23'07.6" S 30°36'06.7" E*

BATTLE OF ISANDLWANA 141

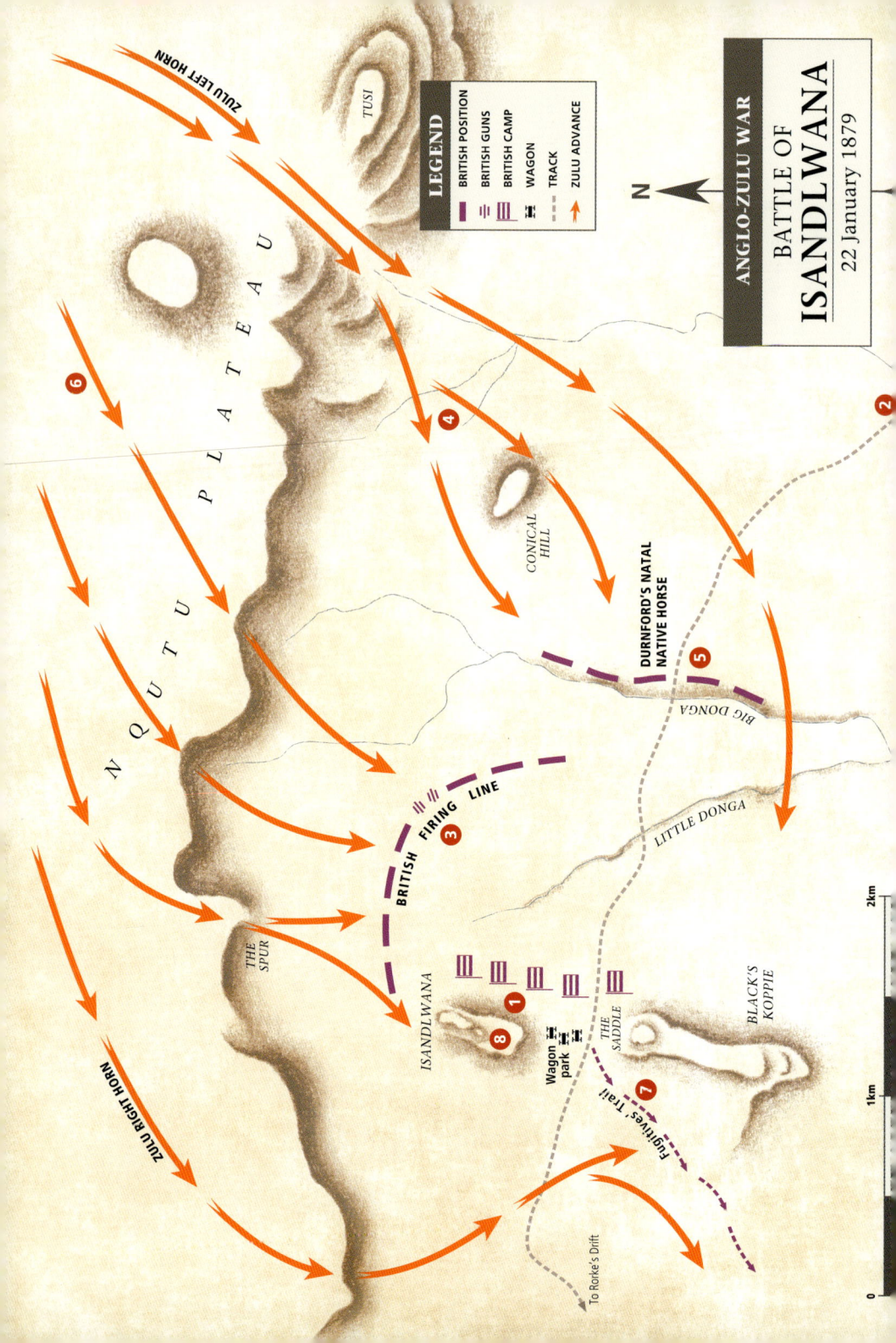

BATTLE OF ISANDLWANA
ANGLO-ZULU WAR
22 January 1879

LEGEND
- British Position
- British Guns
- British Camp
- Wagon
- Track
- Zulu Advance

N

ZULU LEFT HORN

TUSI

NQUTU PLATEAU

CONICAL HILL

DURNFORD'S NATAL NATIVE HORSE

BIG DONGA

LITTLE DONGA

BRITISH FIRING LINE

THE SPUR

ISANDLWANA

Wagon park

THE SADDLE

BLACK'S KOPPIE

Fugitives' Trail

ZULU RIGHT HORN

To Rorke's Drift

0 — 1km — 2km

Monument to the Natal Carbineers who fell at Isandlwana

1 This is the site of the British camp, chosen for its good field of fire, proximity to water, prominent and distinct appearance, and the fact that there was vegetation growing on the rear face of the hill that could be used for firewood. It straddled the track between Rorke's Drift and Ulundi, making it easy to supply.

2 Chelmsford, with his strongest infantry battalion and four of the six guns, went off in this direction early on 22 January.

3 This was the British firing line, a long way from the camp, facing north and east. The line was put out after reports were received of Zulu sighted on the Nqutu plateau moving towards the west, and of a belligerent Zulu attack on a British picket east of Conical Hill early in the morning of 22 January.

4 This is where the rocket battery was cut off and destroyed.

5 Durnford and his mounted Natal Native Horse took up a position in this big donga.

6 The main body of the Zulu army was discovered at around 11h15 in this vicinity by Raw and Shepstone, two of Durnford's men.

7 The men fleeing the battlefield took this route, as the road to Rorke's Drift was blocked by the right horn of the Zulu army.

8 One company of the British defenders, under the command of Captain R. Younghusband, made a fighting withdrawal to this point on the shoulder of the mountain, where they made a brave, last stand.

Battle of Rorke's Drift
22 January 1879

HOW TO GET THERE
Drive from Dundee towards Vryheid on the R33. After 6km turn right onto the R68 towards Nqutu. The turn-off to Rorke's Drift is on your right after 26km. After about 6km there is a T-junction where you turn left. Continue to the entrance gate to Rorke's Drift Museum. The red-roofed building on the terrace ahead of you is the old hospital, now the museum, rebuilt on the foundations of the original building. Behind it rises Shiyane Mountain (Oscarberg). Zulu snipers occupied the sandstone caves you can see on the lower slopes. The church to your left was the storehouse at the time of the battle. There were no other buildings at the time, nor were there trees or any other form of cover. The cattle kraal left of the church was in the same place during the battle, albeit with higher walls. Stones laid out in the ground between the museum building and the church mark the perimeter barricade thrown up by the British using biscuit boxes and mealie meal bags. The barricade also lined the top of the terrace, which was steeper at the time of the battle than it is now.

Entrance gate to Rorke's Drift Museum: 28°21'28.3" S 30°32'06.3" E

Context
Rorke's Drift was the most used of the three drifts (crossing points) across the Buffalo River, which was then the border between Natal and Zululand. It was named after Irishman James Rorke, who had built his house near here and farmed the land on the Natal side of the river. His house had several rooms for paying lodgers. The rooms all had doors to the outside but had no interleading doors to the rest of the house. This layout was to have a bearing on the defence of the building during the battle.

After Rorke died, missionary Otto Witt moved in with his wife and young children and converted Rorke's storehouse into a church. When war broke out between the Zulu and the British in 1879, Lord Chelmsford appropriated the buildings for use as a hospital and a store for ammunition, guns and supplies. When the main column invaded Zululand, the post was left in the hands of a few fit soldiers and 39 sick men in the hospital. The battle occurred straight after the Battle of Isandlwana. Some 4,000 Zulu warriors attacked the small garrison.

Action
When the British column invaded Zululand on 10 January 1879, the soldiers left behind at Rorke's Drift included only 104 men of the 2nd Battalion, 24th Regiment, 39 sick men in the hospital and 300 members of the Natal Native Contingent, who were responsible for loading and offloading the stream of wagons needed to supply the army. The most senior officer

remaining at Rorke's Drift was Major Henry Spalding, with Lieutenant Gonville Bromhead as second in command. After Chelmsford's departure and some days before the battle, a member of the Royal Engineers arrived at Rorke's Drift to build a better crossing over the Buffalo River and so ease the supply problems of an army operating in enemy territory. His name was John Chard and he held the same rank as Bromhead.

Very early in the morning on 22 January a messenger from Lord Chelmsford at Isandlwana arrived at Rorke's Drift, ordering Colonel Durnford to Isandlwana 'in support'. This was the first indication the men at Rorke's Drift had that action was expected in Zululand. Lieutenant Chard had left Rorke's Drift early that same morning, hoping to meet Chelmsford at Isandlwana and clarify his orders. When he arrived there, he was disturbed to hear that Zulu soldiers had been seen running west, in the direction of Rorke's Drift, and so he returned to his post without delay.

Later that morning firing was heard from the direction of Isandlwana, but nothing could be seen from the post. Spalding departed for Helpmekaar to request reinforcements for Rorke's Drift in case of attack, which left Bromhead and Chard in command. An older, more experienced man – Assistant Commissary Officer James Langley Dalton – stressed the futility of trying to flee and recommended that they construct a barricade around the hospital and storehouse buildings instead. This was done, using mostly biscuit boxes and large bags of mealie meal, each weighing 90kg.

The museum at Rorke's Drift and models of two soldiers (inset)

Timeline

1849
James Rorke, the son of an Irish soldier, sets up a trading post on the Buffalo River near the crossing-point between Natal and Zululand.

1856
The Battle of Ndondakasuka sees Cetshwayo emerge as a strong leader of independent Zululand.

1875
James Rorke dies. The Norwegian Missionary Society negotiates to buy the trading post from his family.

1878
A Swedish missionary, Otto Witt, takes occupation of Rorke's house. The store is converted into a makeshift church. Chief Sihayo's sons pursue their father's adulterous wife over the river into Natal at Rorke's Drift, where they put her to death. This incident becomes one of the issues in the British ultimatum, which is presented to the Zulu in December.

1879
The British invade Zululand and are defeated by the Zulu at Isandlwana on 22 January. On the same afternoon the Zulu attack the military garrison at Rorke's Drift. The Battle of Ulundi in July marks the end of the Anglo-Zulu War.

1880–1881
The Boers in the Transvaal fight to win back their independence. They do, at the Battle of Majuba Hill.

1899
The 2nd Anglo-Boer War breaks out.

1902
The Peace of Vereeniging brings to an end the war in South Africa.

BATTLE OF RORKE'S DRIFT   145

This monument at Rorke's Drift marks the mass grave of Zulu who fell during the battle.

Meanwhile, the Zulu had attacked at Isandlwana and defeated the British. About 4,000 of them were on their way to Natal, either in pursuit of fugitives or in the hope of doing some looting. Mostly men who had not had an opportunity to participate in the fighting at Isandlwana, they were disobeying the orders of the Zulu king by invading Natal.

Back at the post, the 300 soldiers of the Natal Native Contingent deserted when some of Durnford's horsemen arrived to report what had happened at Isandlwana. This left only 104 men (instead of 400) to defend a barricade more than 400m in perimeter. Dalton quickly recommended and supervised the construction of an intersecting wall of mealie meal bags and biscuit boxes to reduce the size of the defensive area.

Shortly afterwards the Zulu appeared on the shoulder of Shiyane Mountain. The first attacking wave fell on the rear barricade, where the warriors were repulsed with huge loss. They attempted a second attack and then retired to take up positions in some dead ground to the west of the hospital verandah. Here they were close to the hospital building, where each room with an outside door had been barricaded up and loopholed for defence by men armed with Martini-Henry rifles.

The attackers managed to break into the building, but there were few interleading doors and the defenders dug holes in the internal clay walls through which they escaped into consecutive rooms. Each hole was defended with a bayonet until all the men could be evacuated into the next room.

The memorial in the small cemetery at Rorke's Drift

146   DUNDEE REGION

In their frustration, the Zulu set fire to the thatched roof, but the grass was wet and burned slowly. At last all the men were in the room overlooking the storehouse and the smaller entrenchment and were able to escape the burning building through a small window. Covered by the fire of their colleagues behind the barricades, some brave volunteers from the entrenched area in front of the storehouse carried the sick out of the burning building into the safety of the smaller entrenched area. The Zulu attacked the new position throughout the night, at one time gaining entry to the cattle kraal that was part of the defensive square. They were driven out by soldiers with bayonets. Gradually, the attacks became less frequent.

Lord Chelmsford

At first light, the defenders saw the enemy massing on a hill nearby and feared a concerted attack by daylight. Inexplicably, the warriors turned for the river and melted back into Zululand without another shot being fired. They had seen Chelmsford and the remains of his force returning from Isandlwana and, according to one Zulu report, feared that these were the ghosts of men they had killed the day before.

Aftermath

Only 17 British soldiers were killed, but over 800 Zulu lay dead around the post. The award of 11 Victoria Crosses to the defenders was unprecedented in an action of this scale, and was perhaps sanctioned to focus the British public's attention on the glorious defence of Rorke's Drift, rather than the shocking defeat at Isandlwana that had occurred on the same day.

Principal combatants

Zulu: nDluyengwa, uDloko, uDlondlo and uThulwana regiments.
British: B Company of the 2nd Battalion, 24th Regiment.

The Defence of Rorke's Drift by Alphonse de Neuville, 1880

BATTLE OF RORKE'S DRIFT   **147**

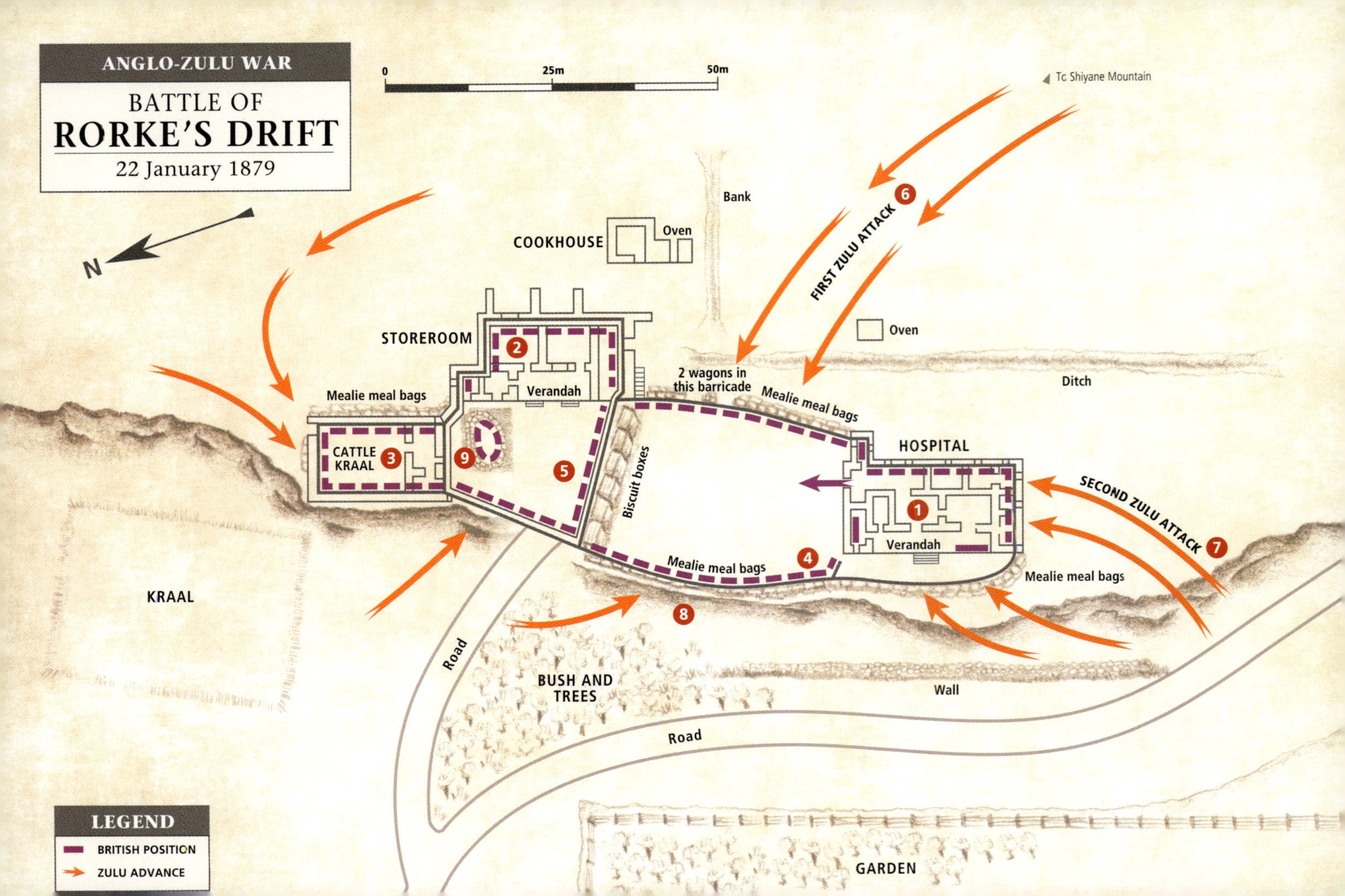

ANGLO-ZULU WAR
BATTLE OF
RORKE'S DRIFT
22 January 1879
0
25m
50m
Tc Shiyane Mountain
N
Bank
COOKHOUSE
Oven
FIRST ZULU ATTACK
6
STOREROOM
2
Verandah
Oven
2 wagons in
this barricade
Mealie meal bags
Ditch
Mealie meal bags
CATTLE
KRAAL
3
9
5
Biscuit boxes
HOSPITAL
1
Verandah
SECOND ZULU ATTACK
7
4
Mealie meal bags
Mealie meal bags
KRAAL
8
Road
BUSH AND
TREES
Wall
Road
GARDEN
LEGEND
BRITISH POSITION
ZULU ADVANCE

The church at Rorke's Drift stands where the storehouse was at the time of the battle.

1 This was the house originally built by James Rorke and later occupied by missionary Otto Witt and his family. When Chelmsford arrived with his army, the house was converted into a hospital. Most of the rooms had no interleading doors because James Rorke used to take in lodgers. The privy was outside and there was no need for the lodgers to enter any other rooms in his house. During the battle the men dug their way through the walls to get from one room to the next as they retreated ahead of the Zulu warriors.

2 This was a storeroom Otto Witt had converted into a small church. It was thatched, with a verandah on the western side. Chelmsford used the building to store the provisions, arms and supplies required by his army.

3 This stone-built cattle kraal is in the same place as the present one, although the walls were higher at the time of the battle. At one point during the night, warriors managed to gain entrance to this kraal and had to be driven out at bayonet point.

4 The first barricade was built to include the hospital building, storeroom and small cattle kraal. The perimeter was 400m. When the 300 Natal Native Contingent troops abandoned their positions, a second line of defence was thrown up to reduce the size of the area to be defended.

5 This is the defensive wall built to reduce the extent of the barricade. The entrenched position now encompassed only the storehouse and the small cattle kraal a perimeter not more than 100m.

6 The first Zulu onslaught came from this direction. The attackers stormed off the shoulder of Shiyane Mountain and fell on the barricade that incorporated the two wagons. They were mown down in swathes by the defenders in the firing line.

7 Another wave of attacks came from the dead ground west of the hospital building. It was through this wall that the Zulu managed to gain entrance to the building.

8 Corporal Schiess, a Swiss national, earned his Victoria Cross by bayoneting a Zulu below the lip of the terrace, in front of the post. The Zulu man was firing into the entrenchment with a muzzle-loading gun at almost point-blank range.

9 This was the redoubt built on the recommendation of Walter Dunne, commissary officer. The raised ground in the redoubt gave a platform from which the defenders could fire over the heads of those manning the barricade. It also offered refuge to the wounded.

Death of the Prince Imperial of France
1 June 1879

HOW TO GET THERE

From Dundee travel east on the R68 to Nqutu. At the four-way stop in the town, continue straight on towards Nondweni. After 10.6km, turn left and continue for 8.6km to cross the Jojosi River, where you will see the monument to the Prince Imperial on your left. The graveyard marks the place where the prince fell. Since the watercourse was diverted when the cemetery was prepared, this area no longer looks the way it did at the time of his death.

Turn-off to Jojosi River: 28°11'20.57" S 30°46'07.73" E
Prince Imperial monument: 28°07'55.65" S 30°47'50.49" E

Context

The Prince Imperial, Louis Napoleon, was the great-nephew of Napoleon Bonaparte and the last of this dynasty. Along with his father, Napoleon III, and his mother, Princess Eugénie, the prince was exiled to England while still a boy. He later attended the Royal Military Academy at Woolwich, where he was popular with the other students and proved himself a good horseman. When the Anglo-Zulu War broke out he was desperate to join his friends who were fighting in Africa. Although Eugénie was reluctant to let him go, she eventually begged on his behalf that he be allowed to accompany Lord Chelmsford as part of the second invasion of Zululand. He was strictly prohibited from participating in any fighting, and his role was to reconnoitre and observe only.

He was a troublesome charge, over-eager to prove his bravery, and Colonel Redvers Buller soon refused to have him anywhere near him on patrol. When the column entered Zululand, scouts were sent ahead to secure the route to Ulundi. It was on one of these expeditions that the prince was killed by a party of Zulu warriors.

Commemorative cross erected by Queen Victoria for Louis Napoleon, who was killed on an expedition by the Zulu

150   DUNDEE REGION

Action

Scouting expeditions were usually uneventful and, on the day that the prince accompanied such a trip, the land had been scouted over before and found safe. On the morning of 1 June, Louis Napoleon joined a scouting party accompanied by a personal friend, Lieutenant J. B. Carey, who spoke French. The escort, made up of Carey and six horsemen of Bettington's Horse, was not as large as it should have been because some of the mounted African auxiliaries had not reported for duty that morning, and so the party left without them.

They rode to a ridge overlooking a river, where the prince spent some time sketching the landscape. At about 15h00 he proposed that they should ride down the hill to some deserted Zulu huts close to the river and there unsaddle for coffee. The huts were checked and found empty, so the party did as he suggested and the horses were let loose to graze.

There were signs that the huts had been recently visited, but the party continued to enjoy their refreshments. Then one of the men reported seeing a Zulu in the long grass. The order was given to fetch the horses and saddle up. The prince, who had requested to be in command, insisted that they all mount together according to military protocol, but as he gave the order a volley crashed around them, causing their horses to shy away.

Those who could mount galloped away. The prince was unable to get onto his horse and was dragged some distance, during which time he lost his Napoleonic sword. (This has been disputed.) When his horse stampeded off, Louis found himself surrounded by Zulu men and deserted by his escort. He tried to shoot the attackers with his revolver, but missed and was killed by numerous assegai wounds, one through his eye. Scouts themselves, the Zulu who killed the prince had taken the opportunity offered by the vulnerable position of the British to make their attack.

This graveyard marks the place where the Prince Imperial was killed. After his death, his body was sent to England for burial.

Timeline

1852
Napoleon III, the nephew of Napoleon Bonaparte, becomes Emperor of France.

1870
Napoleon surrenders at the Battle of Sedan. The French Third Republic is proclaimed and the monarchy abolished. Napoleon is exiled, with his wife, Eugénie, and son, Louis, to England.

1873
Napoleon III dies in England. His widow and son are treated kindly by Queen Victoria. The prince attends the Royal Military Academy at Woolwich.

1879
The Anglo-Zulu War breaks out in Natal and the prince is determined to take part. He is eventually allowed to travel to South Africa to accompany Lord Chelmsford's second invasion of Zululand. He is killed when his scouting party is ambushed by Zulu scouts.

1880
Princess Eugénie and her entourage are accompanied to the site of her son's death by General Evelyn Wood.

1881
The Transvaal is once more an independent Boer republic. Paul Kruger (right) becomes president.

1884–1888
Civil war prevails among the Zulu in Zululand.

1887
Zululand is annexed to the Crown.

DEATH OF THE PRINCE IMPERIAL OF FRANCE

The beautiful Sophie Botha

Louis Napoleon, the Prince Imperial

When the Prince Imperial of France arrived in South Africa in 1879, a naval ball was held in his honour in Simon's Town. There he met Sophie Botha of the farm Hoogekraal, near George, who was visiting Cape Town at the time. The prince enjoyed many dances with this beautiful girl and made arrangements to see her again at her home. When his ship left Cape Town it docked near George and the prince rode, with other young officers, to visit Sophie at Hoogekraal. They had a picnic near the Maalgate River and, while the young men went off to hunt bush pig, the girls bathed in the river. When the prince returned earlier than expected, Sophie was taken by surprise. In her hurry to get out of the water she slipped and fell, hitting her head on a rock. By the time she was found she had drowned. Her death was a heartbreaking experience for the young prince and may have accounted for his reckless behaviour in Zululand.

Aftermath

The prince's untimely death had repercussions internationally, as he was the last of the Napoleonic dynasty. It did not, however, influence the course of the second invasion of Zululand, which ended with a British victory at Ulundi. His mother was heartbroken and later made an epic journey to the place of his death in the company of Colonel Evelyn Wood. Carey was court-martialled for not coming to the prince's aid, but pardoned thanks to Eugénie's pleas for clemency. However, he never regained the respect of his regiment.

The funeral procession of the Prince Imperial

Principal combatants

Zulu: Scouting party consisting of members of the iNgobamakhosi, uMbonambi and uNokhenke regiments.
British: The Prince Imperial of France; Lieutenant J. B. Carey; Six members of Bettington's Horse; Zulu guide.

Battle of Talana Hill
20 October 1899

HOW TO GET THERE
From Dundee, get onto the R33 towards Vryheid. As you leave Dundee, you will see the Talana Museum (your destination) on the left, with Talana Hill looming above it. The big, flat-topped mountain north of Talana Hill is Impati Mountain. Walk a short way up Talana Hill on the path and then turn and look back at the museum buildings below. The British camp site was a long way off, beyond the town. The small hill to your left, on the other side of the tarred road, is Lennox Hill. The Boers held the high ground on which you stand. The British approached across the flat plain through which runs a stream (notice the bridge where the R33 crosses the stream, then follow the stream bed to your right). The eucalyptus-tree wood, visible below you, still exists, but it is not as thick as it used to be. Major General Penn Symons fell at the base of the hill further to your right. A triangular monument marks the spot.

Talana Museum: 28°09'26.6" S 30°15'34.7" E

Context
When the Boer ultimatum to the British expired on 12 October 1899, President Paul Kruger knew that troops from India and Great Britain would soon be despatched to reinforce the British garrisons in South Africa, and the Boers lost no time in invading the British colonies of the Cape and Natal. The Boers' best chance of victory would be to take the small British garrisons while they were still unprepared. However, the British were unconcerned, reasoning that an army of farmers would be no match for trained and disciplined British soldiers. Contrary to all expectations, the war was to drag on for almost three years. The Battle of Talana Hill was the Boers' first attack on the British garrison in Dundee.

Action
Boers, young and old, left their farms and rode to the borders of the British colonies of Natal and the Cape. Those who gathered in the hills north of Natal were disappointed at the total lack of organisation. The weather was cold and wet, there was no food and the

Boer general Lucas Meyer

BATTLE OF TALANA HILL

Timeline

1850
Coal is discovered on Peter Smith's farm in northern Natal. The town of Dundee develops rapidly into an important settlement.

1879
Captain William Penn Symons visits Dundee with the 24th Regiment during the Anglo-Zulu War.

1899
Penn Symons (now a major general) is posted to Dundee to take precautionary measures against the Boers on the northern frontier of Natal.

In October, the Battle of Talana results in the withdrawal of the entire Dundee garrison to Ladysmith. Penn Symons dies of wounds received during the battle and the Boers occupy Dundee. The Battle of Rietfontein is fought outside Ladysmith.

In November Ladysmith is surrounded and besieged for 118 days. The battles of Belmont, Graspan and Modder River are fought in the west.

1900
In February the battles of Vaalkrans and Tugela Heights are fought north of Colenso. Ladysmith is relieved.

In May Dundee is reoccupied by the British and the war moves north into the Transvaal.

At the onset of war Boers suffered from a dire lack of supplies and equipment.

men had to fend for themselves in the open veld while commandos were formed and strategies were developed. Boer general Piet Joubert, by this time in his 60s and a well-respected leader, proposed a three-pronged movement into Natal aimed at Ladysmith, where the 9,000-strong British garrison was stationed. General Lucas Meyer, a well-known Boer leader with a luxurious white beard, would command the eastern column. In the centre, General 'Maroela' Erasmus, who was known not to get on with Meyer, would lead. To the west, General Kock would advance with the Hollander Corps. There was little or no communication between the columns from the moment they crossed into Natal.

The British retained the small garrison stationed in Dundee, against the advice of General Sir George White, who recommended its withdrawal to Ladysmith, or even the Tugela River, once the ultimatum had expired. The general commanding the Dundee garrison, Major General Sir William Penn Symons, was confident that he could hold his own against the Boers and was reluctant to leave the British citizens of Dundee at the mercy of the invading enemy. He had been well treated by them as a young officer during the Anglo-Zulu War of 1879.

Some 4,000 men made up the British garrison, which had its camp in an exposed position on sloping ground west of the town centre. The regiments included the Leicesters, Royal Dublin Fusiliers, Royal Irish Fusiliers, King's Royal Rifle Corps and Artillery. There was also a squadron of mounted men led by Colonel Moller and it was these men, on a rainy misty night, who came across mounted Boer scouts in the nek between Talana and Lennox hills, east of the town. Shots were exchanged but neither side incurred casualties. Penn Symons was not perturbed by the encounter and did not consider it necessary to place sentries, lookouts or pickets on Talana Hill or Impati Mountain, although they both overlooked the town and the army camp.

During the night of 19 October, the Boers were able to drag a 75mm Krupp gun and a Maxim Nordenfeldt gun up the east-facing slopes of Talana Hill, and marksmen positioned themselves among the rocks on the crest of the flat-topped summit.

Erasmus's men manhandled a huge 155mm Creusot gun with an effective range of 10,000m into position on Impati Mountain. Fortunately for the British, mist prevailed on the following day, making it impossible for Erasmus to shell the British camp.

At first light the Boers on Talana Hill fired a Krupp shell into the British camp site.

A mounted British scout

Their aim was accurate and it was lucky for Penn Symons that the ground was wet and that the shell, which landed close to his tent, did not explode. He ordered his artillery to return the fire, but the British guns did not have the range and had to be sent forward before they could engage. Accompanied by the Royal Dublin Fusiliers, the Royal Irish Fusiliers and the

The cemetery at Talana Museum with Talana Hill in the background

King's Royal Rifle Corps, the field artillery ran their guns up to the Sandspruit (now called Steenkoolspruit) from where they fired at the Boers. One Boer gun was disabled and, at 06h30, the three infantry battalions in the stream bed were ordered to attack. It was their first experience of being fired on by a Pom-Pom.

The Royal Dublin Fusiliers formed the firing line, with the King's Royal Rifles in support. They had to advance over open ground and soon came under fire from the Boer Mausers on the slopes of Talana. As they neared the base of the hill, they entered a small forest of eucalyptus trees, about 400m wide, which gave some shelter and took them up against a stone wall ringing the base of the hill.

Penn Symons rode forward, his orderly with a red pennant beside him, to urge the men forward. He made an easy target and was mortally wounded in the groin. He stiffly remounted his horse and rode back to the camp, where he died three days later.

The advance continued under the command of Colonel James Yule. Two charges were made, the second being successful in taking the crest of the hill. Captain Weldon of the Dublins was the first officer to fall; he was killed while saving a wounded man. He was popular with everyone and his fox terrier, Rose, that had accompanied him to the fight, was reluctant to leave his dead body.

As the British reached the crest, friendly fire raked their lines. Private Flynn walked under fire down the hill to deliver a message to redirect the artillery shells, which only then

Colonel Yule force-marches the Dundee garrison to Ladysmith in sodden conditions.

succeeded in lessening the Boer fire. The British soldiers close to the summit fixed their bayonets and charged. The Boers, who had no bayonets and feared the glinting blades, fled taking their guns with them. The hill had been taken and a cease-fire was ordered. Reports say that the British were angry at not being allowed to pursue the fleeing enemy. There were many casualties on both sides.

Meanwhile, the cavalry, which had been sent around the back of the hill after the fleeing Boers, had to withdraw before superior numbers and the men got lost. They found themselves under Impati Mountain, which was occupied by General Erasmus's men, and took cover on Adelaide Farm, where they were surrounded and forced to surrender.

The Boer gun (155mm Creusot) on Impati Mountain began shelling

This stone cairn, near the Talana Museum, marks the spot where Major General Penn Symons was mortally wounded.

the British camp at first light the next day, eventually leaving the garrison no choice but to withdraw from Dundee under cover of darkness. Led by Yule, the entire garrison made its way out of Dundee on the night of 22 October to join General George White and his 9,000 troops in Ladysmith four days later. Shortly thereafter, the Boers besieged the town for 118 days.

Aftermath

Both sides claimed this battle as a victory. The Boers succeeded in occupying the town, but could not prevent the 4,000-strong garrison from reaching and supporting Ladysmith. The British learned that their field guns could not match the range of the Boer Creusot and Krupp artillery pieces. General Sir Redvers Buller, in overall command of the British army in South Africa, would have to use the naval guns from warships to match the Boer guns.

Principal combatants
British: 18th Hussars; Imperial Mounted Infantry; King's Royal Rifle Corps; Royal Dublin Fusiliers; Royal Field Artillery; Royal Irish Fusiliers.
Boers: Commandos from Bethal, Krugersdorp, Middelburg, Piet Retief, Pretoria, Utrecht, Vryheid and Wakkerstroom; Hollander Corps; Staatsartillerie.

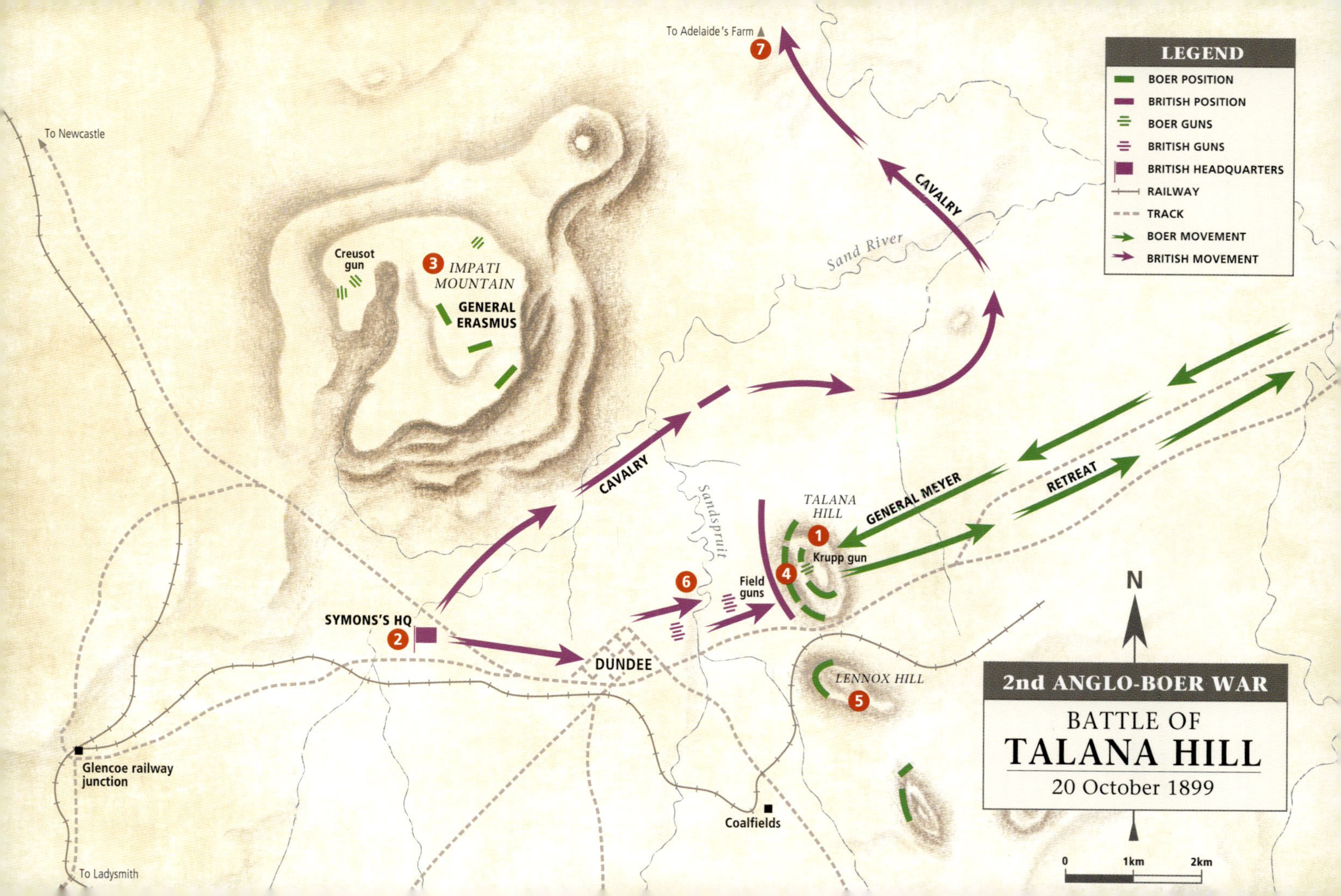

2nd ANGLO-BOER WAR
BATTLE OF
TALANA HILL
20 October 1899
LEGEND
BOER POSITION
BRITISH POSITION
BOER GUNS
BRITISH GUNS
BRITISH HEADQUARTERS
RAILWAY
TRACK
BOER MOVEMENT
BRITISH MOVEMENT
N
0
1km
2km
To Adelaide's Farm
7
To Newcastle
Creusot gun
3
IMPATI MOUNTAIN
GENERAL ERASMUS
CAVALRY
Sand River
CAVALRY
Sandspruit
GENERAL MEYER
RETREAT
TALANA HILL
1
Krupp gun
4
Field guns
6
SYMONS'S HQ
2
DUNDEE
LENNOX HILL
5
Glencoe railway junction
Coalfields
To Ladysmith

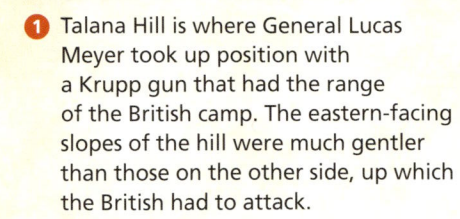

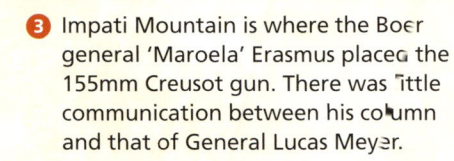

LEFT: The military graves at the Talana battle site
ABOVE: The road sign to the Talana Museum

1. Talana Hill is where General Lucas Meyer took up position with a Krupp gun that had the range of the British camp. The eastern-facing slopes of the hill were much gentler than those on the other side, up which the British had to attack.

2. This is the site of the British camp where Major General Sir William Penn Symons and a 4,000-strong garrison had their headquarters.

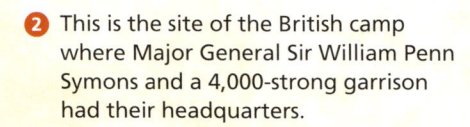

3. Impati Mountain is where the Boer general 'Maroela' Erasmus placed the 155mm Creusot gun. There was little communication between his column and that of General Lucas Meyer.

4. This is the plantation of eucalyptus trees where the initial British infantry advance faltered when the men came up against a stone wall and where Penn Symons was mortally wounded in the groin.

5. Boers lay here on Lennox Hill, pouring crossfire into the ranks of the British troops advancing on Talana Hill.

6. It was from this deep stream bed of the Sandspruit that the British artillery engaged the Boer guns on Talana Hill.

7. This is Adelaide Farm, where Moller's cavalry was surrounded by men from Erasmus's column. The British soldiers were forced to surrender.

Boers manning a 155mm Creusot gun (Long Tom)

Artillery during the 2nd Anglo-Boer War

By the end of the 19th century the word 'gun' had replaced 'cannon' for breech-loading artillery pieces; the old muzzle-loading weapons were known as cannons. It is, therefore, incorrect to use the word 'cannon' to describe the artillery used by both sides during the 2nd Anglo-Boer War.

The Jameson Raid of 1896 had convinced President Paul Kruger of the South African Republic that war with Britain was likely and that his small nation was ill equipped for such an event. He sent emissaries overseas to purchase state-of-the-art weaponry from Europe, including 155mm and 75mm Creusot guns from France, and 75mm Krupp guns from Germany, the first-mentioned accurate to a distance of 10,000m. In addition, he ordered 22 37mm Maxim Nordenfeldt (Pom-Pom) guns and four 120mm Krupp Howitzers.

The men detailed to these guns were known as the Staatsartillerie, the only Boer force that was uniformed and organised in the manner of a conventional regiment. The Boer gunners were trained in Germany by Krupp to use a forward observation officer to direct the line of fire from the gun, which could remain in a position concealed from the enemy.

The standard gun used by the British field artillery at that time was the 15-pounder 7-cwt (hundredweight) breech-loading gun, with an effective range of 3,750m. British gunners were still placing their guns in positions where they could see the enemy. However, smoking black powder had recently been replaced by a smokeless variety, which meant that guns could be concealed from the enemy, who would then be unable to return the fire.

British naval long 12-pounder

It was not long before the British generals realised the superior range of the Boer artillery and resorted to using Royal Navy guns. The ships' guns had a much longer range than those of the Royal Field Artillery and a number of them were taken off ships in Cape Town harbour, mounted on makeshift gun carriages and taken to the war front to counter the Boers' fire power. The naval guns included the 4.7-inch (120mm) gun, with a range of 8,950m, and the naval long 12-pounder (Long 12), with a range of 7,800m.

The breech-loading Long 12, which weighed over a ton, should not be confused with the smaller 12-pounder, a carriage-mounted ship's gun that was used on land by the Naval Brigade and could be dismantled and carried over difficult terrain. The Long 12 was not mobile, but it had a greater range than the smaller, wheeled 12-pounder. To transport the naval long 12-pounders to the front, Captain Percy Scott, Royal Navy captain of the warship *The Terrible*, used the railway workshops to make up limbers for the heavy guns.

During his third attempt to liberate Ladysmith, at the Battle of Vaalkrans (see p. 92), General Sir Redvers Buller is said to have requested that guns be placed on the summit of a big, flat-topped hill known as Swartkop (Black Mountain). While the Royal Field Artillery waited for the engineers to build a road to run the guns up the steep slopes, the men of the Naval Brigade are reputed to have taken the matter into their own hands. Using muscle power, steel hawsers and pulleys, they hauled six Long 12s up the almost sheer, rocky slope to the summit, where they were used to great effect.

This was perhaps the origin of the British Royal Navy's Field Gun competition, held during the annual Royal Tournament of the British Forces, where teams competed against each other to get the smaller 12-pounder across obstacles in the best time. In KwaZulu-Natal, an annual event in Ladysmith, known as the Swartkop Challenge, sees teams compete against the clock to get an original Long 12 up a steep, rocky slope on Wagon Hill.

Men of the South African National Defence Force haul a period naval gun up Wagon Hill during the Ladysmith Swartkop Challenge.

Battle of Blood River
16 December 1838

HOW TO GET THERE
Leave Dundee on the R33 towards Vryheid. About 20km from Dundee, turn right and follow the signs saying 'Blood River Battlefield'. A good dirt road will take you to the entrance gate, which is close to a big concrete wagon. Pay the entrance fee and then walk or drive down the track to the ring of bronze wagons. As you stand in the middle of this ring looking towards the river, a deep donga (gully) appears on your right. The Zulu came from the Nqutu area, which is to your front left (north-east). The first attack came from behind where you are standing and from the right. The next one came from across the river, straight in front of you.

After you have seen the exhibits in the building where you bought your entrance ticket, take the road that leads across the bridge to visit the Ncome Museum on the other side of the river. This gives the Zulu perspective on the battle and has information about the Zulu kings and Zulu culture.

Context
Voortrekker leader Andries Pretorius led a commando of 460 trekkers and three British settlers from present-day Estcourt to invade Zululand, with the intention of avenging the killing of Piet Retief and his 70 companions that had occurred earlier in the year (see p. 28).

Action
The Voortrekker force, accompanied by about 340 black servants with 650 ox-drawn wagons and some 750 horses, crossed the Tugela River at Skietdrift (near Winterton) and advanced cautiously in the direction of umGungungdlovu, King Dingane's headquarters.

The Zulu army of about 15,000 men commanded by Ndhlela nTuli was on its way to meet the Voortrekkers as they crossed the Buffalo River and progressed further into Zululand. On 15 December the Voortrekkers reached the Ncome River, a tributary of the Buffalo, and, hearing that the Zulu were close by, they laagered themselves in a strong defensive position on the banks of this river. The wagons were bound together and wooden gates placed between front and rear wheels to create a barrier that was stuffed with thorn trees. The Voortrekker laager was constructed in such a way that one side bordered a deep donga and the other the Ncome River, which made an enemy attack from these directions very unlikely. The river was deep and fast-flowing due to recent rains and crossing it would have been slow and difficult, especially under fire. The camp site had plentiful water and good grazing for the livestock and the surrounding country was open and devoid of cover in the form of trees or hills, which afforded an open field of vision and fire, and made pursuit on horseback possible. About 600m downstream of the camp was a frequently used drift, while above the confluence with the donga there was a deep hippo pool. Slightly upstream from this spot, the river was fordable. The river banks were covered in dense reeds, making the river look wider than it does today. The water level would have been higher, too.

The Zulu attack came early on the morning of 16 December 1838. Some warriors crossed the river at the downstream drift, circled to their right and advanced on the laager from the west. The Voortrekkers' muzzle-loading guns and two or three cannons mowed them down in swathes. As the Zulu were unable to advance any closer to the tightly entrenched wagon laager, the attack waned.

However, when the Voortrekkers fired across the river into the ranks of those not yet engaged, they were so enraged that a frontal attack was launched from across the eastern plain. When the hot fire of the Boer guns made it impossible to cross the river immediately opposite the laager, the attackers veered left towards the drift, downstream of the donga.

Seizing his opportunity, Pretorius charged out with a mounted commando of 160 men and galloped between the two Zulu columns, firing into both. To escape the deadly fire, some warriors plunged into

A section of the vast bronze laager displayed at the Blood River Museum

Timeline

1809
The Hottentot Proclamation gives Khoikhoi farm workers in the Cape Colony the right to lay complaints against their employers.

1813
In the eastern Cape, a Khoikhoi servant lays a complaint against Freek Bezuidenhout. When troops are sent to arrest the man, he resists and is killed.

1815
Rebel farmers, protesting against the shooting of Bezuidenhout, are confronted by an armed force of British soldiers at the top of Slagtersnek. Rebel farmers who protested against the shooting of Bezuidenhout are hanged.

1834–1835
The Sixth Frontier War is fought in the eastern Cape.

1836
The Great Trek begins when Dutch farmers trek northwards to escape British rule.

1837
Voortrekkers led by Piet Retief enter Natal.

1838
Retief and his party are killed by Dingane's warriors, who subsequently rampage among Voortrekker families in the Bloukrans and Bushmans River valleys. They are countered unsuccessfully at Italeni and Tugela, but the Battle of Blood River is a resounding victory for the Voortrekkers.

1839
The Voortrekkers proclaim the Republic of Natalia.

1842
The Battle of Durban (Congella) results in most Voortrekkers leaving Natal.

BATTLE OF BLOOD RIVER   163

the river, only to be shot down in the water. The Ncome River ran red with their blood and was subsequently known as Blood River. Some Zulu fled to the drift below the donga, hotly pursued by the mounted Voortrekkers, who stayed on their heels for about three hours. It is said that some 3,000 Zulu were killed. The plain where many died was named the Place of Bones.

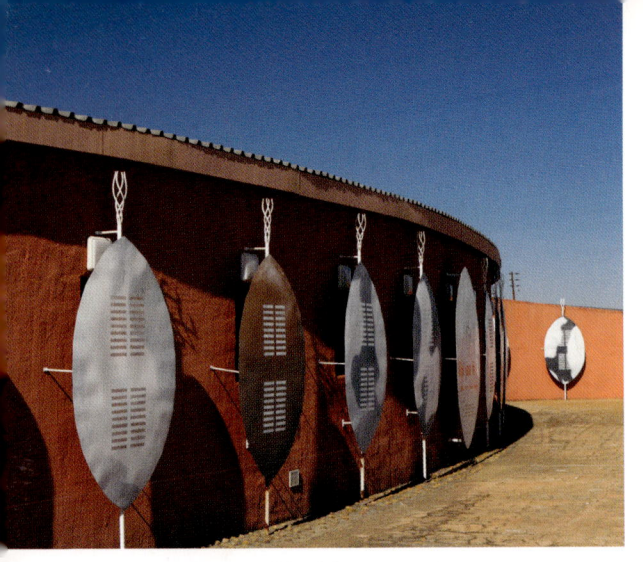

Display of Zulu shields at the Ncome Museum, across the river from the bronze wagon laager (see p. 163)

Aftermath

The Boers had only four men wounded, whereas about 3,000 Zulu were killed. This battle marked the end of Dingane's power and the beginning of a brief dominance of the Voortrekkers in Natal. When the Voortrekkers proclaimed the Republic of Natalia, in March 1839, Dingane fled to Swaziland, where he was later killed. The Boers then supported King Mpande who was, for a time at least, something of a puppet king. Mpande was a peace-loving ruler and when Britain annexed Natal in 1843 he enjoyed good relations with the Lieutenant Governor, giving Natal almost 40 years of peace between black and white.

Principal combatants
Voortrekkers: Trekkers as well as three British settlers; Black servants.
Zulu: Warriors commanded by Ndhlela nTuli.

The Day of the Vow

As the Voortrekkers passed through Wasbank near Dundee, they vowed to build a church and give thanks every year should God grant them victory over the Zulu. When the Voortrekkers defeated the Zulu army at the Battle of Blood River on 16 December 1838, they kept their promise: a church was built in Pietermaritzburg and the 16th of December was designated as a day of thanksgiving. It eventually became a national holiday, known as the Day of the Vow. When apartheid ended in 1994, it was renamed Day of Reconciliation.

Battle of Blood River Poort
17 September 1901

HOW TO GET THERE
This battle took place on an open plain near a poort through which the Blood (Ncome) River flows. Take the R33 from Dundee towards Vryheid and, 47km from Dundee, turn left onto the R34 to Utrecht. Five kilometres from this junction, turn right onto a district road to Blood River Poort and Viljoenspos. Pass two farms and after about 8km turn left at the sign for Goedekloof farm. Follow the farm road for 1km until you see the cluster of walled-in graves on the right. The battle took place north of the cemetery on the open plain between the poort through which the Blood (Ncome) River flows and the grave site. The officers are buried in the Vryheid military cemetery.

Blood River Poort graves: 27°46'56.6" S 30°32'08.7" E

Context
Hoping to divert attention away from the beleaguered Boer commandos in the Transvaal, General Louis Botha invaded Natal for a second time on 10 September 1901 with a force of 1,000 men. The British had tried to protect Natal from such an invasion by building a line of entrenchments and blockhouses between Wakkerstroom and Piet Retief, but this was not yet complete. When they learned of Boer movements towards the borders of Natal, columns of mounted infantry were despatched to Wakkerstroom and Dundee to counter a possible Boer incursion. However, Botha's commando was able to enter Natal uncontested from the district of Ermelo. They rode south, in pouring rain, via Piet Retief. It was the British column based at Dundee that engaged the commando at Blood River Poort.

Action
Botha rested his men at Rooikraal, south of Piet Retief, before riding further south in very wet conditions, to meet up with another 700 men in the vicinity of Scheeper's Nek. A further 300 joined the commando as it neared Vryheid, giving him about 2,000 men altogether, although many of them were out of action because their horses were fatigued and ill due to the incessant rain.

The Dundee-based British column commanded by Colonel Hubert Gough comprised three companies of mounted infantry with two guns. When they arrived at De Jager's Drift, not far north of Dundee, Gough heard news of the Boer movements and, on 17 September, he advanced north towards Blood River Poort. Gough was with the advance party when

Timeline

1899
President Paul Kruger's ultimatum to Great Britain makes war inevitable. The Boers invade the Cape and Natal.

1900
Set-piece battles are fought in Natal and the Cape. The sieges of Ladysmith, Kimberley and Mafeking are eventually relieved. Guerrilla warfare intensifies.

1901
General Jan Smuts (below) invades the Cape, hoping to provoke an uprising against the British by the colony's Afrikaans citizens. His commando is engaged at Moordenaarspoort near Dordrecht. General Louis Botha leads an invasion into Natal.

In September the Battle of Blood River Poort is fought and won by the Boers. Botha's commando subsequently fights at Fort Itala and Fort Prospect. Immediately upon their return from Natal, the men support a successful attack against a British column at Bakenlaagte.

In December, on Christmas day, General Christiaan de Wet defeats a British column at Groenkop.

1902
One final battle is fought at Roodewal before peace is negotiated in Vereeniging.

---

they spotted some horses grazing close to the Blood River, where it passes through the poort at Aasvoëlkrans. Believing there were only a few hundred Boers, he galloped forward to engage them. The Boers were quick to deploy and moved around to attack his right flank and rear. This they did both mounted and dismounted, an unconventional practice on an open plain.

The British guns were now surrounded by about 400 Boers under General J. D. (Koot) Opperman, who was calling on the drivers to surrender. Lieutenant Price-Davies of the King's Royal Rifle Corps demonstrated almost insane bravery by charging in among them, brandishing his revolver in a futile effort to prevent the guns from being lost. He was shot, though not mortally, and later awarded the Victoria Cross for his actions. The British were forced to surrender.

The Boers who triumphed at Blood River Poort went on to attack Fort Itala.

Aftermath

Casualties among the British were high, with 44 killed and wounded and 241 prisoners taken. The guns were lost. Boer losses were negligible. Gough was humiliated, although he escaped that night and made his way back to Dundee. The Boers had nowhere to put the other prisoners and so they stripped them of their clothes and weapons and sent them back to their own lines. Botha went on to penetrate further east into Natal via Babanango.

Principal combatants

British: Johannesburg Mounted Rifles; Mounted infantry under Colonel Gough; Royal Field Artillery.
Boers: Commandos from Utrecht, Vryheid, Wakkerstroom and Swaziland; Members of the Piet Retief Commando.

Battle of Scheeper's Nek
20 May 1900

HOW TO GET THERE
Take the R33 from Dundee towards Vryheid. Approximately 60km from Dundee, look on your left for a sign that marks the position of the British cemetery. Continue on the R33 for about 100m until you reach a dirt track on the left that leads back towards the cemetery and monuments to British soldiers who fell during this battle. The high ridges to the north and east were occupied by the Boers, while the British approached from the south-west. The battle took place on the open plains between the nek and the cemetery.

Cemetery and monuments: 27°51'0.9" S 30°40'02.7" E

Context

Once Ladysmith had been relieved, at the end of February 1900, General Sir Redvers Buller took until May to rest his men before proceeding north. At Helpmekaar in Natal he defeated the Boers, who then retreated over the border into the Transvaal. However, one Boer commando remained in the Nqutu area and a column of mounted infantry, commanded by Lieutenant Colonel E. C. Bethune, was despatched from Dundee to engage it. Once that commando, too, had been overpowered, Bethune proceeded north in the direction of Vryheid; on the way there his column was ambushed at Scheeper's Nek.

The Boer commando in Nqutu with a Maxim Nordenfeldt gun

Action

The five squadrons of mounted infantry commanded by Bethune had with them a Maxim and two Hotchkiss guns. After fulfilling their duty in Nqutu, they rode north to join the track between Dundee and Vryheid, close to where the present road passes through Scheeper's Nek, a defile between two ridges.

It was a Sunday, and about 75 Boers from the Swaziland Commando under Commandant Koot Opperman, with another five of the Vryheid Commando, were attending a church service in a camp just north-east of the nek. When an advance squadron of the British column came across the Boer guards, they galloped back to sound the alarm. The Boers deployed quickly and attacked the British squadron. Captain W. E. D. Goff, commanding the mounted

Timeline

1899
At the outbreak of the war, Sir Edward Bethune, major of the 16th Lancers, raises in Durban Bethune's Mounted Infantry, consisting of mostly colonial horsemen.

1900
In February Bethune's Mounted Infantry is present at the Relief of Ladysmith.

In March General Christiaan de Wet scores a dramatic victory over a British column at Sannaspos.

In May General Sir Redvers Buller (above) drives the Boers off the Biggarsberg and goes on to occupy Dundee. On 20 May Boers ambush five companies of Bethune's Mounted Infantry at Scheeper's Nek, which lies north of Dundee. At the end of the month, the Battle of Doornkop marks an unsuccessful attempt by the Boers to keep the British out of Johannesburg. In the Orange Free State, the Battle of Biddulphsberg is fought, but neither side gains much advantage from it. General Abraham de Villiers is mortally wounded.

In June Buller's army enters the Transvaal. The British attempt to clear the Boers from Diamond Hill, an area east of Pretoria, is unsuccessful.

In August Buller is victorious at the Battle of Bergendal, east of Pretoria.

In December he celebrates his 61st birthday.

Memorial to the 31 members of Bethune's Mounted Infantry who are buried here

men, found himself in an exposed position with only anthills for cover. He attempted to withdraw, but the main column was too far behind to support him, and, when the Boers took up positions on the ridges east and north, he found himself under withering fire.

Captain Goff was killed, although the Maxim gun had been used to good effect to keep the Boers at bay. The rest of Bethune's column was unable to offer much assistance because the Boers had set the dry winter grass alight, releasing acrid grey smoke into the air that obscured the vision of the soldiers. In addition, reinforcements arriving from the south could not fire at the Boers for fear of hitting their own men. Brave attempts were made to rescue wounded men from the approaching flames but the Boers took the would-be rescuers prisoner.

Aftermath

Reports vary as to how many British casualties were incurred, some putting the figure at 30 killed, 30 wounded and 18 prisoners, others at 21 killed, 23 wounded and 18 missing. The Boers put the number of prisoners higher. One man was killed and one wounded on the Boer side.

Bethune withdrew his depleted force to Nqutu, and eventually back to Dundee. The Boers had shown their talent for opportunism and guerrilla-type warfare, which they were to use extensively and very successfully over the next two years.

Principal combatants

British: Bethune's Mounted Infantry; Royal Field Artillery.
Boers: Five men of the Vryheid Commando; Swaziland Commando.

Battle of Hlobane
28 March 1879

HOW TO GET THERE
This battlefield is clearly visible from the road between Vryheid and Louwsburg. Twenty-two kilometres after leaving Vryheid on the R69, stop and park your vehicle on the left-hand side of the road. From here, you will see a flat-topped mountain against the skyline on your left (north). This is Hlobane Mountain. The view from the top is spectacular but, at the time of writing, the access road was not easy to find and was badly eroded.

The lower plateau to the left of the summit is Ntendeka, and the slope that joins the plateau and the summit is the notorious Devil's Pass. The track leading to the top of the mountain on the right-hand (eastern) end of the summit was the route taken by Colonel Redvers Buller, whereas Lieutenant Colonel Cecil Russell ascended from Ntendeka. Colonel Evelyn Wood's fiasco, which led to the killing of his staff officers, occurred under the cliffs that ring the summit, not far from the track that ascends the eastern end of the hill. The high ground to the right of the mountain was where the abaQulusi came from to surround Colonel Frederick Weatherley and others trying to escape the main Zulu force that was approaching the mountain from the south.

The gravestones of the translator Llewellyn Lloyd and Captain Ronald Campbell are on the left-hand side of the track if you are walking or driving up the hill. At the time of writing, these graves were not clearly marked and thus difficult to find without the help of a guide. *Guide recommended*

Context
This Anglo-Zulu War battle took place three months after the disastrous defeat of the invading British central column at Isandlwana (see p. 134) and the besiegement of Pearson's coastal column in Eshowe. The northern column, under the command of Colonel Evelyn Wood, was secure at Khambula (see p. 173), a well-defended position near present-day Vryheid. Wood had been instructed to wait there for further orders, which duly came towards the end of March in the form of a request by Lord Chelmsford for diversionary action to attract attention away from his relief column, which was approaching Eshowe.

This gave Wood and his mounted infantry, most of them keen for an adventure, the excuse to do some cattle-rustling on the nearby Hlobane Mountain (Painted Mountain), which was used by the abaQulusi to graze their herds. Hlobane's flat summit stretches almost 5km from east to west and is approximately 2km wide in some places. It is ringed with boulders, some of which the herdsmen had used to make rough walls along the perimeter of the summit wherever the slopes beneath were gentle enough to encourage the cattle to stray.

Timeline

1878
The British present an ultimatum to the Zulu king, leading to the outbreak of the Anglo-Zulu War.

1879
In January the British invade Zululand in three separate columns. The central column is defeated at Isandlwana, and the coastal column is besieged in Eshowe.

In March, General Evelyn Wood (above), commander of the northern column, is told to create a diversion to draw Zulu attention away from the relieving force approaching Eshowe. He does so by engaging the abaQulusi on Hlobane Mountain. His camp at Khambula is subsequently attacked by the Zulu. General Sir Redvers Buller wins a Victoria Cross for his role at Hlobane.

In June Louis Napoleon is ambushed and killed in Zululand. A month later the British are victorious over the Zulu at the Battle of Ulundi. The Zulu king flees, later to be captured and exiled in Cape Town.

1902
In May, during the final stages of the 2nd Anglo-Boer War, 56 Boers are killed by the abaQulusi at Holkrans, close to Hlobane.

It was a formidable stronghold, and there were only two practical ways up the mountain, one on the west end that adjoined a lower plateau, called Ntendeka, and one on the eastern end of the mountain. The western route onto the lower plateau was a short, steep slope studded generously with enormous boulders. The eastern path was narrow and dominated by the craggy cliffs that towered above it. However, as Wood and his force would disastrously discover, it was the western end that proved impossible for horses and cattle to descend.

Action

The force Wood assigned to the task of assaulting the mountain was made up of one squadron of Imperial Mounted Infantry (or what was left of it after the Battle of Isandlwana) and eight other mounted units of mostly volunteer horsemen. There were also about 1,000 African auxiliaries on foot and 200 Zulu warriors led by Chief Hamu, who had defected to the British. Altogether there were about 1,400 men, divided into two columns.

Wood planned to send both columns up the mountain simultaneously, one up the eastern pass and the other up the western slope, from the lower plateau. On the summit they were to deal with the abaQulusi defenders and round up the cattle and herd them down the western slope (the one closer to Khambula) to the camp.

Buller led the first column of horsemen to climb the eastern end of the mountain, leaving before Lieutenant Colonel Cecil Russell's second column, as he had further to go. With Buller's column was a unit called the Border Horse, under the command of a colourful character called Colonel Frederick Weatherley who was accompanied by his two sons, the younger of whom was only 14.

Buller camped the first night a little distance from Khambula and left at noon the following day to skirt the southern slopes of Hlobane towards the east. Due to a misunderstanding, Weatherley's Border Horse were left behind and the men of the unit slept the following night some distance south of the rest of the column. One of the officers scouted forward and came across a huge Zulu force bivouacked not far from where the unit was positioned. The Zulu soldiers were sent by Cetshwayo to attack Wood's column at Khambula and they were to co-operate with the abaQulusi the next day.

Buller left his camp site at 03h00 on the morning of 28 March to begin the difficult ascent. He and his men drew fire from the abaQulusi as they rode up the steep and narrow eastern pass. Casualties began to mount, but they managed to gain the summit and clear the defenders off the eastern rim before riding along the top towards the west, where they hoped to rendezvous with Russell, rustling the plentiful cattle along the way.

Hlobane Mountain; abaQulusi herdsmen grazed their cattle on its flat summit.

Russell, meanwhile, had reached the lower plateau with his force and soon ascertained that the precipitous boulder-studded slope was impassable for anything other than men on foot. He sent an officer up to tell Buller that they would have to get the cattle off the mountain another way.

While Buller and Russell explored the higher and lower reaches of Hlobane, Colonel Wood was riding along the southern slopes when he came across Weatherley's Border Horse. He ordered them forward to join Buller and followed with his personal escort, choosing to disregard reports that a large Zulu army had been spotted approaching from the south.

Accompanying Wood were several of his personal friends. One was his translator, Llewellyn Lloyd, another his chief staff officer, Captain Ronald Campbell, and a third, the young Lieutenant Henry Lysons. As they neared the eastern cliffs, they came under fire from abaQulusi marksmen hiding in the caves. Covered by fire from the Border Horse, Wood and his escort went towards the enemy, and Lloyd was mortally wounded. He was carried back to a stone cattle kraal while Wood advanced once more. This time his horse was shot and fell, trapping him beneath it. He told Campbell to order the Border Horse forward, but there was a delay and his personal escort, led by the eager young Lysons, with Campbell close behind, rushed forward to the rocky recess. Campbell was shot through the head. Wood insisted that the bodies of Lloyd and Campbell receive a proper burial and sent his young bugler back up the mountain under heavy fire to retrieve the prayer book that was in his saddle bag. The graves had to be dug with assegais, as nothing else was to hand.

It was now after 09h00 and Wood decided to ride back along the southern base of the mountain towards the west. By this time both Russell and Buller had seen the approaching Zulu army in the south and had given up the hope of getting the cattle off the summit. The priority was a safe escape to Khambula and Buller issued an order to retire.

Buller was awarded a Victoria Cross for rescuing several men.

BATTLE OF HLOBANE 171

Some Swazi soldiers joined as mercenaries to fight with Wood's Irregulars. On the right is the medal presented to British men who fought in the Anglo-Zulu War.

The Border Horse was on its way down the eastern pass when it met the forerunners of the Zulu army. Turning tail and retreating towards the north-east, they were met on the nek by the abaQulusi, who were attacking down the slopes of the mountain adjoining Hlobane on the east. They made a desperate charge and some 20 men cut their way through, only to face a sheer drop to the plain below. Weatherley had his wounded teenage son with him on his horse when they were surrounded and cut down in a flurry of assegais. The few men who made it to the plain below were pursued; some were killed as they fled towards Khambula.

Meanwhile, Buller's column was making a desperate escape down the brutal Devil's Pass. Many horses fell as they tried to negotiate a passage between the huge boulders. Once on the lower plateau, no unmounted man had a chance, as the fleet-footed abaQulusi were ready to pursue and kill.

Wood observed the retreat from a safe distance. Russell, claiming to have misunderstood his orders, was also a long way away, close to Khambula camp, and offered no support to the fleeing men. Buller was extremely brave and was to be awarded the Victoria Cross for his actions.

Aftermath

Apart from Isandlwana, this was Britain's most disastrous defeat at the hands of the Zulu. Losses are thought to have been about 130 colonials, among them Piet (Petrus Lafras) Uys, who was killed at the foot of Devil's Pass (his grave can be seen on the Ntendeka plateau). Two imperial soldiers were killed and as many as 250 of the Native Levies were probably also killed while trying to retain the cattle they had managed to get off the hill. Wood, however, retained his good reputation, thanks to his decisive victory at Khambula the next day.

Principal combatants

Zulu: abaQulusi; Zulu army.
British: 1st and 2nd Battalions (mainly Swazi); Baker's Horse; Border Horse; Burgher Force; Colonial units; Frontier Light Horse; Hamu's Warriors; Imperial Mounted Infantry; Kaffrarian Rifles; Natal Native Horse; Royal Artillery; Transvaal Rangers; Wood's Irregulars.

Battle of Khambula

Also known as *Battle of Kambula*

29 March 1879

HOW TO GET THERE

Take the R33 from Vryheid towards Paulpietersburg and eMkhondo (Piet Retief). The turn-off to Khambula battlefield will be on your left, approximately 5km from the junction of the R33 with the R34, just outside Vryheid.

Follow the track north-west for about 5km to find the site. It may be useful to take a specialist guide with you, as there was no official entry gate to this battlefield at the time of writing. As you pass through the fence, you will recognise the battlefield only by a stony ridge on your right (the only high ground nearby) marked by a stone plinth and the remains of the British fort. Walk up the hill to what was once a redoubt built around the stony crest. Two seven-pounder guns were in the fort and there were others in the open, close to the present plinth. The right horn of the Zulu army attacked over the open ground in front of you and to your left.

With your back to the entry gate, look down the slopes. The right horn of the Zulu army attacked over the open ground in front of you and to your left. In the distance you will pick out a walled cemetery. You can drive there by continuing on the dirt track.

As you look towards the British cemetery, the main British camp was 150m to your left (west of the fort), and was big enough to shelter about 1,800 soldiers, the hospital tent, ammunition, supplies and close to 700 horses. There was a smaller cattle laager made up of about 40 wagons behind the fort (south of the hill), connected to the fort with a high palisade fence. The steep valley through which the left horn advanced is close to this laager, to the south.

Walk down towards the road and then cross it to look down into the valley. It was here that the Zulu were able to break into the British cattle laager and almost take the position. ***Guide recommended***

British cemetery: 27°41'15.5" S 30°40'04.4" E

Context

After the British defeat at the Battle of Hlobane the day before (see p. 169), Colonel Evelyn Wood prepared his men for the Zulu attack he was sure would follow. The Battle of Khambula was his successful defence of the British camp in the face of a determined attack by 21,000 warriors.

Timeline

1859
Sir Henry Evelyn Wood is awarded a Victoria Cross for his actions in India.

1873
Wood serves under Major General Sir Garnet Wolseley (below) in the Ashanti Campaign, a successful military expedition against the new Ashanti king who dominates tribes on the Gold Coast (now Ghana).

1875
Major General Wolseley is placed in command in Natal. He leaves Natal at the end of the year, but is recalled at the outbreak of the Anglo-Zulu War.

1878
Wood serves with General Thesiger (later Lord Chelmsford) (left) in the Gaika War (Ninth Frontier War) in the eastern Cape Colony.

1879
The outbreak of the Anglo-Zulu War sees Wood commanding a column as lieutenant colonel. He is engaged at Sihayo's kraal, Hlobane, Khambula and Ulundi. Wolseley replaces Chelmsford after early British defeats and closes the campaign with the capture of Cetshwayo (right).

1880
Wood accompanies Empress Eugénie and her entourage to the place where her son, Louis Napoleon, died.

1880–1881
The 1st Anglo-Boer War (Transvaal War of Independence) is fought and won by the Boers. Wood serves on the committee that negotiates the restoration of the Transvaal's independence.

1897
Wood is appointed adjutant general of the British army.

Action

On the morning of the battle, Wood insisted that the men eat a good breakfast before taking up their positions. Meanwhile, the Zulu gathered to the south-east of the camp and began to deploy in their horns-of-the-buffalo formation (see p. 139). While the left horn ran around to take up position to the south behind the British camp, the right horn gathered in the north-east. Wood provoked them into premature attack by sending Colonel Redvers Buller and his horsemen out of the camp to fire into their ranks and then withdraw. This tactic succeeded in drawing the warriors on and the horsemen found themselves hard-pressed to get back into the laager before the Zulu were upon them.

The cannons on the high ground, together with concentrated fire from the infantry regiments in the laager, inflicted many casualties and drove the Zulu back. However, by this time, the left horn was in position in the dead ground down in the valley and the stream bed to the rear of the camp. From there, some warriors

General Evelyn Wood

The cemetery at Khambula

174 DUNDEE REGION

were able to get into the cattle laager and the main British position was in danger of being overrun. Reinforcements were sent in and the Zulu were driven back into the ravine, but at the cost of many British casualties. Once back in the dead ground, Zulu marksmen were able to fire into the camp, causing yet more casualties. There was another attempt by the right horn to gain the main laager, but this too was repulsed. When the Zulu withdrew, Wood sent his mounted men after them in pursuit. The horsemen slew the fleeing warriors without mercy and no prisoners were taken.

Chief Hamu defected to fight with the British.

Aftermath

This was counted as a major victory for the British and the ferocity of their pursuit was due to their determination to avenge the deaths of their comrades at the Battle of Isandlwana (see p. 134) two months earlier. There were 83 British casualties, including 18 dead. The Zulu probably lost as many as 2,000 warriors and never again fought with as much bravery and vigour.

Weakened by successive battles, the Zulu were in a vulnerable position when the British invaded Zululand for a second time in 1879. When the British finally defeated the Zulu army at the Battle of Ulundi (see p. 53) in July of that year, it marked the beginning of the fragmentation of the Zulu kingdom.

Principal combatants

Zulu: 11 regiments commanded by Mnyamana, Tshingwayo and Zibhebhu.
British: 13th and 90th Light Infantry; Baker's Horse; Border Horse; Burgher Force; Colonial units; Frontier Light Horse; Imperial Mounted Infantry; Kaffrarian Rifles; Natal Native Horse; Royal Artillery; Transvaal Rangers; Wood's Irregulars.

BATTLE OF KHAMBULA

ANGLO-ZULU WAR
BATTLE OF KHAMBULA
29 March 1879

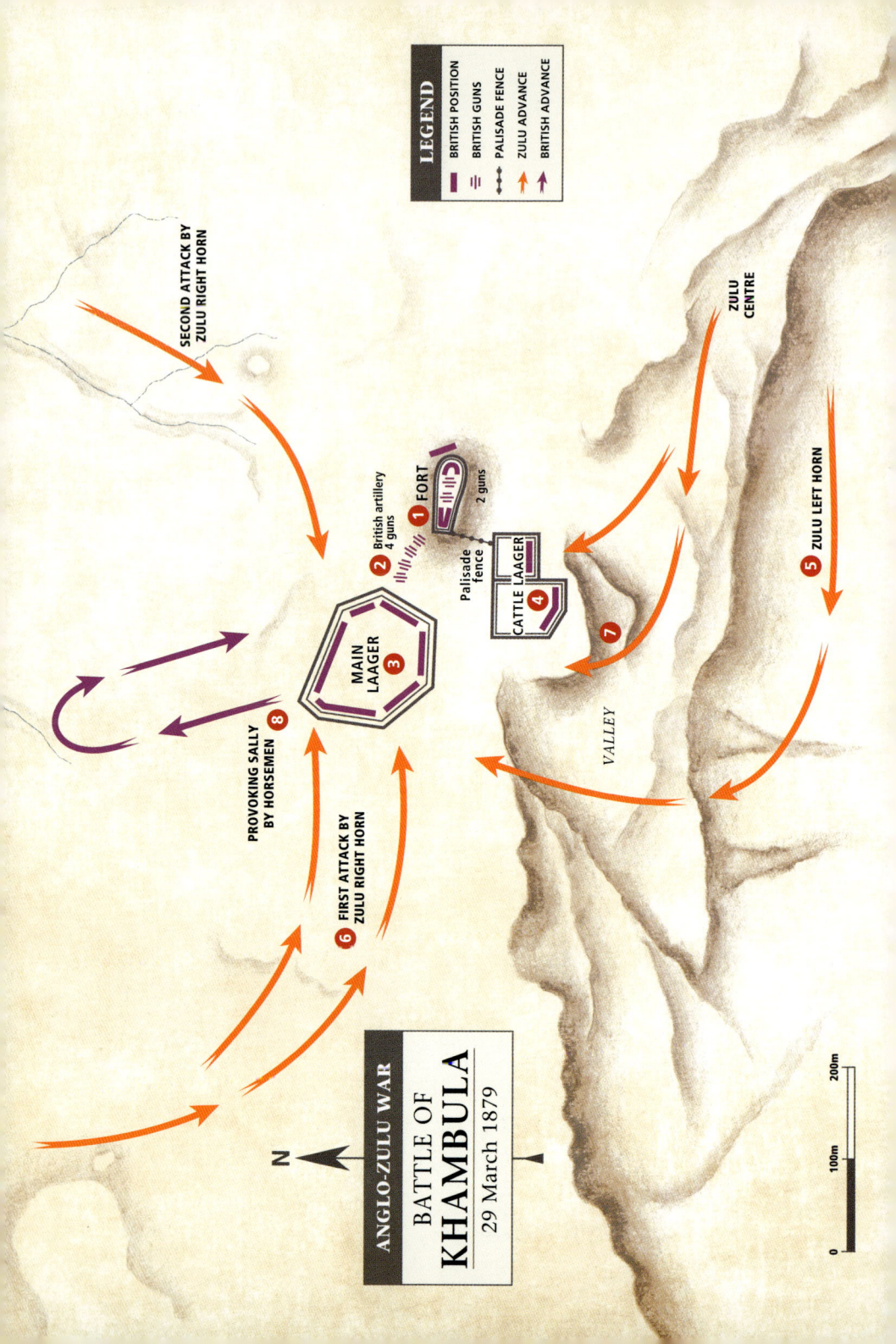

LEGEND
- BRITISH POSITION
- BRITISH GUNS
- PALISADE FENCE
- ZULU ADVANCE
- BRITISH ADVANCE

- SECOND ATTACK BY ZULU RIGHT HORN
- ZULU CENTRE
- ZULU LEFT HORN
- 1 FORT — 2 guns
- 2 British artillery 4 guns
- Palisade fence
- 3 MAIN LAAGER
- 4 CATTLE LAAGER
- 5 Zulu Left Horn
- 6 FIRST ATTACK BY ZULU RIGHT HORN
- 7
- 8 PROVOKING SALLY BY HORSEMEN
- VALLEY

N

0 — 100m — 200m

The right horn of the Zulu army attacked the British camp over this open ground. The Khambula cemetery (inset) lies north-west of the battlefield.

1. The main British position was on this outcrop, which was fortified.

2. The artillery was in the open, enabling the gunners to aim their fire over a wide arc.

3. The main laager was large enough to hold a sizeable number of infantry soldiers, as well as the cavalry and their horses.

4. The cattle laager stood behind the fort and was connected to it by a palisade fence. One side of this laager was close to the steep valley and proved vulnerable to attack.

5. The left horn of the Zulu army approached from this direction.

6. The right horn of the Zulu army launched two attacks: the first against the front and left of the main laager and the second against the right face of the laager. Both were repulsed.

7. There was a concerted effort by the Zulu to gain entrance to the cattle laager and some of them succeeded. Brave efforts by British soldiers drove them out again.

8. Buller and his horsemen went out of a corner of the laager to provoke the Zulu army into attack; some men barely made it back to the safety of the laager. After the battle, Wood sent them out in pursuit of the fleeing Zulu. Terrible slaughter ensued.

Battle of Holkrans
6 May 1902

HOW TO GET THERE
Take the R33 between Vryheid and Paulpietersburg. After driving north for about 23km, turn right towards Zunguin, at the brown signboard to Holkrans. Follow this road for about 15km, passing the farm Holkrans on your right. Then look out for another Holkrans signboard and a track leading off to the right. Follow this track over a small bridge and drive onto the spur of the mountain. Turn right at a junction onto a very rough track that leads to the Boer monument. *Guide recommended*

Context

By April 1902 the 2nd Anglo-Boer War was nearing its end. However, the British had been unable to corner General Louis Botha's commando of about 500 Boers, which was still active in north-eastern Natal. The Boers' resources were depleted, which had necessitated raiding cattle and grain from local Zulu, particularly the abaQulusi, who lived near Hlobane, east of Vryheid. The ill-feeling caused by these raids was fuelled by resentment stemming from the Battle of Tshaneni (see p. 56) in 1884, where the abaQulusi's support of Botha's commando had gone largely unrewarded. Relations between the Vryheid Commando and the abaQulusi had been further soured when, in March 1902, the abaQulusi joined Dinuzulu's warriors to assist General Bruce Hamilton's operations against the Boers in northern Natal.

There was an incident in April when some Boer farmers were killed by the abaQulusi in the vicinity of Vryheid. At the end of April, several abaQulusi homesteads were burnt down on General Botha's orders, in retribution.

In early May, an independent Boer commando led by Field Cornet Jan (Mes) Potgieter, a man who had a history of poor relations with the abaQulusi, attacked and burned the chief's settlement near Hlobane, taking 3,800 head of cattle. Chief Sikhobobo was insulted when Potgieter challenged him to come and get them back. The chief and his people were forced to shelter in the Vryheid garrison under British protection. They subsequently attacked the Boers at Holkrans.

Action

A Boer commando of 73 men under Field Cornet Jan Potgieter had made their camp not far from Chief Sikhobobo's burnt homestead. As an armistice with the British was in place while peace negotiations to end the 2nd Anglo-Boer War were in process, the Boers had taken very few precautions against a surprise attack.

Jan Potgieter

The last page of the Treaty of Vereeniging which concluded the 2nd Anglo-Boer War

On 5 May the men spread out to sleep on a slope stretching between a stone cattle kraal and the banks of a stream about 300m away. Although there was a guard over the cattle, sentries had not been posted. A warning rifle shot woke some of the Boers shortly before dawn the next day, but they had no time to prepare for the onslaught by about 300 abaQulusi. Many Boers were killed before they could retreat. The survivors fled up the hill, pouring rifle fire into the approaching enemy, who took shelter in the long grass. However, as soon as the Boers rose from their firing positions the abaQulusi overwhelmed them with superior numbers. During hand-to-hand fighting some Boers got away, but most were killed.

Aftermath

Of the 73-strong Boer force, 56 men were killed, among them seven Hollanders. The abaQulusi also lost heavily, with 100 dead or wounded. They took three Boer prisoners, all boys under 16 years of age, whom they handed over to the British authorities. The Boers viewed the killings as murders because peace negotiations were under way, and accused British magistrate A. J. Shepstone of complicity in the attack. The chief had informed Shepstone of his intention to retrieve the stolen cattle, yet Shepstone had not informed the officer commanding the garrison, nor warned the Boers.

This incident is said to have been a decisive factor in persuading the Boers to accept the peace agreement; Botha stated that they could not hope for victory if the black man also sided against them. He used this as a powerful argument to persuade the bittereinders, who wanted to fight 'to the bitter end' to accept the peace.

Principal combatants
abaQulusi: Warriors commanded by Chief Sikhobobo.
Boers: Utrecht Commando; Vryheid Commando.

Timeline

1879
The abaQulusi engage the British during the Battle of Hlobane. They are supported by the Zulu army and inflict a notable defeat on the colonial horsemen opposing them. Later in the year, the Zulu are defeated at the Battle of Ulundi and Zululand is divided into 13 separate chiefdoms.

1884
Dinuzulu (right), King Cetshwayo's son, enlists the aid of Louis Botha in a campaign against Chief Zibhebhu. abaQulusi warriors join the Boers and Dinuzulu's warriors to defeat Zibhebhu at Tshaneni.

1886
Louis Botha marries Annie Emmett and settles on his farm east of Vryheid.

1886
Gold is discovered in the Transvaal. There is an influx of foreigners to the Transvaal, most of them British.

1899
The 2nd Anglo-Boer War breaks out. The protagonists agree that black men will not be armed or deployed against the enemy. Louis Botha is appointed commandant of the Vryheid Commando.

1902
In early May, Boer commandos, isolated by the British blockhouses and with insufficient food to survive, raid abaQulusi farms. At Holkrans the abaQulusi attack a Boer commando. Later in May, peace is concluded with the Treaty of Vereeniging.

1910
The Union of South Africa is declared, and General Louis Botha becomes its first prime minister.

BATTLE OF HOLKRANS

Newcastle region

The battles that took place in the mountainous area north-west of Newcastle involved the passage of troops between the British colony of Natal and the neighbouring Boer republics of the Orange Free State and the Transvaal. In this region, the historic road and railway leading from the Natal coast to the Transvaal ran close to the formidable Drakensberg mountain range.

The British remount depot in Newcastle during the 2nd Anglo-Boer War

The many mountain passes leading between Natal and the Orange Free State must have provided a considerable logistical challenge to any British commander. Not only were they steep and difficult to traverse with wagons and long baggage trains, but they were also easily defended by the Boers, providing natural fortresses and plentiful cover. British columns, cumbersome and slow, would have been clearly visible from the high ground and ambushed by the more mobile Boers.

The early history of the area north-west of Newcastle is diverse. The first inhabitants were probably Khoikhoi and San people, who were displaced when Nguni clans migrating from the north settled here. The Ngwane lived in the area in the early 19th century, but it seems

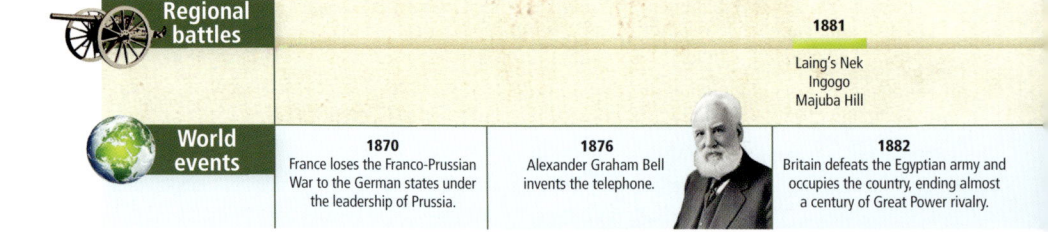

Regional battles

1881
Laing's Nek
Ingogo
Majuba Hill

World events

1870
France loses the Franco-Prussian War to the German states under the leadership of Prussia.

1876
Alexander Graham Bell invents the telephone.

1882
Britain defeats the Egyptian army and occupies the country, ending almost a century of Great Power rivalry.

Newcastle Town Hall, 1900

Battlefields

1. Ingogo 1881
2. Botha's Pass 1900
3. Laing's Nek 1881
4. Majuba Hill 1881
5. Alleman Nek 1900

that they moved on in 1818, after being attacked by the Ndwandwe. Voortrekkers settled their farms in fertile valleys after 1830 and, following the Battle of Blood River, they proclaimed the independent Republic of Natalia. However, the republic was short-lived: Great Britain annexed Natal in 1845. In the years following annexation, an increasing number of British immigrants settled in the region.

The town of Newcastle was surveyed in 1864. It was named for the Duke of Newcastle, the British colonial secretary at the time. Coal was discovered in the region in 1881, and the rock continues to be mined there. The area is also an important centre for the steel industry.

The area to the north of Newcastle, where the modern-day town of Volksrust is located, featured prominently in both the 1st and 2nd Anglo-Boer wars. During the first war, Transvaal Boers used the site as the marshalling point for commandos. It is said that the town was named Volksrust (People's Rest) because it was the place where the Boer troops rested between battles. Volksrust was officially laid out in 1888 and is now the commercial centre for the surrounding farming community.

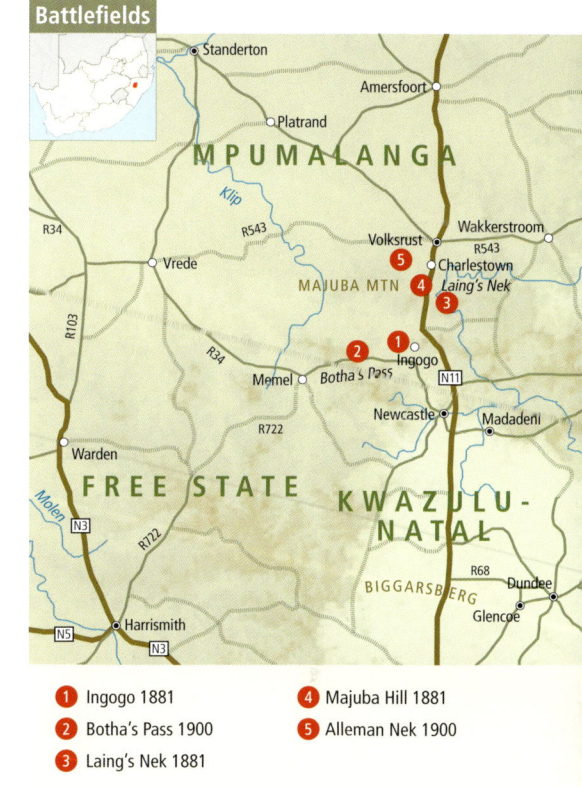

1885 General Gordon is killed at Khartoum trying to evacuate Egyptian forces.

1893 Cecil John Rhodes's British South Africa Company (BSAC) crushes the Ndebele uprising against the Company in Southern Rhodesia.

1896 Nobel prizes for peace, science and literature are established.

1900 Botha's Pass Alleman Nek

1902 A peace treaty ends the 2nd Anglo-Boer War between Britain and the Boer republics

NEWCASTLE REGION 181

Battle of Ingogo
Also known as *Battle of Schuinshoogte*
8 February 1881

HOW TO GET THERE
From Newcastle, take the R34 north-west towards Memel; after about 11.5km turn right onto a gravel road. Continue for another 2.5km until you reach the graves and monuments that mark the battlefield, visible on both sides of the road.

Graves and monuments: 27°36'57.12" S 29°52'39.84" E

Context
After the reverse at Laing's Nek on 28 January 1881 (see p. 187), General Sir George Pomeroy Colley and the Natal Field Force were forced to wait at their camp at Mount Prospect for reinforcements that would enable them to continue their advance to the Transvaal, where the Boers, who had declared independence from Britain in December 1880, had besieged all British garrison towns. Colley's force was supplied from Newcastle and convoys travelling between the town and the camp were continuously harassed by roving bands of Boers under Commandant J. D. Weilbach. On 8 February Colley accompanied a convoy leaving Mount Prospect for Newcastle with the aim of escorting another convoy coming from Newcastle back to his camp. His force was attacked at Schuinshoogte.

Action
Colley left Mount Prospect at 08h30 on 8 February 1881, expecting to be back in the afternoon. He had under his command about 270 men, four artillery guns and a small detachment of mounted infantry. When they reached the Ingogo River, he left two half-companies of infantry and two seven-pounder guns on high ground north of the double drift (the crossing was just above the confluence of the Harte and Ingogo rivers and involved crossing two streams). A message was sent back to the camp ordering an infantry company to relieve the men left at the drift, so that they could rejoin the main force, which then continued up the hill to the Schuinshoogte plateau.

General Nicolaas Smit, who led the Boer attack

182   NEWCASTLE REGION

British soldiers in Pretoria's Church Square just before the outbreak of the 1st Anglo-Boer War, 1880

When the men reached the highest point, the Boers on their right flank opened fire. Colley ordered his artillery to return the fire and deployed his men in a semicircle straddling the road, with the open end to the north-east, and the right flank parallel to the road.

Led by General Nicolaas Smit, the Boers used the dead ground on the perimeter of the plateau to creep closer. There were probably about 200 Boer fighters when the battle commenced. With the arrival of reinforcements during the course of the day, the Boers were able to surround the British position and pour accurate rifle fire into the soldiers. The British artillery guns were used to good effect, but nearly all the men serving the guns were wounded or killed. The mounted infantry, led by Major William Brownlow, attempted a charge against the Boer left flank, but, when the Boers shot nearly all the horses, Brownlow was forced to call off the attack.

At around 14h30, the Boers threatened to outflank Colley's men east of the road, causing him to order a company from his right flank to move east across the road and over open ground to counter the movement. Led by Captain MacGregor, the men advanced boldly to prevent the flanking movement. For a while, they held the position, but by the end of the day MacGregor and nearly the entire company were dead or wounded. Injured horses stampeded across the plateau, bleeding men cried for water, and anyone who dared fire above the rock parapet surrounding the plateau was himself shot as he did so. At about 17h00 a severe thunderstorm broke, torrential rain giving welcome relief to the parched British soldiers. The men had ventured into battle without a water cart, as Colley had presumed they would be back at camp by 16h00.

As darkness fell, the firing lessened and the Boers withdrew to a nearby farm, expecting to resume battle in the morning. Colley, however, was determined to withdraw under cover of darkness. Enough horses could be

Timeline

1845
Natal becomes a British colony.

1852
The Transvaal becomes an independent Boer republic, followed two years later by the Orange Free State.

1871
The Keate Award puts the lucrative diamond fields near Kimberley into Griqua territory. The Orange Free State enjoys revenue associated with trade to the diamond fields, but Boers in the Transvaal are becoming more impoverished.

1877
The Transvaal is annexed to Great Britain.

1879
The Anglo-Zulu War is fought in Natal. The Battle of Isandlwana in January is a disastrous defeat for the British, but they prevail over the Zulu at Ulundi six months later.

1880
The Boers in the Transvaal rise in revolt. British troops are sent to Pretoria to counter the revolution but suffer a severe reverse at Bronkhorstspruit.

1881
British troops approaching the Transvaal from Natal are repulsed at Laing's Nek and again defeated at Ingogo (Schuinshoogte). After the Battle of Majuba Hill, the independence of the Transvaal is restored.

1884
The London Convention decrees that the Transvaal be named the South African Republic; it enjoys virtual independence.

BATTLE OF INGOGO 183

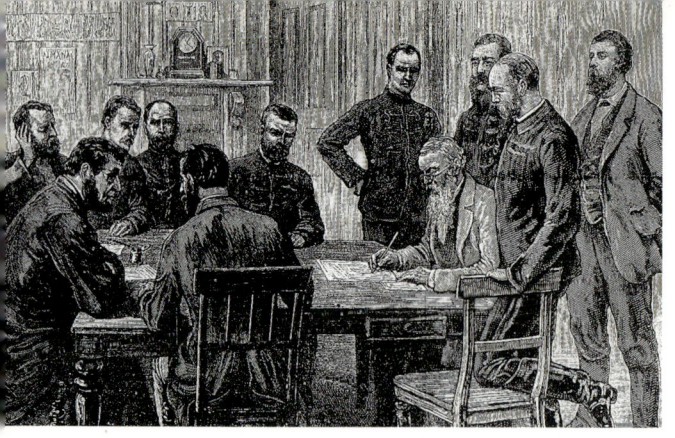

Shortly after the Battle of Ingogo, the Transvaal regained its independence when a peace treaty was signed with Britain. Signatories included President Brand (writing) and General Sir Evelyn Wood (second from right).

harnessed to draw the guns and one ammunition wagon. When it was quite dark, the retreat began. Taking a circuitous route, the party reached the river below the double drift and attempted the difficult crossing. The river was in spate due to the heavy rain and seven men were drowned, but the rest crossed undetected by the Boer patrols and got back to camp the next morning.

Aftermath

British casualties were high – estimates indicate 142 casualties, almost as many dead as wounded – while the Boers had only 10 dead and four wounded. Eight dead Boers were buried on the farm Geelhoutboom, 5km west of the battle site. The deceased British officers were reburied at Fort Amiel; the other men found their last resting place on the battlefield.

The Boers had proved that they were more than a match for Colley's force. Still, Colley's night retreat with the guns, undetected by the foe, was an amazing feat. Only 19 days later Colley again advanced against the Boers, this time at Majuba (see p. 189).

Principal combatants

British: 21st Regiment; 58th Regiment; 60th Rifles (changed in 1881 to King's Royal Rifle Corps); Mounted Squadron; Naval Brigade; Royal Artillery; Royal Engineers.
Boers: About 500 men commanded by General Nicolaas Smit.

Fort Amiel

North of Newcastle, on the road (R34) to Memel, stands Fort Amiel. It was built by the Staffordshire Volunteers (80th Regiment) under Lieutenant Colonel Amiel to counter any possible unrest following the British annexation of the Transvaal Republic in 1877. Used during the Anglo-Zulu War in 1879 as a hospital for Colonel Evelyn Wood's column, it has been much altered since then and now houses the Newcastle Museum.

Battle of Botha's Pass
8 June 1900

HOW TO GET THERE
Botha's Pass is about 40km north-west of Newcastle, on the R34 to Memel. There is nothing obvious here to indicate the battle, apart from a few Boer trenches north-east of the pass that are difficult to access. *Guide recommended*

Context
General Sir Redvers Buller was on his way from Natal with about 24,000 troops, supported by naval and field guns, to join Roberts's army in the Transvaal. Instead of trying to force a passage through the Boer defences at nearby Laing's Nek, he chose to bypass their main positions by taking the route through the hills at Botha's Pass.

Action
After the siege of Ladysmith was lifted on 28 February 1900, Buller forced an easy passage through Boer entrenchments in the Biggarsberg to reach the foot of the Drakensberg and the passes that led into the Orange Free State. Determined to secure his supply, Buller spent some time repairing the railway from Durban. This afforded him the opportunity to consolidate his forces and consider how best to push through the Boer defences on the Orange Free State border.

He had fought with the Boers against the Zulu in 1879 and had no wish to inflict more suffering on a people whose courage and fighting prowess he admired. Without consulting Roberts he arranged a meeting with General Christiaan Botha (Louis Botha's brother) to try to persuade him to lay down arms and encourage his fighters to return to their farms. The offer was relayed to other Boer leaders during a three-day armistice, which gave Botha time to strengthen his defences.

Buller's offer was rejected and he had to advance. Avoiding the road through Laing's Nek, which was extremely well defended, he settled instead on a flanking movement to the north-west, using a brigade of about 3,000 men to move in that direction while another 10,000 distracted the Boers below Laing's Nek.

On 6 June the brigade took Van Wykskop and Spitskop, two hills east of Botha's Pass,

Boers lay fire to Botha's Pass.

BATTLE OF BOTHA'S PASS 185

Timeline

1896
A disastrous attempt, sponsored by Cecil John Rhodes, to overthrow the Transvaal government steels President Paul Kruger's resolve to keep foreigners out of his republic.

1899
The 2nd Anglo-Boer War breaks out. Ladysmith, Kimberley and Mafeking are besieged by the Boers.

1900
The siege of Ladysmith is relieved in February. British forces in Natal prepare to join the British army in the Transvaal.

In May the Orange Free State is annexed and Johannesburg is occupied by British troops.

In June Pretoria, too, is taken by the British, but General Christiaan de Wet's successful raid at Rooiwal on 7 June serves to renew Boer determination to continue fighting. General Sir Redvers Buller's army bypasses the Boer defences at Laing's Nek and pushes into the Orange Free State through Botha's Pass. At the Battle of Diamond Hill, the Boers fail to prevent the British army from pushing further east.

In December Lord Roberts (below) sails from Cape Town, believing the war is almost over. He leaves Kitchener in command in South Africa.

1901
The guerrilla war escalates. Thousands of Boer women and children are interred in concentration camps.

1902
The Treaty of Vereeniging, signed in May, ends the war.

British troops haul artillery to the top of a hill.

encountering little resistance. They spent the next day manhandling field and naval guns to the high ground they had won, 500m above the plain and 7,000m from the pass.

On 8 June the infantry advanced, covered by artillery shells that fell just ahead of them as they climbed the steep slopes. The force of 24,000 men advanced over a front 6km wide. The 2,000 Boers holding the top of the pass were forced to retreat and set alight the dry grass to cover their flight.

Aftermath

The British spent the night on the top of the pass without blankets, in freezing weather, as the wagons had not yet arrived. But Buller was through into the Orange Free State, having taken the Boers by surprise and incurring only 15 casualties. This was a cause of great satisfaction to him, as he had been told by Roberts not to risk the advance through the Drakensberg passes because it would result in an unacceptably high toll of dead and wounded.

Buller was unable to pursue the fleeing Boers, as he had to wait for his supplies. This gave Botha time to prepare the Boers' next line of defence at Alleman Nek (see p. 196).

Principal combatants

British: 1st Royal Dragoons; 5th Lancers; 18th and 19th Hussars; Devonshire Regiment; Dorsetshire Regiment; East Surrey Regiment; Gordon Highlanders; Lancashire Fusiliers; Lancashire Regiment; Middlesex Regiment; Natal Volunteers; Naval Brigade; Queen's (West Surrey) Regiment; Royal Dublin Fusiliers; Royal Field Artillery; Royal Horse Artillery; Royal Lancaster Regiment; South African Light Horse; South Lancashire Regiment; Thorneycroft's Mounted Infantry; West Yorkshire Regiment.

Boers: Commandos from Carolina and Lydenburg.

Battle of Laing's Nek
28 January 1881

HOW TO GET THERE
Drive from Newcastle towards Volksrust on the N11. At the spot where the road passes through Laing's Nek, there are signs to the battlefield. The battle took place mostly east (to the right) of the road, where Brownlow's Koppie and Deane Hill may be identified. Be aware that signage to the sites is poor or non-existent in places.

Mount Prospect is a little more than halfway between the Ingogo River in the south and Laing's Nek. It is on private land and permission to access the site has to be obtained from the owner. *Guide recommended*

Context
The Transvaal was annexed to Britain in 1877. There was cause for much dissatisfaction on the part of the Boers, who had first moved from the Cape to escape British rule only to be forced, again by the British, to give up their republic in Natal when it was annexed to the Cape in 1843. Growing Boer opposition, marked by protest rallies and ongoing unrest, culminated in the ambush of Colonel Philip Anstruther's column at Bronkhorstspruit (see p. 212). Troops were despatched from Natal to the beleaguered Transvaal garrisons and these troops engaged the Boers in battle at Laing's Nek.

Action
General Sir George Pomeroy Colley – recently arrived in South Africa as governor, commander-in-chief and high commissioner – would have preferred to avoid conflict with the Boers. However, British garrisons in the Transvaal were already besieged and he had no choice but to send troops north, from Pietermaritzburg via Newcastle, to relieve them.

The Natal Field Force assembled at Fort Amiel near Newcastle and, accompanied by Colley, moved forward to reach Mount Prospect on 26 January. The weather was wet and misty, forcing them to set up camp there instead of pressing on to Laing's Nek.

The troops totalled about 1,400 men, comprising infantry (58th Regiment), a naval detachment with Gatling guns and rocket tubes, a recently formed squadron of mostly mounted infantry, two artillery batteries and some seven-pounders, and about 70 colonial Natal Mounted Police.

The Boers, commanded by General Piet Joubert, were entrenched on both sides of the road through Laing's Nek, an extremely strong defensive position that Joubert used to its full advantage. He had over 1,000 men laagered in two places on the reverse slopes of the hills, west and east of Laing's Nek. Trenches and stone sangars were constructed on both sides of the road, as well as on the hill east of the nek now called Deane Hill. Joubert also placed men

Timeline

1835
George Pomeroy Colley is born in Dublin, Ireland.

1852
The Sand River Convention grants independence to the Boer republic of the Transvaal. Colley joins the 2nd Queen's Regiment.

1854
The Bloemfontein Convention grants the Orange Free State its independence. Now a lieutenant, Colley comes to the Cape as a magistrate on the frontier. He also leads an expedition that kills the Xhosa chief Tola.

1860
Colley serves with his regiment in China.

1873
Lieutenant Colonel Colley serves under Sir Garnet Wolseley in the Ashanti Campaign in today's Ghana. In Natal, Sir Theophilus Shepstone crowns Cetshwayo king of the Zulu nation.

1879
The Anglo-Zulu War breaks out in Natal. Colley is Lord Chelmsford's chief of staff.

1880
Colley is promoted to major general. He becomes governor of Natal and high commissioner of South East Africa.

1881
Colley commands the British forces during the battles of Laing's Nek in January and Ingogo and Majuba (where he is killed) in February. The Transvaal Republic wins back its independence.

---

on the smaller hill, now called Brownlow's Koppie, approximately 1km south of Deane Hill and at right angles to the expected line of attack.

Colley moved his men out of camp to advance on the nek on the morning of 28 January. The attack began at 09h30 with an artillery bombardment from guns placed west of the road, on a spur of Majuba Mountain. The Boers did not respond. The foot soldiers, commanded by Colonel Bonar Millet Deane, were then ordered to advance against the flat-topped hill immediately east of the road.

They were supported on their right flank by the mounted infantry under Major William Brownlow, who soon came under fire from Boers on the small hill (Brownlow's Koppie) south of the main position. Brownlow wheeled his men right and galloped up the hill to engage them, but the slope was so steep that the horses were exhausted before they reached the crest. Brownlow's horse was shot and the other troops withdrew in confusion before they reached the Boer positions.

Meanwhile, the infantrymen were advancing in close order. About 1km north of their starting point the troops were at the base of the hill and under fire. The officers, unusually, were on horseback as they led the attack up the steep slopes. Bullets whistled around them and Deane attempted to get his men into open order, but the steepness of the slope made it difficult to for them to spread out. In desperation, as increasing numbers of men fell around him, Deane called for a bayonet charge. When his horse was shot from under him he led the men on foot, advancing under fire from Boers who, in some places, were only 40m away. Deane and another four officers fell. Major Edward Essex, the only surviving infantry officer, retreated the infantry down the slopes under covering fire from the artillery. It was during this retreat that the colours were saved and Lieutenant Alan Hill earned a Victoria Cross for rescuing a wounded men.

Aftermath

The Boers succeeded in preventing the British from getting into the Transvaal. In the process, they lost 24 men, 14 of them dead. The British suffered heavily: Colley lost all but one staff officer. Altogether there were 193 British casualties, including 144 dead. Colley could advance no further until reinforcements arrived. He moved the camp to a more defensible position and took over command of the Natal Field Force.

Principal combatants

British: 21st Regiment; 58th Regiment; 60th Rifles; Mounted Squadron; Natal Mounted Police; Naval Brigade; Royal Artillery.
Boers: 400 men commanded by General Piet Joubert.

Battle of Majuba Hill
27 February 1881

HOW TO GET THERE
Drive north on the N11 from Newcastle towards Volksrust. The turn-off to the battlefield is about 8km before Volksrust on your left. From the car park, walk towards the path that leads up the northern slopes of the mountain to the summit. Take a sketch map with you so that you can identify Gordons' Knoll on the way up on the right and MacDonald's Hill in front of you. Make your way across the summit to the hollow where General Sir George Pomeroy Colley fell, and from there look back to the ridge that marked the last desperate line of British defence. Here, on your right, you will also see Hay's Hill. Continue to the south-eastern crest to look down the ascent route of the British and the sheer cliffs over which the terrified soldiers fled.

Context

Sir George Pomeroy Colley had recently arrived in Natal to take up the position of governor, high commissioner and commander-in-chief of all British troops in Natal and the Transvaal. He had hoped to promote peaceful relations between Boer and Brit in South Africa, but when the Boers surrounded the British garrisons in the Transvaal he had no choice but to go to war.

The Boers had taken up strong defensive positions in the mountain passes leading through the Drakensberg into the Transvaal and Colley had suffered a severe reverse at Laing's Nek (see p. 187). A few weeks later, when he accompanied the troops sent to escort a supply column from Newcastle, he was surrounded by the Boers and was lucky to escape by night over the double drift at Ingogo (see p. 182). Colley was eager to win a decisive victory to restore his reputation and avenge these two defeats at the hands of the Boers. The Battle of Majuba Hill was his second failed attempt to break through the Boer defences and enter the Transvaal.

Action

Reinforcements from Britain and India were despatched to Fort Amiel in Newcastle. Five days after their arrival, the entire force, led by Colley but under the nominal

Fort Prospect cemetery with Majuba Hill in the background

BATTLE OF MAJUBA HILL 189

Timeline

1834
Petrus (Piet) Jacobus Joubert's father dies in Pietermaritzburg and Piet moves with his family to the Transvaal.

1851
Joubert moves to Wakkerstroom where, 15 years later, he serves on the Wakkerstroom District Volksraad.

1875
He becomes acting president of the Transvaal during President Burgers's term.

1879
Lieutenant Ian Hamilton serves in the Afghan War under Lord Roberts and is appointed his aide-de-camp.

1880
At the start of the 1st Anglo-Boer War, Piet Joubert is appointed commander-in-chief of the Republican forces.

1881
The Boers commanded by Joubert and Nicolaas Smit defeat the British at the Battle of Majuba Hill. Hamilton is seriously wounded during this battle.

1896
Joubert becomes vice president of the independent Transvaal. He stands against Paul Kruger in the presidential elections but is defeated.

1899
Joubert is commander-in-chief of the Boer forces at the outbreak of the 2nd Anglo-Boer War. He is mortally injured when he falls from his horse near Willowsgrange in Natal. Ian Hamilton becomes chief of staff to General Sir George White in Natal. He fights at Elandslaagte where he is recommended for a Victoria Cross, which is not awarded.

A drawing of the battle on Majuba Mountain, viewed from the hill above the British camp at Mount Prospect

command of Colonel Bonar Millet Deane, advanced to the border between Natal and the Transvaal. The disastrous defeat at Laing's Nek where Deane was killed persuaded Colley that it was imperative to hold the high ground and that the force that held it could not be dislodged. This goes some way to explaining his actions at Majuba.

Peace negotiations with the Boers were in progress, as the recently elected Liberal government of William Gladstone had no wish to be involved in a war in South Africa. Consequently, after the reverse at Ingogo, Colley was instructed to wait for instructions from London before proceeding.

From his camp at Mount Prospect Colley could see Majuba Mountain dominating the road that led over Laing's Nek and into the Transvaal. The flat-topped summit overlooked the Boer positions on both sides of the nek that they held with such strength and Colley was sure that he could force them to retreat – if only he could get his men onto the high ground and shell the Boers from above.

A Zulu scout reported that the Boers did not occupy the mountain at night, but came down to their camp to sleep. And so, with the greatest secrecy, Colley planned to take Majuba by night. He chose a mixed force of about 600 men, some of whom would remain in reserve. They were chosen from four different regiments – Gordon Highlanders, 58th Regiment in their red jackets, 60th Rifles and a section of the Naval Brigade – and perhaps this is why they seemed to lack esprit de corps. The reality was that the men were unfamiliar with the senior officers of regiments other than their own and did not know whom to follow, even later as their own officers were killed during battle. However, as his force

190 NEWCASTLE REGION

moved quietly out of their Mount Prospect camp on a moonless night at 22h00 on 26 February 1881, Colley had no doubt that victory was within reach.

It took them until daybreak to gain the summit. There is only one difficult route onto the summit from the south-west and the last scramble up the slippery grass-covered slope left the men exhausted and in disarray. There were some who got lost altogether

Fleeing British troops plunged over these cliffs.

and had to be tracked down and redirected. It was 05h30 by the time everyone was on top.

Colley deployed the men around the perimeter of the roughly triangular, basin-like summit – each man about 12 paces away from the next – but there were fatal weaknesses in his defensive position. The enemy on what later became known as Gordons' Knoll would be dangerously close to British soldiers holding the crest. On the opposite, south-eastern side of the hilltop there was another small rise; when this crucial position, known as Hay's Hill, was taken by the Boers, the summit became virtually indefensible. The third prominent feature on the summit was MacDonald's Hill, south of Gordons' Knoll and north-west of Hay's Koppie. Men on this hill were vulnerable to Boer snipers on the western slopes and many were shot in the back as they stood to fire at Boers on the summit. However, this position was bravely held to the end by Lieutenant Hector MacDonald and some of the Highlanders.

As dawn lit the sky, Lieutenant Ian Hamilton, who was in command of the false northern crest, immediately saw the importance of occupying Gordons' Knoll, the detached hill close to the British-held crest. He sent some men forward to take up positions there, but had too few to spare.

The Boers spotted the British lining the summit. It is said that the wife of the Boer commander Piet Joubert saw them first and was scandalised because there would be fighting on a Sunday. However, when some of the volunteers called up by her husband showed reluctance to climb the steep hill, Mrs Hendrina Joubert gave them the sharp edge of her tongue and sent them straight up after the English.

Brilliantly commanded by Nicolaas Smit, many of the younger men began to scale the steep north-eastern slopes that provided dead ground and lush gullies – cover through which they could approach unseen. Soon there were Boers concealed behind rocks all around the summit, some of them very close to the British lines.

Sir George Pomeroy Colley, shortly before he was shot

BATTLE OF MAJUBA HILL   191

O'Neill's Cottage below Majuba Mountain, where peace terms between Britain and the Transvaal were negotiated

The Highlanders, who had been sent forward by Hamilton to occupy Gordons' Knoll, were forced off by the attacking Boers, who were then able to fire on the extended British line on the north-eastern crest from the flank and rear. The terrified men broke and fled, allowing the Boers to gain a rocky ridge that formed the last line of the British defence. Colley seemed to have underestimated the danger and reacted slowly to reports of Boers approaching ever closer. When they appeared at almost point-blank range he was in the centre of the summit, pistol in hand, trying vainly to rally his men. There are different accounts of his death: he was shot in the back of the head, some say, by a 12-year-old boy; Boer accounts suggest that he was shot through the top of his skull from the front and died instantly; other reports insist that his last words were, 'But they couldn't hit an elephant at this dist...'.

An unlikely hero

Ian Hamilton, a young British officer, was badly wounded in the wrist during the Battle of Majuba Hill. He was taken prisoner on the summit, but, when the Boers saw the severity of his injury they sent him back to the British camp for medical attention. Hamilton made his way down the steep path, but he had lost so much blood that he fainted and fell unconscious. There he may have remained and died, had it not been for his dog.

Hamilton's terrier, Patch, had been left behind in the safety of the Mount Prospect camp when the British force left for battle the night before. When evening fell and his master had not returned, Patch was frantic. He managed to slip away from his minder and followed Hamilton's scent until he found him, face down, in the grass. Patch pawed the wounded man until he rolled over, and then licked his face so persistently that Hamilton regained consciousness. He managed to get back to camp where he was tended and was sent back to Britain for recuperation.

Although Hamilton never regained full use of his wrist, he went on to enjoy an illustrious military career, playing important roles in the 2nd Anglo-Boer War and World War I. Patch lived to a ripe old age and enjoyed attention from all under Hamilton's command.

Boer general Piet Joubert and his men at breakfast near Newcastle

The soldiers who ran away threw themselves headlong over the southern crest and many died as they fell down sheer ridges onto the boulders below. Others hid among the scrub in ravines and were able to stagger back to camp when night fell. Some were killed on the summit and those who surrendered were taken prisoner.

The Boers had won a decisive victory. They treated the wounded kindly and the dead with great respect. General Joubert himself returned MacDonald's sword, saying that a brave man and his sword should not be parted. Wounded men were sent back to the British camp for medical care.

Aftermath

More than 280 British men were killed, wounded or captured, while the Boers had one man killed and five wounded, one of whom was to die later. The Boers attributed their spectacular victory to God, claiming divine intervention. The new British Liberal government was not willing to get involved in a war in South Africa and could see no good reason for wanting to regain control of the Transvaal. When peace was negotiated, the Transvaal became an independent Boer republic once more. Its first president was Paul Kruger (see p. 218).

The battle left its bruising mark on the losing army: 'Remember Majuba!' became a rallying cry for the British during the 2nd Anglo-Boer War.

Principal combatants

British: 21st Regiment; 58th Regiment; 94th Regiment; 92nd Highlanders; Naval Brigade.
Boers: Various Boer commandos under generals Piet Joubert and Nicolaas Smit.

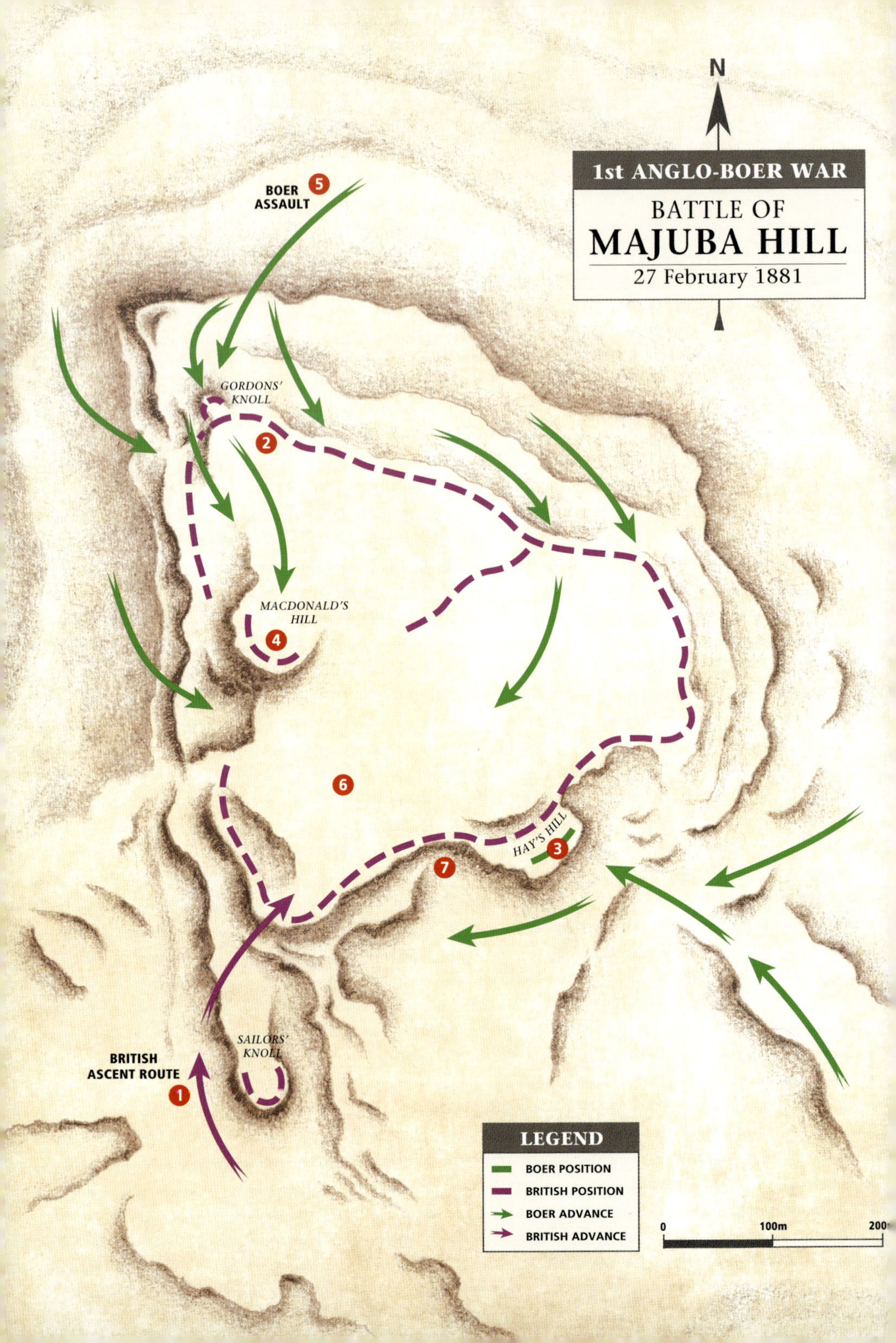
1st ANGLO-BOER WAR
BATTLE OF
MAJUBA HILL
27 February 1881
N
BOER ASSAULT
5
GORDONS' KNOLL
2
MACDONALD'S HILL
4
6
HAY'S HILL
3
7
SAILORS' KNOLL
BRITISH ASCENT ROUTE
1
LEGEND
BOER POSITION
BRITISH POSITION
BOER ADVANCE
BRITISH ADVANCE
0
100m
200m

Majuba Mountain today

1 This was the route followed by the British on the night of 26 February 1881. The slopes of the hill were steep and slippery and it took the troops until 05h30 the following morning to gain the summit.

2 This was the false crest of the summit, another one being below on the lip of the detached hill now known as Gordons' Knoll. Ian Hamilton, on placing men on this sector of the British line of defence, realised its vulnerability and sent some soldiers forward to occupy Gordons' Knoll. However, they were driven back by the attacking Boers.

3 This outcrop, known as Hay's Hill, was taken by the Boers, putting them dangerously close to the British defending the summit.

4 Hector MacDonald and the Highlanders held this koppie bravely throughout the battle, although they were vulnerable to Boer sharpshooters on the western slopes behind them and many fell, shot in the back.

5 The Boers, encouraged by Mrs Hendrina Joubert, the wife of the Boer commander, first assaulted the hill up these north-eastern slopes.

6 General Colley fell at this point. There are conflicting reports of how he died.

7 The Boers pursued the fleeing British soldiers, many of whom plunged over these steep southern slopes to die on the rocks below.

The Boers defeated the British at Majuba.

Battle of Alleman Nek

Also known as *Battle of Allemansnek* and *Battle of Almond's Nek*

11 June 1900

HOW TO GET THERE

The pass through the Iketeni ridge lies 20km west of Volksrust on the R543 to Vrede. From Newcastle, drive through Volksrust on the main road. In the middle of the town turn left onto the road signposted 'R543' to Vrede and Johannesburg. This tarred road leads out of town in a westerly direction and will pass through Alleman Nek. Take the turn-off to Memel on the left and you will find the Boer monument.

Turn-off to Memel: *27°23'13.89" S 29°41'53.60" E*

British troops en route to Johannesburg

Context

General Sir Redvers Buller, commanding a force of 24,000 men, had successfully outflanked Boer defences at Laing's Nek and had forced his way from Natal through Botha's Pass (see p. 185) to enter the Orange Free State. It now remained for him to enter the Transvaal where he was to meet up with Lord Roberts's army, which had just successfully occupied both Johannesburg and Pretoria. He had to confront the last Boer-held position on his route to the Highveld at Alleman Nek. The battle took place when the passage of his column was contested by Boers holding the nek.

Action

Buller and his army were almost through to the Transvaal. As Buller advanced towards Gansvlei stream, General Joachim Fourie hastily posted 3,000 Boers with four guns on both sides of the wagon road where it passed through Alleman Nek. There was no time to build the usual, well-prepared trenches and emplacements.

On 10 June the South African Light Horse took Gansvlei Kop, a hill south-west of Alleman Nek, and the next day Buller launched his attack from a ridge immediately south of the plateau leading to the nek. The mounted men under Lord Douglas Cochrane, the 12th Earl of Dundonald, took a hill on the extreme right, while two long-ranging 4.7-inch

The Royal Field Artillery on parade with a 15-pounder gun. These guns were used at Alleman Nek to bombard the hills prior to the infantry advance.

(120mm) naval guns were set up on the plateau about 2,500m from the Boer trenches. Buller had more than 40 guns and had learned to use them to create a creeping artillery barrage behind which his infantry could advance.

East of the road and south of the nek was a conical hill, which was bombarded first with lyddite shells, then with shrapnel and finally with small shells from the Vickers machine gun. Under cover of the bombardment, infantry brigades were sent forward over the plateau that separated the British ridge from the Boer positions. One brigade approached the right face of the conical hill, the other the centre. The Maxim Nordenfeldt gun of the Boers dropped shells among the advancing infantry. When the infantry reached the base of the hill, about 1,800m from the enemy, the Boers opened fire with their Mauser rifles.

Using what cover they could find, the British scrambled upwards and eventually it was the 2nd Battalion of the Dorsetshire Regiment that reached the crest and charged. The Boers fled, leaving the Dorsets to cross the saddle separating the conical hill from the main ridge behind it, east of the road.

Meanwhile, another infantry brigade was engaged on the wooded bluff west of the road. The Boers contested this position

Musicians from the Royal Dublin Fusiliers

Timeline

1899
General Sir Redvers Buller commands the British army tasked with the relief of Ladysmith.

1900
In February the siege of Ladysmith is relieved.

In May General Buller commences his advance from Ladysmith, drives the Boers off the Biggarsberg and occupies Dundee, while the main British army defeats the Boers at Doornkop and occupies Johannesburg.

In June the British occupy Pretoria, while Buller's army captures Botha's Pass, bypassing Boers in Laing's Nek. Buller fights at Alleman Nek on 11 June, the same day that the forces of Lord Roberts (below left) engage the Boers at Diamond Hill. Buller occupies Volksrust and the Boers evacuate Laing's Nek.

In August Buller is close to joining up with Roberts's army when he fights the Battle of Bergendal, the last set-piece battle of the 2nd Anglo-Boer War.

1901
The guerrilla war against British supply columns in South Africa intensifies.

1902
Britain wins the 2nd Anglo Boer War.

BATTLE OF ALLEMAN NEK   197

Royal Dragoon Guards were part of the composite cavalry commanded by Lord Douglas Cochrane, the 12th Earl of Dundonald, which took one of the hills at the outset of the battle at Alleman Nek.

sharply, but, once they realised that the British had occupied the ridge on their left and could enfilade their positions with artillery, they withdrew in good order, setting the veld alight behind them. Retreating Boer commandos occasionally employed this technique to decrease visibility, thereby concealing their departure.

Aftermath

Casualties on the British side consisted of 28 men killed and 134 wounded. Most of the British soldiers who were killed were reinterred in the Garden of Remembrance in Volksrust. The Boers had lost four men.

The British did not pursue the retreating Boers, who fell back into the Transvaal. Buller was able to occupy Volksrust on 12 June. He had succeeded in outflanking all the Boer positions on Laing's Nek. Soon thereafter, the Boers withdrew from Natal, retreating to the Orange Free State and the Transvaal.

Principal combatants

British: Devonshire Regiment; Dorsetshire Regiment; East Surrey Regiment; Lancashire Fusiliers; Lancaster Regiment; Middlesex Regiment; Mounted infantry; Naval Brigade; Queen's (West Surrey) Regiment; Royal Artillery; Royal Dublin Fusiliers; South Lancashire Regiment; West Yorkshire Regiment.
Boers: Commandos from Bethal, Lydenburg, Pretoria, Soutpansberg, Standerton, Swaziland, Utrecht and Wakkerstroom.

The uniform of a private in the Royal Dublin Fusiliers

198   NEWCASTLE REGION

Logistical challenges of war

Relocating the British army to the battleground and then supplying it provided considerable logistical challenges. During the 2nd Anglo-Boer War, rail was the preferred mode of transport, but once the army moved away from the line it had to rely on ox- and mule-drawn wagons to transport its ample supplies.

Each battery of artillery (six guns) was served by 131 horses and three transport wagons. Oxen were used to draw the big 4.7-inch (120mm) naval guns that were too heavy for horses or mules. Each infantry division, consisting of more or less 10,000 men, was accompanied by about 1,700 horses, 500 mules and 280 wagons or carts drawn by horses, oxen or mules. These cumbersome vehicles carried pontoon bridges, tools, medical supplies, ammunition, tents, equipment, water and food for the men and the animals.

Given the limited availability of grass hay, fodder for the horses and mules had to be imported, adding a substantial burden to the load that needed to be ferried. Oxen, although they were slower than mules, had the advantage of finding their own food, provided enough time – a minimum of eight hours per day – was allowed for grazing. Another eight hours had to be granted for resting, because a more strenuous schedule led to rapid loss of condition and death.

The Remount Service provided a total of 518,794 horses and 150,781 mules and donkeys to the British army in South Africa during the war. Of these, about 350,000 horses and 53,000 mules died. At least 13,000 horses died on board ship and many more on the railway trucks transporting them to the war front. Remount stations were supposed to keep the horses until they had recovered from their journey, but the need for horses at the front was always so urgent that they were sent away before they were properly fit. Horses were initially sourced from Argentina but were also purchased from Spain, the USA, Italy and Australia.

Hex
Bethany
Hebron
Wonderboom
PRETORIA
Hencops
Thorndale
ANGLO-BOERE OORLOG
1899-1902

Gauteng & Surrounds

Long Tom Pass, Mpumalanga

Pretoria, Johannesburg & surrounding regions

Wrought from the ravages of conflict and the promise of hope, the Zuid-Afrikaansche Republiek (ZAR) was established at the Sand River Convention of 1852. The custodians of the new state, the Voortrekkers, had been living on the Highveld ever since their arrival in the region north of the Vaal River in the late 1830s. Farmers of mostly Dutch descent, they had migrated from the British-ruled Cape in search of land, security and freedom from colonial rule. Now, with the signing of the convention, Britain formally recognised the new republic's right to self-rule.

The Rissik Street Post Office was built in 1897 on Market Square, the hub of early Johannesburg.

The Voortrekkers made Pretoria their new capital in 1853, naming it after Great Trek leader Andries Pretorius who had a farm near the junction of the Crocodile and Tshwane rivers. The name 'Tshwane' is derived from the moniker of a Sotho chief who settled with his people on the banks of the river in about 1825. The watercourse has since been named the Apies River, and Pretoria is settled around it.

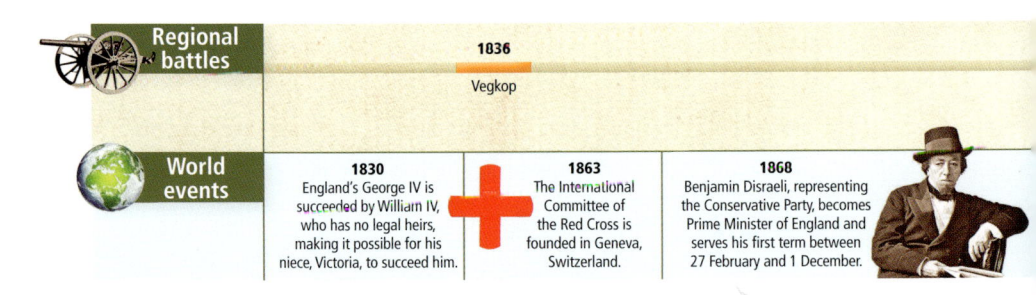

Regional battles

1836 — Vegkop

World events

1830 — England's George IV is succeeded by William IV, who has no legal heirs, making it possible for his niece, Victoria, to succeed him.

1863 — The International Committee of the Red Cross is founded in Geneva, Switzerland.

1868 — Benjamin Disraeli, representing the Conservative Party, becomes Prime Minister of England and serves his first term between 27 February and 1 December.

Battlefields

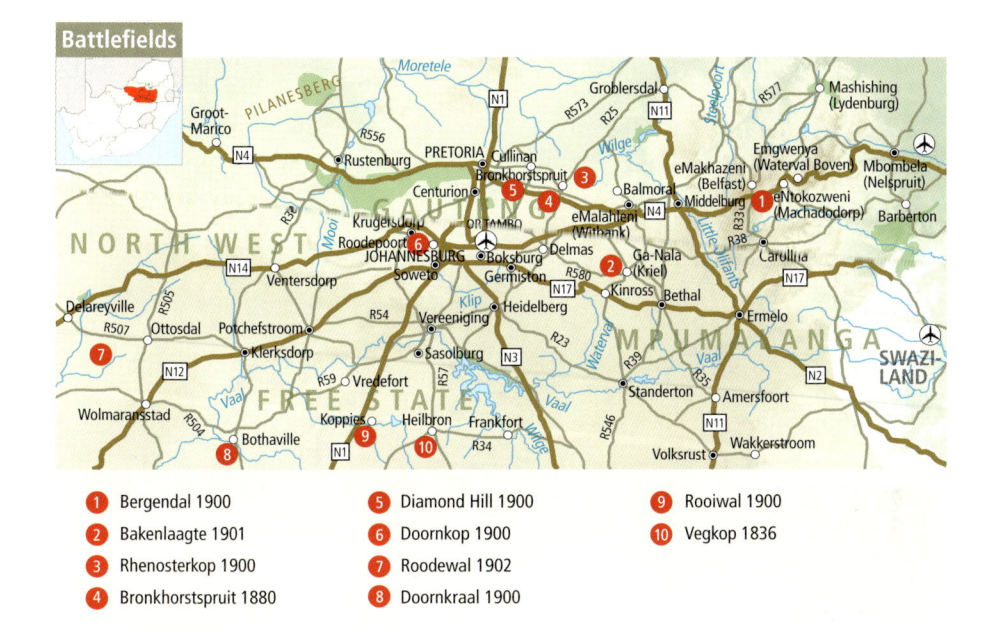

1. Bergendal 1900
2. Bakenlaagte 1901
3. Rhenosterkop 1900
4. Bronkhorstspruit 1880
5. Diamond Hill 1900
6. Doornkop 1900
7. Roodewal 1902
8. Doornkraal 1900
9. Rooiwal 1900
10. Vegkop 1836

Sir Theophilus Shepstone

Life for the 20,000 burghers who made their homes there was difficult. They suffered hardships that included skirmishes with indigenous African societies, a weak economy and political infighting. Soon the early republic was in dire straits, with not enough money to sustain an economy or protect itself from hostile attacks on and from within its borders. So precarious were its financial affairs and security situation that Britain intervened, in the guise of Theophilus Shepstone and a handful of Native Police (plus Rider Haggard as a clerk), and annexed the Transvaal, as it was known to the British, in April 1877.

British defeat of the Zulu nation in July 1879 meant that the Transvaal burghers no longer feared incursions

1880	1900	1901	1902
Bronkhorstspruit	Doornkop Rooiwal Diamond Hill	Bergendal Doornkraal Rhenosterkop	Bakenlaagte	Roodewal

1885	1900	1901	1902
Major General Charles George Gordon is killed fighting the warriors of the Mahdi in the Sudan.	On the first day of the new year, Britain declares northern Nigeria a protectorate.	Oil is discovered in Texas, USA.	The Peace of Vereeniging is signed, ending the 2nd Anglo-Boer War in South Africa.

PRETORIA, JOHANNESBURG & SURROUNDING REGIONS   203

Gold mining is a key feature of modern Gauteng's economy.

from the Zulu on their southern border, thereby diminishing the need for British protection. This, along with a list of grievances against the British administration, ultimately led to the 1st Anglo-Boer War (1880–1881). Following the Battle of Majuba Hill, the Transvaal regained its independence. Paul Kruger became its first president.

The discovery of gold in unprecedented quantities under the Witwatersrand in 1886 led to an influx of settlers, mostly of British origin, and the rapid development of a new economic centre, Johannesburg. Tensions between the burghers and the Uitlanders (foreigners) were used by politicians to provoke the outbreak of the 2nd Anglo-Boer War in October 1899.

Conflicts in this region include a battle between the Voortrekkers and the Ndebele (Vegkop) and one between the Boers and the British in 1880 (Bronkhorstspruit). The rest are all engagements fought during the Anglo-Boer War between May 1900 and the end of the war in May 1902.

Today it is worth visiting the Voortrekker Monument in Pretoria to gain a feeling for the soul of the Afrikaner nation – the Battle of Blood River, the different routes taken by the Voortrekkers on their journey from the Cape, the death of Trekker leader Piet Retief and his followers, the tragic end of Pieter Uys and the massacre at Bloukrans are all portrayed.

Also in Pretoria, both Melrose House, where the Peace of Vereeniging was signed on 3 May 1902, and Paul Kruger's former home are open to the public. A little way out of town, in Irene, is the former farm of Jan Smuts and the site of the Irene concentration camp.

Gold prospectors' shanties, 1889

204   PRETORIA, JOHANNESBURG & SURROUNDING REGIONS

Battle of Bergendal

Also known as *Battle of Dalmanutha*

27 August 1900

HOW TO GET THERE

From Middelburg, drive east towards eMakhazeni (Belfast) on the N4. At the junction of the R33 and the N4, near eMakhazeni, there is a bridge and a service station. From there, continue on the N4 for nearly 5km until you see the gate to the monument on your right. Behind the monument is Bergendal Koppie and the original farmhouse.

The main memorial contains the graves of many Boers who died elsewhere and who were exhumed and reinterred here. There is also a smaller memorial at the site, dedicated to the Rifle Brigade.

Main monument: 25°44'04.8" S 30°06'12.3" E

Context

Lord Roberts was planning to converge his 20,000 troops for a decisive action against Boer commandos east of Pretoria. President Paul Kruger was in Machadodorp, which was the new seat of the Boer government. The Boers intended to use strong positions north and south of the railway line near Belfast to halt the British advance towards Machadodorp.

Action

Roberts's force was advancing eastward from Middelburg and General Sir Redvers Buller was on his way north from Natal to join him. Roberts had planned a pincer movement to trap the Boers between Machadodorp (further east) and Belfast. However, Buller had 9,000 men, 82 guns and provisions for each man for three weeks, all of which slowed his progress. This persuaded him to continue north, instead of progressing east towards Machadodorp through swampy land to outflank the enemy.

British memorial to members of the Rifle Brigade

Timeline

1899
Ladysmith is besieged on 2 November; on 15 December General Sir Redvers Buller tries, unsuccessfully, to force his way through the Boer line to relieve Ladysmith at the Battle of Colenso.

1900
Between February and May there are unsuccessful attempts at Spioenkop and Vaalkrans until the siege is eventually relieved. Buller prepares to move his army north into the Transvaal. Bloemfontein is occupied by the British on 13 March and Johannesburg is captured at the end of May. The Boers resolve to use guerrilla warfare against British columns.

In June Pretoria is occupied and Buller's army enters the Transvaal. General Christiaan de Wet (left) is successful in his attack on a British depot at Rooiwal, while General Louis Botha leads the Boers at the Battle of Diamond Hill east of Pretoria.

On 23 August Buller's army, on its way north, confronts Boers at Amersfoort and Geluk, where the talented Boer leader, Captain von Dalwig, is seriously wounded. British cavalry general Pole-Carew advances along the railway to occupy Belfast a day later. On 27 August the Battle of Bergendal is fought.

In November Lord Kitchener takes over from Roberts as commander-in-chief of the British army.

1901
The blockhouse strategy is adopted to round up Boer guerrillas. Jan Smuts invades the Cape, which has been placed under martial law. Louis Botha (right) invades Natal. On the way back to the Transvaal his commando assists in the Boer defeat of a British column at Bakenlaagte.

Site of the original Bergendal farmhouse

At the beginning of August 1900, Buller's army had confronted Boers at Amersfoort. They retreated after a skirmish and Buller continued north to the farm Geluk. There, on 23 August, Buller's forces engaged the Boers again and the talented Boer leader Captain von Dalwig was seriously wounded. Meanwhile, British cavalry general Reginald Pole-Carew was advancing along the railway to reach and occupy Belfast on 24 August.

Boer General Louis Botha had positioned his 5,000 men in a defensive line over 80km long, stretching north and south of the railway. The centre of the line lay near Belfast, on the farm Bergendal, which was close to and south of the railway line. Botha expected the British to attack his flanks with cavalry, as they had often done in the past. With this in mind, he had used most of his meagre force to strengthen the ends of the line at the expense of the centre. He had four Long Toms (155mm Creusot guns) each with a range of 10,000m. However, the attack on the centre of his line took him by surprise and most of the guns were too far away to be of any help.

Buller had decided to concentrate his attack on a small hill (Bergendal Koppie) south of the railway line. At dawn on 27 August his artillery moved forward to find its range and by 11h00 shells were falling on the hill at a rate of four or five a minute. The shells included 50-pound lyddite bombs that covered the position in acrid yellow fumes. The hill was held by only 74 members of the Johannesburg Police (Zuid-Afrikaansche Republiek Politie, or ZARP) and, despite the scale of the bombardment the men had to endure for three hours, not one of them left his post. Their commander, Commandant Sarel Oosthuizen, was seriously wounded by shrapnel and their ammunition was running low, but still the men held on.

206 PRETORIA, JOHANNESBURG & SURROUNDING REGIONS

They had with them a Maxim Nordenfeldt gun that was used to good effect against the British infantry, which eventually came forward under cover of the artillery.

When the infantry reached the foot of the hill, the men fixed their bayonets and charged. It was only then that the ZARPs fled, some of them reaching their horses and galloping away to fight again. Only 30 of the initial 74 men remained unharmed. When the Boers holding the rest of the line learned that a hole had been made in their centre, they melted away.

G. M. J. van Dam (centre) was the founder and commanding officer of the ZARPs.

Aftermath

Roberts's plan to catch the Boers in a pincer movement and defeat them decisively had failed. The British suffered 300 casualties between 21 and 27 August, most of them incurred on the last day, when 13 men were killed. The Boers had about 78 men in the same period; of these 14 were killed and 19, including Oosthuizen, were taken prisoner.

The British were able to occupy Waterval Boven, while the Boer government took its railway carriage further east to Nelspruit.

As a result of this defeat the Boers released 2,000 British prisoners from the camp near Barberton. Bergendal represented the last pitched battle of the 2nd Anglo-Boer War; after this, the guerrilla war began in earnest.

Principal combatants

British: Devonshire Regiment; Dragoon Guards; Gordon Highlanders; Inniskilling Fusiliers; King's Royal Rifle Corps; Liverpool Regiment; Manchester Regiment; Mounted infantry; Naval Brigade; Rifle Brigade; Royal Artillery; Royal Engineers; Warwickshire Regiment.

Boers: Commandos from Bethal, Carolina, Germiston, Heidelberg, Johannesburg, Krugersdorp, Lydenburg and Middelburg; German Corps; Johannesburg Police (ZARP); Staatsartillerie.

The distinctive monument at Bergendal marks what the war correspondent F. W. Unger called a 'British victory without glory and a Boer defeat without shame'.

Battle of Bakenlaagte
30 October 1901

HOW TO GET THERE
Situated in Mpumalanga, the battle site lies south of eMalahleni (Witbank) and the Matla power station. From Kinross, on the N17, take the R547 to Ga-Nala (Kriel), then turn left onto the R580. Drive about 1km past the entrance to the farm Onverwacht and look over to the east to see Gun Hill in the middle distance. This is the place to pull off the road and explore on foot, with permission of the landowner.

The 73 British soldiers who were killed in the battle were buried on Gun Hill. Their bodies were later exhumed and reburied in Germiston's Primrose Cemetery. Lieutenant Colonel George Benson's grave is there too.

Stopping place below Gun Hill: *26°19'49.9" S 29°07'10.9" E*
Benson's grave: *26°11'45.20" S 28°8'46.05" E*

Context
During the latter part of the 2nd Anglo-Boer War, Lieutenant Colonel George Benson's Flying Column continuously threatened the Boer commandos with successful night raids, forcing them to move their camps every two days and to saddle up at 03h00 every morning in order to avoid capture. General Sarel Grobler and his commando had been following Benson's trail for some time, harassing his rearguard and waiting for an opportunity to attack. The Boers desperately needed to deal with this column, but it was not until General Louis Botha and his commando joined up with Grobler that an attack was driven home.

Benson, needing to resupply his men and horses, was on his way to Balmoral, a town on the railway line to Lourenço Marques (Maputo). His column of over 300 wagons, 800 horses and 600 infantry stretched out over a distance of more than 2km during the march. The Boers took the opportunity offered by the column's relative isolation to attack its rearguard.

Action
At 05h00 on 30 October Benson's column set out from Syferfontein to march north-west to Bakenlaagte farmstead, where Benson intended to camp. The advance guard reached Bakenlaagte at about 09h00. Camp was set up, but at midday the rearguard was still some distance off, in wet conditions where visibility was poor. One of the rearmost wagons got stuck in mud crossing a drift and had to be abandoned, as Boers were close by and threatening to attack.

Benson, who had ridden back from the camp towards the rear of his column, ordered the placing of two field guns on a stony ridge between the rearguard and the camp. He was on his way to rescue the wagon with two squadrons of Scottish Horse, when Botha with

800 horsemen appeared through the mist. He was on his way back from an unsuccessful invasion of Natal, having completed the last 40km of a 70km ride without a pause in order to join Grobler's attack on the hated British column.

When Benson realised his danger, he ordered a retreat to Gun Hill where he had placed the guns. He had earlier ordered two companies from the camp to Gun Hill in support. Expecting them to arrive at any moment, he then sent some of the rearguard forward to protect the north-east aspect of the camp. This created a gap through which the Boers attacked, using the uneven terrain to approach to within 300m, before charging in on the enemy and shooting at almost point-blank range.

The Boers overran the position and, using the dead ground, advanced on Gun Hill. Out of the 280 British soldiers on the ridge, there were 231 casualties. Benson himself received many wounds, which proved fatal. Before he died, he sent a messenger to the camp with orders for their guns to fire on Gun Hill and clear it of the enemy; this, in spite of the danger to himself and his men. The shelling forced the Boers back, but approaching ambulance wagons provided cover for their further advance. They captured the two guns, despite heroic attempts by the British gunners to protect them, and trained them on the camp at Bakenlaagte. However, Botha did not follow up with an attack on the camp, believing there were women and children with the troops.

Aftermath

The British were defeated, but Botha did not follow up his victory and the British camp was left untouched. The Boers lost nearly 100 men and decided to take what they could from the battlefield and withdraw. British reinforcements reached Bakenlaagte the next morning, but were unable to find the Boers, who retired undisturbed with their spoils.

Principal combatants

British: Lieutenant Colonel Benson's Flying Column; Buffs; Mounted infantry; Royal Engineers; Royal Field Artillery; Scottish Horse.

Boers: Six commandos, including Carolina, Ermelo and Vryheid; Swaziland Police.

Timeline

1900
By June both Johannesburg and Pretoria are occupied by the British. Operations in the Brandwater Basin result in the surrender of more than 4,300 Boers to the British, who destroy nearly 2,000,000 rounds of ammunition. The Boers resort to guerrilla warfare.

1901
Lord Roberts proclaims the annexation of the Transvaal. General Jan Smuts invades the Cape, hoping to garner support for the Boers from burghers living in the colony. Louis Botha invades Natal, attacking the British at Blood River Poort, Fort Itala and Fort Prospect. Later in the year, Botha's commando re-enters the Transvaal and engages the rearguard of Lieutenant Colonel George Benson's Flying Column at the Battle of Bakenlaagte.

1902
The massacre at Holkrans persuades many Boers to capitulate to the British and peace is eventually signed at the end of May.

1910
The Union of South Africa is proclaimed, with Louis Botha elected prime minister.

The British defend Gun Hill against the advance of the Boers.

Battle of Rhenosterkop

Also known as *Battle of Renosterkop*

29 November 1900

HOW TO GET THERE
Take the R25 from Bronkhorstspruit towards Groblersdal and drive about 30km north until you see Rhenosterkop, a prominent hill on your right. The turn-off to the site is approximately 30km from the N4/R25 interchange at Bronkhorstspruit. The British attack came from the north and the battle would have straddled the present-day R25. The ravines, which were where the Boers retired after the battle, are to the east of the hill, and can be accessed via the district road south of the hill past the farms Trichardspoort and Kranspoort.

Context
The British were trying to round up a Boer commando operating north-east of Pretoria. There was desultory skirmishing for a few days until the Boer commander, Ben Viljoen, determined to make a stand in a ridge of small hills dominated by Rhenosterkop.

Action
On 27 November the Boers were warned that a 5,000-strong British column led by Major General Arthur Paget had left Pretoria and was approaching in their direction. Commandant (later General) Ben Viljoen sent out a patrol to assess the strength of the column, while the rest of his men built entrenchments on the ridge. His entrenchments stretched almost 5km between flanks and his Maxim Nordenfeldt, 15-pounder and Krupp guns were distributed along its length. However, the 15-pounder was in ill-repair, there were only 14 shells for the Krupp and overall ammunition supplies were low. In his book *My Reminiscences of the Anglo-Boer War*, Viljoen stated that he had scarcely 500 men under his command, although British reports put the number at 2,000.

The British column engaged and then pursued the Boer patrol, which was made up of men of the

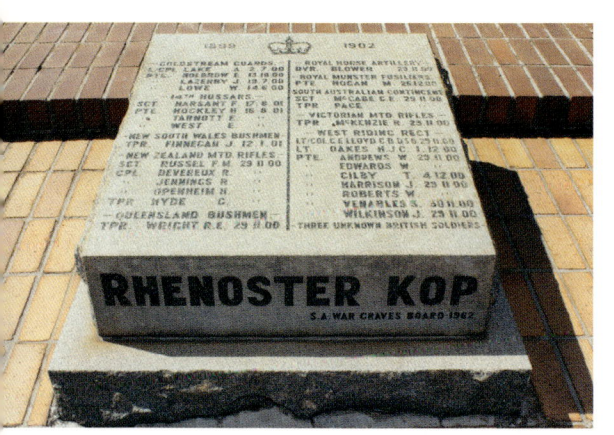

British memorial at Diamond Hill cemetery

210   PRETORIA, JOHANNESBURG & SURROUNDING REGIONS

Boksburg Commando, under Chris Muller, who withdrew to join Viljoen's defensive line along with men of the Johannesburg Commando and the Johannesburg Police.

The next morning began with a British artillery bombardment of the Boer position, which lasted all day. At dawn on 29 November a frontal attack was launched. Paget's first attempt was an infantry charge against the Boer left, which was repelled by shells from the Maxim Nordenfeldt as well as accurate rifle fire, causing heavy losses to the British. The second attempt came against the Boer centre and was also countered by the Boers, who, after two volleys, had forced every approaching soldier to take cover.

The third attempt was also a frontal attack, this time on the Boer right, where Viljoen himself was placed. Once again, the British, and particularly the New Zealanders, incurred heavy losses. Viljoen was puzzled as to why a flanking movement was not attempted. However, Paget's objective was not to take the Boer position, but to defeat the Boers and remove them from the conflict altogether. The British settled down for the night near the crest. The Boers, although victorious, withdrew under cover of darkness. They were short of food and ammunition and their wagons were a long way off.

Aftermath

The British lost heavily, suffering 106 casualties, 15 of whom were killed. The Boers had 22 wounded and two dead. The British who died in the battle are buried in the cemetery at Diamond Hill (see p. 215).

Principal combatants

British: 2nd and 3rd New Zealand contingents; Queen's Lancers; Royal Munster Fusiliers; Victorian Mounted Rifles; Welsh Regiment.
Boers: Commandos from Boksburg, Johannesburg, Middelburg and Pretoria; Johannesburg Police; Theron's Scouts; Theunissen's Scouts.

Colonel George Evan Lloyd

During the Battle of Rhenosterkop the Boers were impressed by a British officer, Colonel Lloyd, whose leg was smashed by a shell but who nonetheless, leaning on his rifle, shouted orders and encouragement to his men. He was eventually killed.
A few months after the event, General Ben Viljoen visited the battlefield and placed a wreath on Lloyd's grave with the inscription, 'In honour of a brave enemy'.

Timeline

1899
Colonel Arthur Paget (below), commanding officer of the Scots Guards fighting between Belmont and Magersfontein, is promoted by Lord Roberts to major general of the 20th Brigade.

1900
Boer general Ben Viljoen is wounded at the Battle of Vaalkrans in February; six months later he returns to the front to fight in a key position at the Battle of Bergendal. In the meantime, both Johannesburg and Pretoria are occupied by the British and President Kruger has moved east from Pretoria on the railway line to Machadodorp.

On 29 November a British column commanded by Paget eventually drives Viljoen's Boers out of their positions on Rhenosterkop. President Kruger leaves on a Dutch ship bound for Europe where he hopes to generate support for the Boer cause.

In December generals Viljoen and Chris Muller capture a British naval 4.7-inch (120mm) gun at Helvetia, 10km north of Machadodorp.

1901
Queen Victoria dies at the age of 81, after having ruled Britain for almost 64 years. Paget relinquishes his command and returns to England where he has a wife and family. He is knighted in 1906.

1902
Ben Viljoen is captured and exiled to St Helena where he writes his reminiscences of the war.

BATTLE OF RHENOSTERKOP   211

Battle of Bronkhorstspruit
20 December 1880

HOW TO GET THERE
Take the R42 from Delmas to Bronkhorstspruit. At the intersection with the R25, near Bronkhorstspruit, turn right and continue north on the R25 for just over 1km to find the monument on your right. There is another monument, set back and not easy to spot, on the opposite side of the road.

Monument next to the road: 25°50'25.7" S 28°44'30.3" E

Context
After the annexation of the Transvaal Republic by Britain in 1877, there was rising discontent among the burghers, who particularly resented Colonel Owen Lanyon, the autocratic British administrator based in Pretoria.

In November 1880, an incident in Potchefstroom involving the Bezuidenhout family and unpaid tax sparked an uprising. When the misdemeanour was punished by the confiscation of a wagon, a mass meeting of Transvaal burghers was held. They gathered at Paardekraal, between 8 and 16 December 1880, where they elected a triumvirate, reinstated the Republic of the Transvaal and arranged the printing of a proclamation to that effect.

Lanyon was initially unperturbed, but Lieutenant Colonel William Bellairs, commander of armed forces in the Transvaal, ordered troops from the outlying garrisons in Marabastad and Lydenburg to march to Pretoria for fear of an armed Boer incursion. There were other British garrisons in Rustenburg, Wakkerstroom and Standerton.

The Boers wanted to prevent the concentration of British troops in Pretoria and sent one commando, under Frans Joubert, towards Middelburg and another towards Standerton to oppose the approaching British columns. It was the commando led by Frans Joubert that came up against the British column marching to Pretoria from Lydenburg.

Action
The departure from Lydenburg of the British column, under the command of Lieutenant Colonel Philip Anstruther, was delayed due to difficulties with the procurement of transport wagons. Anstruther wanted more wagons than regulations allowed his

Frans Joubert

small force of 247 men and this infringement slowed the procurement process. Eventually, a full nine days after receiving the order, the column departed for Pretoria with a long train of 34 wagons that included three women and three children who were related to men in the troops. Progress was slow, especially as heavy rains made the roads soft and time was wasted hauling wagons out of deep mud.

Meanwhile, Bellairs was informed that Boer commandos were riding from their camps to oppose the advancing British columns. He sent a message to Anstruther, delivered to him at Middelburg on 17 December, warning him that armed Boers were heading for Potchefstroom and instructing him to scout thoroughly the route ahead of his column. He also advised that the wagons should be laagered at night. It seems that Anstruther proceeded with no urgency. The 40-strong band played as they marched and only two scouts went ahead, but at no great distance, with another two scouts following behind the 2km-long column.

At mid-morning on 20 December the men were about 1.5km from Bronkhorstspruit, where they intended to camp that night, when Boers were sighted on a low ridge 500m away, left of the road. The band had been playing, the men were carrying only half the regulatory ammunition and many had left their heavy rifles on the wagons for ease of marching. Anstruther was riding with conductor Egerton; they were about 400m behind the front scout and 50m ahead of the band. The band was followed by half a company of red-coated soldiers of the 94th Regiment and the Colour party. Behind them were more soldiers ahead of the wagons, which were strung out along the road with a thin line of armed troops marching next to them. A rearguard of about 20 men followed 200m to 300m behind the wagons.

Home-made Boer cannons were used in the 1st Anglo-Boer War.

Timeline

1852
The Sand River Convention grants the Transvaal its independence.

1877
The Transvaal is annexed to Great Britain. The threat of hostile tribes on its borders is one of the reasons for the annexation, but many Boers are opposed to it.

1879
The Battle of Isandlwana, a crushing defeat for the British in Zululand, persuades some Boers in the Transvaal that they, too, can defeat the British. The end of the Anglo-Zulu War in July destroys the power of the Zulu nation and the threat it posed to the farmers on its borders.

1880
Rising dissatisfaction with British governance in the Transvaal culminates in a Boer proclamation, restoring the republic. British troops are sent from various towns in the Transvaal to quell a possible uprising in Pretoria, the capital. One of these columns is confronted by Boers at Bronkhorstspruit, where a bloody battle ensues.

1881
Troops sent from Natal to counter the Transvaal rebellion are defeated at Laing's Nek, Ingogo and Majuba. A peace favourable to the Boers is signed on 23 March and the Transvaal regains its independence.

1886
Large gold deposits are discovered on the Witwatersrand. Foreigners flock to the Transvaal.

1896
The Jameson Raid persuades President Paul Kruger that the British want his land. He resolves to fight.

1899
The 2nd Anglo-Boer War breaks out.

The band stopped playing as the men halted and watched the Boers, almost 150 strong, on the ridge. A man with a white flag came forward with a message from the commandant. Egerton received it and passed it on to Anstruther. It said that a proclamation had been issued reinstating the Transvaal Republic and that, until the Transvalers had received a response from Owen Lanyon, they did not know whether a state of war existed or not. Under these circumstances, they demanded that Anstruther and his men advance no further towards Pretoria. Anstruther replied that his orders were to proceed to the capital and that he would do so.

This monument marks the Battle of Bronkhorstspruit.

The dispatch was delivered as Anstruther gave orders for the wagons to close up and the men to deploy in skirmishing order. There was a scramble for rifles and ammunition, but, before the men could spread out, a hail of lead hit them from Boer rifles. The Boers had increased in number to over 200 and had come to within 200m of the men and their wagons.

Within a few minutes all the British officers were dead or wounded. Anyone approaching the ammunition wagons was killed and Anstruther was hit six times in the legs. Oxen were shot and band boys lay in pools of blood as the Boers closed in. Anstruther surrendered, perhaps with the thought that someone had better remain alive to tell the tale.

The Boers ceased firing when the flag of truce was shown and came in to take those who were not wounded as prisoners. Conductor Egerton was allowed to ride to Pretoria to get medical help and a camp was set up for the wounded. Anstruther would die nearly a week later, following the amputation of one of his legs.

Aftermath

The British casualty rate was astounding – more than half the column was either dead or wounded in the space of about 15 minutes. Even though the Boers were solicitous of the wounded, especially when they found a woman among them, the action was described as a massacre, as it is said that Anstruther and his men had not had time to respond to the message before the Boers opened fire. However, the British did return the fire and Anstruther had certainly been forewarned that his passage would likely be opposed. The British casualties numbered 157, with 77 of these dead. The Boers had one killed and one wounded.

The engagement shocked Lanyon into the realisation that the Boers meant to fight for their independence. The troops that were on their way to the Transvaal from Natal were instructed to make haste, but were opposed between 28 January and 27 February 1881 in the passes through the Drakensberg. These setbacks culminated in the British defeat at Majuba (see p. 189). Peace was signed on 23 March and the Transvaal regained its independence.

Principal combatants
British: 94th Regiment; Army Hospital Corps; Army Service Corps.
Boers: Led by Commandant Frans Joubert.

Battle of Diamond Hill

Also known as *Battle of Donkerhoek*

11–12 June 1900

HOW TO GET THERE

The battle was fought along a ridge that dominates the road and the railway line about 30km east of Pretoria on the way to Middelburg. Drive east on the N4 from Pretoria, then take the exit to Cullinan (R483 and R515). Turn right and travel south on this road until you see a sign on the right to Galagos Estate. Follow this road to the boom gate and ask for directions to the cemetery and monuments.

Alternatively, continue south on the tarred road past Galagos Estate until you see a sign to Donkerhoek. The war graves are on your right a little further on. Note that the gate to the cemetery may be locked. There is a memorial to the Boers who fell in this battle at the top of the ridge above the cemetery and there are remains of Boer entrenchments in the surrounding hills.

Cemetery: 25°48'22.3" S 28°29'23.7" E
Entrance gate: 25°48'02.2" S 28°29'41.9" E

Context

When Lord Roberts's huge army occupied Pretoria, the capital of the Transvaal, the British expected the Boers to surrender, but this did not happen. The Boers moved their capital to Machadodorp and Kruger steamed east on the railway to the new seat of government.

The Orange Free State Boers under President Steyn and led by General Christiaan de Wet were determined to fight to the bitter end. This revitalised the Transvaal commandos, especially those led by General Louis Botha. To prevent the British army from moving east along the railway towards Machadodorp, Botha established a strong line of defence along the ridge on both sides of the railway line some 30km east of Pretoria. He cleverly positioned about 3,500 men in the hills and trained his long-range artillery pieces on the areas where he imagined the British would attempt to pass through the high ground.

The British, with nearly 5,000 mounted men and over 8,000 infantry, equipped with about 70 guns, advanced against the Boers on 11 June 1900. Their declared aim was not to pursue the president, but to clear the Boers from the areas close to Pretoria.

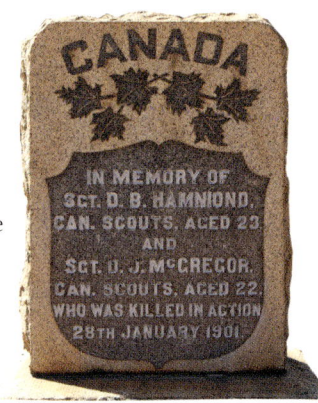

A memorial at Diamond Hill for two Canadian scouts

Timeline

1897
Louis Botha, born in Greytown, Natal, is elected to the Transvaal Volksraad.

1899
War breaks out between the Boer republics and Britain. Botha is elected commandant of the Vryheid Commando and then becomes assistant commandant general under Lucas Meyer.

1900
In February Ladysmith and Kimberley are relieved.

In March Botha is appointed commandant general of the Boer forces.

In June, when Pretoria is occupied, President Paul Kruger leaves the city for Machadodorp. General Christiaan de Wet scores a dramatic victory at Rooiwal in the Orange Free State and Botha commands a Boer force during the Battle at Diamond Hill east of Pretoria.

In July De Wet narrowly escapes capture in the Brandwater Basin. Over 4,300 Boers surrender to the British.

The Transvaal is annexed in September, and President Kruger leaves for Europe from Lourenço Marques.

1902
Botha is one of the signatories of the peace treaty that brings the 2nd Anglo-Boer War to an end.

1907
Botha is elected president of the Transvaal.

1910
Botha becomes the first premier of the Union of South Africa.

Action

Botha had concentrated his greatest firepower on both ends of his defensive line, assuming the British would attempt to outflank his force by simultaneously attacking the areas north and south of the railway line. His guess proved correct when, on 11 June, British cavalry brigades attacked both ends of the Boer line, with the infantry, supported by artillery, advancing towards the centre of the position.

In the north, Boer general Koos de la Rey was able to prevent General John French's 1,400 horsemen from making further progress. British cavalry, trying unsuccessfully to outflank the Boers in the south, resorted to an expensive charge led by the 12th Lancers that resulted in 19 casualties. Meanwhile, General Hamilton was attempting to push forward with his infantry brigade in the centre, under Diamond Hill. By nightfall on 11 June he found part of his force almost surrounded.

On 12 June the British mounted a strong attack against Boers on the western slopes of Diamond Hill. The Boers eventually fled, but only to take up positions on surrounding hills from where they could enfilade the British lines.

An advance by the New South Wales Mounted Rifles later in the day gave the British a position on the ridge near the centre and it was this success that led Botha to withdraw his men under cover of darkness

Protective stone shelters used by the Boers during the Battle of Diamond Hill

This Boer monument overlooks the British cemetery at Donkerhoek (Diamond Hill) near Cullinan.

that night. He realised that his line would be impossible to hold once the British had placed artillery in their newly won position and, not wishing to lose valuable fighting men, decided to leave the field to fight another day. The Boers left with a sense of victory, believing they had succeeded in their objective.

Aftermath

The British suffered about 180 casualties while the Boers lost 30 men, of whom 11 were killed. The battle gave the Boers a valuable boost to their morale and made them more determined not to accept peace terms, but to continue to fight. The war was to carry on for nearly two more years.

Principal combatants

British: 10th and 14th Hussars; 12th Lancers; Australian Horse; Coldstream Guards; Derbyshire Regiment; Dragoon Guards; Gordon Highlanders; Grenadier Guards; Horse Guards; Household Cavalry; Inniskilling Dragoons; Life Guards; Lincolnshire Regiment; Mounted infantry; New South Wales Mounted Rifles; Queen's Own (Cameron Highlanders); Royal Artillery; Royal Engineers; Royal Sussex Regiment; Royal Warwickshire Regiment; Scots Guards; Tasmanian Contingents; Welsh Regiment; Western Australian Mounted Infantry; Yorkshire Regiment.

Boers: Commandos from Bethal, Carolina, Ermelo, Heidelberg, Johannesburg, Krugersdorp, Lichtenburg, Lydenburg, Marico, Middelburg, Potchefstroom and Rustenburg; German Corps; Staatsartillerie.

Paul Kruger

Paul Kruger was born in 1825 to a farming family near Colesberg. His mother died when he was only six years old and his father remarried a year later.

The boy Paul matured early. He was strong and agile, and excelled at sports. He is said to have vaulted over the oxen to get to the other side of a wagon train, and he shot and killed his first lion at the age of 14 years. No runner could surpass him and there are stories about how he once challenged some Zulu men to a cross-country race. Apparently Kruger outpaced them to such an extent that he was able to call in on a friend for coffee on the way to the finish. In general, though, the tales of his prowess are so amazing that truth is difficult to separate from fiction.

In 1835 stock theft and poverty forced the family to move north of the Orange River, an area that was mostly uninhabited and where there were vast herds of game. When Kruger was almost 11 years old, he fought in the Battle of Vegkop (see p. 231). Kruger is also reputed to have visited Gert Maritz and the Voortrekkers in Natal in 1838 and to have been in the Retief laager when the Zulu impi attacked.

By the time he was 16 years old, Kruger had married his first wife and taken possession of his first farm (he would later own several) in the Pilanesberg, where he grew citrus. His wife died in childbirth in 1845, and in 1847 he married her first cousin. Together they had 16 children.

President Paul Kruger

This monument at Vegkop depicts a man, gun pointing downwards and spears broken, entreating for a peaceful future.

Kruger fought against the British in the Battle of Boomplaats in 1848 and was present in 1852 at the Sand River Convention, which gave the Transvaal its independence. He accompanied and fought in various raids against indigenous groups and met, and is said to have liked, Moshoeshoe of Basutoland. He also tried to broker peace between Moshoeshoe and the leaders of the Orange Free State.

At the age of 32 he had a deep spiritual experience and became a strict Dopper, or member of the Gereformeerde (Reformed) church, believing implicitly in the Bible, which is said to have been the only book he had ever read. He disapproved of dancing, drinking or frivolity of any kind. He did, however, enjoy a practical joke and often made amusing comments.

President Paul Kruger and his second wife Gezina

Kruger proved himself a hero during the affair in Makapan's cave, when he crept under cover of darkness into a cave to confer with fugitives of the Ndebele under Chief Makapan. His growing reputation as a leader and his stubborn bravery and strength had already earned him enormous respect by the time he was elected commandant general of the Rustenburg area. From then on he divided his time between war and state affairs, as there was constant squabbling among the Boer leaders. When diamonds were discovered and land claims disputed, Kruger served on various commissions.

In early 1877, Thomas Burgers, President of the Transvaal, forced Kruger to resign as commandant general. Kruger was a thorn in his side and the Boer leader, in turn, disliked Burgers for his lack of both religious zeal and fighting skill. Many burghers supported Kruger and he was eventually voted vice president of the republic. Following British annexation of the Transvaal in April 1877, Kruger led delegations overseas in protest. His reputation as a skilled statesman grew and, in 1883, he was elected president of the new independent Transvaal Republic established in the wake of the 1st Anglo-Boer War.

The discovery of gold under the Witwatersrand led to an influx of miners and fortune seekers, mostly of British descent, that threatened to engulf the Transvaal. If Kruger had granted them franchise, their sheer numbers might have seen him voted out of power. Small wonder, therefore, that he was determined to protect the hard-won independence of the republic and his people, a position he held throughout his political career and which, no doubt, contributed to the outbreak of the 2nd Anglo-Boer War.

Battle of Doornkop

Also known as *Battle of Johannesburg, Battle of Crows' Nest Hill, Battle of Klipriviersberg* and *Battle of Doringkop*

29 May 1900

HOW TO GET THERE
The ridge of low hills where the battle took place lies in Soweto, about 10km south-west of Roodepoort. Take the R41 from Randfontein towards Roodepoort and drive for about 11km until you reach the intersection with the R588 (Adcock Street). Turn right here to reach the centre of the ridge where the battle was fought.

Context
The British were advancing on Johannesburg, and the Boers took up their last defensive position on the Klipriviersberg, a ridge of low hills running parallel to the Klip River, about 4km further east. Doornkop was the high ground in the centre of the position, immediately left of the road leading into Johannesburg. Once the British had crossed the Klip River, the Boers opposed their further advance from extended positions along the Klipriviersberg ridge.

Action
This engagement was part of a three-day battle beginning on Sunday 27 May 1900, when General John French's cavalry brigade, in the vanguard of the approaching British army, was forced back across the Klip River by the Boers.

General John French

Led by General Koos de la Rey, the Boers were in positions stretching for more than 3km west of the road leading to Johannesburg. They were supported by three guns and a Maxim Nordenfeldt, but did not pursue the fleeing British column. Major Erasmus of the Staatsartillerie had prepared, over the previous five days, an extended line of fortified positions on the Klipriviersberg ridge and it was into these positions that De la Rey and his men settled. That night the Staatsartillerie placed a further seven artillery pieces in carefully chosen positions on the ridge.

The next day, 28 May, General French sent cavalry forward, but the men were repulsed by the Boer guns and forced to retire south of the Klip River, leaving the Boers to hold the Klipriviersberg ridge that night. There were few of them, though, as many had deserted. In the meantime, the British infantry, commanded by Colonel Ian Hamilton, had arrived at the Klip River. His men were on half rations because the baggage train had been delayed.

On the morning of 29 May, some of the British cavalry moved around to the west of the Boer right flank and attacked the ridge. The soldiers were unable to dislodge the Boer guns, and it fell to the infantry to launch a frontal attack. The Gordon Highlanders led the infantry assault in the centre, calmly marching forward, under continuous fire, in two long, straight lines. They were driven back from the main Boer position twice, but succeeded on their third attempt – although they suffered over 100 casualties.

On their right, the Royal Canadian Regiment and the City Imperial Volunteers made clever use of the ground, advancing in short dashes up the long slope. They had to contend with flames and smoke as exploding shells had set the grass on fire. They lost fewer men than the Gordons and by dusk the ridge had been taken.

Meanwhile, French's cavalry had successfully outflanked the Boers to the west, where General Sarel Oosthuizen's commando was forced to withdraw. The road to Johannesburg was open.

London (City) Imperial Volunteers proved to be good soldiers.

Timeline

1899
In October war breaks out in South Africa. Boers invade the British colonies of Natal and the Cape. Kimberley and Mafeking are besieged, followed by Ladysmith in November.

1900
In January the Battle of Spioenkop is fought in Natal but the British fail to reach Ladysmith.

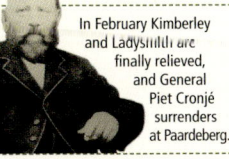

In February Kimberley and Ladysmith are finally relieved, and General Piet Cronjé surrenders at Paardeberg.

In March the British occupy Bloemfontein. A Boer deputation leaves for Europe in an attempt to gain foreign support.

In April Mafeking is still under siege, but a month later it is relieved.

On 26 May British forces cross the Vaal River south of Johannesburg and on 29 May they break through the Boer line on Klipriviersberg (Doornkop) to occupy the city. The overseas Boer delegation receives a hero's welcome in America but little concrete support for its cause.

In June Pretoria falls to the British and Kruger leaves for Machadodorp, the new seat of the Boer government.

1901
Peace negotiations between General Louis Botha and Lord Kitchener in Middelburg fail, largely due to Lord Milner's influence. The war continues for another year.

BATTLE OF DOORNKOP 221

The smartly uniformed Staatsartillerie, equipped and trained in Germany, played an important role in the Battle of Doornkop.

Aftermath

The British suffered about 250 casualties, with 47 men killed. The number of Boer casualties is uncertain. Commandant Frederick Krause rode south out of Johannesburg to meet the leaders of the British force and persuaded them to delay occupation for 24 hours to prevent the possibility of street fighting. The city was peacefully taken on 30 May.

Principal combatants

British: Cameron Highlanders; Canadian Mounted Rifles; Cheshire Regiment; City Imperial Volunteers; Coldstream Guards; Derbyshire Regiment; Dragoon Guards; Duke of Cornwall Regiment; Gordon Highlanders; King's Shropshire Light Infantry; Mounted infantry; Royal Artillery; Royal Canadian Dragoons; Royal Canadian Regiment of Infantry; Royal Horse Guards; Royal Sussex Regiment.
Boers: Commandos from Heidelberg, Johannesburg; Rustenburg and Waterberg; Staatsartillerie.

The origin of Brits

Johannes Nicolaas Brits, the first white man to settle in Bloemfontein, sold his farm there to the British in 1846. It was to become the home of the British Resident, Major Henry Warden. Johannes Brits then moved north to the Transvaal to lay out a farm called Roodekopje, 48km west of Pretoria. When the railway line was constructed between Pretoria and Rustenburg in 1906, a station built on the farm was named Brits after the first owner. Over time, a small, prosperous town developed here.

Battle of Roodewal

Also known as *Battle of Rooiwal*

11 April 1902

HOW TO GET THERE

From Ottosdal, travel west along Voortrekker Street (R507) towards Delareyville. About 30km from Ottosdal, there is a turning to the right to Sannieshof. Continue for another 6km past this turning, then veer left at the sign to Migdol. Drive for about 2.4km, then turn left again where the sign indicates 'Migdol and Glaudina'. Cross the Brakspruit, then continue for another 2km. Turn left at the T-junction (there is a farmhouse on your left). Continue for 700m, before turning left onto a track that leads to the Boer graves 800m further along, on your left. ***Guide recommended***

Turn-off (36km) from Ottosdal: *26°48'2.72" S 25°38'44.47" E*
Graves: *26°50'1.68" S 25°39'17.42" E*

Context

Lord Kitchener was trying to trap Boer general Koos de la Rey's commandos in the western Transvaal by sweeping thousands of British mounted infantry and cavalry in long lines across the countryside, with the aim of driving the commandos up against the blockhouse lines (see p. 225).

In March 1902 De la Rey's commandos in the western Transvaal had their main camp on a farm called Roodewal (Rooiwal). De la Rey and President Steyn had already left the camp to attend peace talks in Klerksdorp when two British mounted columns approached. This battle resulted when the Boers attempted to break through the British line to escape capture.

Context

General Horatio Kitchener had organised over 16,000 mounted men into four columns, stretched out in a line more than 40km long. They were advancing south, under the overall direction of General Ian Hamilton. The columns were south of Delareyville when a miscommunication led to a change in the direction of one column, which inadvertently resulted in two columns converging in the vicinity of the farm Roodewal.

General Horatio Kitchener

Timeline

1902

In January Commandant Gideon Scheepers is shot by a British firing squad despite objections that he should have been treated as a prisoner of war. Skirmishes continue in the Transvaal. General Ben Viljoen is captured near Lydenburg amid suspicions that he was betrayed.

In February a report drawn up by the Ladies' Commission (Fawcet Commission), highlighting the shocking conditions in the concentration camps, is published in London.

In March General Lord Methuen is wounded and captured by General Koos de La Rey's commando at Tweebosch.

In April Boer leaders travel to Klerksdorp to take part in peace negotiations. In their absence, the Battle of Roodewal is won by the British on 11 April. Also in April, General Jan Smuts lays siege to the copper-mining town of Okiep in Namaqualand.

In May, 56 Boers are killed by members of the abaQulusi in Natal. Peace is proclaimed with the Treaty of Vereeniging, ending the 2nd Anglo-Boer War.

De la Rey had left General Jan Kemp in command of about 2,600 men. Kemp realised that his force was in danger of an attack by an overwhelming number of British horsemen, and he decided to attempt to break through their line at a point where his scouts had reported a gap. The change of plan by the British had, on the contrary, made this section of the line particularly strong.

Early on the morning of 11 April a British advance party of about 40 mounted infantry was confronted by hundreds of Boer horsemen galloping uphill towards them. Not certain if they were their own men, the British held their fire until the Boers were within rifle range. The Boers, led by Commandant Ferdinand Potgieter, were shooting from the backs of their horses. They were met with answering fire, but the British mounted infantry shot very wide and the Boers continued to charge, causing the British advance party to flee in some disarray.

However, a little further north were another 3,000 British mounted infantry, dismounted, with field guns and a Maxim gun. The terrain forced the Boer horsemen to bunch together as they continued their wild charge, and the enemy guns tore through them, wounding and killing many. When Potgieter fell at about 08h00, only 60m from the British line, the rest of the Boers fled. British General Robert Kekewich was slow to order a pursuit and those Boers who were not killed or wounded managed to get away.

General Jan Kemp

Aftermath

This brave attempt by the Boer cavalry charge against overwhelming numbers was admired by the British. The Boers lost Potgieter, who fell with three bullet wounds in his body, as well as 50 others who were killed. They also lost 10 field guns and a Maxim Nordenfeldt. British losses were 12 men killed and 75 wounded. In addition, the British lost 300 horses, killed in the initial action and during the pursuit. Scarcely a month later peace was proclaimed and the war was over, making this loss of life even sadder.

Principal combatants

British: 3rd, 7th, 13th, 14th, 19th and 20th Hussars; Dragoon Guards; Leinster Regiment; Mounted infantry; Royal Horse Artillery.
Boers: Commandos from Krugersdorp, Pretoria West and Rustenburg; Members of Transvaal commandos under General Jan Kemp.

Blockhouses

By October 1900, the British thought the war was won. Lord Roberts sailed home believing all that was left to do in South Africa was some 'mopping up'. But, despite major towns being occupied by the British, the Boers continued to fight. Roving bands of horsemen attacked British convoys at will, while those skilled in explosives (many of them Irishmen) blew up bridges, railway lines and stations. To defend these strategic places, stone blockhouses of various designs were constructed by the British. However, there were not enough of them and Boers still managed to sabotage vital links in the British lines of communication.

Lord Kitchener, who had been left in South Africa to bring the war to a conclusion, realised that it would be necessary to do more than defend a few places along the railway line. He launched his notorious scorched-earth tactic, which involved burning farms that supplied the Boer guerrilla bands and rounding up Boer commandos by driving them into British-manned lines of interconnected blockhouses.

The latter necessitated the building of so many blockhouses that a design for a corrugated-iron construction was adopted. These structures were quicker and cheaper to erect than stone and masonry ones. The design was drawn up by the Royal Engineers and manufactured in kit form in a factory in Middelburg. The kits were delivered by rail to the station nearest to their ultimate destination and then transported by ox-wagon.

Royal Engineer records indicate that 7,447 corrugated-iron blockhouses and 441 stone or brick blockhouses were built during the latter stages of the war. Each was surrounded by a sentry trench and barbed-wire entanglements. They were linked by fences, equipped with searchlights and manned by armed soldiers, some of them black men.

Today, the legacy of the blockhouses remains. Several stone blockhouses have survived to be used for other purposes, including serving as barns on private farm land. On the other hand, few corrugated-iron blockhouses have lasted. A replica of one can be seen close to the bridge near the Modder River battlefield site.

TOP: Stone blockhouse at Aliwal North
LEFT: Replica corrugated-iron blockhouse near the Modder River battle site

Battle of Doornkraal

Also known as *Battle of Bothaville*

6 November 1900

HOW TO GET THERE

Take the R30 south out of Bothaville in the Free State. Drive for 1.5km, going across the Vals River to the intersection with the R59. Turn right here onto the R59, heading in a southerly direction. Continue for 7km, until you reach a road going off to the left. At this intersection there is a memorial commemorating the Battle of Doornkraal. Turn left into the road; the Boer mass graves are about 100m along on the left-hand side. There is also a war memorial in the gardens of the Dutch Reformed Church in Bothaville itself.

Mass graves: 27°27'30.78" S 26°34'41.73" E

Context

General Christiaan de Wet knew there were burghers in the Cape who sympathised with the Boers. He wished to go there and encourage them to join their cause. President Steyn, who also wished to meet with the Cape burghers, went with him.

They were on their way south with 800 men and had reached the town of Bothaville when they encountered a strong British force. There was a skirmish on 5 November resulting in a British withdrawal out of range of the Boers' Krupp guns. De Wet made camp that night under a hill south of the town and the river, believing the position to be safe. They were surprised early the following morning by an advance guard of 600 British mounted infantry.

Action

De Wet's camp was about 10km south of Bothaville, while the British camp was north of the river and at least 11km away. The Boer outposts were placed close to the river and were told to keep watch on the British camp and to report any movement. Unfortunately for De Wet and his men, the sentries fell asleep. Waking shortly before dawn, they saw smoke rising from the British camp and a corporal reported to De Wet that all was well. However, the mounted infantry of 600 men commanded by Colonel Philip le Gallais had moved forward before dawn to a small hill only 300m from the Boer camp. While the Boers were still waking up, the British opened fire.

There was panic in the Boer camp. President Steyn escaped safely because his adjutant always kept a horse saddled and ready to go. Only about 150 Boers stayed to fight, the rest scrambled onto their horses bareback and galloped away. De Wet attempted in vain to rally them, but, each time he succeeded in stopping one group of burghers, another would gallop

President Steyn (seated), with members of the Orange Free State commandos

past him and, when he followed that group, the first would follow. Eventually nearly the whole commando was out of range of the firing.

The Boers who stayed to fight took shelter in some farmhouses, while the British found other farm dwellings where they did the same. For nearly four hours field guns and rifles exchanged lethal fire at almost point-blank range. Eventually General Charles Knox arrived with the rest of the British column and one of the mounted infantry officers led a bayonet charge. The Boers surrendered, giving up four Krupp guns, two field guns that they had previously captured from the British, and one Maxim Nordenfeldt. There was no pursuit of the Boers who had fled as the British were too busy looting the camp and loading its spoils.

Aftermath

The British lost about 38 men who were either killed or wounded. Le Gallais died of his wounds that night. The Boers lost valuable weaponry (although De Wet said that they had no ammunition for the Krupp guns at that stage). Nine Boers were killed (some reports say 25), about 30 wounded and 100 taken prisoner. However, De Wet was soon at work again – only weeks later he attacked the British once more.

Principal combatants

British: Durham Light Infantry; Members of the Buffs; Mounted infantry; Royal Horse Artillery.
Boers: Commandos from Bothaville, Heilbron and Vrede; Orange Free Staters under General Christiaan de Wet.

Timeline

1882
Marthinus Theunis Steyn, educated at Grey College in Bloemfontein and trained as an advocate at Leiden University and the Inner Temple in London, begins to practise law in Bloemfontein.

1889
Steyn is appointed state attorney.

1896
Steyn is elected president of the Orange Free State.

1898
Steyn arranges a meeting between President Kruger and Lord Milner to try to avert war with Britain.

1899
War breaks out, and Steyn agrees to support the Transvaal. He is young enough (42) to participate in the fighting and joins the burghers in the field.

1900
Bloemfontein is abandoned and Steyn accompanies General Christiaan de Wet's (right) commando. Steyn narrowly avoids capture when De Wet's commando is surprised at Doornkraal.

1901
Steyn participates in De Wet's invasion of the Cape. He then protests against the Transvaal government for considering a ceasefire without consulting the Orange Free State government. Steyn is determined to fight to the bitter end.

1902
Steyn becomes ill and is forced to resign. De Wet signs the peace treaty as acting president of the Orange Free State. Steyn travels to Europe with his wife to seek a cure for creeping paralysis. Steyn and his wife return to South Africa and work at rebuilding the Boer nation.

1914
Steyn tries to prevent hostilities during the 1914 Boer Rebellion against the Union government.

1916
Steyn collapses and dies while addressing a women's meeting in Bloemfontein.

Battle of Rooiwal

Previously known as *Battle of Roodewal*
(Changed in 1929)

7 June 1900

HOW TO GET THERE
The Rooiwal battle site lies south-west of Koppies in the Free State, close to the Bloemfontein–Vereeniging railway line. From Sasolburg, drive south on the R57 to the intersection with the R82. Turn right onto the R82 and drive to Koppies. Rooiwal is about 9km south-west of Koppies.

Context

Bloemfontein, the capital of the Orange Free State, was occupied by the British in March 1900. Two months later, at the end of May, the Orange Free State was declared a British colony. Lord Roberts and his vast army then advanced north to Johannesburg and on to Pretoria, with both towns falling to the British. The Transvaal burghers all but gave up when President Kruger retreated to Machadodorp, the new capital of the Transvaal, but a pocket of Boer resistance, in the north-eastern Orange Free State, remained. Here, a force of about 8,000 burghers, under the command of General Christiaan de Wet, was determined to restore Boer morale by scoring some decisive victories against the British columns operating in the Orange Free State.

General Christiaan de Wet

Action

As the Boer commandos left Johannesburg, they blew up the railway lines to the coast behind them. By the beginning of June the British had repaired them only as far south as Vredefort. Supplies and ammunition destined for the British army – by this time numbering about 100,000 men – had accumulated 35km south of Vredefort at Rooiwal station garrison, waiting for the line to be reopened.

With this rich prize in mind, De Wet planned three simultaneous attacks at different points along the railway line. He sent one commando to engage the British guarding Vredefort station, about 35km north of Rooiwal, and another to the Renoster River Bridge post, 5km from Rooiwal. As the bridge was heavily guarded, De Wet sent 300 men with two Krupp guns and a Maxim Nordenfeldt gun. He led the attack on Rooiwal himself, and was accompanied by only 80 men and one Krupp gun. He had expected to come up against

This Distinguished Conduct medal (for non-commissioned personnel) was awarded to a company sergeant major of the Railways Pioneers.

about 100 men defending the supply depot, but there were more than 170 men holding the post under the command of Captain A. G. W. Grant, many of them members of the newly founded Railway Pioneers.

De Wet led his force by night to within 800m of the station. At dawn he sent a burgher forward under a flag of truce to say that the station was surrounded by 1,000 men with four guns and that the British should therefore surrender. Grant replied that he had no intention of doing so.

De Wet's men lay flat on the open ground and opened fire on the station. Grant's men, entrenched east of the railway line, returned the fire. De Wet's Krupp was in an exposed position; fearing it would be hit, he ordered his men to withdraw it to a position 3,000m away and then to open fire. Meanwhile, the garrison at Renoster River Bridge had surrendered without firing a shot. As soon as he heard this news, De Wet ordered the two Krupp guns supporting that commando to be sent to Rooiwal, where they soon arrived and were duly put into action.

The British had no artillery and could not withstand the long-range shells from three artillery pieces, which soon rent holes in their entrenchments. Grant was forced to surrender, leaving enormous amounts of booty for the victorious Boers.

The Boers, and especially the Irish pro-Boers, were skilled in the use of explosives and blew up bridges to destroy British lines of communication wherever they could.

Timeline

1854–1873
Christiaan de Wet is born on a farm in the south-eastern Orange Free State, a recently proclaimed independent Boer republic. In the 1870s he works as a transport rider to the Kimberley diamond fields. He marries in 1873, when he is 19.

1881
Having moved to the Heidelberg district in the Transvaal with his family, De Wet joins protests against the British annexation of the Transvaal and fights the British at Laing's Nek, Ingogo and Majuba.

1885
De Wet becomes a Volksraad member of the Lydenburg area, his domicile after the Transvaal regains its independence. After attending only one session, he moves back to the Orange Free State.

1887
De Wet supports President Steyn in the presidential elections in the Orange Free State.

1889
De Wet is elected a member of the Orange Free State Volksraad.

1899
De Wet sends his son to buy him a mount for the approaching war. The white horse, Fleur, becomes De Wet's inseparable companion. He joins the Heilbron Commando and is sent to Natal with three of his sons. He excels at the Battle of Nicholson's Nek and is appointed fighting general on the western border of the Orange Free State.

1900
In March Bloemfontein is occupied by the British and De Wet achieves an overwhelming success at Sannaspos. In May he defeats a British force at Reddersburg. On 7 June, shortly after the British occupy Pretoria, De Wet scores a welcome victory at Rooiwal. A month later he escapes the Brandwater Basin, following the Battle of Surrender Hill, which sees General Marthinus Prinsloo surrendering to the British.

1901
In February De Wet invades the Cape, but is forced back into the Orange Free State. He scores a brilliant success at Groenkop on Christmas day.

1902
The Peace of Vereeniging is signed.

BATTLE OF ROOIWAL 229

British troops in Church Square, Pretoria, on the annexation of the Transvaal in September 1900

Aftermath

Seven British soldiers were killed and 23 wounded, and about 140 prisoners were taken. Boer losses were only two burghers wounded.

The spoils of the battle were considerable. The Boers gained a significant amount of ammunition of varying calibres, which would prove to be immensely valuable. There were also large numbers of British army winter uniforms and plentiful food supplies of every description. The champagne and cigar cases were broken open and the men enjoyed whatever they could before De Wet forced them to move on. When they had all they could carry, quantities of ammunition were blown up and the rest of the food and supplies burnt. The railway line to the north was broken up as they left – over a distance of more than 12km.

Just as important was the morale boost this victory gave the Boers – especially the Transvaal commandos – who were at a low ebb. This action gave them the will to continue the war against the British and to fight with renewed vigour.

The secret stash

Some of the Lee-Metford ammunition the Boers took at Rooiwal was hidden in a cave near Harrismith and used in the later stages of the war, when nearly all the Boers were armed with British rifles.

Principal combatants

British: Railway Pioneer Regiment.
Boers: Orange Free State Boers.

Battle of Vegkop

Also known as *Battle of Vechtkop*

15 October 1836
(Some reports say 2 October, 19 October or 20 October)

HOW TO GET THERE
The Vegkop battlefield site lies south of Heilbron in the Free State. Take the R34 between Frankfort and Heilbron. Just before Heilbron, cross the road to Petrus Steyn and continue until you see a sign to Vegkop on your left. Turn in here and drive for 20km until you see signs to the battlefield on your left.

Entrance gate: 27°28'09.7" S 27°54'24.3" E
Memorial: 27°28'42.4" S 27°54'46.3" E

Context
The Ndebele had successfully raided parties of Voortrekkers north of the Vaal River in August 1836. The acquisition of livestock was the main reason for the attacks and the Ndebele were able to take off with such large numbers of animals that they were tempted to raid the Voortrekker camps south of the river too. Voortrekker leader Hendrik Potgieter prepared a strong defensive position at Vegkop and successfully fought off the attack when it came.

Action
Hendrik Potgieter, an active if taciturn man, had taken a small party over the Vaal River in August 1836 to explore the country further north. Meanwhile, the Ndebele people had come across a hunting party north of the Vaal River and killed many of them, taking their oxen and livestock. A further attack north of the river on the Liebenberg family left 13 dead.

When Potgieter heard of these attacks he returned south of the river and recommended that all the Voortrekkers withdraw to a single, strong position and prepare there for the Ndebele attack he was sure was imminent. The place he chose was between the Renoster and Wilge rivers, near an isolated small hill now named Vegkop (Vechtkop).

Fifty wagons were securely lashed together to form a sturdy laager. The gaps between the wheels were filled with thorn bushes, and ammunition was prepared for the muzzle-loading flintlock (snaphaan) guns. Each man had at least two weapons and the women accompanying their husbands knew how to reload the guns with the requisite powder and shot.

Vegkop Memorial

Timeline

Sometime after 1821
Mzilikazi flees Shaka in Natal to assert his influence north of the Vaal River. His followers are known as the Ndebele.

1823–1827
The Ndebele spread out over a wide area on the banks of the Vaal River near present-day Vereeniging. They acquire large herds of cattle.

1827
The Ndebele move further north to avoid cattle raiders and settle in the vicinity of present-day Pretoria.

1829
Mzilikazi meets Kuruman missionary Robert Moffat and strikes up a friendship that lasts many years.

1832
The Ndebele move further west to the Marico Valley.

1836
The Great Trek begins as Voortrekkers leave the Cape to escape British rule. Voortrekker hunters crossing the Vaal River are mistaken for Griqua raiders and are killed by the Ndebele. Voortrekkers led by Hendrik Potgieter defeat the Ndebele at Vegkop.

1837
The Voortrekkers attack Mzilikazi's capital at Mosega and the Ndebele flee north to Gabeni. After subsequent attacks from both Zulu and Voortrekker forces, Ndebele refugees move further north to cross the Limpopo River.

1838
Potgieter travels to Natal to assist the Voortrekkers after Retief's murder. The Zulu defeat his force at Italeni. He establishes Potchefstroom in the Transvaal.

The Liebenberg girls

When the Ndebele attacked the Liebenberg family near the Vaal River in 1836, three girls were taken alive. Two of the little girls were reputed to have survived to accompany the group into what is now Zimbabwe.

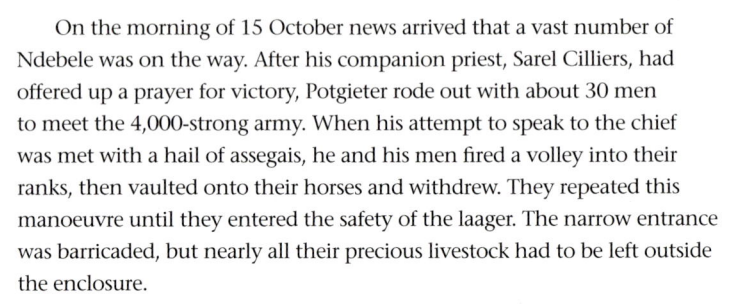

On the morning of 15 October news arrived that a vast number of Ndebele was on the way. After his companion priest, Sarel Cilliers, had offered up a prayer for victory, Potgieter rode out with about 30 men to meet the 4,000-strong army. When his attempt to speak to the chief was met with a hail of assegais, he and his men fired a volley into their ranks, then vaulted onto their horses and withdrew. They repeated this manoeuvre until they entered the safety of the laager. The narrow entrance was barricaded, but nearly all their precious livestock had to be left outside the enclosure.

The Ndebele squatted on their shields around the laager, waiting to launch their attack. This delay caused extreme tension among the Trekkers, some of whom threatened to break out to fight the enemy in the open. Potgieter knew this would spell disaster. He had to provoke an attack as soon as possible and did so by waving a red flag tied to the end of a whip at the encircling army. This galvanised them into making an onslaught against the laager.

Many reached the wagons, in spite of the hot fire from the defenders' guns. They tore at the sailcloth and thorn tree branches that were used to reinforce the laager, bravely trying to gain entry. However, the Voortrekkers kept their nerve and fired steadily. Eventually the warriors were forced to withdraw, leaving swathes of dead bodies behind them.

Unable to use their killing assegais, the Ndebele resorted to hurling their throwing spears over the ringed wagons into the laager, killing two and wounding at least 12 men. The women and children were sheltered in a roofed, square enclosure in the centre of the circle. More than 1,113 assegais were later collected from inside the laager.

The warriors, assembled just out of range, were again waiting to attack. The Trekkers watched the men lying on the ground around the laager and shot those who were sweating, as that alone revealed which ones were alive and waiting to attack once more.

Potgieter initiated a second confrontation by riding out and firing into the ranks of the attackers. The next onslaught by the Ndebele was nearly as ferocious as the first, but ended sooner, as the brave warriors found it impossible to penetrate the laager. They retreated out of range

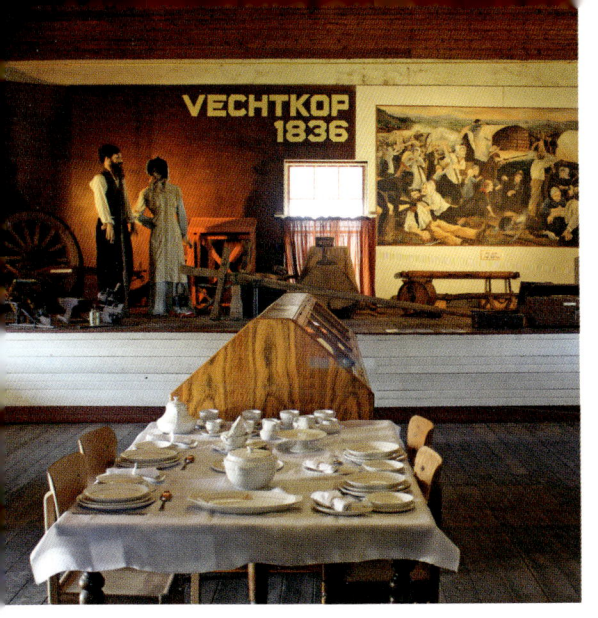

Museum at Vegkop, near Heilbron

and then departed, taking with them over 5,000 head of cattle, 100 horses and a large number of sheep.

A prayer of thanks was offered up by the Voortrekkers when they realised they were safe. However, they were in dire straits with no oxen to draw the wagons and dwindling food supplies. A message was sent to Thaba Nchu requesting help from the party of Trekkers that had settled there from Graaff-Reinet, under Gert Maritz. Reverend Archbell, who had established a Wesleyan mission at Thaba Nchu, spared no effort to gather a rescue party to send to Vegkop.

Aftermath

Although the Voortrekkers successfully drove off the enemy, killing about 160 of them, they lost nearly all their livestock and were vulnerable to further attacks. They were forced to unite with the main camp at Thaba Nchu and steps were taken to draw up a constitution and establish a form of government. Punitive raids were launched against the Ndebele, who were eventually forced, a year after the Battle of Vegkop, to flee to present-day Zimbabwe. This left the Highveld open for further parties of Voortrekkers to settle.

Principal combatants

Voortrekkers: Trekkers led by Hendrik Potgieter.
Ndebele: Warriors led by Mkalipi.

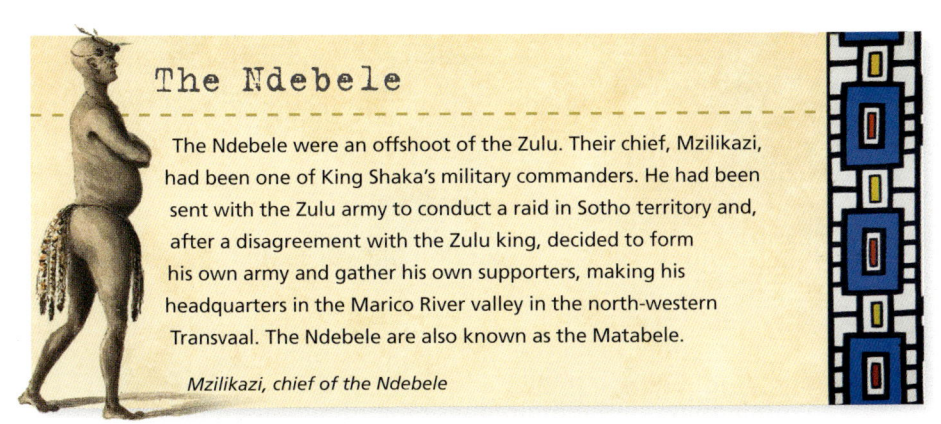

The Ndebele

The Ndebele were an offshoot of the Zulu. Their chief, Mzilikazi, had been one of King Shaka's military commanders. He had been sent with the Zulu army to conduct a raid in Sotho territory and, after a disagreement with the Zulu king, decided to form his own army and gather his own supporters, making his headquarters in the Marico River valley in the north-western Transvaal. The Ndebele are also known as the Matabele.

Mzilikazi, chief of the Ndebele

BATTLE OF VEGKOP

TRANSVAAL
ORANGE FREE STATE
RELIEF OF KIMBERLEY
VICTORIA REGINA ET IMPERATRIX
STATE
Brandfort
WINBURG
Senekal
Modder R.
BLOEMFONTEIN
Ladybrand

Free State & Northern Cape

Brandwater Basin, Free State

Bloemfontein & Kimberley regions

The vast plains and mountainous ramparts that constitute central South Africa were the arena of widely diverse conflicts over several decades. Today, this huge area of mostly flat, open terrain – stretching from the Kalahari Basin north-west of Kimberley to the well-watered farms that lie east of Bloemfontein along the western border of Lesotho – encompasses the provinces of the Free State and Northern Cape.

San people living in the area between the Orange and Vaal rivers were displaced as far as the Kalahari Desert by Tswana-speaking groups, including the Kwena and Taung.

The first white family to settle near Bloemfontein, in 1840, was that of Johannes Nicolaas Brits, a Voortrekker from the Cape. British influence made itself felt in 1846, when Major Henry Warden, the British Resident, settled in Bloemfontein. Almost a decade later, in 1854, the Orange Free State became an independent republic, with Bloemfontein as its capital.

The McGregor Museum, Kimberley, was once a sanatorium where Cecil John Rhodes lodged.

When, in 1870, diamonds were discovered on the republic's western border – in the Kimberley district of the Cape Colony – a land dispute arose, with the Cape Colony, the Orange Free State and the Griqua, who had been granted land west of Kimberley by the British, all claiming ownership of the territory. The Keate Award gave the diamond fields to the Griqua, who ceded the land to Britain as Griqualand West.

When the 2nd Anglo-Boer War broke out, Orange Free State burghers under President Steyn joined the Transvaal to fight against Great Britain. Towards the end of the war, when the Transvaal

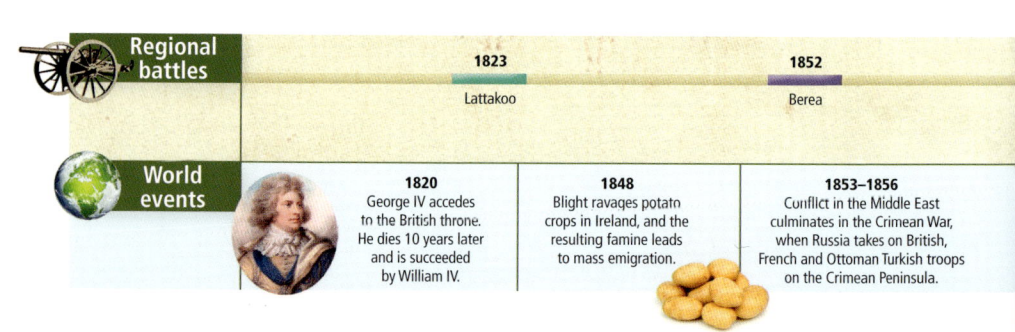

Regional battles
- 1823 Lattakoo
- 1852 Berea

World events
- 1820 George IV accedes to the British throne. He dies 10 years later and is succeeded by William IV.
- 1848 Blight ravages potato crops in Ireland, and the resulting famine leads to mass emigration.
- 1853–1856 Conflict in the Middle East culminates in the Crimean War, when Russia takes on British, French and Ottoman Turkish troops on the Crimean Peninsula.

Battlefields

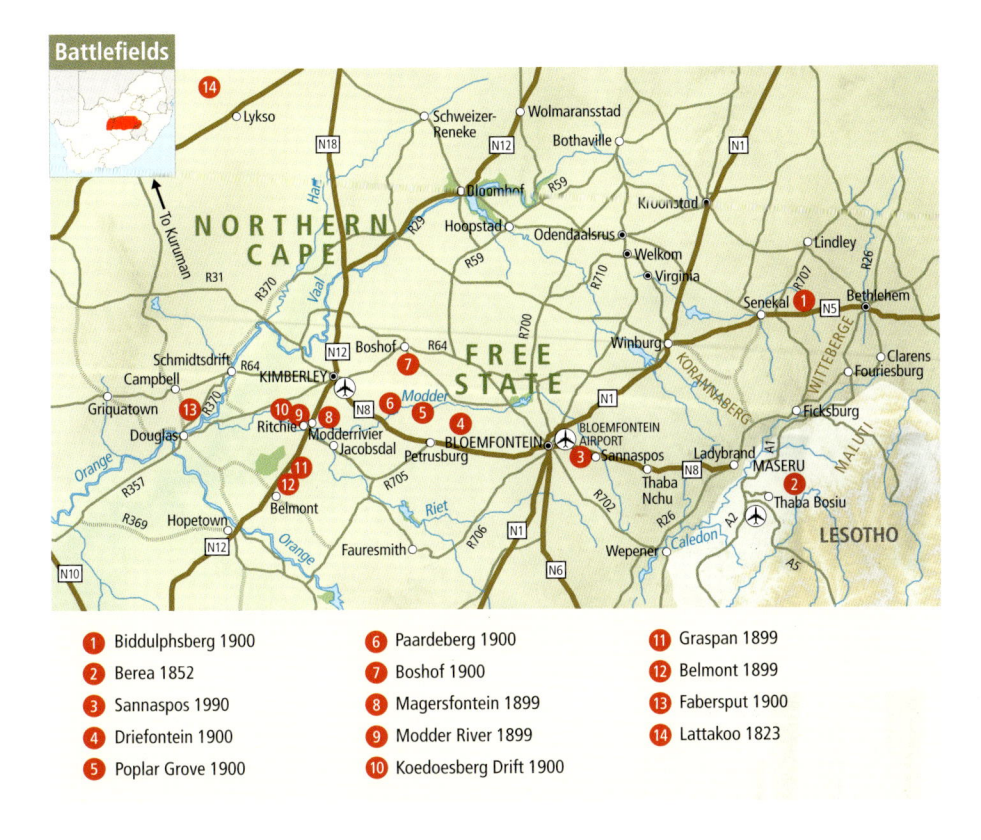

① Biddulphsberg 1900	⑥ Paardeberg 1900	⑪ Graspan 1899
② Berea 1852	⑦ Boshof 1900	⑫ Belmont 1899
③ Sannaspos 1990	⑧ Magersfontein 1899	⑬ Faberput 1900
④ Driefontein 1900	⑨ Modder River 1899	⑭ Lattakoo 1823
⑤ Poplar Grove 1900	⑩ Koedoesberg Drift 1900	

Boers were talking of giving up, it was the Orange Free State contingent, led by some of the war's best commanders, who galvanised the Boers when they promised to fight 'to the bitter end'.

A general lack of water for people and animals in the region posed a huge problem for the British army, while heat and flies caused great discomfort to men and animals alike. Unsanitary conditions in the crowded army camps and, later, in British concentration camps, gave rise to typhoid and dysentery, which killed hundreds of thousands of soldiers and civilians. The President Brand cemetery in Bloemfontein is a stark reminder of those who succumbed to disease during the war.

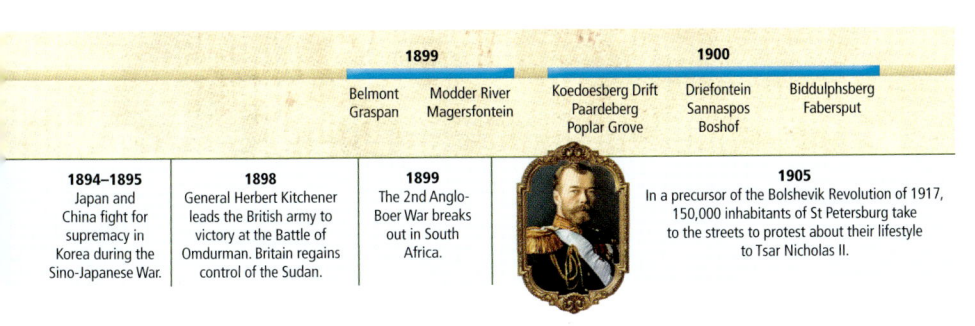

	1899		1900	
Belmont Graspan	Modder River Magersfontein	Koedoesberg Drift Paardeberg Poplar Grove	Driefontein Sannaspos Boshof	Biddulphsberg Faberput

1894–1895	1898	1899	1905
Japan and China fight for supremacy in Korea during the Sino-Japanese War.	General Herbert Kitchener leads the British army to victory at the Battle of Omdurman. Britain regains control of the Sudan.	The 2nd Anglo-Boer War breaks out in South Africa.	In a precursor of the Bolshevik Revolution of 1917, 150,000 inhabitants of St Petersburg take to the streets to protest about their lifestyle to Tsar Nicholas II.

BLOEMFONTEIN & KIMBERLEY REGIONS

The concentration camp at Bloemfontein

Concentration camps

As early as March 1900, General Lord Roberts was moving refugee Boer women and children into camps where they were to be fed and cared for by the British. The Boer generals were initially relieved that the task of providing for these displaced farming families did not fall to their stretched resources.

However, when General Kitchener embarked on his scorched-earth policy, every Boer farm was laid to waste to prevent Boer commandos from drawing support from them. Even those farmers who had signed the oath of neutrality were not be trusted, as they would often be forced to supply the Boer commandos or would disregard the oath they had taken when they were asked for help – and so Kitchener ordered every farm dwelling in the areas of operation to be burnt, all food crops destroyed and every animal killed.

The trickle of Boer refugees to the concentration camps quickly became a flood. The camps were intended to be places of safety, where the refugees could be conveniently provided for. There were different camp rules, however, for women whose husbands were dead or had surrendered and for those whose husbands were still on commando. The latter received meagre rations, were kept under close surveillance, and were often cruelly treated.

The detainees were initially housed in wooden huts constructed near railway lines for ease of supply, but the huts were

Thousands of displaced women and children, black and white, lived under terrible conditions in the concentration camps.

238 BLOEMFONTEIN & KIMBERLEY REGIONS

soon replaced with tents that were stifling in summer and freezing in winter. The provisions supplied were lacking in fresh produce and important trace elements, causing the camp dwellers to develop scurvy and rickets. The deficiency of vitamins also lowered their resistance to other sicknesses and they fell ill with a variety of diseases that spread like wildfire due the crowded conditions and lack of hygiene. Tents were infested with lice; in summer clouds of mosquitoes were a curse for any camps close to water.

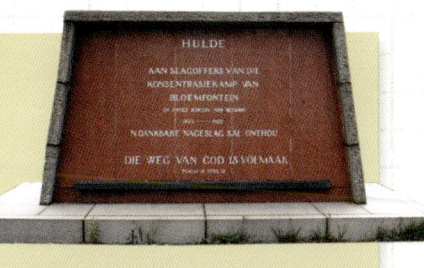

Memorial plaque, Bloemfontein concentration camp

Particularly vulnerable to disease were the children, whose isolated living conditions on big farms meant that they had had little prior exposure and thus no resistance to the likes of measles, influenza, gastro-enteritis, bronchitis and other common ailments. It was not unusual for a mother to come into a camp with six children and have to bury them all before the end of the war. Over 26,000 women and children died in these camps.

Black people living in the war areas were also removed from their homes and put into camps that were usually separate from those where the whites were housed. Conditions in these camps were even worse than in those for whites, and it is estimated that over 30,000 black inmates died due to the squalid conditions.

Women and children survived as best they could in the camps.

Graves at the site of the concentration camp in Aliwal North, where 716 men, women and children died

CONCENTRATION CAMPS 239

Battle of Biddulphsberg
29 May 1900

HOW TO GET THERE
In the Free State, travel on the N5 from Senekal towards Bethlehem. After about 16km, at a signboard, turn left onto a dirt road. Follow this road west around the Biddulphsberg, which you will see on your left. The road eventually links up with the R707 to Lindley.

Context
The British were working their columns through the Orange Free State towards the Transvaal. One such column was threatened by Boers as it approached Lindley. In order to create a diversion and draw the Boers south, Lieutenant General Leslie Rundle attacked the Boer commandos that were entrenched in the Biddulphsberg Hills.

Action
A British column approaching the town of Lindley found Boers there in force and telegraphed Rundle in Senekal for help. Instead of risking a 60km march to Lindley, Rundle decided to attack the Boer commandos 13km east of Senekal, in this way forcing Boers to come from Lindley in support and enabling the stranded column to gain the town.

Boer general Abraham de Villiers, leading a force of 400 men, saw the 4,000-strong British column approaching and planned his defence. He had two Krupp guns, a Maxim Nordenfeldt and (possibly) one other gun. The Maxim Nordenfeldt was placed on the north-eastern slope of the hill and his men entrenched themselves on the high ground on the north-western, northern and north-eastern slopes. There were also 40 riflemen in a donga beneath the hill in the centre of his position.

Artillery on both sides exchanged fire, but, when the Boer Pom-Pom ceased firing, the British thought the Boers had fled. The infantrymen were sent

Blinding smoke and flames worsened the plight of wounded Grenadier Guards, many of whom were badly burnt.

240   BLOEMFONTEIN & KIMBERLEY REGIONS

The Maxim Nordenfeldt gun inflicted heavy casualties on advancing British infantry.

forward, only to be met by a hail of bullets. Rundle attempted to outflank the Boers on their right and sent the Grenadier Guards forward. The riflemen at the foot of the hill held their fire until the Guards were almost upon them before unleashing a fearsome fusillade. The battalion lost 41 per cent of its men, more than it did in any other battle in the war.

Things were made worse by a raging grass fire caused by a carelessly tossed match or an exploding shell. Some wounded were unable to escape the flames and died in agony, while others were badly burnt.

Rundle eventually ordered a retirement and De Villiers sent his men forward in pursuit. However, the retirement was covered by British artillery and De Villiers himself was badly wounded in the jaw. There was no doctor with the commando and De Villiers was tended by the British doctor. He was given the undertaking that he would not be made prisoner, should he recover, but would be released. However, his injury proved fatal.

Aftermath

The British lost heavily with 37 men killed and over 130 wounded. The Boers lost only their general. The battle had no effect on the fate of the column requesting aid; it was besieged in Lindley by the Boers.

Principal combatants

British: Driscoll's Scouts; Grenadier Guards; Imperial Yeomanry; Royal Field Artillery; Scots Guards; West Kent Regiment.
Boers: Commandos from Ficksburg, Ladybrand, Senekal, Smithfield, Thaba Nchu and Wepener; Orange Free State Artillery; Scouts.

Timeline

1880–1881
Sir Leslie Rundle serves in South Africa during the 1st Anglo-Boer War.

1899
The 2nd Anglo-Boer War commences. Lieutenant General Rundle is given command of the 8th Division and later becomes known as Sir Leisurely Trundle.

1900
In February Kimberley is relieved and British forces make their way towards the Transvaal. Boer general Piet Cronjé surrenders at Paardeberg.

In March the British occupy Bloemfontein.

In May British forces occupy Winburg and the annexation of the Orange Free State is proclaimed. Rundle and his division fight Boers entrenched in the Biddulphsberg. A Boer force overpowers a British force at Lindley. At the end of the month, the British occupy Johannesburg, and Pretoria is occupied a few days later.

In July Rundle achieves a notable victory in the Brandwater Basin when 4,300 Boers surrender.

In August General Christiaan de Wet escapes Rundle and British forces in the Magaliesberg.

In September the Transvaal is annexed by a formal proclamation.

Battle of Berea
20 December 1852

> **HOW TO GET THERE**
> The Berea plateau lies in the mountain kingdom of Lesotho, and can be reached from the capital, Maseru, about 145km from Bloemfontein. From Maseru, take the main road (A2) south to Mafeteng/Roma. After about 12km, turn left onto the A3 towards Roma/Thaba Seka. Drive for about 6km; when you see the sign to Thaba Bosiu, turn left onto the B20. Thaba Bosiu is about 9km along this road. The Berea plateau is about 5km north of Thaba Bosiu and can be seen from there.
>   Visitors must ensure they have the necessary travel documents for entry into Lesotho.
>
> Thaba Bosiu (mountain): 29°20'47.35" S 27°39'50.95" E
> Thaba Bosiu cultural village: 29°20'50.65" S 27°39'46.67" E

Context

In June 1852 the British Resident in Transorangia (the area between the Orange and the Vaal rivers) suffered a humiliating defeat at the hands of the Sotho at Viervoet. The governor of the Cape, Lieutenant General Sir George Cathcart, thought it important to restore the prestige of British troops north of the Orange River before withdrawing them in accordance with the Sand River Convention of the same year. At the same time, he hoped to recover livestock stolen by the Sotho from Boers in Transorangia and from the Tlokwa, Rolong and Kora. These groups had been granted land by the British in areas that the Sotho regarded as their territory.

Action

Cathcart gathered about 2,500 troops comprising cavalry, infantry and artillery at his camp site at Platrand, west of the Caledon River. He then met with Moshoeshoe, ruler of the Sotho, and demanded a large fine of 10,000 cattle and horses as punishment for the stolen cattle.

Moshoeshoe agreed, but asked for more time. Cathcart grudgingly agreed to extend the time from three to four days, but was unwilling to make any other concessions.

On the third day, after only a third of the cattle and half the number of horses had been delivered, Cathcart crossed the Caledon River with his army to advance on Thaba Bosiu, Moshoeshoe's stronghold, with the aim of gathering cattle as he pushed forward. Cathcart had been told that 30,000 beasts, along with women and children, had been sent to the Berea plateau, north of Thaba Bosiu –

Lieutenant General Sir George Cathcart

this was his target. He left some men to guard the camp and others to watch over the drift across the Caledon. The remaining troops were divided into three columns, each taking a different route to the valley below Thaba Bosiu, where they were to converge with the cattle and horses they had rounded up on the way.

The left column, comprising 233 cavalry under the command of Lieutenant George Napier, was to ride eastward below the north face of the Berea plateau and then skirt south around the eastern end, intercepting any cattle that came down from the top. In reality, the column had to ascend the plateau because its north-eastern face adjoins the eastern high ground. The central column was made up of about 400 mostly infantry men, led by Lieutenant Colonel William Eyre. He was instructed to ascend the plateau from the west, herd together as many cattle as he could and descend down the southern face to join Cathcart in the Phuthiastana River valley at midday. Cathcart himself led the third column, consisting of fewer than 400 men and two field guns, directly to the valley below and south of the Berea plateau, about 5km north of Thaba Bosiu.

Napier's mounted men rounded up 4,500 cattle on the north-eastern nek of the plateau. Some women and children who fled before them were pursued and shot. However, when Napier's men attempted to drive the beasts back towards the British camp, they were attacked by 700 Sotho – good horsemen, well mounted, and many carrying flintlock muskets. They managed to trap a group of Lancers in a dried watercourse that the soldiers had mistaken for

Thaba Bosiu (in the foreground) was Moshoeshoe's stronghold. The Berea plateau, not visible in this photograph, lies to the left of the mountain.

Timeline

1837
Adam Kok III becomes chief of the Griqua; he has his headquarters at Philippolis, named after Dr John Philip, of the London Missionary Society.

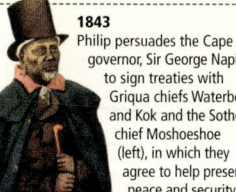

1843
Philip persuades the Cape governor, Sir George Napier, to sign treaties with Griqua chiefs Waterboer and Kok and the Sotho chief Moshoeshoe (left), in which they agree to help preserve peace and security.

1844
Voortrekker leader Hendrik Potgieter offers a treaty to Adam Kok.

1845
Kok (below) complains of cattle theft by the Boers and hands over to the British a group of Boers wanted for murder. The Cape governor, Sir Peregrine Maitland, appoints a British Resident to Transorangia to settle disputes between Voortrekkers and Griqua.

1848
Cape Governor Sir Harry Smith defeats the Voortrekkers at Boomplaats.

1849
Moshoeshoe accepts an unfavourable boundary known as the Warden Line.

1852
Lieutenant General Sir George Cathcart replaces Sir Harry Smith as Cape governor. He continues the fight on the frontier. On 20 December Cathcart leads 2,000 men against Moshoeshoe. He is defeated at the Battle of Berea.

1854
The British government cedes Transorangia to the Voortrekkers under the name of Orange Free State.

1867
After a final battle with the Voortrekkers, Moshoeshoe appeals to Queen Victoria, who agrees to make Basutoland a British protectorate.

1869
Britain signs a treaty with the Boers that defines the boundaries of Basutoland; it reduces Moshoeshoe's kingdom to half its previous size.

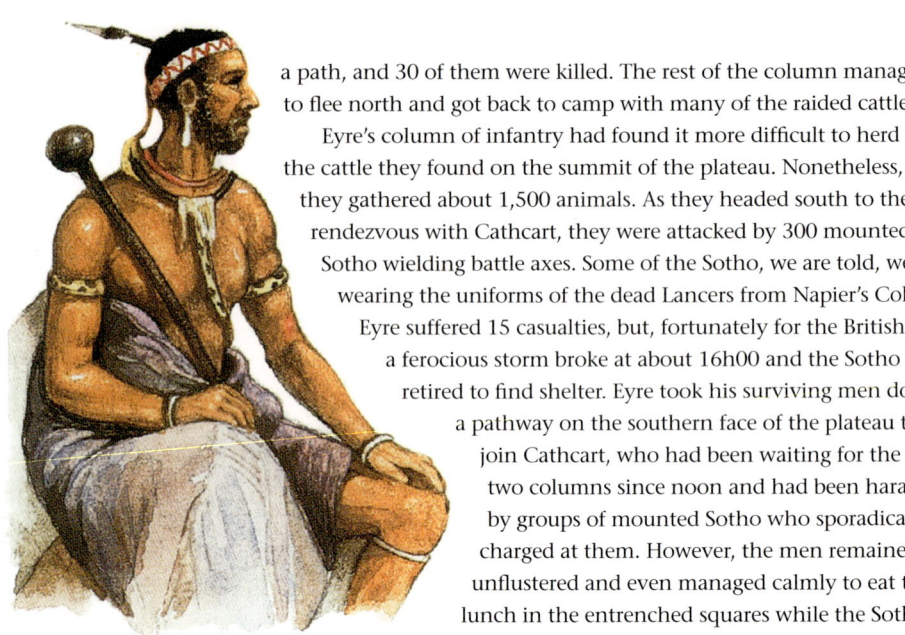

a path, and 30 of them were killed. The rest of the column managed to flee north and got back to camp with many of the raided cattle. Eyre's column of infantry had found it more difficult to herd the cattle they found on the summit of the plateau. Nonetheless, they gathered about 1,500 animals. As they headed south to their rendezvous with Cathcart, they were attacked by 300 mounted Sotho wielding battle axes. Some of the Sotho, we are told, were wearing the uniforms of the dead Lancers from Napier's Column. Eyre suffered 15 casualties, but, fortunately for the British, a ferocious storm broke at about 16h00 and the Sotho retired to find shelter. Eyre took his surviving men down a pathway on the southern face of the plateau to join Cathcart, who had been waiting for the other two columns since noon and had been harassed by groups of mounted Sotho who sporadically charged at them. However, the men remained unflustered and even managed calmly to eat their lunch in the entrenched squares while the Sotho demonstrated around them.

Moshoeshoe was leader of the Sotho and an astute statesman.

Once Eyre's men had joined with Cathcart's, both sides were about equal in number. The Sotho, no doubt infuriated by the huge herd they saw being taken off, mounted an attack but were held at bay by the cool firing of Cathcart's men. At about 17h00 Cathcart's men were led back to bivouac in some rocks nearby. The Sotho attacks continued until about 20h00.

Meanwhile Moshoeshoe had met with his advisers; he knew he stood no chance against the organised, well-armed forces ranged against him. Missionary Eugène Casalis helped him draft a letter that, in a triumph of diplomacy, allowed Cathcart to claim to have won the battle and thus save face. Moshoeshoe requested politely that Cathcart stop punishing him, that he had learned his lesson and only wanted peace. Relieved at this opportunity to salvage his pride and reputation, Cathcart sent back a message saying there would be no more fighting. He withdrew on 21 December, leading his men back across the Caledon River.

Aftermath

Moshoeshoe's masterful diplomacy enabled him to retain good relations with the British and saved Lesotho from being annexed by the Orange Free State in 1867. Cathcart had learned that Moshoeshoe was a force to be reckoned with and that the Sotho were an enemy not easily defeated.

Principal combatants
British: 12th Lancers; 43rd, 73rd and 74th Regiments; Cape Mounted Rifles; Queen's Regiment; Rifle Brigade; Royal Field Artillery.
Sotho: Warriors, some of them mounted.

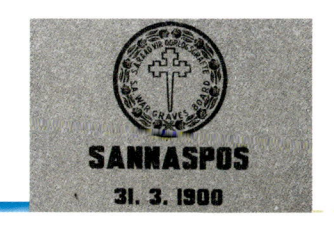

Battle of Sannaspos

Also known as *Battle of Koornspruit*

31 March 1900

HOW TO GET THERE

Leave Bloemfontein on the N8 towards Thaba Nchu. After about 30km, look out for a sign and a white monument on the right-hand side of the road. If you stand on the monument and look east towards the Modder River, the donga in front of you is the Koornspruit, site of the ambush. The Boers had positions along the stream to your left and right. The British wagons were approaching the drift across the spruit from the east (in front of you). The battery that got away would have taken up a position about 1,200m away on the other side of the stream, to your right. There were some tin huts there that gave the defending British some shelter. Their line of retreat was to your right and then behind where you stand, to Bloemfontein. If you drive about 2km further, you will reach the station buildings at Sannaspos and the site of the waterworks on the right-hand side of the road. There is a cemetery here.

Monument: 29°09'19.8" S 26°31'57" E

Context

Bloemfontein was already in British hands and General Frederick ('Bobs') Roberts was on his way to take Pretoria, capital of the Transvaal, and still the Boers refused to give up. With the encouragement of President Marthinus Steyn, the Orange Free State Boers began a different phase of the war, where British columns were harassed by roving commandos of extremely mobile Boers. The action at Sannaspos on 31 March 1900 marked the first time that the guerrilla-style tactics of General Christiaan de Wet proved spectacularly successful.

The Modder River intercepts the road and railway line about 30km east of Bloemfontein on the Thaba Nchu road at Sannaspos, a siding on the new line east to Ladybrand. Nearby were the waterworks, a pump station on the Modder River that supplied Bloemfontein's water.

De Wet, with a force of about 1,500 men, had planned to attack the British garrison, about 200-strong, at Sannaspos and take the waterworks. As he neared the position, he realised that a much larger force (1,800 men and 12 guns) under Brigadier General Robert Broadwood was approaching Sannaspos from Thaba Nchu. De Wet was a master of opportunity and he planned an ambush for the approaching column.

Action

De Wet and about 400 men took up positions in a deep donga through which ran the Koornspruit that runs parallel to the Modder River, about 2km west of the waterworks

Timeline

1895
After service in the Afghan War as general, and later as commander-in-chief in India, Lord Roberts is promoted to field marshal.

1899
Roberts supersedes General Sir Redvers Buller as commander-in-chief of all British troops in South Africa.

1900
In February Roberts's army forces the surrender of General Piet Cronjé at Paardeberg.

In March Roberts's army takes Bloemfontein. General Christiaan de Wet scores a notable victory at Sannaspos.

In May British forces under Roberts occupy Kroonstad, and Mafeking is relieved. The British annex the Orange Free State and occupy Johannesburg.

In June Roberts enters Pretoria. De Wet scores another success when he captures Rooiwal station, a British supply depot.

In October Roberts turns over his position to Horatio Kitchener, who appoints Frank Maxwell aide-de-camp.

1914
Roberts dies in France while visiting Indian troops there during World War I.

1917
Now a brigadier general, Maxwell is killed in action near Ypres in Flanders.

and the station. Where the road entered the stream bed, it narrowed to a wedge, forcing wheeled transport into single file as it entered the drift. The general's brother, Piet de Wet, and about 1,100 men with five Krupp guns were positioned in some small hills north-east of the Modder River, within range of the station and the waterworks.

The British force from Thaba Nchu arrived at Sannaspos late in the evening of 30 March and slept the night in a camp straddling the road close to the station. When they broke camp at first light, the Boers on the other side of the Modder River began to shell the position. This precipitated a rapid retreat west towards Bloemfontein. The transport, comprising over 100 wagons driven by civilian drivers, rushed towards the Koornspruit Drift, ahead of the composite cavalry regiment and its two supporting batteries of Royal Horse Artillery. Q and U batteries consisted of 12 12-pounder breech-loading guns, 402 horses and 22 carts manned by 377 men. As the transport wagons entered the steep defile into the donga, armed Boers were waiting. The soldier-guard that accompanied each wagon was held up and disarmed by Mauser-wielding Boers as soon as the wagon was below the skyline and invisible to the following wagons. Each driver, upon entering the dead ground, was directed to proceed alternately right and left, and the wagons were lined up in the spruit on each side of the drift. Some of the men were so surprised that they surrendered their arms before they were even asked to do so. De Wet later complained that the Boers wasted time in asking where they should put the rifles – there were so many.

Meanwhile, the Boer guns were still dropping shells into the camp site and so wagons continued to rush towards the wedge-shaped trap.

The U Battery of the Royal Horse Artillery followed the transport wagons into the stream bed and was surrounded by Boers. It was then that the first shot was fired and the officer commanding the battery managed

The railway siding, near where the British soldiers camped on their first night in Sannaspos

246 BLOEMFONTEIN & KIMBERLEY REGIONS

to gallop off to warn the horsemen following behind. Roberts's Horse was the leading squadron and was about 200m from the Koornspruit when the men received the news that the Boers were taking prisoners. The order was given at once to turn about and withdraw. As they did so, the Boers opened fire on the retreating men and horses.

The other Royal Horse Artillery battery, Q Battery, had not yet reached the donga and was fired on as it fled, but the retreat was covered by some men of Roberts's Horse and five out of six guns got clear. These guns were halted about 1,200m clear of the spruit and wheeled round into a firing position to go into action against the Boers, so covering the retreat of the troops. Men and guns found some cover behind tin sheds and an embankment south-west of the ambush.

> ### Maxwell's VC
>
> During the retreat from Sannaspos a lieutenant of Roberts's Horse, Frank Maxwell, rescued a wounded man under fire and then helped, again under fire, to take ammunition to the guns. Finally, he assisted in dragging the guns to safety – by hand – and stayed with the last one until it was abandoned. For these brave actions he was awarded a Victoria Cross.

In spite of mounting casualties of men and horses, the gunners calmly manned their weapons. When the ammunition had been exhausted and most of the horses killed, ammunition limbers were dragged up to the guns by hand. Many gunners were killed in the hail of Boer bullets and soon only two of the guns were firing. For three hours these kept the Boers at bay. When eventually the order was given for all guns to retire, the gunners' commander, Phipps Hornby, sent back messages saying he could not get the guns away. Volunteers went forward with horses and limbers to extricate them, and four guns and limbers were bravely rescued under fire.

One gun belonging to U Battery had escaped capture when the gunners were all killed in the spruit and the horses stampeded to the rear, dragging the gun along. The other guns belonging to U Battery were already across the donga and in Boer hands before the alarm was given for the retreat to begin.

Aftermath

The retirement south and then west towards Bloemfontein was well executed by the composite cavalry, which covered each others' half-companies. The fleeing soldiers were not followed up with any great determination by the Boers. However, the British lost 578 men, including those killed, wounded or made prisoners of war. The loss of the seven guns was keenly felt. The Boer loss is estimated at six killed (some reports say three) and 11 wounded. Five Victoria Crosses were awarded for the rescue of the guns.

Principal combatants

British: 10th Hussars; Burma Mounted Infantry; Household Cavalry; New Zealand Mounted Infantry; Rimington Guides; Roberts's Horse; Royal Field Artillery; Royal Horse Artillery.
Boers: Commandos from Bloemfontein, Kroonstad and Winburg.

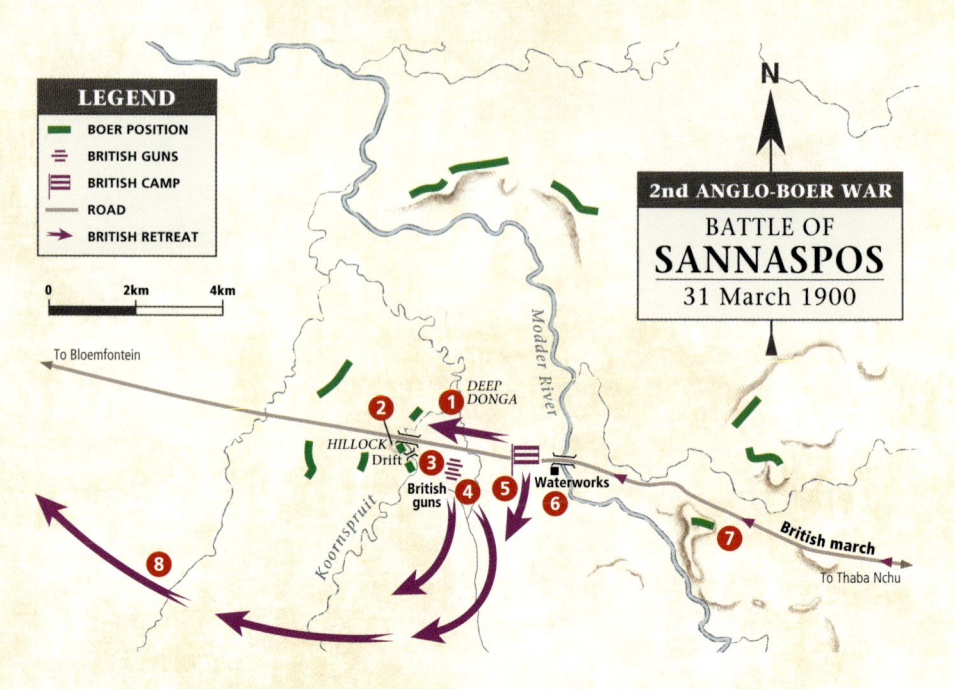

LEGEND
- BOER POSITION
- BRITISH GUNS
- BRITISH CAMP
- ROAD
- BRITISH RETREAT

0 2km 4km

2nd ANGLO-BOER WAR
BATTLE OF SANNASPOS
31 March 1900

To Bloemfontein

DEEP DONGA

Modder River

HILLOCK
Drift

Koornspruit

British guns

Waterworks

British march
To Thaba Nchu

Amid explosions, maddened horses bolt at Sannaspos.

1 This was the deep donga over which the wagons had to pass on their way from Thaba Nchu to Bloemfontein.

2 The present-day monument stands on this hillside. Boers were in this position prior to the ambush.

3 This is where the British guns of Q Battery took up position to wheel around and fire at the Boers, covering the retreat of the wagons behind them.

4 Tin huts in this area gave shelter to British guns and soldiers, allowing some of them to retreat safely to Bloemfontein.

5 This was the site of the British camp.

6 The waterworks were De Wet's original target before he learned of Broadwood's force approaching from Thaba Nchu.

7 There were Boers in these hills.

8 This was the line of the British retreat.

Battle of Driefontein

Also known as *Battle of Abrahamskraal*

10 March 1900

HOW TO GET THERE
This battle was fought over a 20km front stretching south from the Modder River to the Driefontein Hills, approximately 66km west of Bloemfontein. To find the Driefontein Hills, drive from Bloemfontein towards Kimberley on the N8. Turn right at the Immigrant railway siding turn-off and follow this road north. The hills may be seen to your right, after about 15km. *Guide recommended*

Context
Lord Roberts's army was advancing east towards Bloemfontein in three huge columns. On 7 March the Boers had been forced back from Poplar Grove to Abrahamskraal, a farm on the south bank of the Modder River, west of Bloemfontein. This battle occurred when Roberts's northernmost column engaged the Boers at Abrahamskraal, while the centre encountered the Boers' left flank 20km further south in the Driefontein Hills.

Action
Many Boers had fled after Cronjé's surrender at Paardeberg (see p. 254) and the subsequent battle at Poplar Grove (see p. 251). It is probable that Boer commanders Christiaan de Wet and Koos de la Rey had only 3,000 men to prevent the British pushing through to Bloemfontein. Only 1,500 Boers actually fought in the Battle of Driefontein.

Lord Roberts had divided his force into three columns, each comprising over 10,000 men. Accompanied by 30 guns, they advanced along three parallel roads from Poplar Grove towards Bloemfontein. The left column marched close to the south bank of the Modder River, the centre column was on a road that passed through the Driefontein Hills, and the right-hand column progressed along the Petrusburg road. General John French commanded the left, Roberts accompanied the centre column, and the right was led by General Charles Tucker.

Early on 10 March, British scouts encountered Boers at Abrahamskraal, close to the Modder River. Leaving part of his column to hold this position, French took his cavalry south, intending to drive the Boers out of the Driefontein Hills, where they lay in Roberts's path.

At 10h00 French and his men came across 1,500 Boers with two Creusot guns and a Maxim Nordenfeldt in the Driefontein Hills. They were unable to prevent them from pouring hot fire into Roberts's approaching column, forcing the British to retire out of range. The British field guns were then brought to bear on the hills and a heavy artillery duel ensued. The Boers used their Maxim Nordenfeldt gun cleverly against the British 12-pounders and it was a long time before the British were able to send the infantry forward again.

Timeline

1899
During the siege of Ladysmith, the British succeed, one December night, in storming a Boer gun emplacement overlooking the town. The Long Tom gun is damaged. A Boer commandant, J. D. Weilbach of the Heidelberg Commando, is blamed, although his negligence is never proven.

1900
In February the siege is relieved. British forces begin outflanking the Boers in their entrenched positions in the Magersfontein Hills. Kimberley is relieved and Piet Cronjé surrenders at Paardeberg.

In March the President of the Transvaal, Paul Kruger, narrowly avoids capture at the Battle of Poplar Grove. The Battle of Driefontein sees the British push forward towards Bloemfontein, but the Boers are able to retreat in an orderly fashion without undue loss, thanks to the heroic actions of J. D. Weilbach. Bloemfontein is taken by the British in the same month. In a war council meeting, the Boers decide to concentrate on destroying the enemy's lines of communication rather than attacking from defensive positions. The guerrilla war begins in earnest.

In April Boers under the leadership of a French general, Georges de Villebois-Mareuil, are surrounded and defeated at Boshof, north of Kimberley.

In May Mafeking is relieved and British forces occupy Johannesburg.

In June Pretoria falls to the British.

At noon there was an attempt by the British to outflank the position to the south and it was only the brave leadership of Commandant Johan Weilbach of the Heidelberg Commando that prevented the turning movement.

At 14h00 Lieutenant General Thomas Kenny led his men in a frontal assault on a hill in the centre of the position, believing the Boers had retired. Suddenly his infantry were caught in a barrage of Mauser bullets that hit more than 300 men. Those remaining charged the crest, using a final bayonet charge to clear the Boers. There were reports on both sides of unethical use of the white flag and the British later accused the Boers of using expanding (dum-dum) bullets. At around 18h00 the Boers ran short of ammunition and retired, taking most of their goods and equipment with them.

Commandant Johan Weilbach

Aftermath

The British lost 400 men, 60 of whom had died. The Boers evacuated the position that night, having counted 32 men dead and 20 taken prisoner. The road was open to Bloemfontein, which was occupied by the British at midnight on 12 March.

Principal combatants

British: 10th and 14th Hussars; 9th, 12th and 16th Lancers; Australian Horse; Coldstream Guards; Dragoon Guards; Dragoons; Essex Regiment; Gloucestershire Regiment; Gordon Highlanders; Life Guards; Naval Brigade; New South Wales Lancers; New South Wales Mounted Infantry; Oxfordshire Light Infantry; Roberts's Horse; Royal Field Artillery; Welsh Regiment; Yorkshire Regiment.

Boers: Commandos from Boksburg, Fordsburg, Heidelberg and Winburg; Johannesburg Police.

Battle of Poplar Grove
7 March 1900

HOW TO GET THERE
The Poplar Grove battle site lies close to the Modder River between Kimberley and Bloemfontein. To reach the site of General Christiaan de Wet's laager at Poplar Grove, drive east from Kimberly on the N8 until you reach Petrusburg, where you turn left (north) onto a gravel road. Poplar Grove is just south of the Modder River, to the right of the road.

Site of De Wet's camp: 28°54'32.6" S 25°21'52.1" E

Context
The commander-in-chief of the British army in South Africa, Lord Roberts, was on his way to occupy Bloemfontein, capital of the Orange Free State. The last natural line of defence between Kimberley and Bloemfontein was a line of small hills stretching for about 14km on both sides of the river, west of the Poplar Grove camp, where the Boers had dug themselves into well-entrenched positions. The battle occurred when the British attacked and threatened to outflank the Boers, who later fled.

Action
General Christiaan de Wet believed that Roberts would march north towards Johannesburg and Pretoria without making a detour to occupy Bloemfontein. Consequently, the Boers were taken by surprise when the British attacked early on 7 March 1900.

Roberts was determined to take Bloemfontein, the Orange Free State capital. Its occupation, he believed, would demoralise the Boers. There were about 5,000 Boers and seven guns in positions on the line of small hills that stretched from Leeuwkop (or Loogkop), on the north bank of the Modder River, to the Seven Sisters, about 14km further south. Roberts's battle plan was to use his cavalry to outflank the Boers on their left by riding south and then east. Once past the end of the Boer line, the British

Memorial at Poplar Grove

BATTLE OF POPLAR GROVE 251

Timeline

1900
In February General John French's (above) cavalry relieves Kimberley. Boer general Piet Cronjé surrenders at Paardeberg. General Philip Botha, elder brother of Louis Botha, fights bravely to prevent the encirclement of Cronjé's laager. Lord Roberts and his army surprise the Boers by moving east towards Bloemfontein, instead of marching north into the Transvaal.

In March Philip Botha fights a rearguard action at Poplar Grove, enabling the Boers to withdraw with few casualties. Shortly thereafter, Roberts occupies Bloemfontein.

In May, in an attempt to divert Boer forces from Lindley, the British attack Boer commandos at Biddulphsberg, south of Kroonstad. Johannesburg falls to the British in the same month. Pretoria is occupied by Roberts's army, and President Paul Kruger leaves Pretoria on an eastbound train.

In June General Louis Botha commands the Boers during the Battle of Diamond Hill, east of Pretoria.

In July Philip Botha escapes the British in the Brandwater Basin. He is accompanied by General Christiaan de Wet and President Marthinus Steyn.

1901
Philip Botha is killed during a skirmish with the British in the Ventersburg district.

---

soldiers were to attack the Boers from the rear. At the same time, British artillery and infantry would attack the enemy's centre, which was close to the south bank of the river, and right, which was north of the river on Leeuwkop. Roberts hoped the Boers would flee into the arms of the cavalry behind them.

De Wet was at the laager at Poplar Grove, east and behind the Boer centre, where he was expecting a visit from President Paul Kruger, who was coming to encourage the men.

At 03h00 the British cavalry left the camp and rode south. It comprised Lancers, Dragoons, Hussars, Canadian and Australian mounted infantry, as well as City Imperial Volunteers. The division was commanded by General John French. Although a speedy advance was necessary for the success of Roberts's plan, French ordered a halt and waited for daylight before progressing east towards the Boer left flank. This delay was to prove costly. To the left of the cavalry, three infantry divisions moved forward while 42 British guns, including the 4.7-inch (120mm) naval gun, bombarded the hills.

The Boers on the south end of the line were commanded by General Philip Botha, older brother of Louis Botha. When he saw the cavalry threatening to outflank his position, he ordered a line of men to spread out eastward and fire into the ranks of the approaching horsemen. This move delayed the British advance and prevented the cavalry from gaining the rear of the Boers. However, the Boers in the centre had been under severe bombardment since first light and, when they saw the British cavalry threatening to outflank them, they panicked and fled.

In the meantime, Kruger had arrived at the Poplar Grove camp in a pony cart at 10h00, and De Wet met with him before sending him away as quickly as possible, as his capture by the British would have been disastrous for the Boer force. De Wet then galloped to the centre of the Boer line and did all he could to keep the retreat orderly. He organised a skilful rearguard action that kept the cavalry from closing the gap between the south bank of the river and the fleeing Boers.

Meanwhile, Major General Sir Henry Colville's division, including the Highland Brigade and the

General John Pinkstone French

252   BLOEMFONTEIN & KIMBERLEY REGIONS

The abandoned attachés

During the Battle of Poplar Grove, the military attachés for Russia and the Netherlands were captured by the British. They had accompanied the Boer forces in a mule cart, but, when the British gained the upper hand, the fleeing Boers appropriated their mules to get their own transport away, stranding the two foreigners.

Second and third from the left are the military attachés for the Netherlands and Russia respectively.

Shropshire Light Infantry, had taken and held the north bank of the river. The Boers were forced to abandon their Krupp gun on Leeuwkop, which was joyfully claimed by the Shropshire Light Infantry, whose soldiers were first up the hill.

General French was later blamed for his slowness. Had he managed to trap the enemy between his cavalry and the river, 5,000 Boers would have been captured, as well as their president. French, on the other hand, blamed the condition of the horses for the fact that they could not raise a gallop; they lacked fodder, he maintained, because Roberts had mounted so many colonials that there was insufficient feed for the regular cavalry mounts. French also blamed Roberts's transport arrangements for the hungry men's lack of food and supplies.

Aftermath

The Boer defence had crumbled, forcing the Boer fighters to withdraw to a line of defence further east. De Wet's skilful rearguard action meant that Boer casualties, apart from the Krupp gun, were minimal. The Boers had only one killed and one wounded, and they managed to get most of their equipment away. The British had eight killed and 49 wounded.

Principal combatants

British: 9th and 12th Lancers; Australian mounted troops; Canadian Regiment; City Imperial Volunteers; Coldstream Guards; Dragoon Guards; Gordon Highlanders; Hampshire Regiment; Inniskilling Dragoons; Life Guards; Lincolnshire Regiment; Mounted infantry; Naval Brigade; Norfolk Regiment; Oxfordshire Light Infantry; Royal Field Artillery; Royal Horse Artillery; Royal Horse Guards; Shropshire Light Infantry; Welsh Regiment.
Boers: Commandos from Bethlehem, Bloemfontein, Boshof, Edenburg, Heidelberg, Ladybrand, Philippolis, Potchefstroom, Senekal and Winburg; Staatsartillerie.

Battle of Paardeberg
17–27 February 1900

HOW TO GET THERE

Leave Bloemfontein on the N8 towards Kimberley. Turn right after about 35km and follow the signboard saying 'Perdeberg'. Follow the road over the railway line and turn left at the T-junction. The Paardeberg Museum is visible a little way along this road on your right. The battlefield is about 8km on from the museum. To reach the site, retrace your steps to the T-junction and then follow the road left. After about 8km there is a diorama to the right of the gravel road, on the banks of the river, where the main laager was. From this position you can trace the course of the battle. The Boers occupied the river banks for about 12km up- and downstream from this point. The Oskoppies (Kitchener's Hill) is on the skyline in front of you. The hills behind you to the right had British artillery on them, as did the high ground in front of you. Colonel Ormelie Campbell Hannay made his suicide charge across the flat ground behind you. His grave is there, on the opposite side of the road in an open field. The monument to the Boers is behind you and those to the British are a little further east. Many Canadians lie in the graveyard.

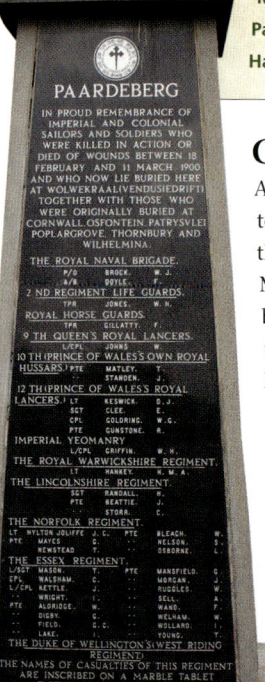

Main laager and battlefield: 28°56'41.8" S 25°08'49.7" E
Paardeberg Museum: 28°58'57.2" S 25°04'52.2" E
Hannay's grave: 28°56'22.3" S 25°08'51.3" E

Context

After the Battle of Magersfontein (see p. 260), General John French took his cavalry to Kimberley in a wide, flanking movement that steered clear of the Boers in entrenched positions in the Magersfontein Hills. Men and horses were driven to exhaustion by the speed of the advance in scorching weather and over rough terrain, where water was scarce. At the expense of many dead horses, French and his troops rode into Kimberley from the south-east on 15 February 1900, meeting with little resistance. The siege was over.

This left Boer commander Piet Cronjé in a precarious position. Since early December he had occupied fortified positions at Magersfontein, where he and his men had made themselves comfortable with their wives and other non-combatants.

Paardeberg monument

Piet Cronjé (centre) surrenders at Paardeberg. As a result, more than 4,000 men are made prisoners of war.

But there were now British soldiers in force to the north and south of his position, as General Frederick Roberts's force, with some of Lieutenant General Lord Paul Methuen's men from Modder River, was approaching from Jacobsdal. Cronjé realised he would have to retire to Bloemfontein, capital of the Orange Free State, as soon as he could.

His passage eastward along the north bank of the Modder River was slow. He had to stay close to the river, as he needed water for his livestock and trek oxen. He was also encumbered by the more than 400 wagons carrying women and supplies. The convoy was spotted by British scouts and they reported the news to General French. French left Kimberley to pursue the convoy. The battle was Cronjé's desperate defence against the British attack.

Action

Before the British made contact on 17 February 1900, Cronjé had reached Vendutie Drift, east of Paardeberg Drift, and managed to get half his wagons across the swiftly flowing river. When the convoy was attacked, Cronjé's men fought an effective rearguard action and secured the remaining wagons in a strong defensive position on the north bank of the river, close to the drift. Marksmen took up positions in deep trenches on both sides of the river. British troops were unable to get to the laager and heavy casualties resulted from

Timeline

1892
Horatio Herbert Kitchener, governor general of the Eastern Sudan, is promoted to the command of Egyptian forces.

1896
During the Jameson Raid, the abortive attempt to overthrow the Boer government in Johannesburg, Commandant Piet Cronjé captures the invaders. He is appointed a member of the Executive Council of Johannesburg.

1898
Kitchener conquers the Sudan.

1899
Kitchener (left) comes to South Africa as chief of staff to Lord Roberts. Cronjé is appointed assistant commandant general. Colonel Ormelie Hannay arrives in South Africa. He commands a division of Roberts's mounted infantry.

1900
In February Kitchener temporarily replaces Roberts's command, as the British army encircles the embattled Cronjé at Paardeberg. Hannay is mortally wounded when he gallops alone at the Boer defences to prevent others from obeying Kitchener's suicidal orders. Cronjé surrenders to the British. The defeat impacts on the Battle of Tugela Heights in Natal, where the British break the Boer line to relieve the siege of Ladysmith. Their success is mainly due to the demoralisation the Boers feel at Cronjé's surrender. Cronjé is exiled to St Helena.

In November Kitchener replaces Roberts as commander-in-chief.

1902
Largely due to the success of Kitchener's scorched-earth policy, the Boers surrender and the peace of Vereeniging is signed, ending the war.

1904
On his return from exile, Cronjé travels to the USA to give realistic displays of Boer military experience, for which he is ridiculed.

1916
Kitchener drowns when his ship hits a mine on its way to Russia.

their attempts to do so that day. Further attacks were made from the north and the south, and along the river banks.

On 18 February Roberts was ill, leaving General Lord Kitchener, who was chief of staff, in command. He ordered a frontal attack on the main laager, which was certain to be suicidal. Colonel Hannay, commanding the mounted infantry, raced forward on his own to save others in his regiment from certain death. He was killed in the open by the Boer marksmen commanding a clear field of fire. The disastrous British frontal attacks continued all day, with men making brave but futile attempts to break through the Boer defences. There were more British soldiers killed that day than the total number of casualties suffered by them between leaving Modder River in December 1899 and occupying Bloemfontein on 13 March 1900.

After this huge loss of life, Roberts forbade any further frontal attacks when he was back in command. Instead, he gathered 70 guns together to shell the Boer laager. He had 40,000 troops and almost 100 guns against the 4,000 Boers with only five guns.

Boer scout Danie Theron

General De Wet had meanwhile arrived to help Cronjé out of his predicament and had taken control of some hills about 4km south of the river, known to the Boers as Oskoppies and to the British as Kitchener's Hill. Cronjé sent the men who had horses to join De Wet, but out of a total of 50 only 20 got through. The rest were killed or taken prisoner.

Roberts then sent a message to Cronjé, offering safe passage for the women and children, but this was refused as the women were not willing to leave. On 23 February Boer scout Danie Theron got through the British lines from De Wet's position to deliver a message to Cronjé to the effect that he should attempt to break out to the south, where he would be supported by De Wet's men. However, Cronjé's officers refused to agree to this, saying that

The gallant Colonel Hannay

Colonel Ormelie Campbell Hannay received an order from Kitchener to charge the Boer camp, an order that he knew would lead to the death of those who obeyed it. To save his men, he galloped ahead alone against the centre of the Boer position. When he was only about halfway there his horse was shot from under him, but he got up and continued the charge on foot. He was hit several times before he fell. His brave act was a forcible demonstration against Kitchener's practice of sacrificing men by giving them orders that would undoubtedly result in death.

This memorial in the cemetery at Paardeberg is dedicated to the Boers who fell during the battle.

the river, which had come down in flood, would be impossible for the wagons to cross without a bridge. Attempts were made to build a chain bridge, but it was swept away. The battle became a siege that was to last until 27 February. The Boers in the laager suffered terribly in incessant rain, the carcasses of dead horses and oxen polluting their camp, while the British subjected them to an almost continuous bombardment. On 27 February, on the anniversary of the Battle of Majuba Hill (see p. 189), Cronjé surrendered.

Aftermath

Following their surrender, 4,085 Boers were made prisoners of war. British casualties were high, with 303 men dead, 906 wounded and 61 missing. The surrender had a dreadful effect on Boer morale and was a contributory factor to the Boer defeat in Natal, at the Battle of Tugela Heights (see p. 98), which preceded the relief of Ladysmith.

General Piet Cronjé (front row, centre) in exile on St Helena Island

Principal combatants

British: 10th and 14th Hussars; 9th, 12th and 16th Lancers; Argyll and Sutherland Highlanders; Australian Horse; Bedfordshire Regiment; Black Watch; East Kents Regiment; Essex Regiment; Gloucestershire Regiment; Highland Light Infantry; Household Cavalry Regiment; Mounted infantry; New South Wales Lancers; New South Wales Mounted Rifles; Oxfordshire Light Infantry; Royal Canadian Regiment of Infantry; Royal Field Artillery; Royal Irish Regiment; Royal Warwickshire Regiment; Scandinavian Corps; Seaforth Highlanders; Welsh Regiment; West Riding Regiment; Wiltshire Regiment; Worcestershire Regiment; Yorkshire Regiment.
Boers: Members of commandos from Bloemfontein, Ficksburg, Ladybrand, Potchefstroom and Winburg; Boers under the command of General Piet Cronjé; Staatsartillerie.

Battle of Boshof

Also known as *Battle of Tweefontein*

5 April 1900

HOW TO GET THERE
From Kimberley, travel towards Bloemfontein along the R64 to reach Boshof/Dealesville. In the middle of Boshof, turn right into Voortrekker Street. After 500m, turn right into Oranje Street. This is the road to Bosvark. Continue on this road for approximately 9km, then turn left onto the road to the farm Middelkuil. After about 6km, you will reach the battlefield and the memorial to General De Villebois-Mareuil. There is also a war memorial in the grounds of the Dutch Reformed Church in Boshof.

Context
Comte De Villebois-Mareuil, commander of the European Legion in South Africa and holding the local rank of vechtgeneraal (combat general), was critical of the Boers' lack of discipline and fighting methods. He recommended a form of guerrilla war against the cumbersome British columns operating in the Orange Free State. The attack on Boshof was designed to demonstrate the effectiveness of this type of fighting. He planned an elaborate night attack on the town, but the British sent out a column, which surrounded the approaching Boers.

Action
De Villebois-Mareuil was organising foreign troops in South Africa into a European legion to fight against the British. He planned to use 100 of these men to launch a night attack on Boshof, which had been held by a small British garrison. However, General Paul Methuen had recently arrived in the town with a column of more than 7,000 men and 12 field guns.

Although De Villebois-Mareuil was informed by Boer scouts that reinforcements had reached Boshof and that his small force would be countered by thousands – rather than hundreds, of troops – he refused to abandon the attack. However, he approached the town with caution, camping the night of 4 April on the farm Tweefontein, 8km south-east of Boshof.

British scouts reported the approach of De Villebois-Mareuil's horsemen. At first light on 5 April, Methuen sent a column comprising six companies of infantry (many of them Imperial Yeomanry), one field battery and the Kimberley Mounted Volunteers to locate and capture them. They came across the enemy on two small hills.

The Comte De Villebois-Mareuil

258 BLOEMFONTEIN & KIMBERLEY REGIONS

The hills were surrounded and three field guns supported the soldiers, who approached on foot to within 50m of the Boers. The Boers urged De Villebois-Mareuil to surrender, arguing that they were up against superior numbers supported by artillery, of which they had none. But De Villebois-Mareuil refused, preferring to fight rather than to be taken prisoner.

When the British were about to charge forward, with bayonets fixed, one of the Boers showed the flag of surrender. However, when the British came forward to take prisoners, other Boers fired into them. This abuse of the white flag caused the battle to rage on. The British guns again poured deadly shrapnel into the Boers on the crest. De Villebois-Mareuil was one of the first to be hit and die. Most of the remaining men surrendered, although a few managed to get away.

Aftermath

Thirteen Boers were dead and 54 prisoners were taken. They had lost a brave man and a talented leader in the Comte De Villebois-Mareuil. Lord Methuen arranged for his burial in the Boshof churchyard, but the body was later reinterred at Magersfontein. The British had three dead and seven wounded.

Methuen's reputation, suffering after his defeat at Magersfontein, was restored through this successful action at the Battle of Boshof. At the same time, the Imperial Yeomanry had shown that they could be relied upon.

Principal combatants

British: Imperial Yeomanry; Kimberley Mounted Volunteers; Royal Field Artillery.
Boers: Commandos from Bloemfontein, Boshof and Hoopstad; French Corps.

In spite of not being formally trained soldiers, the Imperial Yeomanry showed their mettle during the Battle of Boshof.

Timeline

1870–1871
Georges de Villebois-Mareuil, an officer in the French army, fights bravely in the Franco-Prussian War. He is promoted to the rank of captain.

1895
He resigns from the French army because he is not given an active command.

1899
In September De Villebois-Mareuil arrives in South Africa to fight for the republican cause. General Piet Joubert appoints him military adviser to the Boers, ahead of the outbreak of the war a month later.

In December De Villebois-Mareuil is present at the Battle of Colenso. After this clash, the British need reinforcements. A corps of mounted men drawn from organised regiments of Yeomanry is formed. Termed the Imperial Yeomanry, the men are sent to the Cape Colony to join General Lord Methuen's (right) force.

1900
At a meeting in Kroonstad, the Boers agree to adopt a different method of warfare. De Villebois-Mareuil is appointed fighting general in the Boer army and tasked with mobilising and commanding a 'European legion' of foreign volunteers. A month later he is killed at the Battle of Boshof.

1902
Methuen is defeated by General Koos de la Rey at Tweebosch.

1907
Methuen becomes commander-in-chief in South Africa.

1909
Methuen becomes governor of Natal until union in 1910.

Battle of Magersfontein
11 December 1899

HOW TO GET THERE
From Kimberley, take the N12 south. After about 28km (before you cross the Modder River), turn left. Drive a further 1.5km until you reach the sign to the battlefield, where you turn left. Drive 8km until you see the gate to the battlefield on your left.

Drive through the gates and follow the track around the main hill to the restaurant and car park. Follow the concrete path that leads up the hill behind the restaurant to the lookout point. From here, you are close to the sites of the Boer Krupp gun and the Boer trenches, which were below. The Modder River lies to the south. It was over this flat terrain that the British approached before dawn on the day of the battle.

The museum is situated on the opposite side of the car park, a little way up the smaller hill. It has excellent displays showing the course of the battle. On the hill behind the museum is a memorial to the Highland Brigade. To visit the graves of 11 Transvalers, as well as the Scandinavian memorial, drive back the way you came in and take the track to the left. There is a walking trail to these sites. The Black Watch memorial is on the other side of the road from the entrance gate. The Boer memorial is about 4km down this road if you turn left (north) towards Kimberley on leaving the battlefield.

Entrance gate: 28°58'13.4" S 24°42'17.7" E
Boer memorial: 28°57'12.2" S 24°44'02.1" E

Context

After the Battle of Modder River (see p. 268), Lord Methuen made his comfortable headquarters on the north bank of the river and waited for reinforcements to arrive. There were good reasons not to move forward sooner; repairs were needed to the railway bridge, his army was exhausted, his supplies were depleted, and Methuen himself was still recovering from a thigh wound sustained at the Battle of Modder River. Furthermore, the besieged in Kimberley had managed to send a message, advising that they had supplies to last for another 40 days at least.

On 4 December supplies and reinforcements began to arrive. The additional troops included the kilted Highland Brigade, commanded by Major General Andy Wauchope. With them were the Gordon Highlanders, Canadian and Australian contingents, 12th Lancers and 100 mounted infantry. There was also a battery of Royal Horse Artillery and the 4.7-inch (120mm) naval gun known as Joe Chamberlain.

Memorial stone, Magersfontein Museum

260 BLOEMFONTEIN & KIMBERLEY REGIONS

Armoured trains, such as this one at Magersfontein, were used extensively during the 2nd Anglo-Boer War.

Methuen then made his battle plans: he would proceed towards Kimberley, cutting the Boer defensive line east of the railway at a line of low hills known as the Magersfontein Koppies. The Highland Brigade would be given the honour of launching the attack, which was to be preceded by a night march from the British camp to the place Methuen had selected for the start of the attack.

Action

Methuen's army at this stage numbered over 11,000 men, but less than a third of these were involved in the battle. The Highland Brigade was made up of three battalions and numbered about 3,500 men. The battalions included the Black Watch, the Seaforth Highlanders, the Argylls and Sutherlands and the Highland Light Infantry. All wore kilts, apart from the Highland Light Infantry. The Highlanders had learned the hard way that the dark kilt with its light-coloured sporran made an excellent target for Boer marksmen. On this occasion, no sporrans were worn and each man had a khaki apron covering the front of his kilt.

On 10 December the British artillery batteries were moved to within range of the line of low hills and began their bombardment. They were aided by the Naval Brigade's answer to the Boer Long Tom: a 4.7-inch (120mm) naval gun with a range of close to 10,000m. The hills erupted in dirty yellowish clouds of dust

Timeline

1899
In November Boers led by General Koos de la Rey oppose General Lord Methuen on his way to the besieged town of Kimberley. Battles are fought at Belmont, Graspan and Modder River, where De la Rey is wounded and his son is killed. Methuen, commanding the British forces, is also wounded.

In December, Major General Andy Wauchope (right), commanding the Highland Brigade, arrives to reinforce Methuen's division. Boer general Piet Cronjé replaces the wounded De la Rey to command the Boers at Magersfontein, implementing a battle strategy planned by De la Rey. The Highland Brigade leads the way at the Battle of Magersfontein and Wauchope is killed. The Battle of Colenso is fought and lost by the British in Natal. General Lord Roberts supersedes General Buller as commander-in-chief of the British army in South Africa and takes over from Methuen as commander of the 1st Division.

1900
In January General John French's cavalry engages De la Rey's commandos near Colesberg.

In February Lord Roberts (left) renews the offensive and French's cavalry bypasses the Boer defences in the Magersfontein Hills to relieve the siege of Kimberley, while Roberts approaches Bloemfontein.

In March Bloemfontein is occupied.

In May Roberts's army takes Johannesburg. Pretoria falls a few days later, on 5 June.

BATTLE OF MAGERSFONTEIN 261

The unknown soldier

A young Scottish bandsman died on the battlefield at Magersfontein where he was found by the victorious Boers. The Boers buried him with their dead and gave him a memorial stone, even though his name was not known at the time. He was later identified as William Milne, of the Seaforth Highlanders. His name now appears on an extra tablet on his gravestone at the Boer monument in Magersfontein.

and rocks as the high-explosive lyddite shells rained down, but the Boers were elsewhere. During the entire bombardment only three men were wounded.

They marched in close formation (quarter column), struggling over the rough terrain to hold a body of 3,500 men in a rough rectangle about 45m across and 160m long. Each man held on to his neighbour's clothing, and guide ropes were used to keep the half-companies aligned in the pitch darkness. The men were ably guided by Major George Benson, with a compass in each hand. He had done a reconnaissance of the ground that morning and eventually succeeded in getting the men to a point very close to that which Methuen had indicated. When they were within 1,200m of the Magersfontein Hills, dawn was only half an hour away and the silhouette of the dark high ground could be seen against a lightening sky. The men halted, ready to deploy. This would have opened the packed mass of troops facing the hills, but Wauchope, anxious that they would lose direction, ordered them to advance a little further before breaking the formation.

The Boers were commanded during this battle by Piet Cronjé. They had been inspired by the arrival of President Steyn in Jacobsdal, where he had made an impassioned speech urging them to support General De la Rey, who had planned the Boer strategy. At the time, De la Rey was receiving treatment for a shoulder wound he had sustained at the Battle of Modder River.

The Boers' defensive line stretched from a drift across the Modder River, east of Magersfontein, through the high Magersfontein ridges and then west of the railway line as far as Langberg Hill, visible from the present-day N12, which lies south of Kimberley. De la Rey had ordered the construction of a network of interleading trenches at the foot of the Magersfontein Hills. Coils of barbed wire covered the approaches to the trenches and branches concealed each

Lord Methuen observing the battle

262 BLOEMFONTEIN & KIMBERLEY REGIONS

Interred in the crypt of the Magersfontein Burgher Monument are the remains of those who fell within a 100km radius, among them Adriaan de la Rey, the Comte De Villebois-Mareuil and Scandinavian volunteers fighting for the Boers.

excavation. The bombardment on the morning of 10 December had warned the 8,000 Boers that an attack on Magersfontein was imminent and they manned these trenches, waiting for the infantry to arrive.

The Boers heard the British before they saw them, the crunch of boots warning them that the attack would come at first light. It was when the Boers saw the packed men about to deploy and open their order that the firing began – an opening barrage of rifle shots that was described by survivors as 'a river of fire'. The Highland Brigade was prevented from moving rapidly into open order by thick patches of thorn bush in the line of their advance and bullets ripped into the closely packed men. Within minutes most of the officers fell, as well as hundreds of men. General Wauchope gave the order to reinforce to the right; his aide-de-camp went to relay the order and, on his return, found the general dead. The Boers were firing on the stricken mass of prostrate, kilted figures.

However, the British were meanwhile deploying to the right and left, and the battle was by no means over. Reinforcements were sent forward and some men found a gap in the centre of the Boer line, through which they advanced to take up positions on the rising ground. From there they were able to fire into the Boer rear,

General Koos de la Rey

BATTLE OF MAGERSFONTEIN   263

The open ground over which the British advanced on the Magersfontein Hills

Lord Horatio Kitchener with his aide, Lieutenant Frank Maxwell

but were forced back by a band of men led by Cronjé, who was in the right place by chance, having got lost in the thunderstorm.

By mid-morning the sun was fiercely hot and the Highlanders, lying flat with the backs of their knees exposed, suffered severely. Fire from the Boer trenches was accurate and unremitting. Any movement, to get water or to shift an aching limb, attracted a bullet from the invisible enemy.

The British observation balloon had, by this time, found the whereabouts of the Boer trenches and shells were falling close to them, keeping their rate of fire down. Under such cover, some British soldiers were able to reach the eastern slopes of the hill to the right of the main position, where they engaged the Scandinavians, who were fighting as

264   BLOEMFONTEIN & KIMBERLEY REGIONS

volunteers for the Boers. The Scandinavians were nearly all killed, after fighting ferociously, none of them willing to be taken prisoner by a Scot.

It was a little after 13h00 that the Boers managed to make their way around the right of the British, forcing the commanding officer in that sector to order his men to withdraw slightly to the rear. At the same time, the Boer guns opened up on the retreating men. This was the final straw for the Highlanders. They broke and fled, despite frantic threats from their remaining officers. Many were killed as they ran back towards the camp.

Wauchope had been mortally wounded. Most officers had suffered the same fate and there was no-one left to lead a concerted attack on the Boer positions. As the shadows grew longer, Methuen realised that further advance was impossible and ordered a general withdrawal. Many more were killed as the men retreated back towards the Modder River. At about 18h00 the Boers indicated that they would not shoot wounded men on the battlefield, and clambered out of their deep trenches. An armistice was declared as both sides collected their dead and wounded.

Aftermath

There were 192 British dead and more than 690 wounded. The Boers lost 71 men, and a further 184 were wounded, although different reports give different figures. This defeat, and the British reverse at Stormberg (see p. 301) the day before, persuaded General Sir Redvers Buller to launch an ill-prepared attack on Colenso (see p. 69) in Natal on 15 December. Kimberley was eventually relieved by General John French and his cavalry forces, leaving Methuen's division to enter the occupied town almost unnoticed.

Principal combatants

British: 9th and 12th Lancers; Argyll and Sutherland Highlanders; Black Watch; Grenadier Guards; Highland Light Infantry; King's Own Yorkshire Light Infantry; Loyal North Lancashire Regiment; Manchester Regiment; Northamptonshire Regiment; Northumberland Fusiliers; Royal Engineers; Royal Field Artillery; Royal Horse Artillery; Scots Guards; Seaforth Highlanders.

Boers: Commandos from Bloemfontein, Bloemhof, Fauresmith, Ficksburg, Hoopstad, Jacobsdal, Klerksdorp, Kroonstad, Ladybrand, Lichtenberg, Potchefstroom, Senekal and Wolmaransstad; Scandinavian Corps.

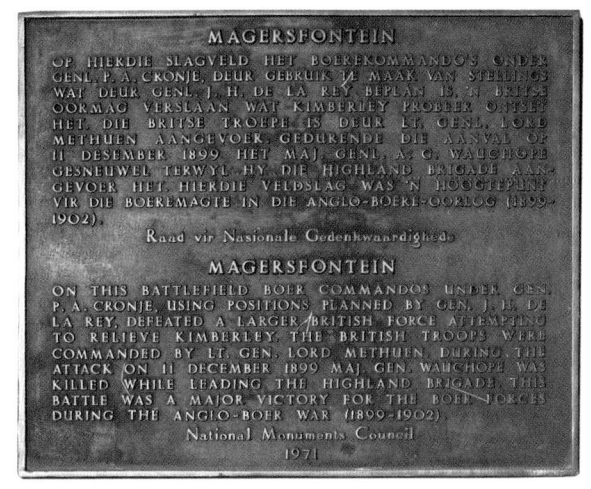

A plaque at the Magersfontein Battlefield Museum, indicating that it is a heritage site. The museum was opened in 1971.

BATTLE OF MAGERSFONTEIN   265

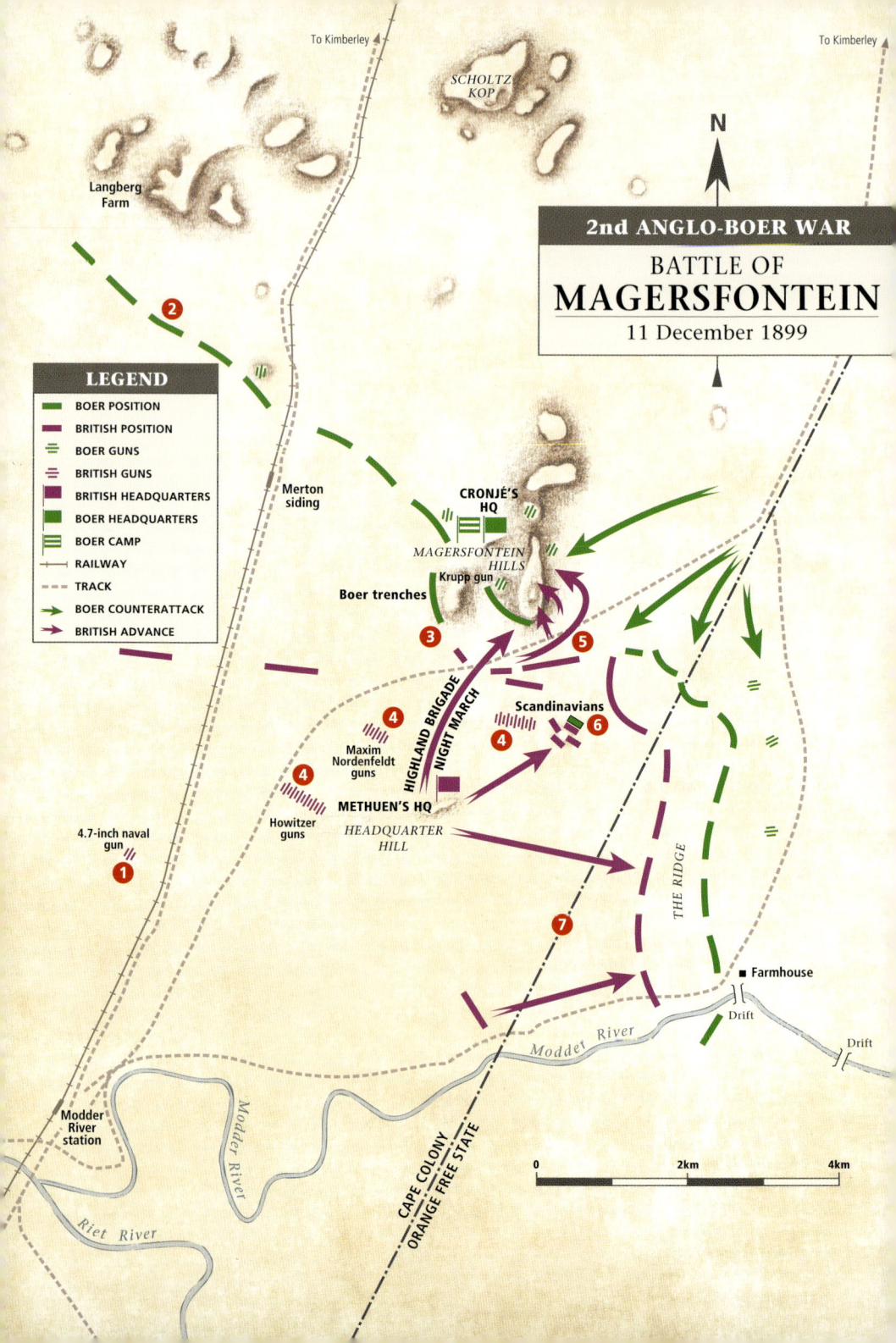

2nd ANGLO-BOER WAR
BATTLE OF MAGERSFONTEIN
11 December 1899

LEGEND
- BOER POSITION
- BRITISH POSITION
- BOER GUNS
- BRITISH GUNS
- BRITISH HEADQUARTERS
- BOER HEADQUARTERS
- BOER CAMP
- RAILWAY
- TRACK
- BOER COUNTERATTACK
- BRITISH ADVANCE

To Kimberley

SCHOLTZ KOP

Langberg Farm

Merton siding

CRONJÉ'S HQ

MAGERSFONTEIN HILLS

Krupp gun

Boer trenches

HIGHLAND BRIGADE NIGHT MARCH

Maxim Nordenfeldt guns

Scandinavians

METHUEN'S HQ

Howitzer guns

HEADQUARTER HILL

THE RIDGE

4.7-inch naval gun

Modder River station

Modder River

Riet River

CAPE COLONY | ORANGE FREE STATE

Farmhouse

Drift

0   2km   4km

Boers lay concealed in trenches in front of these hills at Magersfontein.

1 The British 4.7-inch (120mm) naval gun in this position opened an artillery bombardment against the Magersfontein ridges on 10 December, the day before the battle.

2 The Boer line stretched from here, close to Langberg Hill in the west, reaching over the Magersfontein Hills to end close to the Modder River in the east.

3 Boer General Koos de la Rey had placed trenches stretching along almost 1km of flat ground at the base of the hills in this area.

4 British artillery batteries were placed on both sides of the line of advance of the Highland Brigade. Shells from these guns forced the Boers to take cover and enabled British infantry to gain the slopes of the hills to the east.

5 A gap in the Boer line made it possible for the British to get through the Boer defences and gain the slopes of the hill behind the trenches. The arrival of Piet Cronjé and his commando forced the British back.

6 Here the British engaged a Scandinavian contingent fighting as volunteers for the Boers. They fought exceptionally bravely and were nearly all killed.

7 The border between the Orange Free State and the Cape Colony ran through these hills.

Memorial for the men of the Highland regiments who fell at Magersfontein

Battle of Modder River

Also known as *Battle of Twee Riviere*

28 November 1899

HOW TO GET THERE

Drive from Kimberley on the N12 towards Hopetown. Right after crossing the Modder River Bridge, follow the signs to the battlefield on the left. The road will take you down to the river and under the railway bridge. As you face the water, the confluence of the Riet and Modder rivers is on your right. The Boer trenches and rifle pits were close to where you stand, to the right and left. The British were approaching from behind you. Some of them got across the river, left of the railway line, and into the village on the north bank. There were Boer guns on the north bank of the river.

South of the river and on the east side of the railway line is a stone blockhouse constructed in 1901. Near the parking area is a model of a corrugated-iron blockhouse of the sort that was used in numbers during the latter stages of the war.

To reach the village of Modder River, drive over the bridge to the north bank of the river and follow the signs into the village. The Crown & Royal Hotel, site of the British headquarters after the battle, is on the main road.

Confluence of the Riet and Modder rivers: 29°2'20.3" S 24°37'29.8" E

This posed photograph of Cape Garrison Artillery officers aiming at Boers across the Modder River was taken before the battle.

Context

General Lord Paul Methuen and his troops were on their way to Kimberley, having defeated the Boers at both Belmont (see p. 280) and Graspan (see p. 277) a few days earlier. General Koos de la Rey had realised from these battles, where the British had twice broken through the Boer defensive line, that it was not always advantageous to hold positions on the high ground. British artillery firing shrapnel could make a hilltop untenable and, if the sides of the hill were steep, the enemy was afforded dead ground through which it could advance unharmed.

At Modder River, he chose his defensive positions differently. He planned to halt the British advance by using the low-lying land, where the road and railway bridges cross the Modder and Riet rivers close to their confluence, for his trenches and rifle pits.

During the wait after the battle, some of the officers rigged up shelters to escape the baking sun.

Action

Deep, concealed trenches were dug in the south banks of the river, extending east and west of the railway bridge. The trenches were well constructed and camouflaged with branches and soil. His men were instructed to hold their fire until the British were at close range.

Methuen had believed the Boers to be in retreat, until he received intelligence that they had been seen on the north bank of the Modder in the vicinity of the railway bridge. He planned an attack in order to clear the way for his advance across a river that, he had been told, was easily fordable in many places at this point – information that turned out to be incorrect.

His troops left camp at 04h00 on 28 November and the battle began with the British artillery bombarding the north banks of the river, the shells passing harmlessly over the heads of the Boers in their trenches on the south side. Methuen sent his troops forward in open order, the whole formation marching over the flat terrain as if on parade. They were horribly surprised by the barrage of rifle and gunfire that met them about 1,000m before the river.

Contrary to De la Rey's orders, some of General Cronjé's Orange Free State Boers lost their nerve and fired too soon. What could have been a massacre became, instead, a gruelling duel that was to last 10 hours and end with a Boer withdrawal by night.

De la Rey led his men from the centre of his Transvaal commandos, close to the railway bridge. The open ground suited the Mausers to perfection and Major Friedrich Albrecht of the Staatsartillerie used his 75mm Krupp guns to good effect, pinning the British down in the broiling sun as the Boers poured fire into anything that moved.

Timeline

1899
The war in South Africa begins in October and Boers invade the Cape and Natal. Boers led by General Koos de la Rey capture an armoured train near the western border of the Transvaal. In Natal there are battles at Dundee, Elandslaagte, Rietfontein and Ladysmith.

In November Ladysmith is besieged and British forces commanded by General Lord Methuen gather at Orange River station, where the railway line from Cape Town to Kimberley crosses the Orange River. Battles are fought at Belmont and Graspan. De la Rey (below) returns from Mafeking to command the Boers around Kimberley. At Modder River, Methuen is opposed by De la Rey's forces.

In December the British, under General William Gatacre, are defeated at Stormberg. Methuen is defeated again at Magersfontein. The Battle of Colenso in Natal results in 1,450 casualties. Lord Roberts takes over from General Sir Redvers Buller as commander-in-chief of the British army in South Africa.

BATTLE OF MODDER RIVER 269

Koos de la Rey

During the Battle of Modder River, General Koos de la Rey carried no weapons, but he had with him a leather sjambok that he sometimes used to lash his men into obedience. At his side was his eldest son, Adriaan, who was to be killed that evening during the battle – two days after his 19th birthday. There is a memorial to him in the Jacobsdal Garden of Remembrance.

The Highlanders in their kilts suffered greatly as the backs of their bare legs were exposed to the burning sun all day. Both sides suffered from ferocious thirst, but the Boers – in the shelter of their trenches and with the river close at hand – were better off.

Apart from causing many casualties, the Boers' Maxim Nordenfeldt gun, with its murderous one-pound shells, had an enormously demoralising effect on the British infantrymen, caught as they were in the open without cover. For a while it seemed the British had been beaten. However, there were no Boer guns west of the railway bridge, which meant that the British on the left were not pinned down by shellfire and could use whatever cover they could find to creep in on the Orange Free Staters holding the extreme right of the Boer line. These Boers had suffered worst during the defeats at Belmont and Graspan. Demoralised and undisciplined, they were commanded by a weak leader, Jacobus Prinsloo. When the British approached with bayonets fixed, they fled.

Some of the British soldiers on the left flank waded across the river, using the dam weir to get across the swirling water and storm the high ground north of the river. They occupied buildings in the village and drove out occupants at bayonet point. De La Rey himself led a furious counterattack to send many British back across the river. But some held their positions

The Garden of Remembrance in Jacobsdal contains memorials to both British and Boer soldiers.

BLOEMFONTEIN & KIMBERLEY REGIONS

on the north bank even as darkness was falling. De la Rey was slightly injured in the shoulder. Worse still, his son Adriaan had received a stomach wound from a spent shell. He was carried to hospital in a blanket and died shortly afterwards.

Aftermath

Apart from his personal grief at losing his son, De la Rey was bitterly disappointed that the Orange Free Staters had fled, saying

The original Crown & Royal Hotel served as the British headquarters after the battle.

that, if they had only held on, the British would have had to go back to the Orange River for water and that many would have perished in the sandy wastes between the rivers. However, without the support of the Orange Free State men on the right of the Boer line, De la Rey saw no alternative but to withdraw and take up another defensive position further north, below the Magersfontein Hills.

Seventy British soldiers were killed and 413 wounded, while 16 Boers were killed and 66 wounded. An additional 13 Boers were taken prisoner. Lord Methuen had sustained a painful flesh wound in the thigh, making this the only time that both commanders were wounded in the same engagement in the war. Because the railway bridge had been damaged by Boers, Methuen now had to wait for reinforcements before attempting the repair needed to get his troops across the river. Certain reports claim that some of his troops secretly left Modder River to join Lord Roberts's approaching army.

Principal combatants

British: 9th Lancers; Argyll and Sutherland Highlanders; Black Watch; Coldstream Guards; Colonial Mounted Irregulars; Diamond Fields Horse; Grenadier Guards; Highland Light Infantry; Kimberley Light Horse; Loyal North Lancashire Regiment; Naval Brigade; New South Wales Lancers; Northamptonshire Regiment; Northumberland Fusiliers; Rimington's Scouts; Royal Field Artillery; Royal Horse Artillery; Seaforth Highlanders; South African Reserve; Yorkshire Light Infantry.
Boers: Commandos from Bloemfontein, Bloemhof, Fauresmith, Ficksburg, Hoopstad, Jacobsdal, Klerksdorp, Kroonstad, Ladybrand, Lichtenburg, Potchefstroom, Senekal and Wolmaransstad; Staatsartillerie.

Christmas presents arrive for British troops.

BATTLE OF MODDER RIVER 271

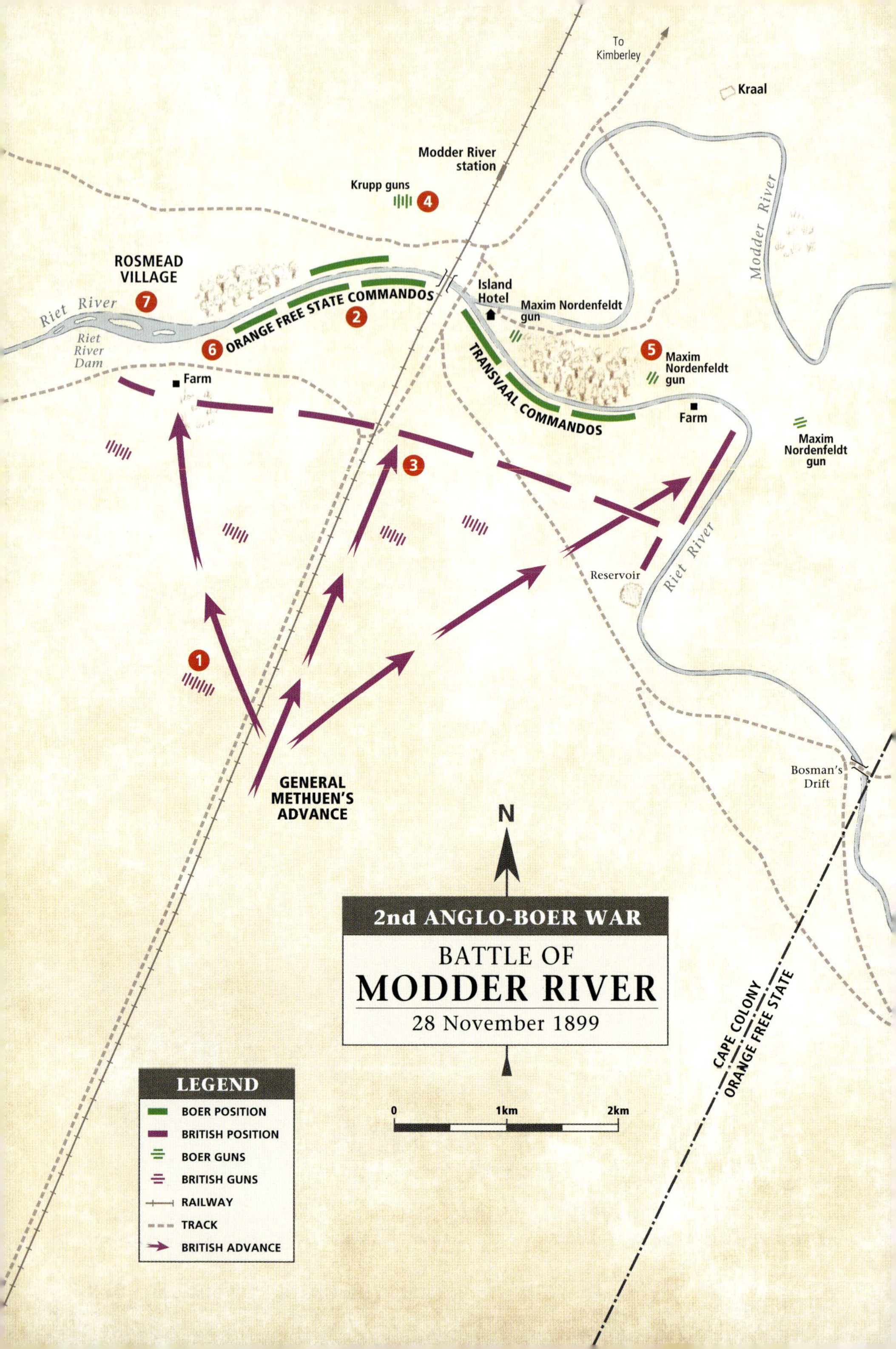

2nd ANGLO-BOER WAR
BATTLE OF
MODDER RIVER
28 November 1899
To Kimberley
Kraal
Modder River station
Krupp guns
ROSMEAD VILLAGE
Riet River
Riet River Dam
ORANGE FREE STATE COMMANDOS
Island Hotel
Maxim Nordenfeldt gun
TRANSVAAL COMMANDOS
Maxim Nordenfeldt gun
Modder River
Farm
Farm
Maxim Nordenfeldt gun
Reservoir
Riet River
Bosman's Drift
GENERAL METHUEN'S ADVANCE
N
0
1km
2km
CAPE COLONY
ORANGE FREE STATE
LEGEND
BOER POSITION
BRITISH POSITION
BOER GUNS
BRITISH GUNS
RAILWAY
TRACK
BRITISH ADVANCE

① The British advance began with an artillery bombardment from these guns, aimed at the north bank of the river. The shells passed harmlessly over the heads of the Boers concealed in trenches on the south bank of the river.

② The Boer trenches stretched along the river east and west of the bridge. The Boer commander, Koos de la Rey, was with his Transvaal commandos close to the centre of the defensive line.

③ The British advanced across this open flat ground, which offered little cover from the Boer bullets and shells. De la Rey had ordered his men to hold their fire until the British were at close range, but some men of the Free State commandos fired prematurely and thus prevented a complete massacre and a decisive Boer victory.

④ The Boer Staatsartillerie fired shells from their German Krupp guns into the lines of advancing British soldiers.

⑤ The Boer's Maxim Nordenfeldt guns, located east of the bridge, had a demoralising effect on the British, who were forced to lie flat in the hot sun all day because any movement would attract shells, which exploded with dreadful regularity.

⑥ Boers on this end of the line did not have artillery support and the British were able to creep forward, using whatever cover they could find to get very close to the river and to the positions of some of the Orange Free State Boers.

⑦ When the Boers in these trenches fled, some British soldiers forded the river, using the dam weir to aid their crossing. They got into Rosmead village and began to advance on the Boers north of the river. De la Rey mounted a furious counterattack.

Members of the Royal Field Artillery on their way to Kimberley

Battle of Koedoesberg Drift
5–7 February 1900

HOW TO GET THERE
Take the N12 south from Kimberley towards Hopetown. Turn right at Ritchie and proceed to Kerk Street in the village. Continue on this road for about 25km. Just before you reach a T-junction, turn sharp left towards the Riet River. The place where the gravel road crosses the Riet River on a bridge is close to the old Koedoesberg Drift.

Lord Frederick Roberts

Context

After the Battle of Magersfontein, Lord Methuen waited at Modder River station camp for reinforcements. Meanwhile, the British commander-in-chief, General Roberts, brought cavalry up the line from Colesberg and prepared to pass east of Modder River station to reach Kimberley, relieve the siege and then occupy Bloemfontein. He wished to distract the Boers camped at Magersfontein from his movements and also needed to protect Methuen's line of communication with Cape Town by preventing Boers from moving south over the Riet River at Koedoesberg Drift.

General Hector MacDonald was sent with a force of almost 2,000 men to build a small fort to hold the drift. When Boer scouts reported that a British force was moving west along the river from Modder River camp, Commandant Floris du Plooy, leading 100 men, rode to counter them. His troops were later reinforced by General Christiaan de Wet and a Krupp gun. The battle was a series of skirmishes that took place on and under the Koedoesberg ridge between 5 and 7 February 1900.

The British observe Boer positions across the Modder River.

274 BLOEMFONTEIN & KIMBERLEY REGIONS

On 13 March 1900 Lord Roberts occupied Bloemfontein without opposition.

Action

The Highland Brigade, comprising four battalions, left Modder River station camp on 3 February 1900 to march west along the Riet River. It was exceedingly hot and men were dropping from heat and exhaustion. On 4 February the men reached their destination, a crossing of the river close to the Koedoesberg, a dominant hill on the north bank.

General Hector MacDonald ordered entrenchments to be built on both sides of the river and began the construction, on the north bank, of a small fort to protect the drift. Many men spent the day bathing in the river, welcoming the opportunity to cool down. They were called to arms when 100 Boers, led by Du Plooy, approached the Koedoesberg. Shots were fired and the Boers retired before superior numbers. The next day General De Wet arrived. He had requested more men than he had been granted by Piet Cronjé and arrived with only 300 men. They engaged the British on the river banks, but neither side was able to force the other back.

On 6 February the Boers cautiously approached the fort that the British were building, but they were unable to take it. Fortunately for the Boers, another 200 men led by Andries Cronjé had arrived. With them came a Krupp gun. De Wet realised that the key to the position was the Koedoesberg ridge, and the Krupp gun was manhandled up onto the northern summit of the hill, from where it fired on the construction works below. The four British guns on the southern summit of the Koedoesberg answered and an artillery duel was fought throughout the day. MacDonald, realising that the battle was to be fought on the hill, not down at the river, sent men to reinforce the Seaforth Highlanders on the southern high ground, while snipers on both sides tried to reach their enemy on the opposite hill.

Timeline

1880
Hector MacDonald (right) works his way through the army ranks to become, at the age of 27, 2nd lieutenant in the 92nd Gordon Highlanders.

1881
A peak on Majuba Mountain is named after MacDonald, who demonstrated exceptional bravery during the Battle of Majuba Hill.

1891
MacDonald is promoted to major general after service in Egypt and the Sudan.

1896
Scottish golfer Freddie Tait, third son of an Edinburgh professor, wins the British amateur golf championship.

1899
The 2nd Anglo-Boer War breaks out. Now an officer in the Black Watch, the former golfer Freddie Tait (left) comes to South Africa as part of the Highland Brigade. MacDonald and the Gordon Highlanders arrive in South Africa to reinforce the Highland Brigade after the Battle of Magersfontein. MacDonald takes over command from Major General Andy Wauchope, who was killed during the battle.

1900
MacDonald commands the battle at Koedoesberg Drift. Cronjé arrives with 200 men and a Krupp gun to bombard the British fort. Lieutenant Tait, leading the Highland Brigade in a charge against the Boers, is shot through the chest and dies.

1902
The 2nd Anglo-Boer War ends.

1929
The Freddie Tait Cup, contested for the first time, is awarded annually to the leading South African amateur. On the cup is the badge of the British Army Golfing Society, of which Tait was a member.

BATTLE OF KOEDOESBERG DRIFT   275

MacDonald sent a message to the Modder River station requesting cavalry and horse artillery. He intended them to approach from the north and surround the Boers on Koedoesberg, thereby forcing them to surrender. General James Babington left Modder River at 11h30 on 7 November with cavalry and 12 guns. By all accounts, the column moved very slowly. By the time Babington reached Koedoesberg, the Boers were gone, having retreated upon news of the approaching column. They withdrew by night, to hills further north.

Aftermath

Three Boers were killed and four wounded. British casualties were also light, with three men killed (one of them the famous golfer Lieutenant Freddie Tait) and four wounded. The British had successfully distracted the Boers away from their eastern line of advance.

Principal combatants

British: 10th Hussars; 9th Lancers; Argyll and Sutherland Highlanders; Army Service Corps; Black Watch; Dragoons; Highland Light Infantry; Naval Brigade; Royal Army Medical Corps; Royal Engineers; Royal Field Artillery; Royal Horse Artillery; Seaforth Highlanders.
Boers: Bethulie Commando; Elements of other Orange Free State commandos; Staatsartillerie.

Siege of Kimberley and the Long Cecil

The inhabitants of besieged Kimberley had at their disposal only artillery guns with relatively short range and small calibre. The surrounding Boer forces knew this and made their positions just out of range of the town's seven-pounders.

Long Cecil was constructed in the De Beers' workshops.

A large-calibre, long-range gun was needed to reach them, and Cecil John Rhodes, who lived in Kimberley for the duration of its siege, made available the workshops of his diamond-mining company, De Beers Consolidated Mining Ltd., for its manufacture. Cleverly designed by George Frederick Labram, an engineer born in Detroit, USA, the gun was ready in a remarkably short time. Its first shell fell close to the pumping station on the outskirts of town, which was occupied by the Boers. The Boers were greatly surprised when the large shell exploded close by.

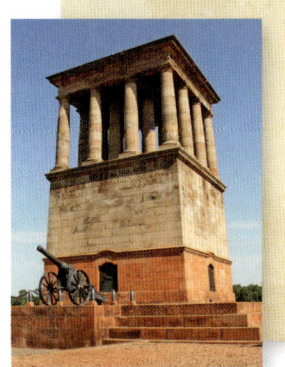

The gun, named Long Cecil, served the town from January 1900 until the siege was lifted on 15 February of that year. Ironically, Labram was killed by a shell from a Boer gun shortly before the siege ended.

The Honoured Dead Memorial where George Frederick Labram, designer of the Long Cecil, is remembered.

Battle of Graspan

Also known as *Battle of Enslin*
and *Battle of Rooilaagte*

25 November 1899

HOW TO GET THERE
Drive south from Kimberley on the N12, continuing for 65km. There is a sign to the battlefield on your left. The battle is variously referred to as Graspan, Enslin and Rooilaagte. Graspan was the name of the railway station, Enslin the name of the siding a short distance further north, and Rooilaagte the name of the farm north-east of the station.

Context
General Lord Paul Methuen's division, on its way to relieve the siege of Kimberley, had forced a way through the Boer defence at Belmont two days before, but failed to capture the enemy. This time, a day's march further up the line, Methuen was determined to do so.

Action
Faulty British intelligence put the number of Boers holding the hills east of Graspan at 400. In reality, there were over 2,000 men. Boer commander Koos de la Rey had arrived to support the Orange Free State burghers under Chief Commandant Jacobus Prinsloo, who had to be persuaded to fight again due to the criticism levelled at him after his poor performance at Belmont (see p. 280). The Boers now had six guns as well as Maxim Nordenfeldt and Hotchkiss machine guns.

On 24 November they fired on a British armoured train from the hills near Graspan and this decided Methuen to launch an attempt to capture the elusive enemy. On 25 November, at 03h30, troops marched north towards the Boer position. The battle began when a single Boer shell was answered by a full-scale bombardment from British guns.

This image, called The Dying Bugler's Last Call, *shows a staged event at the Battle of Graspan.*

Timeline

1899
In October war is declared and Commandant Jacobus Prinsloo leads Boers to surround and besiege Kimberley. In Natal, the Boers take Dundee and Elandslaagte and defeat the British outside Ladysmith.

*V R
RECRUITS
ARE NOW WANTED
For all Branches of
HER MAJESTY'S ARMY.
God Save the Queen.
APPLY TO any RECRUITER or to the nearest POST OFFICE*

In November Ladysmith is besieged. The British army continues to arrive on warships in the Cape Town and Durban harbours. A naval brigade, formed for service on land, entrains in Simon's Town to join General Paul Methuen's column, which is on its way to relieve Kimberley. The brigade joins Methuen's column at Witteputs and proceeds to fight at Belmont, where Prinsloo's Boer force is defeated. Methuen proceeds to Graspan. During this battle in late November, the Naval Brigade is in the forefront of the attack and many of its members are killed. Boer fighters express their dissatisfaction with Prinsloo's leadership, and General Koos de la Rey arrives to take over command of the force. Prinsloo has to be persuaded to fight again.

In December Prinsloo fails in his mission to cut communications between Graspan and the Orange River.

1900
The new year brings battles at Spioenkop and Platrand in Natal. The sieges of Kimberley and Ladysmith are relieved.

Methuen's division comprised the Naval Brigade, Guards' Brigade, 9th Brigade and 900 mounted men. The troops were reported to be hungry, as Methuen had insisted that they march light. He had planned to send his artillery forward on both flanks, using his cavalry on the right to prevent the Boers getting away, but, when he saw that he was strongly opposed, he changed his plan and ordered a frontal assault on the Boer left (east) flank. The hill next to it and further west was to be held, to prevent support being supplied from that quarter.

Both low hills were first bombarded with shrapnel. Shells rained down among the rocks and boulders for half an hour before the advance began. Most of the shells fell harmlessly around the Boers in their trenches, but, when the British soldiers were 600m away, they came under hot fire. The Naval Brigade, made up of 190 marines and 55 sailors, was in the forefront of the assault and was first to come under fire. The troops were not using very open order and, as they neared their target, they converged, going forward in close order, with their officers in front and easily distinguishable by their swords. The brigade was to lose 60 per cent of its officers during the battle.

The hill in the east was manned by the Jacobsdal Commando, led by Commandant W. S. Lubbe. Despite being wounded by shrapnel in his eyes, he continued to encourage his men. Some of the Boers on his right were forced off the high ground, yet they continued to fire at the advancing Naval Brigade from the plain. It was during this battle that De la Rey observed that the Mauser bullet, with its high velocity and flat trajectory, was far more effective when fired from the plain than when

British soldiers guard Boer prisoners during the Battle of Graspan.

fired from the high ground. He was to use this knowledge to his advantage at Modder River three days later (see p. 268). The tactic was again used at Magersfontein two weeks after that (see p. 260).

When the British advance had reached the dead ground at the foot of the hill, the soldiers climbed in short rushes towards the crest, each rush being covered by the men behind them. Once the British neared the enemy trenches, the Boers vacated their positions, retreating northward. As soon as the British had the eastern summit, the rest of the Boer line could be enfiladed, forcing the Boers to retreat, this time in good order. Once again, as at Belmont, Methuen was unable to follow up in pursuit.

The Krupp gun was used to great effect by the Boers.

Aftermath

The British lost 283 men. The Naval Brigade suffered the heaviest casualties, with 11 men dead and 73 wounded. Methuen had learned that the Boers, although greatly outnumbered, were a real threat. Boer losses were 20 dead and 40 wounded. Chief Commandant Prinsloo was replaced by Piet Cronjé, who arrived from Mafeking. His arrival helped to boost Boer morale.

Principal combatants

British: Army Service Corps; Australian Mounted Rifles; Coldstream Guards; Grenadier Guards; King's Own Yorkshire Light Infantry Lancers; Manchester Regiment; Naval Brigade; North Lancashire Regiment; Northamptonshire Regiment; Northumberland Fusiliers; Rimington's Guides; Scots Guards; Royal Army Medical Corps; Royal Engineers; Royal Field Artillery; Royal Horse Artillery.
Boers: Commandos from Bloemfontein, Brandfort, Fauresmith, Jacobsdal and Kroonstad; Transvaal Boers under General Koos de la Rey; Staatsartillerie.

Plumbe's faithful companion

During the Battle of Graspan, Major J. H. Plumbe of the Marine Light Infantry was killed and his body left lying behind a big boulder, unseen by the ambulance men when they collected the dead and wounded. It was the barking of his terrier, devoted and standing next to its dead master, that brought the attention of the ambulance men to the body.

Battle of Belmont
23 November 1899

HOW TO GET THERE
Drive south from Kimberley towards Hopetown on the N12, continuing for about 84km. There is a sign to the battlefield on your left.

Context
War between Britain and the Boer republics broke out in October 1899. The Boers invaded the Cape Colony and invested the garrison towns of Mafeking and Kimberley. In Natal, Ladysmith was besieged. While the overall commander of the British army, General Sir Redvers Buller, concerned himself with events at Ladysmith, General Lord Paul Methuen was sent up the railway line from Cape Town to relieve the siege of Kimberley. The Boers attempted to halt his advance at Belmont.

Action
Methuen, with nearly 9,000 men, had intelligence that more than 2,500 Boers would counter his advance from a line of small hills to the east of Belmont station. He had superior numbers of men and guns and could, perhaps, have bypassed the smaller force, but he was reluctant to leave the railway line open to damage by the Boers, as it was his only way of getting civilians out of Kimberley and back to Cape Town. Besides, he was hampered by a lack of cavalry. With only 900 mounted men in his division, he was not mobile enough to outflank and bypass the enemy easily. His plan was to attack the Boers in the hills and drive them away towards the east, leaving him free to advance uncontested northwards along the railway to Kimberley.

On 22 November the Boers opened fire on the British and their Krupp guns. Methuen sent forward his horse artillery to engage them, exhausting the horses that were still recovering from their long sea voyage. The Boers moved their guns out of range.

On 23 November, at about 02h00, two separate columns of British troops assembled west of the line near Belmont station. The march across the railway line towards the hills 1.5km away began at 03h15. The Guards' Brigade was to launch an attack on Gun Hill, the closest hill and furthest south, while the 9th Brigade marched on Table Mountain, the flat-topped hill further away and north-east of Gun Hill. Behind these features stretched another line of low hills, named Mont Blanc. There were two knolls in this high ground, both south-east of Gun Hill: Razor Back in the centre and Sugar Loaf on the southern end.

The distance to Gun Hill from the railway was greater than Methuen had thought and it took the men until dawn to get there. The Boers opened an inaccurate falling fire, due to the dawn light and their position, and the Guards advanced towards the fire to gain the dead ground directly below the Boers. From there they charged the position, bayonets fixed, which caused the Boers to move back onto Mont Blanc, leaving about 30 horses behind.

Scots and Grenadier Guards take Gun Hill.

Meanwhile, the men of the 9th Brigade had moved north of their intended line of advance because the rising sun made it difficult for them to fire accurately at the Boers when approaching from due west of Table Mountain. Their hot fire on the Boer right flank caused the Boers on Table Mountain to withdraw and take up new positions on Mont Blanc.

Instead of supporting the attack on Table Mountain, the Guards' Brigade swung right to meet the Boer counterattack from Razor Back and Sugar Loaf. Methuen decided to change his plan of action and to support them with everything he had. The reserves joined the attack and the combined forces were too much for the Boers, who fled towards the north-east.

Their retreat was not followed up because of Methuen's lack of cavalry. Attempts to drag one of the naval long 12-pounder guns up Mont Blanc to fire at the retreating enemy were unsuccessful.

Aftermath

Of Methuen's men, 54 were killed and 243 wounded. The Grenadier Guards had lost the most heavily. About 80 Boers died and 70 were taken prisoner. The Boer leader Chief Commandant Jacobus Prinsloo was never to lead the Orange Free State commandos again. The Boers had learned that they needed strong leadership and clever tactics to counter the discipline and numerical superiority of the British army.

Methuen was able to continue his advance up the line. But he was soon to be opposed again, less than a day's march from Belmont.

Principal combatants

British: Army Service Corps; Coldstream Guards; Grenadier Guards; King's Own Yorkshire Light Infantry; Manchester Regiment; Naval Brigade; New South Wales Lancers; Northamptonshire Regiment; Northumberland Fusiliers; North Lancashire Regiment; Rimington's Guides; Royal Army Medical Corps; Royal Engineer; Royal Field Artillery; Royal Horse Artillery; Scots Guards.
Boers: Commandos from Bloemfontein, Brandfort, Fauresmith, Jacobsdal and Kroonstad.

Timeline

1899
In October Paul Kruger sends an ultimatum to the British government which leads to the outbreak of war. Mafeking and Kimberley are besieged and an armoured train is captured by the Boers at Kraaipan. The battles of Elandslaagte and Talana are fought in Natal.

November sees the start of the siege of Ladysmith. Aliwal North on the Orange River is occupied by the Boers. Winston Churchill is captured, but the battle at Willowgrange ends the Boer offensive in Natal. General Lord Methuen fights the Boers at Belmont and Graspan. At Modder River the Boers succeed in halting Methuen's progress towards Kimberley.

In December the battles of Stormberg and Magersfontein are won by the Boers. Churchill escapes from Pretoria. The Battle of Colenso is fought in Natal.

1900
In January the Boers attack Platrand in Ladysmith. General Lord Roberts arrives in Cape Town to supersede Methuen and the Battle of Spioenkop is fought in Natal.

In February battles are fought at Koedoesberg Drift, west of Kimberley, and at Vaalkrans in Natal. Kimberley is relieved, General Piet Cronjé surrenders at Paardeberg, and Ladysmith is finally relieved after the Battle of Tugela Heights.

Battle of Fabersput
30 May 1900

HOW TO GET THERE
From Douglas, in the Northern Cape, take the R370 towards Schmidtsdrift. After about 20km turn left onto a dirt track. The battle was fought about 6km further along this road.

Battle site: 28°53'54.8" S 23°51'41.0" E

Context
General Sir Charles Warren had replaced Lord Robert George Kekewich as military governor of the Cape north of the Orange River and was tasked with clearing the area of rebel groups fighting for the Boers. He made his camp between Douglas and Campbell in order to engage a band of Cape rebels who were active in the district in support of the Boers' campaign against the British. The rebels surrounded and attacked his camp at dawn on 30 May 1900.

Action
Warren's total force of about 2,000 was made up mostly of inexperienced volunteers. On 21 May they had occupied Douglas, driving the rebels north to Campbell. Warren then moved northwards to Fabersput with some 700 men, positioning himself between the two towns to await supplies and reinforcements.

The Boer rebels were commanded by General P. J. de Villiers, a talented tactician and the respected leader of about 400 rebels. He was the elder brother of General Abraham de Villiers, who had been mortally wounded at Biddulphsberg.

The British camp was arranged on a low plain, divided by a valley. Warren had his headquarters in a farmhouse north-east of the valley on rising ground. The Yeomanry and their horses, the Canadian gun crews and Paget's Horse camped near another house, west of the valley.

Pickets surrounded the camp, but the Boers, approaching through the valley, managed to get through the picket lines. Fifty-seven sharpshooters took up their positions in the garden, 30m from the horse circles of the Yeomanry. More Boers, led by Jan Vorster, approached from the hills in the north-east while Commandant N. T. Venter and his men came into the south of the camp. It was the last group that surprised a British picket. When the first shots were fired at the Boers, general firing broke out and confusion reigned as the British tried to find the enemy.

Cape rebels
The term 'rebel' was used to describe those Boers who had been born in the Cape, which was a British colony at the time, and who took up arms against the British during the Anglo-Boer War.

Warren scrambled his men into position and placed his guns. He positioned a Maxim machine gun on the roof of the farmhouse to fire on the Boer sharpshooters in the garden. The Duke of Edinburgh Yeomanry fired their rifles in the same direction.

Meanwhile, many of the horses had stampeded and chaos broke out among the Yeomanry west of the valley. However, Vorster, attacking from the north-east, came under heavy fire and had to withdraw. The British guns were threatening the horse lines of the rebel fighters, which caused them to retire after about two hours.

Aftermath

After the battle, the British counted 15 men dead (some reports say 25) and 30 wounded (some reports claim 37). Fourteen Boers were found dead in the garden. They are buried under the new memorial to the Boers, 4km from the Magersfontein battlefield gate.

This successful attack did much to encourage the Cape rebels, many of whom were not sure whose side they should take. However, Warren was able to progress to Campbell unopposed and he occupied the town on 4 June, where he also found abandoned Boer ammunition and supplies. Thirty-three rebels surrendered on 4 June at Campbell.

Principal combatants

British: Duke of Edinburgh Yeomanry; Imperial Yeomanry; Mounted infantry; Paget's Horse; Royal Canadian Field Artillery; Warren's Scouts.
Boers: Cape rebels mostly from Griqualand West; Marksmen from East Griqualand.

The sentencing of Cape rebels in Graaff-Reinet, circa 1901

Timeline

1878
Sir Charles Warren commands the Diamond Fields Horse during the Griqualand West Rebellion.

1884
Warren returns to South Africa to occupy Bechuanaland (Botswana).

1888
Back in London, Warren is commissioner of the London Metropolitan Police.

1899
Warren is recalled from retirement to serve in South Africa, commanding the 5th division to fight at Spioenkop, where the British are defeated.

1900
In February Warren replaces Lord Kekewich as military governor of the Cape north of the Orange River. Two batteries of the Royal Canadian Field Artillery arrive in Cape Town; they join Warren's force, which is tasked with clearing Cape rebels supporting the Boers out of Griqualand West.

In May Warren's force, comprising largely volunteers, occupies Douglas, driving the Boers north to Campbell. Warren moves to Fabersput, where General Petrus de Villiers leads an attack on his camp. The rebels are forced to withdraw and Warren progresses to Campbell.

In June Warren occupies Campbell and many rebels surrender or are made prisoner of war.

In August Warren is recalled to Britain.

BATTLE OF FABERSPUT

Battle of Lattakoo
26 June 1823

> **HOW TO GET THERE**
> From Kuruman, in the Northern Cape, take the N14 north to Lykso. From this town, drive north for 30km to Dithakong, which is spread over what used to be Lattakoo, once the capital of the Tswana (Tlhaping). At the time of the battle, a second settlement called Lattakoo had been established, as it was customary for the chief to move his capital to a new location after the death of his predecessor.
>
> Tim Couzens, in his book *Battles of South Africa*, covers this seldom-visited site comprehensively. He puts the old town of Lattakoo south of the Moshaweng River, just before the bridge, and describes the second Lattakoo as being on the other side of the river, to the west and north. The battle itself would have been fought over a large area, covering both the old and new settlements of Lattakoo.
>
> *Bridge over the Moshaweng River: 27°05'08.4" S 23°55'21.67" E*

Context
Between 1822 and 1824, three Nguni clans dominated the area between the Vaal and Orange rivers. There was great instability, resulting in three minor Sotho clans moving north of the Vaal. Desperate for food, they scavenged where they could and joined forces to plunder Lattakoo, the capital of the Tswana. The Battle of Lattakoo resulted when a mixed force defended the capital.

Action
The Phuting, Hlakwana and Fokeng clans were forced north of the Vaal River by the warring Ngwane (led by Mathiwane), Ndebele (led by Mzilikazi) and Tlokwa (led by the legendary Mmanthatisi). The Tlokwa were the strongest of the three groups and had gained a fearsome reputation. Led by a bare-breasted female chief, the warriors reputedly gained their strength from drinking her breast milk.

The three refugee clans, numbering between 40,000 and 50,000 men, women and children, were desperate for food, and advanced on Chief Mothibi's capital, Lattakoo. Mothibi sought help from the missionaries at Kuruman, where Robert Moffat of the London Missionary Society had his station. Moffat rode 150km south to Griquatown to request armed support; on his way back he was accompanied by a Cape merchant, George Thompson, who joined him on a scouting trip to find the enemy. Thompson's account

Letters posted here at the Kuruman Mission are franked with a Moffat Mission stamp.

284 BLOEMFONTEIN & KIMBERLEY REGIONS

The homestead of Robert and Mary Moffat, Kuruman Mission

describes how they unexpectedly came across a dense horde of people, whom Moffat mistakenly believed to be the Tlokwa, in the valley between the old and new Lattakoo.

After Sunday service on 22 June, the church in the town of Kuruman was turned into a fort. Supporting Griqua troops, led by Andries Waterboer, arrived that day, much to the relief of Moffat (although apparently he had to repair many of their firearms).

On 24 June, the Tswana troops, accompanied by Moffat, left Kuruman to find the enemy. They tried to parley with them, but their adversaries proved unwilling to talk. It was not until 26 June that the Tswana provoked an attack from the enemy, who had apparently never seen firearms before. Nonetheless, the three clans mounted a brave fight and the battle went on for seven hours. Eventually the invaders were forced back, with the Tswana and Griqua in pursuit slaughtering men, women and children with their battle axes. Over 500 people were killed and more than 1,000 wounded. Moffat was horrified at the slaughter undertaken by his allies, who gave no quarter to the wounded, the women or the prisoners.

Aftermath

It is said that, had the invaders attacked Lattakoo and then fallen on Kuruman, the mission would have been destroyed and there would be no town of Kuruman today. The three Sotho groups that made up the attacking force were eventually integrated with the Tlokwa, resettled in the Philippolis area, or returned south of the Orange River.

Principal combatants

Sotho: Clans of Phuting, Hlakwana and Fokeng.
Tswana: Troops accompanied by Moffat; Supporting Griqua troops.

Timeline

1795
The British occupy the Cape.

1779
The First Frontier War is fought in the Eastern Cape between Xhosa and trekboers.

1818
The Zulu defeat their rivals, the Ndwandwe, at Gqokli Hill and Shaka builds a strong, warlike Zulu nation.

1821
The London Missionary Society founds Kuruman as a mission station run by Robert Moffat.

1823
The Tswana confront warlike Sotho clans approaching from the north at the Battle of Lattakoo.

1824
British traders settle in Durban. King Moshoeshoe makes his stronghold on Thaba Bosiu and builds the Sotho nation.

1828
King Shaka is murdered by his half brother Dingane, who becomes king of the Zulu.

1829
Mzilikazi, leader of the Ndebele tribe, sends messengers to Moffat in Kuruman inviting him to visit. Mzilikazi refers to Moffat from that time onwards as 'the king of Kuruman'.

BATTLE OF LATTAKOO   285

Colesberg region

The small Karoo town of Colesberg lies close to the border between the Free State and Northern Cape and north-east of the boundary that separates the Eastern and Northern Cape provinces. For years, its position in a remote corner of the Cape Colony made it an ideal stopover for travellers, traders and explorers venturing into the southern African interior.

Watercolour of Colesberg by Charles Bell, 1845

Between 1814 and 1816, the London Missionary Society established two mission stations in the area to help bring stability to the colony's northern frontier. Together, the missions attracted more than 1,700 San, much to the consternation of the frontier farmers who complained that their safety was under threat from the San. As a result, in 1818, the Cape governor ordered the closure of the mission stations.

In 1822 Lord Charles Somerset granted land to the burghers farming in the area. The land was administered by the local church council and in 1830 the first plots were sold. The fledgling town was named after Sir Lowry Cole, governor of the Cape from 1828 to 1833.

At the onset of the 2nd Anglo-Boer War in 1899, Colesberg's strategic position was evident to both the British and the Boers. For the British, its close proximity to the railway

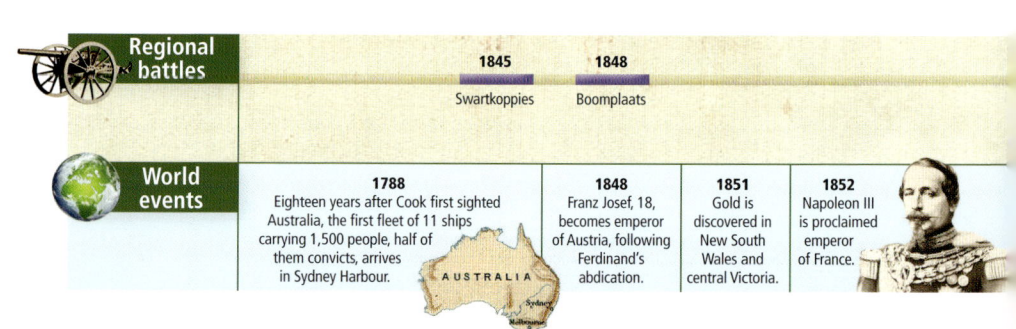

Regional battles

1845	1848
Swartkoppies	Boomplaats

World events

1788	1848	1851	1852
Eighteen years after Cook first sighted Australia, the first fleet of 11 ships carrying 1,500 people, half of them convicts, arrives in Sydney Harbour.	Franz Josef, 18, becomes emperor of Austria, following Ferdinand's abdication.	Gold is discovered in New South Wales and central Victoria.	Napoleon III is proclaimed emperor of France.

junction at Naauwpoort (Noupoort) was crucial, as the army depended on the line for communications and transport. For the Boer commandos, the koppies around the town provided cover for defence and concealment for ambush. The distinctive hill that dominates the town, Coleskop, was used by British soldiers as a site for their artillery. At 1,707m, Coleskop added much-needed height to increase the range of their guns.

Apart from the railway line that runs north through Colesberg, a second line, coming from East London, runs east of the town, passing through Stormberg railway junction. The battle at Stormberg was one of the first engagements of the 2nd Anglo-Boer War and one of three British defeats in seven days. The other two battles fought during what was later to become known as 'Black Week' were at Colenso and Magersfontein. After the reverse at Stormberg, British general Sir William Gatacre was forced to wait for reinforcements and it fell to General Sir John French and his cavalry to prevent the Boers from invading the colony from the Orange Free State.

French used colonial mounted troops, many of whom were from New Zealand, Australia and Tasmania. Their bravery and skill were well demonstrated in the skirmishes around Colesberg, especially those on Pink Hill and West Australia Hill, both occurring in the early part of 1900.

Two other significant engagements took place in the region, both in Labuschagne's Nek (near Dordrecht, east of Colesberg). The second of these, in March 1900, marked the last stand made by the Boers in the Cape before they withdrew to the Orange Free State.

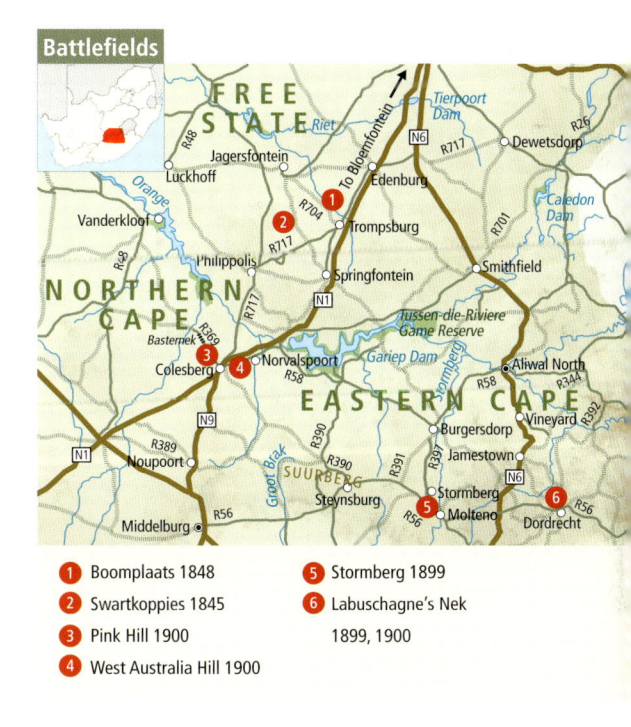

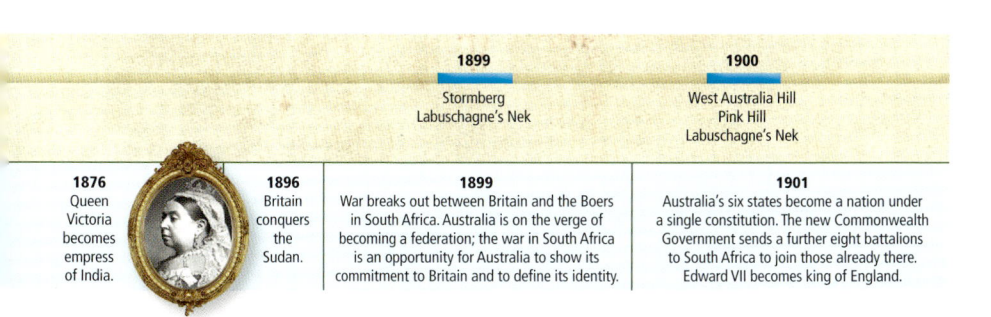

Battlefields

1. Boomplaats 1848
2. Swartkoppies 1845
3. Pink Hill 1900
4. West Australia Hill 1900
5. Stormberg 1899
6. Labuschagne's Nek 1899, 1900

1899
Stormberg
Labuschagne's Nek

1900
West Australia Hill
Pink Hill
Labuschagne's Nek

1876 Queen Victoria becomes empress of India.

1896 Britain conquers the Sudan.

1899 War breaks out between Britain and the Boers in South Africa. Australia is on the verge of becoming a federation; the war in South Africa is an opportunity for Australia to show its commitment to Britain and to define its identity.

1901 Australia's six states become a nation under a single constitution. The new Commonwealth Government sends a further eight battalions to South Africa to join those already there. Edward VII becomes king of England.

Battle of Boomplaats
29 August 1848

HOW TO GET THERE
Travel along the N1 north from Colesberg to Trompsburg, then take the off-ramp into Trompsburg (Louw Street). From there, turn left into Voortrekker Street, then right into Jan Street (R717). Drive for about 1.5km before turning right onto the R704, continuing for 22.5km, then turning right onto a district road towards Jagersfontein and Charlesville. Drive for about 4.5km to reach the Kromellenboogspruit. The battle took place south of this stream and in the koppies north of it. *Guide recommended*

Battle site: *29°50'58.98" S 25°38'45.47" E*

Context

In 1844 Voortrekker leader Hendrik Potgieter assured Griqua chief Adam Kok III that the Voortrekkers who had settled in his territory, north of the Orange River, wished to live there peaceably, enjoying the same rights and privileges as the chief's own people. However, conflicts arose after some Griqua farm workers and servants working for the new settlers complained to Kok of ill-treatment by their employers. Ongoing dissatisfaction led to a clash between the Griqua and Voortrekkers at Swartkoppies in 1845. Cape Governor Sir Harry Smith reacted swiftly by placing the area between the Orange and Vaal rivers (Transorangia) under British rule. The Voortrekkers, opposed to becoming British subjects, called on Transvaal commander Andries Pretorius to help them regain their independence. The Battle of Boomplaats was fought between the Voortrekkers, led by Pretorius, and the British, under Sir Harry Smith, who was determined to enforce British authority in Transorangia.

Adam Kok III

Fort Bloemfontein (Queen's Fort) was built after the Battle of Boomplaats by British Resident Major Warden to protect British interests between the Orange and Vaal rivers.

Action

Sir Harry Smith was first and foremost a soldier. He came to the Cape as deputy quartermaster general in 1828, and in 1834 was sent to the eastern Cape to restore order on the frontier. He was transferred to India in 1840, where he was covered in military glory before returning to the Cape in 1847 as commander-in-chief and governor. He ended the Seventh Frontier War, in 1847, by annexing the area between the Kei and Keiskamma rivers, renaming it British Kaffraria. When there was trouble between the Griqua and the Voortrekkers in the area north of the Orange River, he annexed this territory, too, naming it Transorangia.

Meanwhile, the famous Voortrekker leader Andries Pretorius had left Natal to make his farm in the Magaliesberg in the Transvaal. He strongly opposed the British annexation of Transorangia and the presence of a British Resident in Bloemfontein in the Orange Free State. He proceeded to muster support for his cause from both the Transvaal and areas south of the Vaal River. He was especially successful in the district of Winburg, where 500 men decided to join his commando. By August he had gathered almost 1,200 men and had occupied Bloemfontein, causing Major Henry Warden, the British Resident, to withdraw south of the Orange River to the Cape Colony.

Smith was determined to win back British control over the area and gathered his forces in Colesberg on the northern frontier of the colony. When he had about 1,200 men under his command he rode north to cross the Orange. When the Voortrekkers realised how strong the enemy force

Timeline

1836
A party of trekboers, led by Hendrik Potgieter, fights off an attack from the Ndebele at Vegkop, south of the Vaal River.

1837
Andries Pretorius treks from the Graaff-Reinet area to territory between the Orange and Vaal rivers. At the end of the year he assists Hendrik Potgieter with his attack on the Matabele by guarding his laager. Piet Retief leads a party of Voortrekkers into Natal.

1838
Pretorius leads the Voortrekkers in Natal to a victory over the Zulu at the Battle of Blood River.

1840
Pretorius proclaims Mpande king of the Zulu.

1842
Pretorius besieges a British garrison in the Old Fort in Durban. He is forced to withdraw when British reinforcements arrive on a warship.

1847
Sir Harry Smith is appointed governor of the Cape.

1848
The British annex Transorangia and Pretorius leads a force against them at the Battle of Boomplaats.

1850–1853
Sir Harry Smith fights the Xhosa in the Eastern Cape during the Eighth Frontier War.

1854
The Bloemfontein Convention grants independence to the Orange Free State.

BATTLE OF BOOMPLAATS 289

was, many drifted away, and it is probable that Pretorius was left with fewer than 600 fighting men. Smith and his army moved fast, first to Philippolis, then to the farm Touwfontein (close to the Swartkoppies battle site), and then in the direction of Bloemfontein. Pretorius chose to confront the British on a line of ridges that crossed the road to Bloemfontein, immediately south of the Kromellenboogspruit. He placed his men in a line about a mile long on the high ground spanning the road, in front of the deserted farm Boomplaats. With more ridges to their rear, Pretorius and his men were in a strong defensive position.

When General Smith's forces arrived there on 29 August, the Voortrekkers opened fire prematurely, giving the British an opportunity to charge at their left and centre. The Voortrekkers were driven back through the farm buildings and took up positions on the low koppies further north. The British opened fire with their three field guns, followed by a cavalry charge led by Griqua horsemen and men of the Cape Mounted Rifles. The Trekkers fled northward, but the British followed them into Bloemfontein and as far as Winburg.

Smith had a young prisoner named Thomas Dreyer shot. Born in the Cape, Dreyer was, technically, a rebel – even though he had long since renounced his Cape affiliations. Smith's action caused much bitterness among the Voortrekkers.

Aftermath

The British counted a total of 22 men killed, among them six Griqua. The number of Voortrekker casualties is uncertain, with historical reports citing figures between nine and 49.

Smith accomplished his mission of restoring British control over Transorangia, but his victory was short-lived. Six years later, when the political climate in Britain had changed and support for Smith's expansionist policies had waned, the British government signed the Bloemfontein Convention in February 1854.

With the Bloemfontein Convention, the Imperial government ceded the territory between the Orange and Vaal rivers to the Voortrekkers, which led to the establishment of the independent Boer Republic of the Orange Free State.

The battle, and the subsequent shooting of Dreyer, fuelled the Voortrekkers' hatred of the British. The standing joke among them was that the three curses in South Africa were droughts, locusts and Englishmen.

Andries Pretorius

Principal combatants

Voortrekkers: Supporters from the Transvaal, Winburg and other areas south of the Vaal River, led by Andries Pretorius.
British: 45th and 91st Regiments; Rifle Brigade; Cape Mounted Rifles; Mounted Griqua soldiers.

Battle of Swartkoppies
Also known as *Battle of Zwartkoppies*
2 May 1845

HOW TO GET THERE
Travel along the N1 north from Colesberg to Trompsburg, then take the off-ramp into Trompsburg (Louw Street). From there, turn left into Voortrekker Street, then right into Jan Street (R717). Continue on the R717 for about 1.5km before turning right onto the R704. After about 22.5km, turn left onto a district road towards Jagersfontein. Continue for about 15km, where the road curves sharply north. There is access to the battle site at this point, through a private farm on the banks of the river, the Prosespruit. To reach the site, permission has to be obtained from the owners.

If you continue on the district road for another 2.5km, the low hills on your left, west of the river, are the Swartkoppies.

Swartkoppies: 29°55'35.00" S 25°28'34.00" E

Context
The first white farmers to move north of the Orange River, from the 1820s onwards, were trekboer families in search of grazing land for their livestock. Unlike the Voortrekkers, who followed later, most remained loyal to the Cape government.

Both trekboers and Voortrekkers in southern Transorangia, a territory between the Orange and Riet rivers dominated by the Griqua, had no wish to challenge the authority of the Griqua leaders, including Adam Kok III, who became chief in the Philippolis area in 1837. When the Voortrekkers began to move into the area, Dr John Philip of the London Missionary Society feared that they would challenge the authority of the chiefs. He subsequently persuaded the British government to sign a treaty promising to support the Griqua in the event of a conflict with the newcomers. Therefore, when disagreements between the Voortrekkers and the Griqua escalated into armed conflict in 1845, British troops were sent to the area.

Missionary Dr John Philip

Very little is known about this battle, and the account given here is largely drawn from an article by D. Y. Saks, published in the *Military History Journal* in 1994.

Timeline

1823
The Griqua support the Tswana to defend Kuruman in the Battle of Lattakoo.

1836
Voortrekker leader Hendrik Potgieter fights the Ndebele at the Battle of Vegkop.

1837
The British award land north of the Orange River to the Griqua. Trekboers settle north of the Orange River, in Griqua territory.

1842
Voortrekkers in Durban are defeated by the British at the Battle of Durban.

1843
The British government signs a treaty promising to support the Griqua in the event of a conflict with the Boers in territory north of the Orange River.

1844
Voortrekker leader Hendrik Potgieter assures the Griqua chief, Adam Kok III, that the Voortrekkers wish to live peaceably in the Griqua territory north of the Orange River. However, conflicts arise amid complaints of ill-treatment of Griqua in the employ of Voortrekkers.

1845
Griqua, supported by the British, clash with Voortrekkers at the Battle of Swartkoppies.

1848
The area between the Orange and Vaal rivers is annexed by the British and a battle is fought at Boomplaats.

1851
The British Resident in Trans-orangia fights Moshoeshoe's Sotho at Viervoet. The British are forced to withdraw.

1852
Moshoeshoe takes on the British at the Battle of Berea, near Thaba Bosiu in Basutoland (Lesotho).

1854
The Bloemfontein Convention makes the Orange Free State an independent Boer republic.

Sir George Napier

Action

Trouble between the Voortrekkers and the Griqua arose when the Griqua accused Voortrekker commandant Jan Kock and a farmer, Jan Krynaauw, of ill-treating two servants, both of them Kok's subjects. Kok called for the arrest of the two men. When Krynaauw evaded his capturers, his home was burgled by his pursuers and ammunition and guns were taken. The Trekkers rose in revolt, gathered an armed force and made their headquarters on a farm called Touwfontein, north of Philippolis. The Voortrekkers and the Griqua fought several minor skirmishes, but Adam Kok, unable to restore his authority, sent for help.

In terms of the 1843 treaty between the Griqua and Cape Governor Sir George Napier, Kok was supplied with arms, and British troops were despatched from Fort Beaufort in the eastern Cape to reinforce those already in Philippolis. They called on the Trekker force to disband but, as there was no sign of compliance, the troops advanced against the laager at Touwfontein. Armed Griqua were sent ahead to initiate an attack, followed by British infantry patrols and a squadron of Dragoon Guards with 24 Cape Mounted Riflemen.

The latter regiment originated in a corps of Khoikhoi and San soldiers formed by the Dutch administration of 1793. They were kept on by the British, who subsequently occupied the Cape, and had fought with distinction in the early frontier wars. In 1827 the infantry component of the regiment was disbanded, but the cavalry remained and was renamed the Cape Mounted Riflemen.

The Voortrekkers left their laager to skirmish with the Griqua vanguard. By the time the British infantry arrived, fighting had been going on for some time. The Trekkers had taken a position in a row of small hills called the Swartkoppies, from where they advanced towards the enemy on the plains below.

The arrival of the mounted troops took the Voortrekkers by surprise and, when the Dragoons led a charge, the Trekkers retreated to the ridges behind them in confusion. The Dragoons followed up rapidly, compelling the Trekkers to abandon their laager and camp site with everything in it and flee down the reverse slopes of the ridges. The British did not pursue the fleeing men, content to plunder the camp instead.

Aftermath

Three Trekkers were killed and 15 prisoners taken. On the British side only one Griqua had been killed.

Although this was a relatively unimportant skirmish, it was indicative of how aggrieved the Trekkers in Transorangia felt at the British who, they believed, discriminated against them because they were white. It is interesting that, only two years earlier, British troops had been sent, also from the Cape, to counter the Trekkers in what was known as Port Natal. That had triggered the Battle of Durban (see p. 31) and the annexation of Natal to the Cape in 1843. In the area north of the Orange, River, tensions rose subsequent to the Battle of Swartkoppies, culminating, in 1848, in the annexation of the area between the Orange and Vaal rivers by the British and the Battle at Boomplaats (see p. 288).

Principal combatants

Voortrekkers: Trekkers led by Hendrik Potgieter.
Griqua and British: Griqua fighters led by Adam Kok III; Cape Mounted Riflemen; Dragoon Guards; Royal Field Artillery.

Cape Mounted Rifles and Dragoon Guards pursue trekboers who have fled to the hills.

Brits versus Boers at Colesberg

British troops behind an entrenchment, essential cover in the open plains

At the outbreak of the 2nd Anglo-Boer War in October 1899, Boers from the Orange Free State invaded the Cape Colony, occupying Colesberg in mid-November and proclaiming it to be part of the Orange Free State.

General Sir Redvers Buller, at that stage in overall command of the British army in South Africa, allotted to General John Pinkstone French the task of preventing the Boers from progressing any further south into the Cape, protecting the railway lines around Naauwpoort railway junction and removing the Boers from the Colesberg district.

The wide, open, arid plains and lack of vegetation made this area well suited to British cavalry and horse-drawn artillery, as soldiers who were not mounted lacked mobility and could not cover enough ground in a day to traverse the territory occupied by invading Boers. Lord Roberts had recognised the need for more mounted troops and French's cavalry brigade utilised many horsemen from the colonies, including Australians, New Zealanders, Tasmanians, Canadians, Ceylonese (Sri Lankans) and Indians, although the largest colonial mounted contingent was, not surprisingly, from South Africa.

British reinforcements, many of them from Australia and other colonies, landed in Cape Town before being sent to the front.

Remains of a Boer entrenchment in the hills above Colesberg

There were numerous engagements between the Boers and the British cavalry around Colesberg between December 1899 and February 1900 as the tide of the Boer invasion ebbed and flowed.

On 17 December 1899 General French made his headquarters at Arundel, south of Colesberg. The Boers were, by this time, at the Rensburg railway siding between Colesberg and Arundel. But, on 30 December 1899, French and his cavalry (which included many colonial troops) forced the Boers back to Colesberg. The last day of December 1899 saw the British take McCracken Hill west of Colesberg. A severe artillery bombardment caused the Boers to vacate other positions in this area. However, an attempt by the British to take a hill north of the town ended disastrously for them when the Boers pre-empted the night assault and killed and took prisoner a large number of men from the Suffolk Regiment.

On 9 January 1900 the British occupied a position called Slingersfontein, south-east of Colesberg. There were various engagements in this area, as well as some west of the town, but neither side took the upper hand.

General De la Rey arrived with reinforcements for the Boers at the end of January 1900; on 12 February, a determined attempt by the Boers to turn the British right flank resulted in heavy losses on both sides.

By 14 February, the British had withdrawn south to Arundel from where they had set off six weeks earlier. Subsequent attempts by the Boers to get around the British flanks at Arundel failed and, at the end of February, news of the Boer surrender at Paardeberg, the relief of Kimberley and the invasion of the Orange Free State by Lord Roberts persuaded the Boers around Arundel to withdraw in order to lend their support to the push against Roberts's army, which was then approaching Bloemfontein.

General John French commanded mounted troops at Colesberg.

Battle of Pink Hill

Also known as *Battle of Hobkirk's Farm*

12 February 1900

HOW TO GET THERE
Take the R369 from Colesberg and travel north-west for 13km over Bastersnek Pass (10km) to Pink Hill (Hobkirk's Farm). In Colesberg itself, there are several Anglo-Boer War memorials and graves in the local military cemetery, which is on the right-hand side of the road as you enter the town from Bloemfontein on the N1.

Context
In November 1899 the Boers invaded the Cape Colony and occupied Colesberg, a small town on the railway line between Port Elizabeth and Bloemfontein. The British sent troops north on the railway line to counter the invasion, which threatened their communications. The Battle of Pink Hill occurred when the Boers assaulted British positions east and west of Colesberg, hoping to get around the British flanks and force their retreat to Naauwpoort.

Action
General Koos de la Rey recognised that the British were strung out, depleted and less mobile than they had been before Lieutenant General John French and his cavalry departed from Colesberg at the end of January 1900. Major General Ralph Clements had fewer than 7,000 men to defend a line east and west of Colesberg, stretching over 70km. De la Rey decided on a simultaneous two-pronged attack against both flanks of the British-held line.

The western (left) flank of Clements's army stood on a small hill known as Pink Hill, north-west of Colesberg. The high ground was held by only 190 men, many of them members of the Victorian Mounted Rifles, the Victorian Mounted Infantry and several South Australian units. Nearby were two guns and more men of the Victoria Mounted Rifles and New South Wales Mounted Infantry, together with some imperial troops.

At noon on 12 February, about 1,000 Boers attacked the position with such speed that the British were surrounded. This meant that the British positions at Kloof Camp, closer to Colesberg, and Windmill Hill were threatened. Even Coleskop, the hill commanding the town on which the British had mounted their guns, was in danger of falling to the Boers.

Maximum damage

When the British army withdrew from Rensburg Siding to Arundel, the soldiers, in an attempt to deter their pursuers, scattered behind them a mass of bent metal nails intended to penetrate the hooves of the Boers' horses.

Never on a Sunday

The Boer attack on Pink Hill took place on Monday, 12 February 1900, and was part of a two-pronged attack that had been meant to be launched on Saturday, 10 February, at both ends of the British line that extended more than 60km. The reason the attack was delayed was that General Hendrik Schoeman arrived a day late – he was overly cautious and reluctant to take risks (in June 1900 Schoeman was to surrender to the British). General Koos de la Rey did not like to fight on a Sunday if it could be helped and so the battle took place only on the Monday.

Major George Eddy, the Australian commanding the British right flank, defended bravely. Although under heavy fire from Boer Mauser rifles and two Maxim Nordenfeldt guns, he walked about, encouraging his men and placing them where he believed they would be most effective. Eddy delayed the Boer advance for four hours, allowing the infantry on Pink Hill and at Windmill Camp to withdraw. Only at 15h00, when the Boers had finally secured the hill, did Eddy order his mounted men to retire. Just as he did so, he was killed by a head shot.

Aftermath

The Australians lost 40 per cent of their force, with six men killed, of whom three were officers, and 22 wounded. (Some accounts give eight men killed, 13 wounded and 12 taken as prisoners.) The brave stand on Pink Hill gave the artillery enough time to remove most of their guns from Coleskop; one was left behind, which they destroyed. British troops withdrew to Rensburg Siding on 13 February. The order was not received by two companies of the Wiltshire Regiment, and they were surrounded in their camp and forced to surrender.

Principal combatants

British: 5th Australian Corps; South Wales Mounted Infantry; Victorian Mounted Infantry; Victorian Mounted Rifles; Wiltshire Regiment.
Boers: Commandos from Germiston, Heilbron, Johannesburg, Kroonstad, Waterberg and Zoutpansberg; Transvaal Police.

A trooper of the Victoria Mounted Rifles

Timeline

1899
In October, when the ultimatum to the British expires, the Boers invade Natal, fighting the British at Talana, Elandslaagte, Rietfontein and Ladysmith, Kimberley and Mafeking are besieged, followed by Ladysmith a month later. Boers invading the Cape Colony occupy Colesberg, a small town on the railway line between Port Elizabeth and the Orange Free State. The 1st Australian Regiment enrols at Cape Town. This is the first time a regiment is formed for active service comprising troops representing most of the six colonies of Australia.

In November Lord Methuen advances on the Modder River, between Kimberley and Hopetown.

In December the British lose the battles of Colenso in Natal and Magersfontein in the Cape.

1900
In January General Sir John French departs from Colesberg to support Lord Roberts's advance on Kimberley.

In February the Boers fight mostly Australian troops at the battles of West Australia Hill and Pink Hill. British troops withdraw down the line to Rensburg Siding and then to Arundel, which is where they had started from six weeks earlier.

BATTLE OF PINK HILL 297

Battle of West Australia Hill
9 February 1900

HOW TO GET THERE
From Colesberg, take the R58 towards Norvalspont. After about 3.5km, turn right and continue for approximately 11.5km before bearing left. If you continue on this road for just over 4km, you will see the Slingersfontein Hills, of which West Australia Hill is the prominent one, on your left.

Context
Invading Boer commandos had penetrated the Cape Colony from the Orange Free State along the railway line to Colesberg. The defending British troops were stretched in a thin line west and east of the town. The Boers were planning an attack on Slingersfontein, a farm south-east of Colesberg, which was the site of a British camp and hospital; it also formed the British army's right flank. The skirmish on West Australia Hill was an engagement between Australian mounted infantry and 400 Boers who were attempting to approach Slingersfontein undetected.

Action
The Boers around Colesberg numbered about 5,000 men. They were under the overall leadership of the recently arrived General Koos de la Rey, who had placed several of his generals in command of different sections: Freek Grobler was responsible for the west flank, Piet de Wet commanded the middle section, Richard Lemmer and Jan Celliers led the east and south-east sections and Gerard van Dam held sway at the far east. With his troops in place, De la Rey planned to attack both flanks of the British simultaneously.

Slingersfontein had been occupied by the British on 9 January, under the command of Brigadier General Thomas Porter. It was then taken over as part of General Ralph Clements's sector after the action on New Zealand Hill on 15 January, when the camp was reinforced with more troops.

The Inniskilling Dragoons aided the safe withdrawal of the Western Australian Mounted Infantry.

Australia and the 2nd Anglo-Boer War

New South Wales Mounted Rifles in Cape Town

There were Australian-born settlers living in South Africa before the outbreak of the Anglo-Boer War in 1899. Many of them were Uitlanders (foreigners) living in the Transvaal, attracted by the gold that had been discovered in vast quantities under the Witwatersrand in 1886.

The Imperial Light Horse, a regiment raised in Johannesburg at the outbreak of the war, was made up mostly of Australians and had as a senior officer Major Karri Davies, who originally came from New South Wales. Between 5,000 and 7,000 Australians served in 'Irregular' regiments raised in South Africa. The Australian Horse and the New South Wales Lancers played important roles in actions around Colesberg.

When it was found that better mobility was needed to counter the Boers, many of the Australian infantry regiments were mounted. In the early part of 1900. A number of Australian mounted infantry units were used to help Major General Ralph Clements with his task of guarding the right flank of Lord Roberts's army as he prepared to strike at the Boer capitals.

The tough Australian 'bushmen' were particularly valuable as scouts and could match the Boers with their horsemanship, marksmanship and bushcraft. Altogether 16,175 Australian men and 40 Australian women enlisted and about 1,000 were killed in total. However, the Australian contingents were, for the most part, broken up and interspersed with imperial troops, no one contingent ever numbering more than 1,000 soldiers.

On 9 February, a mounted troop of 400 Boers led by Celliers was approaching Slingersfontein from the east when it was spotted by a patrol of Western Australian Mounted Infantry. Unbeknown to Celliers's men, the Boer attack that was intended to happen on 10 February had been postponed by two days.

The Boer troops had to cross an open plain before first light, to avoid being raked by British artillery on Slingersfontein. Under cover of the hilly country, the Boers decided to pass through a nek between West Australia Hill and a small, adjacent hill, from where they aimed to launch a surprise attack on the Slingersfontein camp.

Timeline

1885
The New South Wales Lancers are named in honour of the 5th Royal Irish Lancers, who encamped with the New South Wales Artillery at Handoub in the Sudan after the death of General Gordon in Khartoum.

1899
Volunteers in the New South Wales Lancers arrive in South Africa to join British forces against the Boers. In October the Western Australian government ratifies the formation of a company of infantry, the Western Australian Mounted Infantry, to fight with Her Majesty's forces in South Africa. A month later the men leave for South Africa. Meanwhile, Boers occupy Aliwal North and Colesberg.

1900
In January British soldiers haul a gun to the top of Coleskop in Colesberg. General Koos de la Rey becomes commander of the Boers around Colesberg.

In February Western Australian troops fight at the Battle of West Australia Hill. Further north, Kimberley is relieved.

In March Boers pull back from Colesberg, destroying the bridge at Norvalspont. During the same month, British troops, under the command of Lord Roberts, occupy Bloemfontein.

In December the men of the Western Australian Mounted Infantry leave Cape Town for home.

1901
The Western Australian Mounted Infantry is disbanded.

A 15-pounder belonging to the No. 4 Battery of the Royal Field Artillery is hauled up Coleskop.

Major Hatherley Moore, commanding a troop of 27 men of the Western Australian Mounted Infantry, put his men in positions on the three small hills commanding the nek to prevent the Boers from charging through. The Boers held positions about 400m from the Australian-held koppies, on slightly higher ground.

The fighting continued throughout the day, and Moore stubbornly held the hills in spite of mounting casualties. He sent a message back to the camp to warn the men of the impending attack, allowing them enough time to move the hospital down the line to a position closer to the town. The 27 men opposing 400 Boers were under fire until it got dark, when Moore withdrew his men with the aid of the Inniskilling Dragoons.

Aftermath

Three Australians were killed. Another died of sunstroke and three more were injured. The Australian fighters had covered themselves in glory and demonstrated that they were steady and reliable under fire. A commemorative stone was placed on the hill on the 100th anniversary of the battle.

Principal combatants

British: Inniskilling Dragoons; Royal Field Artillery; Western Australian Mounted Infantry.
Boers: Lichtenberg Commando supported by other commandos.

Lieutenant Geoffrey Hensman

During the battle on West Australia Hill, Lieutenant Hensman was hit by Boer bullets in both legs. He shouted for help and two privates built, under heavy fire, a stone sangar around him to protect him from further injury. While so doing, Private Michael Conway was killed. The other private, Alexander Krygger, was mentioned in dispatches. Sadly Hensman's wounds were fatal.

Battle of Stormberg
10 December 1899

HOW TO GET THERE

To reach the Stormberg railway line junction, where this battle took place, drive south from Burgersdorp towards Molteno. About 5km from Burgersdorp, turn left onto a dirt road, the R397, which is signposted 'Molteno via Stormberg'. There is a blockhouse, about 8km before the junction of the R397 and the R56, close to the road where it crosses the railway line. It is clearly visible on your right (when you are driving south) and signifies that you have arrived. There is another blockhouse on the other side of the line, but it is not visible from the road.

There is a parking sign just after the blockhouse. You can locate Rooikop Mountain on your left (facing south towards Molteno) and Kissieberg, the long ridge stretching further away to your front right, on the other side of the road.

There are memorials and graves on the farm Vegkoppies, which is situated under Kissieberg. To reach the farm from Stormberg, travel west towards Steynsburg and Middelburg on the R56. The farm is 2km from where the R56 meets the R397. This is private property and permission to visit must be sought from the owners.

Stormberg railway line junction: 31°16'44" S 26°17'43" E
Blockhouse: 31°16'56.2" S 26°17'20.9" E

Context

Following the outbreak of the 2nd Anglo-Boer War in October 1899, the British were faced with Boer invasions of the Cape and Natal. General William Gatacre was sent up the railway line from East London to Queenstown to counter the advance of Boers along this route. The Boers had already occupied Stormberg railway junction some 13km north-west of Molteno. It was important for Gatacre to recapture Stormberg because it was there that the railway line branched west to link with the area, in the vicinity of Naauwpoort, where General John French was operating with his mounted troops. The Boers holding Stormberg had effectively destroyed communication between the two. The battle was Gatacre's attempt to take back Stormberg junction.

Action

Gatacre began advancing north from Queenstown in November 1899. He was supposedly in command of a division of 10,000 men, but had sent some men to support Major General Redvers Buller in Natal and others to support General Paul Methuen in the Orange Free State. He had also left men behind to guard Queenstown and so his troops, as he progressed towards Molteno, numbered under 3,000.

Timeline

1883
Jan Hendrik Olivier is elected to the Orange Free State Volksraad.

1895
Sir William Gatacre commands the British army in the Sudan and in the advances on Omdurman and Khartoum.

1899
In November Olivier (below) is commandant of the Rouxville/Zastron Commando; he is tasked with keeping the British south of the Orange River and out of the Orange Free State. He commands a Boer force that occupies Aliwal North, Burgersdorp and other towns in the Cape Colony that border the Orange Free State. Gatacre is given command of the British army's 3rd Division in South Africa; he begins advancing north from Queenstown.

In December Olivier commands the Boers who defeat the British under Gatacre at Stormberg junction. In the same month, the Battle of Magersfontein is fought and lost by the British. The dual defeats at Stormberg and Magersfontein result in an over-hasty attack by British forces, led by General Sir Redvers Buller, on Boer defences at Colenso. Buller is defeated and forced to withdraw with 1,450 casualties.

1900
After the defeat at Colenso, Buller is replaced as British commander-in-chief by Lord Roberts, who arrives in Cape Town, along with Lord Kitchener, in January.

The Boers holding Stormberg were aided by the fact that the Berkshire Regiment, in the northern Cape Colony a month previously, had spent some time entrenching their position before being driven out by the advancing Boers. This meant that the Bethulie, Smithfield and Rouxville/Zastron commandos were able to occupy ready-made trenches. Accompanying them were some Cape rebels from Burgersdorp.

Gatacre's plan was to rail his troops to Molteno on 9 December, rest them there in the afternoon and then embark on a night march to Stormberg, arriving at the Boer position at dawn on Sunday 10 December for a surprise attack. Their rail journey began with three hours of waiting in open cattle trucks for men of the Berkshire Regiment, who never arrived. This was regrettable, as they would have known the route and perhaps prevented the disastrous wrong turning taken later by the guides. Because of the delay, the troops arrived in Molteno only at 19h00, leaving them with less than two hours to rest and eat before embarking on the march to Stormberg.

Gatacre, meanwhile, had received intelligence that the Boers had entrenched themselves strongly on the south slopes of Kissieberg. This proved to be false, but it swayed him to direct his attack on the Boer right flank rather than continue with the frontal attack he had favoured at first.

The Boer commander, General F. A. Grobler, had meanwhile left Stormberg with about 400 men to support the Boer force at Colesberg. This left General J. H. Olivier in command of about 1,000 men and two guns at Stormberg.

The blockhouse at Stormberg junction

The Cape rebels

At the outbreak of the 2nd Anglo-Boer War in 1899, citizens of the Cape Colony who were of Boer descent had to choose whether they would leave their homes to join their compatriots in the independent Boer republics in their fight against Great Britain, or side with Britain as loyal citizens of the Cape.

In Dordrecht cemetery is the grave of a burgher, Petrus Klopper, who surrendered to the British and then, in 1901, fought against them with the Boer commandos. His public execution caused an outcry in South Africa and in Britain. Public executions of Cape rebels during the war were thereafter banned.

Many Boers living in the Dordrecht area chose to support the Boer cause. A Boer named John Baxter was the first to be executed for wearing khaki. He is buried in Aberdeen.

Memorial to the Cape rebels from the Dordrecht area

Gatacre's original, frontal approach would have entailed a night march of about 13km. Instead, he told the guides to take a more circuitous route that first led south and then turned sharply right, to arrive close to the railway junction and under the west shoulder of Rooikop. Unfortunately, his guides missed the turn to the right and the march went on for more than 20km, lasting until daylight and putting the assaulting column on the wrong side of the ridge. The element of surprise was lost when the column stumbled on a Boer laager. Shots were fired and the Boers scrambled to take up their defensive positions along the Kissieberg ridge.

The British came under rifle and artillery fire from the directions of both Kissieberg and Rooikop. The Northumberland Regiment and Royal Irish Fusiliers bravely stormed the ridge, but came up against sheer precipices in some places that were impossible to breach. The two field gun batteries supported the attack, but shells dropped short and killed or wounded many of the two regiments' own men. Gatacre signalled a retreat, and, as the men scrambled back towards Molteno, they came under fire from Boer guns on both hills. The field artillery covered the exhausted, fleeing men as best they could by wheeling round and firing back at the Boers as the British retreated.

Boer artillery detachment at Stormberg

BATTLE OF STORMBERG

British troops, including Australians, arrive at Stormberg junction.

During the protracted night march preceding the battle, 634 men in the advance guard had become separated from the column. Not sure of their position, they slept some of the remaining hours of darkness in a cave. As dawn broke they hurried forward towards the junction, unaware that the rest of the column had retreated. The Boers quickly surrounded them and took them prisoner.

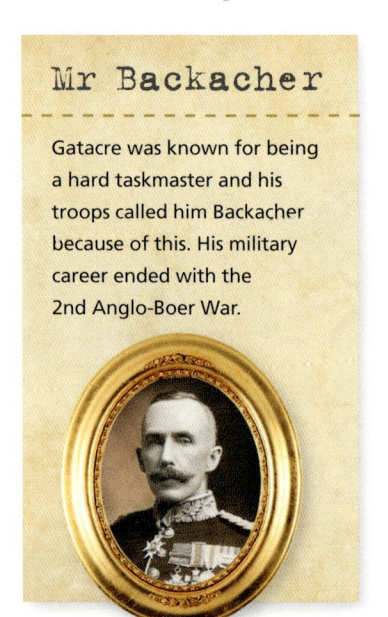

Mr Backacher

Gatacre was known for being a hard taskmaster and his troops called him Backacher because of this. His military career ended with the 2nd Anglo-Boer War.

Aftermath

Of Gatacre's force, 27 men were killed and 57 wounded, and over 600 were captured. It was a huge blow to British prestige and became one of the three incidents known collectively as Black Week (the other two were Colenso and Magersfontein). It was this defeat, as well as the one at Magersfontein, that persuaded General Sir Redvers Buller to make an over-hasty, frontal attack on Colenso, also destined to end in disaster.

Principal combatants

British: Cape Police; New South Wales Lancers; Northumberland Fusiliers; Royal Berkshire Regiment; Royal Engineers; Royal Field Artillery; Royal Irish Rifles; Volunteer mounted infantry.
Boers: Commandos from Bethulie, Rouxville/Zastron and Smithfield; Cape rebels.

Battle of Labuschagne's Nek
30 December 1899 and 4 March 1900

HOW TO GET THERE
Labuschagne's Nek lies about 11km north-west of Dordrecht on the Jamestown road. Drive west out of Dordrecht on the R56 and, before you leave the town, turn right onto a minor road marked 'Jamestown', which weaves up the nek after about 10km.

There were two engagements here, but neither of them is signposted in any way. The first occurred on 30 December 1899, when British scouts led by Captain Raymond de Montmorency were ambushed by 500 burghers. The second occurred on 4 March 1900, with General Brabant forcing the Boers out of their laager and fort on Labuschagne's Nek.

The dead were exhumed and reinterred in Burgersdorp.

Top of Labuschagne's Nek: 31°18'01.3" S 26°56'36.6" E

30 DECEMBER 1899

Context
When the 2nd Anglo-Boer War broke out, the town of Dordrecht was held by Cape rebels – citizens, or burghers, of the British Cape Colony who supported the Boers. It was taken by the British on Christmas Eve 1899, but the burghers were determined to reclaim it. This engagement occurred as a result.

Action
At about noon on 30 December, British scouts led by Captain Raymond de Montmorency encountered a Cape rebel force of about 300 men (the British claimed the number to be 500) with a gun, in the vicinity of Labuschagne's Nek.

De Montmorency, with 30 men, advanced towards them, leaving the main body of troops with the horses in a donga and detaching other men to a position west of the donga. Montmorency followed the donga upwards towards the enemy, but the burghers came around from the flank to attack the 40 men lower down. Horses were killed by shells from the Boer gun and Lieutenant A. G. Warren of Brabant's Horse was badly wounded. Carrying their wounded officer, the men retreated to a nearby hill. They climbed to the summit, where they sheltered among the boulders. Had they left the wounded man, they could have got away; yet they refused to do so. They put themselves in a defensive position among rocks on the crest, and, when the burghers tried to storm their position, they drove them back. These British soldiers were scouts and therefore good hunters, well matched to their opponents.

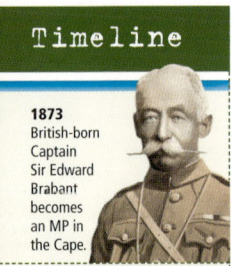

Timeline

1873
British-born Captain Sir Edward Brabant becomes an MP in the Cape.

1878
Brabant raises and commands a mounted unit called Brabant's Horse.

1879
Brabant is colonel of the 1st Cape Mounted Yeomanry.

1887
Captain the Honourable Raymond de Montmorency joins the 21st Lancers.

1898
De Montmorency receives a Victoria Cross for his role in the charge against the Dervishes at Omdurman.

1899
In October the 2nd Anglo-Boer War breaks out. Brabant forms a new Brabant's Horse, serving under General William Gatacre. Dordrecht is taken by Cape rebels.

In December Dordrecht is occupied by British forces. De Montmorency engages a burgher force in Labuschagne's Nek. His troops are forced back to Dordrecht.

1900
In January Boer commandos and Cape rebels reoccupy Dordrecht.

In February the Boers are forced out of Dordrecht yet again. However, there remains a strong force of about 1,100 Boers, commanded by J. H. Olivier, at Labuschagne's Nek. On 23 February De Montmorency is killed at Stormberg.

In March Brabant's Horse captures Olivier's laager in Labuschagne's Nek. This is the last action in the northern Cape before the Boers withdraw to the Orange Free State.

The burghers attempted to take the position by sending black agterryers forward in the guise of British African Police. This ruse was not successful and the British held the burghers off until night fell. The commander then sent five men off under cover of darkness to get back to Dordrecht through the burgher line to summon help. However, their absence had already been noted in Dordrecht and 115 men with two guns were on their way.

De Montmorency, leading 30 of these men, succeeded in reaching the besieged. Their firepower, along with a bombardment from the British guns, led to a burgher withdrawal. By morning De Montmorency and his men were back in the town. The wounded Warren died as they reached Dordrecht.

Aftermath

One burgher died and eight prisoners were taken. The British lost a number of horses and an officer was killed. The British commanding officer, Sir William Gatacre, decided that his troops were too spread out and that it was not worthwhile leaving soldiers in Dordrecht merely to guard the town. It was abandoned and subsequently reoccupied by the burghers.

Principal combatants
British: Brabant's Horse; British scouts; Cape Mounted Rifles.
Boers: Boers, with the support of Cape rebels.

4 MARCH 1900

Context

By February 1900 the British had advanced along the route of the railway lines into the northern Cape towards the Orange River, pushing the Boers back as they went. Gatacre had succeeded in crossing into the Orange Free State at Bethulie, and had sent his mounted men forward to Springfontein, the junction of the East London and Cape Town railway lines. There he made contact with some of Lord Roberts's forces, sent down from Bloemfontein. It fell to General Edward Brabant, commander of the colonial mounted forces, to keep the areas east of Gatacre's centre of operations free of Boers. The attack by Brabant on the Boers at Labuschagne's Nek was intended to force the enemy north across the Orange.

Action

Boer commandos, with the support of Cape rebels from the surrounding districts, had occupied Dordrecht on 3 January. Meanwhile, Lord Roberts was almost in Bloemfontein.

A view from the top of Labuschagne's Nek today

Roberts had arranged for the colonial mounted troops to join forces under the overall command of General Brabant. It was this 1,800-strong force, consisting of colonials as well as a battery of field artillery and some imperial troops, that drove the Boers out of Dordrecht on 18 February. The British troops went on to occupy Jamestown, further north. However, a strong force of about 1,100 Boers commanded by J. H. Olivier remained at Labuschagne's Nek.

Early in the morning of 4 March, Brabant and his men approached the nek from the west. Advancing up the slope of the ridge, they came across the Boer stronghold: a well-entrenched stone fort commanding the nek from the west. Brabant was surprised to find it unoccupied. The Boers had left the fort to sleep in their laager, which was in the valley below the nek. Brabant and his men took up positions in and near the fort and waited for the Boers to return, which they did about an hour and a half after sunrise.

The Boers spotted the British from about 400m away and a fierce gun battle ensued. Although the British had a strong position in the fort and on the hill on one side of the nek, the Boers managed to hold the hill east of the nek and to defend their laager. It was not until evening that Major C. Maxwell led a column that managed to take some of the Boer trenches east of the road and, during the night, to place artillery guns there that threatened the Boer laager. When daylight showed the Boers that the guns commanded their position, they fled towards the north and were soon across the Orange River and into the Orange Free State.

Aftermath

The capture of the Boer laager was the last action in the northern Cape before the Boers withdrew north to the Orange Free State. The Boers lost eight dead and 17 wounded, while the British had 14 killed. The Boer commandos had been forced out of the Cape and the British were now advancing on all fronts.

Principal combatants

British: Border Horse; Colonial mounted troops.
Boers: Boers with the support of Cape rebels.

Smuts – guerrilla leader, military strategist and statesman

Jan Christiaan Smuts was the state attorney of the Transvaal at the outbreak of the 2nd Anglo-Boer War in 1899. He had been instrumental in drafting the ultimatum that preceded the war. He subsequently played dual roles as both military commander and state attorney. He served with the famous Boer general Koos de la Rey in the western Transvaal, where he learned much of military strategy.

After initial Boer victories, the British gained the upper hand and it was decided in 1901 that Smuts should invade the Cape and encourage burghers there to join forces with the Boers. The invasion succeeded in occupying 35,000 well-equipped British soldiers for eight months whose task was to curb the activities of Smuts and his commandos in the Cape during the latter stages of the war. The daring escapades of this tattered and emaciated band of horsemen form the body of Deneys Reitz's journal of the Anglo-Boer War, *Commando*.

Smuts and his men suffered terribly from the cold when they crossed the Orange River to enter the Cape, close to the Natal border. To add to their woes, they were attacked by hostile mounted Sotho sympathetic to the British cause.

The ragged commando passed through Labuschagne's Nek, where the men rode through heavy rains, cold and wind, the cruel weather causing the loss of 30 horses to exposure. When Smuts neared Dordrecht, he rode ahead with four men to make a reconnaissance of the area and was ambushed by British scouts. Charlie, Smuts's horse, was shot from under him and two of his men fell, mortally wounded. By dint of clever running, Smuts managed to hide in a donga, losing only his hat and saddlebag in the process. The latter, when later recovered, was found to contain the New Testament in Greek, Schiller's entire works and the Greek book *Anabasis*, written by a professional soldier, Xenophon, in the 4th century BC.

General Smuts became South African Minister of Defence during World War II.

Smuts did not venture too close to Dordrecht but continued south, where 12 men, unable to continue in the cold, were left behind, presumably to die of exposure.

When the commando reached the railway line from Maclear, they saw a train approaching. Smuts forbade his men to roll rocks onto the line for fear that it contained civilians; to his chagrin he later learned that General French had been aboard.

On 17 September, after a week of incredible hardship during which his commando narrowly escaped a tightening cordon of British soldiers in appallingly cold and wet weather, Smuts and his men came upon a British camp comprising mainly 17th Lancers. The Lancers were taken by surprise and a spirited engagement took place, which resulted in a startling Boer victory. Thirty British soldiers were killed and many more wounded and captured. The Boers lost one fighter and were able to rearm, clothe and horse themselves.

Near the present-day Addo Elephant National Park, Smuts and his men, hungry from surviving on mountain tortoises for a week, feasted on the fruit of the Boesmansbrood (*Encephalartos altensteinii*) and almost died of poisoning. (The fruit of this cycad is edible only at certain times of the year; at the wrong time it contains strong concentrates of prussic acid. For the rest of his life Smuts was to suffer from a weak stomach.) To make matters worse, he had the British on his tail and had to be strapped to his horse to get away.

General Smuts (centre, seated) with some of his fighting men during the 2nd Anglo-Boer War

In Meiringspoort Pass through the Swartberg Mountains Smuts intercepted a British column.

They escaped by a most spectacular route between rocky cliff faces and over steep mountains on a rough track lined with impenetrable walls of thorn trees and scrub – at one place no more than a rocky stream bed between two mountains. The route had been opened up by Harry Smith in the 1850s, during one of the frontier wars.

Smuts stayed away from a Port Elizabeth bristling with British troops, but his men glimpsed the Indian Ocean with great excitement; many of them had never seen the sea before. They travelled further west, through Meiringspoort Pass in the Swartberg Mountains. Here Smuts's commando successfully intercepted a British column and came away, again, with fresh horses and warm clothes. However, the khaki uniforms were speedily abandoned when the men heard of a proclamation that Boers found wearing British uniforms would be shot without trial.

They passed through Calitzdorp, described by Smuts as an oasis complete with palm trees, towards Laingsburg. Smuts had, by this time, split his small force in order to avoid capture. He crossed the railway line and headed for Matjiesfontein, riding past a line of blockhouses east of the village. In Matjiesfontein, British officers living in the Lord Milner Hotel used the building's turrets as lookout points. Not far from here, Smuts narrowly escaped with his life when a shell from an Armstrong five-pounder cannon landed close to him, covering him in sand and dust.

Memorial to fallen Boers in Vanrhynsdorp, the town Smuts occupied in 1901 and where he lived for a while

310 COLESBERG REGION

Smuts's trail led from there into the Boland. Here he ascended the Roggeberge, where piles of tablet-like sandstone form unevenly layered natural castles, marking the boundary between the present-day Northern and Western Cape.

They took a spectacular track that climbed over the Cederberg to intercept the route between Clanwilliam and Citrusdal. Smuts then turned towards the north and progressed, in gasping heat, to reach Vanrhynsdorp at last – the only town that remained in Boer hands throughout the war. Here he paused to consolidate his forces.

Smuts with his granddaughter Mary. He had a large family and numerous grandchildren.

Near the Vanrhynsdorp church stands the oldest existing building in Namaqualand, and it was this house that Smuts used as headquarters. His men scouted as far as the coast, and Smuts himself rode 482km north to Kakamas on the Orange River near the Augrabies Falls. While he was away, an English-speaking man named Lambert Colyn visited the Boer headquarters, claiming that he wanted to fight for them. Fears that he was a spy were confirmed when the house was stormed by the enemy two weeks later. When Smuts returned he attacked a nearby British stronghold, capturing Colyn among others. Colyn was tried, found guilty of treason and executed on Smuts's orders, though he begged for mercy.

A blockhouse near the road is a reminder of Smuts's intention to take control of the copper mines in this area. The towns of Concordia and Springbok surrendered to the Boers, but the officer commanding the Okiep garrison refused to succumb and the town was blockaded.

It was during this blockade that a cart carrying two white flags was seen approaching on the dusty road. It contained a dispatch from General Kitchener requesting Smuts's presence at the peace negotiations. Smuts rode to Port Nolloth from where he took a ship to Cape Town and then an armoured train to Pretoria to negotiate peace at the end of the 2nd Anglo-Boer War in 1902.

Smuts sailed from Port Nolloth (left) to Cape Town and travelled from there to Pretoria for peace negotiations to end the 2nd Anglo-Boer War.

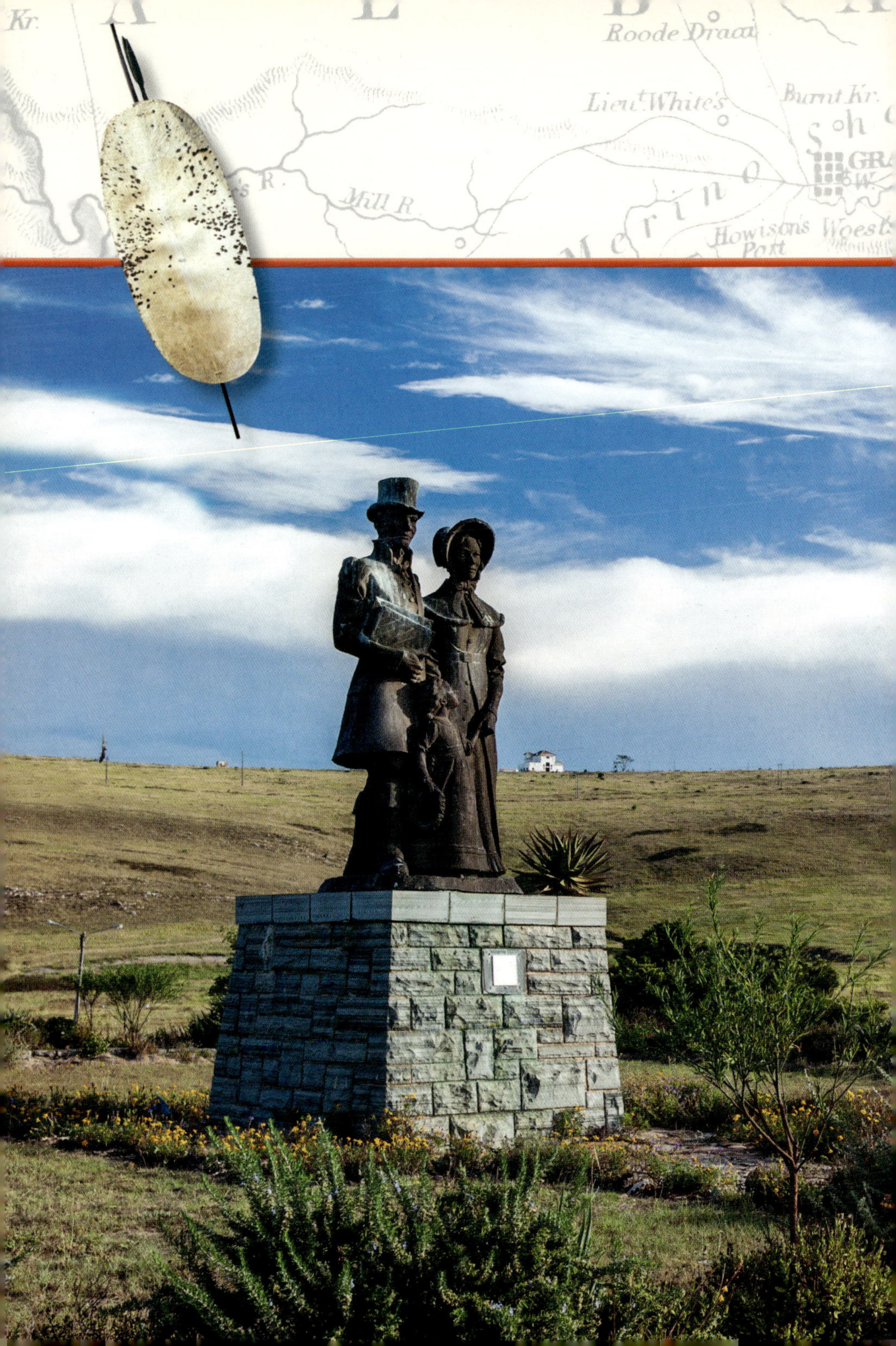

Eastern Cape

Statue commemorating the arrival of the British settlers in the eastern Cape Colony in 1820, Grahamstown

Grahamstown region

This is a wonderful area to explore, rich in history, with forgotten forts and ruins of military outposts to be found in dramatic, rugged countryside. Its history is characterised by clashes between the San, Khoikhoi, Xhosa, trekboers and European settlers, and defining features of its early development are the nine frontier wars that took place between 1779 and 1878.

Grahamstown was founded in 1812 by Colonel Graham as a military outpost to protect the frontier.

At the heart of the conflict was colonial expansion. From the early 1700s, the San, in particular, offered fierce resistance when trekboers, in search of pasture for their livestock, encroached on their traditional hunting grounds. Later, the migrating farmers encountered the Xhosa, and serious clashes ensued as competition for resources intensified and both parties sought to protect their territories and livestock.

In 1778, the governor of the Cape Colony, Joachim van Plettenberg, visited the eastern frontier and proclaimed the upper Fish River and the Bushmans River as the boundary

Regional battles

1815
Slagtersnek Rebellion

World events

1776
America declares independence and breaks all ties of allegiance with Britain. Thirteen American colonies become the United States of America.

1812
Napoleon retreats from Moscow and his reputation as undefeated military hero in Europe is shaken.

1815
The Battle of Waterloo ends 26 years of fighting between the European powers and France.

314   GRAHAMSTOWN REGION

between the colony and the land of the Xhosa. Two years later he pushed the boundary further east by declaring the entire length of the Fish River as the new frontier. This decision was to prove disastrous for peace in the region. In 1786, to quell unrest in this far-flung territory, a drostdy was established at Graaff-Reinet and a landdrost appointed for the region.

Yet clashes continued, and when British rule was imposed at the Cape, first in 1795 and then again in 1806, local administrators tried to enforce greater control over the strife-torn region. However, some measures failed to take into account the complexity of ethnic relationships in the region and served only to fuel volatility. Clashes between and within chiefdoms, such as the Battle of Amalinde, which represented a struggle for supremacy between two Xhosa-speaking groups, were not uncommon.

A further complication was resistance on the part of Dutch farmers to reforms that insisted on fair treatment of Khoikhoi and San labourers. Many farmers employed Khoikhoi and San servants and felt that the new regulations left them, as employers, unprotected. Dissatisfaction eventually led to the Slagtersnek Rebellion in 1815.

Grahamstown was founded as a military outpost after the Fourth Frontier War of 1811–1812. During the war, over 20,000 Xhosa were forced east across the Fish River, thereby dispossessing them of their territory west of this boundary. The Battle of Grahamstown was fought during the Fifth Frontier War, which lasted from 1819 to 1820.

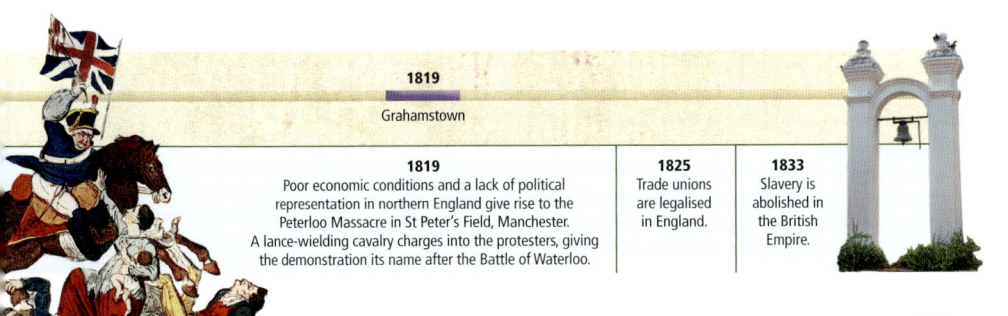

Battlefields

1. Slagtersnek Rebellion 1815
2. Grahamstown 1819

1819
Grahamstown

1819
Poor economic conditions and a lack of political representation in northern England give rise to the Peterloo Massacre in St Peter's Field, Manchester. A lance-wielding cavalry charges into the protesters, giving the demonstration its name after the Battle of Waterloo.

1825
Trade unions are legalised in England.

1833
Slavery is abolished in the British Empire.

GRAHAMSTOWN REGION   315

Gideon Scheepers – a martyr of the 2nd Anglo-Boer War

The military court in Graaff-Reinet where Scheepers was tried and convicted

The beginning of the 2nd Anglo-Boer War was characterised by a series of set-piece battles fought in Natal and the Cape, as British troops moved inland to relieve the sieges of Ladysmith, Kimberley and Mafeking.

However, after initial Boer victories, the sheer force of British troop numbers prevailed and the tide turned against the Boers. Gideon Scheepers, an officer in the Staatsartillerie and a member of General Christiaan de Wet's forces, was appointed as a scout and sent with Boer commander Pieter Kritzinger to the eastern Cape in an attempt to broaden the theatre of war and enlist the support of Cape burghers.

Scheepers proved himself to be a skilful guerrilla fighter and his small force of 279 men caused much mayhem among British columns operating in the southern parts of the eastern Cape Colony.

General John Pinkstone French assigned Colonel Henry Scobell the task of capturing Scheepers, but despite strenuous efforts he evaded capture until, in August 1901, he developed acute appendicitis and became so ill that he could no longer ride his horse. The British were closing in and he had no choice but to tell his men to leave him and save themselves. His men sent a message to the British, informing them of their leader's whereabouts and requesting a doctor, who arrived from Prince Albert. Scheepers was forced to surrender to an officer of the Hussars and was taken to Beaufort West for treatment.

When he was well enough to travel he was transferred to Graaff-Reinet where he was tried by a military court on charges of arson, murder and destruction of trains, although as an officer in the Boer forces he should have been treated as a prisoner of war.

Scheepers was found guilty of all charges and sentenced to death, and his execution by firing squad caused an outcry both locally and abroad. He gained martyr status and his body, which was initially buried where he had been executed, was removed by the British to a place unknown to this day.

A memorial close to the site of his execution on the road to Murraysburg, about 2km out of Graaff-Reinet, was erected by the Graaff-Reinet Afrikaans Cultural Society. There also is an Anglo-Boer War Memorial monument at the corner of Donkin and Somerset streets in Graaff-Reinet itself.

Slagtersnek Rebellion
Also known as *Slachter's Nek Rebellion*
October–November 1815

HOW TO GET THERE
This is not really a battle, as the rebels surrendered without a shot being fired. But the rebellion had far-reaching consequences and deserves a place in this guide. Slagtersnek itself was the site of the surrender. The rebels were hanged at Van Aardspos and there is a memorial there, on the N10 south of Cookhouse. However, the best place to examine this incident is at the Somerset East Museum housed in the old parsonage, where the original hanging beam stands and where the events leading up to the execution are explained in detail.

Somerset East Museum: *32°42'46.5" S   25°35'06.1" E*

Context
Dutch farmers in the eastern Cape Colony were unhappy with the British government's attempts to establish good administration and ensure fair treatment of farm labour. The Hottentot Proclamation of 1809 insisted on a written contract between employer and employee and promulgated strict pass laws. Provision was made for servants to complain about unfair treatment and once a year a travelling circuit court visited each area to hear these cases. The farmers felt that the government was siding with their servants against them and resented having to answer charges laid by their employees. This was exacerbated by the fact that the local military force, known as the Cape Regiment, was made up of Khoikhoi and other 'coloured' soldiers, who were commanded by white officers. The Dutch farmers resented having the law enforced by 'coloured' men. The situation was worsened by a land shortage that had arisen when the British government forbade new settlement east of the Fish River. A number of families were without farms. Known as bywoners, they had to eke out an existence on land belonging to others. Some opted to settle with the Xhosa east of the Fish River and pay tribute to the incumbent chief. It was a combination of all these factors that led to the rebellion.

Action
In 1813 a Khoikhoi servant known as Booy laid complaints against his employer, a farmer named Freek Bezuidenhout. The farmer refused to answer summonses to attend court and finally, in October 1815, two British officers and 12 Khoikhoi troops arrived at his farm to arrest him. Refusing to negotiate, Bezuidenhout and his son fled to a nearby cave, pursued by some of the soldiers. Shots were exchanged and Bezuidenhout was killed.

Timeline

1778
Governor van Plettenberg declares the upper Fish River to be the boundary between the Cape Colony and the Xhosa.

1779–1781
Xhosa raids result in counter-raids, and the First Frontier War ensues. The Zuurveld, south of the Fish River, is later cleared of all Xhosa people.

1793
More raids and retaliatory raids give rise to the Second Frontier War.

1799–1803
The Third Frontier War erupts.

1811–1812
The Fourth Frontier War breaks out when Colonel John Graham forces over 20,000 Xhosa north over the Fish River.

1813
A Khoikhoi servant lays complaints against his employer, Freek Bezuidenhout.

1815
Bezuidenhout is killed after British officers and troops arrive at his farm to arrest him. This leads to a rebellion, which is quelled by British soldiers at Slagtersnek.

1816
The rebels are hanged in March.

1819
The Battle of Grahamstown is fought during the Fifth Frontier War of 1819–1820.

1820
British settlers arrive in the eastern Cape Colony.

1834–1835
The Sixth Frontier War occurs.

1836
Voortrekkers leave the Cape to escape British rule.

1846–1878
There are three more frontier wars.

The museum in Somerset East displays the hanging beam used in the Slagtersnek Rebellion.

At Bezuidenhout's funeral, his brother, Johannes, swore vengeance and his neighbour, Hendrik Prinsloo, promised to support him. Prinsloo sent out letters to other farmers, inciting rebellion. One of these was intercepted and Prinsloo was imprisoned. About 60 rebels joined forces to demand his release.

On the 18 November 1815 they were confronted by an armed force of British soldiers at the top of Slagtersnek and forced to surrender. Not one shot was fired.

Johannes Bezuidenhout was not among those who surrendered, but was ambushed some days later at Madoersdrif by 100 Cape Regiment troops. He resisted arrest and shot a Cape soldier before he was himself mortally wounded and died, sheltering behind the wheel of his wagon with his wife and 14-year-old son.

All of the rebels were charged and six sentenced to death. Governor Lord Charles Somerset pardoned one of them, the other five were to be hanged at Van Aardspos on 9 March 1816. Since the hangman had not been told that there were five men, he had only brought enough rope to hang one and had to find more for the other convicts. Four of the ropes broke and the public pleaded for the lives of these men, but new rope was found and they were hanged again, this time successfully.

Aftermath

This rebellion has been cited as a catalyst for the Great Trek. The descendants of Freek and Johannes Bezuidenhout claim that their forbears' actions caused the migration to the Transvaal and led, indirectly, to the discovery of gold and diamonds, without which South Africa would not be what it is today.

Principal combatants
Dutch: Farmers in the eastern Cape Colony.
British: Cape Regiment.

Battle of Grahamstown
22 April 1819

HOW TO GET THERE
This battle was fought just north-east of Grahamstown's town centre. The British military barracks at Fort England, and the officers' mess were close to where the Grahamstown cathedral now stands. Fort England formed one end of the British line and the modern railway station the other. To the north, the ridge extending to the right of the conical hill, Mount Zion, was the direction from which the Xhosa attack came. The ridge is accessible from Beaufort Street when you drive north-east.

Context

There were two prominent Xhosa factions in the areas near the Fish River, the Rharhabe and the Gcaleka. The heir to the Rharhabe kingdom was Ngqika, but he was too young to rule when his father died and his uncle Ndlambe was appointed regent.

Friction between the regent and his nephew escalated in 1817 when Ngqika concluded an agreement with the governor of the Cape, Lord Charles Somerset, whereby chiefs were rewarded for helping to apprehend cattle thieves. Relations worsened when Ngqika seduced one of Ndlambe's wives and took her for his own. The enmity between the two eventually led to a battle between the warring factions at Amalinde (near King William's Town) in October 1818. The Gcaleka supported Ndlambe, who emerged victorious. Ngqika went to the British for help and revenged himself on Ndlambe by instigating a raid by British soldiers into his territory in November 1818. Led by Lieutenant Colonel Thomas Brereton, they confiscated 23,000 head of cattle, some of which were given to Ngqika.

Still confident after his victory over Ngqika at Amalinde and incensed by the British raid, Ndlambe encouraged his sangoma and right-hand man Nxele (also known as Makana) to lead an army of close to 10,000 warriors over the Fish River to recover the cattle and punish the settlers. They attacked two British patrols, killing one British soldier in each patrol, as well as raiding and burning farms and killing

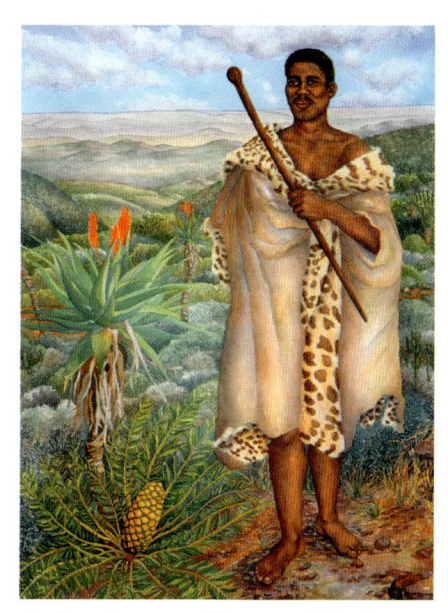

Ngqika, who opposed his regent, Ndlambe, at Amalinde near King William's Town

Timeline

1812
20,000 Xhosa are forced to vacate all territory west of the Fish River. Grahamstown is founded to house the British garrison defending the territory.

1813
Captain Thomas Willshire fights at Vitoria during the Peninsular War (1808–1814) and at the siege of San Sebastian (northern Spain).

1814
Lord Charles Somerset arrives in the Cape to take up the post of governor.

1817
Somerset visits the Cape frontier. The Xhosa chief Ngqika, against the wishes of his uncle and regent, Ndlambe, makes an agreement with Somerset whereby chiefs are rewarded for helping to apprehend cattle thieves.

1818
Lieutenant Colonel Willshire leads his regiment, the 38th Light Infantry, to the Cape. The enmity between Nqgika and Ndlambe leads to a battle between warring Xhosa factions at Amalinde, near King William's Town.

1819
Willshire becomes commander of British Kaffraria. A quarrel between local chiefs leads to an attack on Grahamstown. Willshire defends with only his own company of the 38th and 240 local troops.

1837
Willshire is made brevet colonel, with the local rank of brigadier general, in India.

---

the inhabitants. The British were in the process of putting together a force of more than 3,000 troops to restore order, but this army had not yet left the vicinity of Algoa Bay by the time Nxele launched his attack on Grahamstown.

The battle of 1819 was one of several fought during the Fifth Frontier War of 1819 to 1820.

Action

The garrison town of Grahamstown, with one main street and only 30 houses, had been founded by Colonel John Graham in 1812 after he had forced more than 20,000 Xhosa to vacate all territory west of the Fish River. The garrison consisted of 84 white men and officers, 130 black soldiers and 80 Khoikhoi troops of the Cape Regiment; 32 civilians also lent support.

Ndlambe's force was led by his right-hand man, Nxele. Ndlambe was supremely confident in his numerical advantage and even sent a messenger to the fort the day before the battle, warning that the Xhosa would be in town the next morning.

Commanding officer Lieutenant Colonel Thomas Willshire sent back a message saying that they would be ready, but on 22 April 1819, as he rode out to scout in an easterly direction, he was concerned to see large numbers of warriors in the distance. His small force had been depleted by the earlier departure of 100 infantrymen to investigate a report of unrest towards the east (this report, which came from Ngqika's interpreter, was possibly a ruse).

Nxele divided the 10,000 warriors into three columns and lined them up along the ridge north of the Matyala stream, east of Mount Zion. The forerunners of his army were already in Grahamstown occupying some civilian houses when the main army attacked in the early afternoon – the left flank against the barracks and the right against the High Street buildings and the officers' mess.

The British were lined up south of the stream, facing the ridge. Armed with smooth-

Colonel John Graham

320 GRAHAMSTOWN REGION

bore muzzle-loading muskets, they held their fire until the warriors were within 35m of their position, although the range of their guns was twice that distance. Some of the Xhosa had firearms, but most relied on their sharp throwing spears, lethal over a distance of 50m. When they came in close contact with the enemy they would break off the long handles of the spears and use them as short, stabbing assegais.

The British had the advantage of the rising ground above the stream and were supported by artillery armed with shrapnel that fired over the heads of the foot soldiers and into the approaching warriors. The arrival of a Khoikhoi hunter named Boesak with a group of about 130 good marksmen was very fortunate. They could pick off the Xhosa, who were cut down in swathes, many dying on the banks and in the small stream that ran between them and the defenders. However, the Xhosa's left flank managed to fight its way into the barracks on the British right, and fierce fighting took place there before they were repulsed. Before the remaining invaders could be driven out, 102 Xhosa died inside the perimeters of the barracks. Fighting along the rest of the line lasted little more than an hour before the Xhosa withdrew.

Government Advertisement.

HIS Excellency the Governor and Commander in Chief is pleased to notify and direct, that the present Head Quarter Cantonment of the Cape Regiment, situated in the Zuureveldt, which is also to be the future Residence of the Deputy Landdrost of Uitenhage, shall be henceforward designated, and only acknowledged, by the name of "GRAHAM's TOWN," in testimony of His Excellency's respect for the Services of Lieut.-Colonel GRAHAM, through whose able exertions the Caffre Tribes have been expelled from that valuable District.

Castle of Good Hope, 14th August, 1812.

By Command of His Excellency the Governor,

(Signed)   H. ALEXANDER, *Secretary.*

Cape government notice announcing the naming of Graham's Town in 1812

Aftermath

More than 400 Xhosa were killed, at the expense of three British dead and some wounded.

After this, the area between the Fish and the Keiskamma rivers was ceded to the British and was supposed to be neutral territory, unoccupied by either Xhosa or settlers. In reality it became British territory and was a cause of much resentment among the Xhosa. The frontier was to become a battleground for another three wars owing to the acute land hunger of the Xhosa who, over a period starting in 1812, had been forced out of the land stretching from the areas south-west of the Fish River eastwards, all the way to the Keiskamma River. The shortage of land was exacerbated by the Mfecane in modern KwaZulu-Natal, which forced displaced people southwards and added to the competition for grazing and food.

The power of Ndlambe's chiefdom was never the same after this battle. Nxele handed himself over to the British and was imprisoned on Robben Island. He drowned during an escape attempt. Ngqika, still married to the wife he had taken from Ndlambe, died the year after the battle.

Principal combatants

Xhosa: Supporters of Chief Ndlambe, led by Nxele (Makana).
British: 38th Light Infantry; Boesak's Khoikhoi hunters; Cape Regiment; Civilians; Colonial troops; Royal African Corps.

Hout Bay
Noort Hoch Seal I.
or Slang Kop P. Simons B. Gordon B.
Roman R.
West Hoek Town Whittle R.
Winkle B. Pringle
Olifants-bosch Buffels B. R.
CAPE of GOOD HOPE Anvil
discov.d 1487 BAY
Bellows

SUTHERLAND HIGHLANDERS
93
CAPE OF GOOD HOPE
BALAKLAVA

Western Cape

A view of Cape Town from Blouberg, across Table Bay

Cape Town region

Apart from its spectacular beauty and dramatic mountain scenery, the Cape is noteworthy for its history as a bitterly contested port among the leading trading nations of Europe, whose ships plied a route that took them around the southern tip of Africa to the Far East from the 1600s onwards. During the ensuing two centuries its ownership changed a number of times as a result of complicated European politics.

Ships from Europe, sailing to and from the Far East, called in at the Cape to replenish their supplies.

Both the Muizenberg and Blaauwberg battles, fought along the False Bay and Table Bay coastlines, concerned the strategic value of the outpost to the Dutch, the British and, indirectly, the French in the years after it had been established as a halfway station in 1652. The cosmopolitan character of modern-day Cape Town's population reflects the influences of these nations as well as the East Indian colonies that had been under their control.

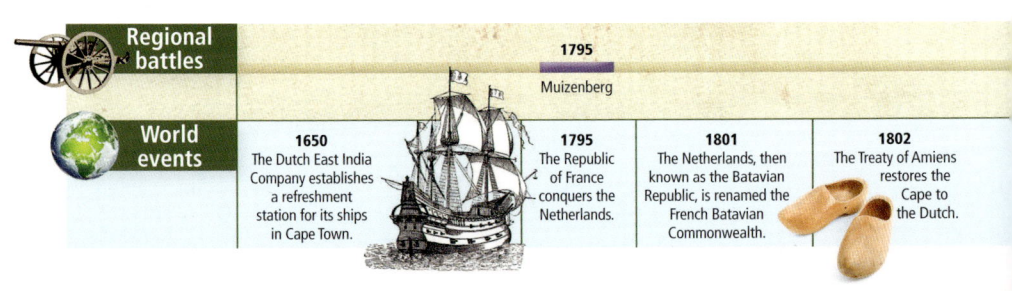

Regional battles

- 1795 — Muizenberg

World events

- 1650 — The Dutch East India Company establishes a refreshment station for its ships in Cape Town.
- 1795 — The Republic of France conquers the Netherlands.
- 1801 — The Netherlands, then known as the Batavian Republic, is renamed the French Batavian Commonwealth.
- 1802 — The Treaty of Amiens restores the Cape to the Dutch.

324   CAPE TOWN REGION

The first Europeans to set foot in the Cape were survivors of various shipwrecks. It was not until 1652 that the first permanent European settlement was established, set up by the Dutch East India Company (Vereenigde Oostindische Compagnie, or VOC) as a refreshment station where ships could replenish water and fresh food supplies, vital for scurvy-ridden sailors on the way to India and beyond. The Cape soon became known as the 'tavern of the seas' as there was always a good supply of fruit and vegetables to be had, grown in the Company's Garden, and meat bartered from the local Khoikhoi, the region's earliest inhabitants.

During the French revolutionary wars, political tensions between France and England fostered fear in Britain that the French-supporting Dutch would refuse to supply British ships visiting the Cape. This threat, as well as the fact that Holland was regarded as an enemy power, led to the first British occupation of the Cape in 1795, achieved after the Battle of Muizenberg. However, the Treaty of Amiens in 1802 saw the Cape restored to Holland, then referred to as the Batavian Republic. Four years later, Napoleon's efforts to expand his empire, coupled with a growing French influence in Holland, led to increasing hostility in Europe and a second British invasion of the Cape of Good Hope in 1806, which was presaged by the Battle of Blaauwberg.

Although neither of these battles was much more than a series of skirmishes, both had far-reaching political implications for the development of the fledgling colony.

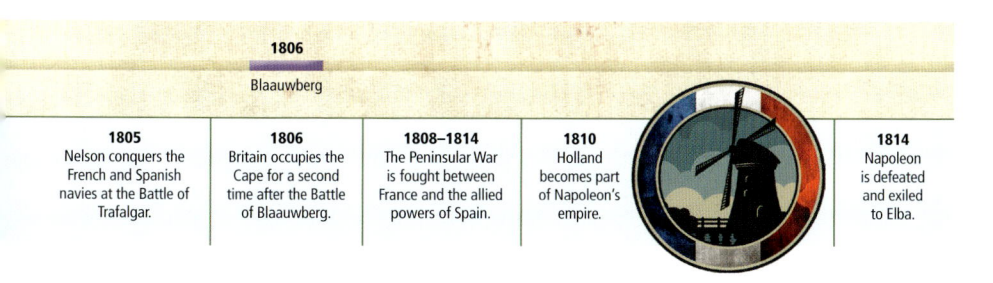

Battlefields

① Muizenberg 1795　② Blaauwberg 1806

1805	1806	1806	1808–1814	1810	1814
Nelson conquers the French and Spanish navies at the Battle of Trafalgar.	Blaauwberg	Britain occupies the Cape for a second time after the Battle of Blaauwberg.	The Peninsular War is fought between France and the allied powers of Spain.	Holland becomes part of Napoleon's empire.	Napoleon is defeated and exiled to Elba.

CAPE TOWN REGION　325

Battle of Muizenberg
7– 9 August 1795

HOW TO GET THERE
Fought between Muizenberg and Wynberg ridge, the Battle of Muizenberg was essentially a series of skirmishes. Remains of the rudimentary Dutch fortifications, prepared in only three days and abandoned on the last day, can be visited on the hillside between St James and Muizenberg beaches. The site can be accessed from the coastal road between Muizenberg and Fish Hoek.

Context

The Cape had been a refreshment station since 1652, when the Dutch had established a garden to supply their ships with fresh provisions. However, by 1795, the once powerful VOC was in decline, while the British East India Company was expanding its influence in India and Ceylon. This was vital to Britain, as the American colonies had been lost and trade with Asia was essential to fill the gap. The Cape was pivotal as a refreshment and supply point for its trading vessels on the long haul to India. Even more important, it had a healthy climate in which troops bound for India, many of them weak from scurvy after the long sea voyage, could recuperate before travelling on.

Leading up to the French Revolution in 1789, unrest in Europe had caused serious ideological rifts in Holland, where some citizens sided with the Royalist supporters of the Prince of Orange and of Britain, and others with the Republicans, known as Patriotten, who supported the French against the British. France was Britain's enemy and it was to England that William V, Prince of Orange, fled when he was forced out by the Republicans. Holland became more and more dominated by France, so much so that by 1801 the Batavian Republic was replaced by the French Batavian Commonwealth and in 1810 Holland became part of Napoleon's Empire.

The British became increasingly aware of the military significance of the Cape and the threat it could pose were it to fall into enemy hands, particularly if that enemy were France. Lord Baring, chairman of the British East India Company, was conscious that French-supporting Dutch in the Cape could very well refuse to supply British ships. It would be even worse if the French were to put an armed force on board a Dutch trading ship bound for the Cape and take possession of it. The Battle of Muizenberg occurred when the Secretary for War in Britain was eventually persuaded to send a fleet of nine ships to the Cape to defend British interests.

Sluysken coat of arms; Abraham Sluysken was governor of the Cape.

Action

The British fleet consisted of two squadrons commanded by Vice Admiral George Elphinstone and Commodore Blankett, with a small army aboard of about 515 soldiers and 350 marines under Major General James Craig. They landed unopposed and occupied Simon's Town in June 1795.

The Cape governor, Abraham Sluysken, agreed initially to supply the ships, but changed his mind when he realised that the British had intentions of wresting control of the Cape from the VOC. The British had expected Sluysken to support them, as they had with them a letter from the Prince of Orange, instructing Sluysken to do so. They had not come in sufficient strength to take the port by force and Sluysken capitalised on this by rallying the Dutch burghers under the VOC banner. Colonel Robert Gordon, the VOC commander-in-chief and senior military man who reported to Sluysken, led a militia force to fortify and hold a position at Muizenberg. The governor then stopped provisioning the fleet in Simon's Town harbour. Negotiations led nowhere and Craig, after assessing the strength of the Dutch, decided to launch an attack on the militia at Muizenberg.

On 7 August some 1,800 of Elphinstone's men marched along the coast from Simon's Town towards the small fort at Muizenberg. Four warships sailed alongside them in support, for Craig did not have ordnance until the arrival of 400 East India Company artillery men on 9 August. The ships fired into Dutch guard posts on the way and, when they reached the fort, bombarded it with their cannons. The Dutch had no answer and withdrew, fighting as they retreated.

British warships sail towards Muizenberg in support of foot soldiers marching parallel on the shore.

Timeline

1666
Construction work begins on Cape Town's Castle.

1761
George Keith Elphinstone joins the British Royal Navy.

1763
Sir James Henry Craig, who grew up in Gibraltar, joins the British army at the age of 15.

1766
Elphinstone leaves the navy to take part in a trading venture to the East, but rejoins two years later.

1771
The boundary of the Cape Colony is established on the Gamtoos River.

1774–81
Captain Craig serves in the American Revolutionary wars and is promoted to lieutenant colonel.

1778
Cape Governor Van Plettenberg pushes the Cape Colony's eastern boundary to the Fish River.

1793
Elphinstone is promoted to rear admiral for the war with France; he serves in the Mediterranean and at the Siege of Toulon.

1795
Craig becomes major general and commands the force that captures the Cape at the Battle of Muizenberg. Elphinstone commands the fleet that seizes Muizenberg. Craig is governor of the Cape until 1797.

Twenty-two 24-pounder cannons formed part of the extensive fortifications built in 1793 to protect Table Bay against invasion.

Craig had done well with the few men at his disposal, especially as 200 of them were ill with scurvy, but his force was not strong enough to defeat the enemy and skirmishes continued for six weeks. Eventually the Dutch were driven back into positions on Wynberg Hill where they held on still. On 3 September the main British reinforcements arrived in Simon's Town harbour and finally drove the Dutch out of their positions on the Wynberg ridge. On 14 September they surrendered and the Cape passed into British hands.

Aftermath

This was a minor engagement with major political implications. Major General Craig became Cape governor when the British fleet, along with Elphinstone, departed for India. Craig was a fair and sympathetic ruler who carried out his task in an even-handed and conscientious manner.

The Cape was to remain under British control until 1804, when it was handed back to the Batavian Republic. In 1806 the British again took control after they attacked and defeated the Dutch at the Battle of Blaauwberg (see p. 330).

Principal combatants
British: Royal Marines and British army under Major General James Craig; Royal Navy under Admiral George Elphinstone.
Dutch: Dutch militia fighting for the Dutch East India Company under Governor Abraham Sluysken and Colonel Robert Gordon.

Vice Admiral George Elphinstone

Colonel Robert Jacob Gordon

Robert Jacob Gordon was born in Holland, of Scottish descent. His father was an officer in the Dutch army. Robert followed in his footsteps, joining the army in 1753 while simultaneously studying at the University of Hardewijk.

He received a broad education and was a talented linguist, speaking most European languages. He would later learn some African languages, too.

He first visited the Cape at the end of 1773 when he made a 10-month journey across the peninsula in the company of a renowned botanist. He was so taken with the country that he arranged his transfer to the VOC Cape garrison. In 1774, before moving to the Cape, he travelled in Europe, where he met research scientists and philosophers whose influence is later apparent in his detailed journals describing his exploratory travels.

He arrived in Cape Town in 1777, taking command of the Cape Castle garrison in 1780. It is possible that the VOC tasked him with assessing the military implications of holding the Cape against a foreign power, as he made four extensive trips into the interior during the period of his duty.

His detailed observations of the indigenous people, plants and animals he encountered and the geology of the terrain he traversed earned him the reputation of an accomplished explorer free of prejudice and possessed of a clear vision and a keen sense of observation.

In August 1795, when the British invaded the Cape, Gordon was the VOC commander-in-chief and the most senior military man in the Cape. The British forced the surrender of the VOC troops, mustered by Governor Sluysken and led by Gordon.

Gordon found himself torn between loyalty to the VOC and his pro-British feelings, especially to the Prince of Orange, who had taken refuge in England. He was viewed as a traitor by the Dutch and was mistrusted by the British. His health was also deteriorating and so, in October, he shot himself.

In those days people committing suicide were not allowed to be buried in consecrated ground and Gordon was placed somewhere in an unmarked grave, the location of which remains unknown.

Robert Gordon, a tragic figure

Cape Town Castle entrance

Battle of Blaauwberg
8 January 1806

HOW TO GET THERE
Approaching in a northerly direction along the R27, you see Blouberg Mountain looming on your right. A fairly unobstructed view is a few kilometres after the left-hand turn-off to Big Bay Boulevard (M120). The battle was fought on the flat plains south-east of the main summit. The lower hill west of the mountain is the Kleinberg. The battlefield is best viewed from the top of Blouberg Mountain, but this can be done only by prior arrangement with the landowners.

Context

After the first British occupation in 1795, the Cape was given back to the Batavian Republic in terms of the Treaty of Amiens of 1802. Now under direct control of the Dutch government, it became more than a refreshment station for ships on their way to the Far East. The inhabitants were now members of a democratic republic, ably governed by Governor General Jan Willem Janssens, who introduced liberal reforms: importation of slaves was no longer permitted, the qualified franchise was non-racial, free trade was encouraged, and Islamic religion was given full legal protection.

However, unrest in Europe was to cause another British invasion and occupation at the Cape. British politicians feared that the French would take control of the port and threaten their naval supremacy. As Napoleon was planning an attack on Britain at the time, he encouraged the notion that France intended to take the Cape, in the hope that Britain would weaken her defences by sending ships and troops to South Africa.

Major General David Baird commanded the British army that took the Cape in 1806.

Governor Janssens was well aware of the threat and feared that his two regular Batavian battalions would be insufficient to resist an invasion. To add to their strength, he cobbled together the best irregular local force he could muster, made up of the Hottentot Light Infantry, a 'coloured' regiment of well-trained soldiers, Waldeck's Battalion, German, Hungarian and Austrian mercenaries, about 240 sailors and marines from a French warship, and a squadron of volunteer burgher cavalry.

British soldiers advance on General Janssens's Dutch troops at Blaauwberg.

Action

The British invasion force sailed from Falmouth and Cork in secret, their stated destinations given as the Far East and the Mediterranean. It was a formidable fleet comprising more than 60 ships and 6,700 troops under the overall command of Commodore Sir Home Popham, with the army under the command of Major General David Baird. The latter had spent a year in the Cape during the first British occupation and knew its defences and the terrain.

The fleet sailed into Table Bay on 4 January 1806, where it was spotted by lookouts on Signal Hill. Popham had decided to land in Table Bay rather than at Simon's Town, in False Bay, as the latter was well defended.

It was the worst possible time for Janssens to call up his troops from their far-flung farms, as it was the middle of cropping season and very hot. A chain of signalling guns fired from hill to hill sent the message 250km inland, but not all the men responded. In the end Janssens had only about 2,000 men at his disposal.

The weather, meanwhile, was causing the British landing problems because the wind and swell were so strong that anchoring close to shore was impossible. On 6 January a small vessel was scuttled off Losperd's Bay (present-day Melkbosstrand) to create a breakwater. The troops were sent ashore in landing vessels, one of which overturned, drowning 36 men.

Shako plate worn on the cylindrical hats of the 59th Regiment, part of Baird's force

Timeline

1588
The destruction of the Spanish Armada allows the British and Dutch to share in the highly profitable East Indies spice trade.

1600
The East India Company is founded by London businessmen to trade with the East.

1602
Dutch merchants and independent trading companies founded the Vereenigde Oostindische Compagnie (VOC, or Dutch East India Company).

1650
The VOC sets up a refreshment station for its ships at the Cape of Good Hope.

1772
Scottish-born Sir David Baird joins the British army, and is sent to India as a captain in the Highland Light Infantry seven years later.

1793
Jan Willem Janssens, born in Holland and serving in the army as a military engineer, is seriously wounded in Flanders during a battle against the French.

1800
Janssens is appointed secretary to the war ministry.

1795
The British occupy the Cape for the first time after the Battle of Muizenberg. Baird is now a colonel and commands the land force that occupies the Cape.

1802
The Cape is restored to the Dutch. Janssens is appointed governor and military commander.

1806
Baird commands the force that conquers the Dutch at the Battle of Blaauwberg and Britain reoccupies the Cape. Governor General Janssens is forced to surrender and is sent back to the Netherlands, which is now under France. Baird is made acting governor of the Cape for a year.

BATTLE OF BLAAUWBERG

On shore, Baird divided his force into two brigades and began the march south towards Cape Town, choosing the route inland of Blaauwberg Mountain rather than the sandy track between mountain and beach. On the left were three regiments of the Highland Brigade and on the right the 24th, 59th and 83rd infantry regiments. They were accompanied by about 600 marines and sailors who dragged two howitzers and a battery of small field guns, battling through the thorny scrub and sand in scorching heat.

Janssens spent the night at Rietvlei, before marching his men north to take up position on the flat plain east of the Blaauwberg Mountain the next day. Joining the mountain to the south is a smaller hill called the Kleinberg. Janssens put a cannon and some mounted troops here to protect his left flank. His firing line stretched about a kilometre and a half across the plain, with the burgher light cavalry on the left, some of the Batavian infantry to their right, the Hottentot Light Infantry next, and then the Waldeck mercenaries in the centre. Next, on their right, were the French seamen and then came more Batavian infantry and light horse regiments to make up the right flank. Janssens himself rode up and down the line, urging his men on.

Commodore Popham

The British fleet sails into Table Bay prior to the Battle of Blaauwberg.

332   CAPE TOWN REGION

The battle began at 05h00 on 8 January 1806, when the British troops on the saddle under the eastern slopes of Blaauwberg Mountain opened with an attack by the 24th Regiment on the mounted burghers on Kleinberg. The burghers were forced off the hill and the left flank of Janssens's army was now unsupported. Meanwhile, the Highland Brigade had been advancing on the centre of Janssens's line, the section held by the Waldeck battalion who were already jittery after a shell had

The Treaty Tree in Woodstock, where Janssens capitulated to the British

landed nearby. When the Highlanders fixed bayonets and sounded the charge on their bagpipes, the Waldeck mercenaries broke and fled. Janssens implored the men to stand, but the Batavian soldiers on the left were the next to retreat. The Hottentot Light Infantry and the French, however, remained and fought valiantly until ordered by Janssens to retire. Almost half the French marines and sailors had been killed and he retired his depleted force to the Hottentots Holland Mountains after sending the Waldeck men back to Cape Town in disgrace. Baird marched on to Cape Town the next day where he encountered no opposition. Capitulation was signed on 18 January and the Cape became a British colony.

Aftermath

A total of 15 British men were killed and about 190 wounded. Janssens's army was shattered, though, with 337 men lost, although not all of them were killed. The Cape became a British colony and its administration gave rise to many grievances among the farmers along the frontier, eventually leading to the Great Trek and the founding of the independent Boer republics of the Orange Free State and the Transvaal. Without this battle, the gold under the Witwatersrand might have remained undiscovered. And perhaps, if this battle had not taken place, the Anglo-Zulu War would not have taken place, as Britain would not have considered confederation had the Cape not been a colony.

Jan Willem Janssens

Principal combatants

British: 60 ships and 6,700 troops under the overall command of Commodore Popham, including 24th, 59th and 83rd infantry regiments, Highland Brigade and Naval Brigade.
Dutch: Dutch militia under Governor General Janssens, including Batavian Infantry, Burgher Light Cavalry, French marines and sailors, Hottentot Light Infantry, Light Horse regiments and Waldeck's Battalion of Mercenaries.

BATTLE OF BLAAUWBERG

Chronology of battles and checklist

BATTLE CATEGORY & BATTLE NAME	DATE	NEAREST TOWN	PROVINCE	PAGE	VISITED
INDIGENOUS BATTLES					
Gqokli Hill	April 1818	Ulundi	KwaZulu-Natal	51	
Lattakoo	26 June 1823	Kuruman	Northern Cape	284	
Ndondakasuka	2 December 1856	KwaDukuza (Stanger)	KwaZulu-Natal	40	
Tshaneni	5 June 1884	Mkuze	KwaZulu-Natal	56	
COLONIAL & FRONTIER BATTLES					
Muizenberg	7–9 August 1795	Cape Town	Western Cape	326	
Blaauwberg	8 January 1806	Cape Town	Western Cape	330	
Slagtersnek Rebellion	October–November 1815	Somerset East, Grahamstown	Eastern Cape	317	
Grahamstown	22 April 1819	Grahamstown	Eastern Cape	319	
Durban	23–24 May 1842	Durban	KwaZulu-Natal	31	
Swartkoppies	2 May 1845	Trompsburg	Free State	291	
Boomplaats	29 August 1848	Trompsburg	Free State	288	
Berea	20 December 1852	Maseru, Bloemfontein	In Lesotho, but accessible from the Free State	242	
Mome Gorge	10 June 1906	Nkandla, Eshowe	KwaZulu-Natal	34	
VOORTREKKER BATTLES					
Vegkop	15 October 1836	Heilbron	Free State	231	
Zaailaager	17 February 1838	Estcourt	KwaZulu-Natal	28	
Italeni	10 April 1838	Babanango	KwaZulu-Natal	48	
Blood River	16 December 1838	Dundee	KwaZulu-Natal	162	
1st ANGLO-BOER WAR BATTLES					
Bronkhorstspruit	20 December 1880	Bronkhorstspruit, Pretoria	Gauteng	212	
Laing's Nek	28 January 1881	Volksrust	Mpumalanga	187	
Ingogo	8 February 1881	Newcastle	KwaZulu-Natal	182	
Majuba Hill	27 February 1881	Volksrust	KwaZulu-Natal	189	

334   FIELD GUIDE TO THE BATTLEFIELDS OF SOUTH AFRICA

BATTLE CATEGORY & BATTLE NAME	DATE	NEAREST TOWN	PROVINCE	PAGE	VISITED
ANGLO-ZULU WAR BATTLES					
Isandlwana	22 January 1879	Nqutu	KwaZulu-Natal	134	
Rorke's Drift	22 January 1879	Nqutu	KwaZulu-Natal	144	
Hlobane	28 March 1879	Vryheid	KwaZulu-Natal	169	
Khambula	29 March 1879	Vryheid	KwaZulu-Natal	173	
Gingindlovu	2 April 1879	KwaGingindlovu	KwaZulu-Natal	43	
Death of the Prince Imperial of France	1 June 1879	Nqutu	KwaZulu-Natal	150	
Ulundi	4 July 1879	Ulundi	KwaZulu-Natal	53	
2nd ANGLO-BOER WAR BATTLES					
Talana Hill	20 October 1899	Dundee	KwaZulu-Natal	153	
Elandslaagte	21 October 1899	Ladysmith	KwaZulu-Natal	120	
Rietfontein	24 October 1899	Ladysmith	KwaZulu-Natal	118	
Ladysmith	30 October 1899	Ladysmith	KwaZulu-Natal	112	
Winston Churchill's capture	15 November 1899	Estcourt, Colenso	KwaZulu-Natal	66	
Belmont	23 November 1899	Hopetown	Northern Cape	280	
Willowgrange	23 November 1899	Estcourt	KwaZulu-Natal	60	
Graspan	25 November 1899	Ritchie	Northern Cape	277	
Modder River	28 November 1899	Kimberley	Northern Cape	268	
Stormberg	10 December 1899	Molteno	Eastern Cape	301	
Magersfontein	11 December 1899	Kimberley	Northern Cape	260	
Colenso	15 December 1899	Colenso	KwaZulu-Natal	69	
Labuschagne's Nek	30 December 1899	Dordrecht	Eastern Cape	305	
Platrand	6 January 1900	Ladysmith	KwaZulu-Natal	106	
Spioenkop	24 January 1900	Ladysmith, Bergville	KwaZulu-Natal	80	
Vaalkrans	5–7 February 1900	Ladysmith	KwaZulu-Natal	92	
Koedoesberg Drift	5–7 February 1900	Ritchie	Northern Cape	274	
West Australia Hill	9 February 1900	Colesberg	Northern Cape	298	
Pink Hill	12 February 1900	Colesberg	Northern Cape	296	

BATTLE CATEGORY & BATTLE NAME	DATE	NEAREST TOWN	PROVINCE	PAGE	VISITED
Tugela Heights	14–27 February 1900	Colenso	KwaZulu-Natal	98	
Paardeberg	17–27 February 1900	Kimberley	Free State	254	
Labuschagne's Nek	4 March 1900	Dordrecht	Eastern Cape	306	
Poplar Grove	7 March 1900	Petrusburg	Free State	251	
Driefontein	10 March 1900	Bloemfontein	Free State	249	
Sannaspos	31 March 1900	Bloemfontein	Free State	245	
Boshof	5 April 1900	Boshof	Free State	258	
Scheeper's Nek	20 May 1900	Vryheid	KwaZulu-Natal	167	
Biddulphsberg	29 May 1900	Senekal	Free State	240	
Doornkop	29 May 1900	Johannesburg	Gauteng	220	
Fabersput	30 May 1900	Douglas	Northern Cape	282	
Rooiwal	7 June 1900	Koppies	Free State	228	
Botha's Pass	8 June 1900	Newcastle, Memel	KwaZulu-Natal	185	
Alleman Nek	11 June 1900	Volksrust	Mpumalanga	196	
Diamond Hill	11–12 June 1900	Pretoria, Bronkhorstspruit	Gauteng	215	
Surrender Hill	28–30 July 1900	Ladysmith, Fouriesburg	Free State	126	
Bergendal	27 August 1900	eMakhazeni (Belfast)	Mpumalanga	205	
Doornkraal	6 November 1900	Bothaville	Free State	226	
Rhenosterkop	29 November 1900	Bronkhorstspruit	On Mpumalanga / Gauteng border	210	
Blood River Poort	17 September 1901	Vryheid	KwaZulu-Natal	165	
Bakenlaagte	30 October 1901	eMalahleni (Witbank)	Mpumalanga	208	
Groenkop	24–25 December 1901	Kestell, Ladysmith	Free State	129	
Roodewal	11 April 1902	Ottosdal, Delareyville	North West	223	
Holkrans	6 May 1902	Vryheid	KwaZulu-Natal	178	

Glossary

agterryer – literally 'after rider', mostly black servants of Boer fighters
assegai – Stabbing spear
biltong – strips of dried, spiced meat, similar to beef jerky
bittereinders – the Boers who, in the latter stages of the 2nd Anglo-Boer War, refused to surrender, vowing to fight 'to the bitter end'
burgher – citizen
bywoners – Afrikaner men, women or families without farms, who made a living on land belonging to other farmers
Cape rebels – citizens of the British Cape Colony, who supported the Boers
donga – dry gully (through soil erosion)
Dopper – a member of the Gereformeerde (Reformed) church, a more conservative institution than the more popular Hervormde (Reformed) church
drift – ford
horns-of-the-buffalo formation – Zulu attack formation
Khoikhoi – name given to describe the original herding people of the Cape
koppie – a small hill
kraal – an enclosure containing animals or a group of traditional huts
kranz (krans) – cliff
laager – an enclosed area formed by a circle of wagons latched together to protect the people inside
landdrost – magistrate with jurisdiction over a particular district
lobola – bride price, paid in cattle
Long Tom – the 155mm French Creusot gun imported by the Boers for use during the 2nd Anglo-Boer War
mealie meal – crushed corn
Mfecane (Difaqane) – a series of wars fought as African societies in southern Africa expanded in size and competed for power, land and other resources from about the 1790s to the 1850s
muti – traditional medicine dispensed by healers
picket (or piquet) – a military term for a small group of men on watch
Pom-Pom gun – the Maxim Nordenfeldt gun, which fires 1lb shells at a rate of 60 per minute, exploding with a regular 'pom pom pom' sound
poort – narrow valley
sangar – an entrenchment built of rocks to protect those inside from bullets and shells
sangoma – traditional healer
sjambok – heavy leather whip
snaphaan gun – flintlock gun
spruit – stream
Staatsartillerie – State Artillery
trekboer – semi-nomadic livestock farmer
Uitlanders – foreigners
umuzi – Zulu homestead
uSuthu – young Zulu warriors under Cetshwayo and Dinuzulu
vechtgeneraal – literally 'fighting general' in the Boer army
VOC – Vereenigde Oostindische Compagnie (Dutch East India Company)
Volksraad – Parliament of the South African Republic
Voortrekker – Afrikaner settlers who migrated from the Cape Colony to Natal and the Transvaal during the Great Trek in the 1830s and early 1840s.
ZAR – Zuid-Afrikaansche Republiek (South African Republic)
ZARP – Zuid-Afrikaansche Republiek Politie (South African Republic Police, also known as Johannesburg Police)

Bibliography

Amery, L. (ed.). 1900. *The Times History of the War in South Africa 1899–1900*, Vol. 11. London: Sampson Low, Marston & Co.

Armstrong, H. C. 1937. *Grey Steel*. London: Methuen & Co. Ltd.

Baring Pemberton, W. 1964. *Battles of the Boer War*. London: B. T. Batsford Ltd.

Barker, D. 2005. *Zulus at Bay – A Colonial Chronicle*. Pinetown: Denis Barker.

Barnard, C. J. 1970. *Generaal Botha op die Natalse Front*. Pretoria: A. A. Balkema.

Becker, P. 1969. *Hill of Destiny – The Life and Times of Moshesh*. London: Longman House.

Bergh, J. S. 1984. *Tribes and Kingdoms*. Cape Town: Don Nelson.

Bourquin, S. B. & Torlage, G. 1999. *The Battle of Colenso*. Randburg: Ravan Press.

Boyden, P., Guy, A. & Harding, M. 1999. *Ashes and Blood – The British Army in South Africa 1795–1914*. London: National Army Museum.

Bradlow, F. 1997. 'The Battle of Boomplaats'. *Military History Journal*, 10(5).

Bridgland, T. 1998. *Field Gun Jack versus the Boers – The Royal Navy in South Africa 1899–1900*. Barnsley, South Yorkshire: Pen & Sword Books Ltd.

Bulpin, T. V. 1952. *Shaka's Country – A Book of Zululand*. Cape Town: Howard Timmins.

Bulpin, T. V. 1965. *Lost Trails of the Transvaal*. Johannesburg: Thomas Nelson and Sons.

Bulpin, T. V. 1976. *The Great Trek*. Cape Town: T.V. Bulpin.

Burleigh, B. 1900. *The Natal Campaign*. London: Chapman & Hall.

Butler, A. (n.d.). 'Kuruman Moffat-sending'. Pamphlet.

Butler, F. 1899. *The Life of Sir George Pomeroy Colley*. London: John Murray.

Cameron, T. & Spies, S. B. 1986. *An Illustrated History of South Africa*. Johannesburg: Jonathan Ball Publishers.

Castle, I. 1996. *Majuba 1881 – The Hill of Destiny*. Osprey Military Campaign Series. London: Osprey Publishing.

Changuion, L. 2001. *Silence of the Guns*. Pretoria: Protea Book House.

Chisholm, R. 1979. *Ladysmith*. Braamfontein: Jonathan Ball Publishers.

Clammer, D. 1977. *The Last Zulu Warrior*. Cape Town: Purnell & Sons.

Clements, W. H. 1936. *The Glamour and Tragedy of the Zulu War*. London: John Lane & Bodley Head.

Coetzer, O. 1966. *The Road to Infamy*. Rivonia: William Waterman Publications.

Coleman, A. D. 2010. 'The Disputed Territory: A New Perspective'. (Unpublished paper).

Couzens, T. 2004. *Battles of South Africa*. Cape Town: New Africa Books.

Creswicke, L. [19–]. *South Africa and the Transvaal War*, Volumes I–VII. London: Blackwood, Le Bas & Co.

Danes, R. 1901. *Cassell's History of the Boer War 1899–1901*. London: Cassell & Co. Ltd.

De Wet, C. R. 1902. *Three Years' War*. New York: Charles Scribner's Sons, Trow Directory.

Doyle, A. C. 1901. *The Great Boer War*. London: George Bell & Sons.

Duxbury, G. R. 1980. 'The Battle of Bronkhorstspruit'. *Military History Journal*, 5(2).

Evans, M. E. 1988. *Encyclopedia of the Boer War*. Oxford: ABC-CLIO Ltd.

Giliomee, H. 2003. *The Afrikaners – Bibliography of a People*. Cape Town: Tafelberg Publishers Ltd.

Gillings, K. (n.d.). *Twenty Significant Battles of KwaZulu-Natal*. Durban: Art Publishers.

Gillings, K. 1989. 'The Bambata Rebellion of 1906 – Nkandla Operations and the Battle of Mome Gorge'. *Military History Journal*, 8(1).

Griffith, K. 1974. *Thank God We Kept the Flag Flying*. London: Hutchinson & Co.

Grobler, J. E. H. 2004. *The War Reporter – The Anglo-Boer War Through the Eyes of the Burghers*. Cape Town: Jonathan Ball Publishers.

Hancock, W. K. 1962. *Smuts Vol. 1 – The Sanguine Years 1870–1919*. Cambridge: Cambridge University Press.

Harrison, C. W. F. 1895. *Port Natal – Illustrated Handbook of General Information Relating to Durban, Port Natal and Railways in Connection*. London: Payne Jennings.

Hillegas, H. C. 1901. *With the Boer Forces*. London: Methuen & Co.

Jones, H. M. & Jones, M. G. M. 1999. *A Gazetteer of the Second Anglo-Boer War 1899–1902*. Milton Keynes: The Military Press.

Knight, I. 2001. *With His Face to the Foe*. Jeppestown: Jonathan Ball Publishers.

Knight, I. & Castle, I. 1994. *Fearful Hard Times*. London: Greenhill Books.

Kruger, R. 1974. *Good Bye Dolly Gray*. London: Pan Books.

Laband, J. 1992. *Kingdom in Crisis*. Pietermaritzburg: University of Natal Press.

Laband, J. & Thompson, P. 1983. *Field Guide to the War in Zululand 1879*. Pietermaritzburg: University of Natal Press.

Lee, E. 1986. *To the Bitter End – A Photographic History of the Boer War 1899–1902*. Middlesex: Penguin Books.

Lock, R. 1995. *Blood on the Painted Mountain*. London: Greenhill Books.

Lock, R. 1995. *Zulu Conquered – The March of the Red Soldier 1828–1884*. London: Greenhill Books.

Lock, R. & Quantrill, P. 2005. *Zulu Vanquished – The Destruction of the Zulu Kingdom*. London: Greenhill Books.

Lourens, J. A. J. & Lourens, J. (n.d.) *The Battle of Groenkop*.

Lugg, H. C. 1949. *Historic Natal and Zululand*. Pietermaritzburg: Shuter and Shooter.

MacKeurtan, G. 1930. *The Cradle Days of Natal*. London: Longmans, Green & Co.

Manning, S. 2007. *Evelyn Wood VC – Pillar of the Empire*. South Yorkshire: Pen and Sword Books.

Maurice, F. 1906. *The History of the War in South Africa*. London: Hurst & Blackett Ltd.

McCracken, D. 2009. *MacBride's Brigade – Irish Commandos in the Anglo-Boer War*. Dublin: Four Court Press.

McCracken, D. (ed.). 2013. *Teddy Luther's War – The Diary of a German-American in an Irish-Boer Commando*. Johannesburg and Solihull: 30 Degrees South and Helion & Co.

McDonald, J. G. 1928. *Rhodes – A Life*. Glasgow: Glasgow University Press.

Morris, D. R. 1965. *The Washing of the Spears*. London: Pimlico.

Mossop, G. 1990. *Running the Gauntlet*. Pietermaritzburg: G. C. Button.

Nathan, M. 1937. *The Voortrekkers of South Africa*. London: Central News Agency and Gordon Gotch.

Nathan, M. 1941. *Paul Kruger – His Life and Times*. Durban: The Knox Publishing Co.

Pemberton, W. 1964. *Battles of the Boer War*. London: B. T. Batsford Ltd.

Powell, G. 1994. *Buller: A Scapegoat? A Life of General Sir Redvers Buller 1839–1908*. London: Leo Cooper.

Ransford, O. 1967. *The Battle of Majuba Hill*. London: John Murray.

Ransford, O. 1974. *The Great Trek*. Indianapolis: Cardinal.

Reitz, D. 1998. *Commando*. Johannesburg: Jonathan Ball Publishers.

Rickard, J. 2007. 'Battle of Driefontein 10 March 1900'. www.historyofwar.org/articles/battles_driefontein.html (Last accessed July 2013).

Ritter, E. A. *Shaka Zulu*. London, New York, Toronto: Longmans Green & Co.

Rundgren, P. (n.d.). 'Battle of Elandslaagte'. (Unpublished paper).

Russell, G. 1971. *The History of Old Durban*. Durban: P. Davis & Sons.

Saks, D. Y. 1994. 'Botched Orders or Insubordination? The Battle of Berea Revisited'. *Military History Journal*, 9(6).

Sandys, C. 2000. *Churchill Wanted Dead or Alive*. London: HarperCollins.

Schoeman, C. 2012. *Brothers in Arms. Hollanders in the Anglo-Boer War*. Cape Town: Zebra Press.

Shamase, M. Z. 1996. *Zulu Potentates*. Durban: S. M. Publications.

Spies, S. B. (ed.). 1989. *A Soldier in South Africa 1899–1902*. Houghton: The Brenthurst Press.

St Leger, S. 1986. *Mounted Infantry at War*. Alberton: Galago Publishing.

Steenkamp, W. 2012. *Assegais, Drums and Dragoons – A Military and Social History of the Cape 1510–1806*. Johannesburg and Cape Town: Jonathan Ball.

Taylor, C. 2003. 'The Site of the Battle of Muizenberg'. www.muizenberg. info/pdf/battleofmuizenberg.pdf (Last accessed July 2013).

Theal, G. M. 1973. *History of the Boers in South Africa*. Cape Town: C Struik (Pty) Ltd.

Trew, P. 1999. *The Boer War Generals*. Johannesburg: Jonathan Ball Publishers.

Unger, F. W. 1901. *With 'Bobs' and Kruger – Experiences and Observations of an American War Correspondent in the Field With Both Armies*. Philadelphia.

Uys, I. 1992. *South African Military Who's Who – 1452–1992*. Germiston. Fortress Publishers.

Uys, I. 1998. *Rearguard – The Life and Times of Piet Uys*. Knysna: Fortress Publishers.

Van Schoor, M. C. E. 1984. *Vegkop*. Pretoria: National Monuments Council.

Viljoen, B. 1902. *My Reminiscences of the Anglo-Boer War*. London: Hood, Douglas & Howard.

Walker, E. A. 1922. *Historical Atlas of South Africa*. London: Humphrey Milford, Oxford University Press.

Walker, E. A. 1934. *The Great Trek*. London: Adam & Charles Black Ltd.

Warwick, P. 1980. *The South African War. The Anglo-Boer War 1899–1902*. London: Longman House.

Watt, S. A. 1991. 'The Skirmish at Senekal: The Battle of Biddulphsberg, May 1900'. *Military History Journal*, 8(6).

Westby-Nunn, T. (compiler). 2000. *A Tourist Guide to the Anglo Boer War 1899–1902*. Cape Town: Westby-Nunn Publishers.

Whitehouse, H. (ed.). 1995. *A Widow-making War*. Nuneaton: Paddy Griffith Associates.

Picture credits

The publisher would to thank the following for permission to reproduce their photographs:

ABBREVIATIONS KEY

b = bottom, **l** = left,
m = middle, **r** = right,
t = top, **TL** = Timeline

ABWM = Ango Bocr War Museum
AEP = Argief, Erfenisstigting, Pretoria
AV = adventtr
AX = Alexan2008
AY = ayzek
BB = *The Natal Campaign* by Bennet Burleigh. London: Chapman & Hall, 1900
BD = bendickson
BHTC = Bell Heritage Trust Collection
BS = Burkhard Schlosser
BT = bortonia
CC = Campbell Collections, University of KwaZulu-Natal
CDA = Charles Aikenhead
CDB = Charles Davidson Bell
CH = *Cassell's History of the Boer War 1899–1901* by Richard Danes. London: Cassell & Co. Ltd, 1901
CMMF = Castle Military Museum Foundation, Cape Town
CS = Chris Schoeman
CW = *South Africa and the Transvaal War*, Volumes I–VII, by Louis Creswicke. London: Blackwood, Le Bas & Co., [19–]

D39 = diane39
DB/VM = Drihan Bester/ Voortrekker Monument and Nature Reserve
DC = duncan1890
DM = Dmstudio
DMC = Donal McCracken Collection
DNY = DNY59
DP = depositphotos
DS = Dirk Schwager
FB = FrankvandenBergh
GH = Graham Horn
GTZW = *The Glamour and Tragedy of the Zulu War* by W. H. Clements. London: John Lane & Bodley Head, 1936
HHS = Himeville Historical Society
HR = hronos7
HVH = Hein von Hörsten
ILN = Illustrated London News
IOA = Images of Africa
IS = iStockphoto.com
JDP = Jéan du Plessis
JH = John Haigh
JJ = jimmyjamesbond
JZ = JOZZ
KM = Kathy Moyze
LC = Liz Clarke
LCW = Loretta Chegwidden
LHMD = Local History Museums, Durban
LM = Linda Muir
LOC = Library of Congress

LP = Library of Parliament
MA = Museum Africa
MC = Mendelssohn Collection
MI = MrIncredible
NASA = National Archives of South Africa
NC = nicoolay
NLSA = National Library of South Africa
NVDH = Nicki von der Heyde Collection
NZAV = NZAV Foto-archives, Netherlands
PG = Project Gutenberg
PJ = Peter Jarvis
RDLH = Roger de la Harpe/ Africa Imagery
RHS = Random House Struik
RL = Raylipscombe
RS = Robin Smith
RT = Roelien Theron
RX = rupertx
SH = Stuart Holmes
SU = source unknown
TG = The Graphic
TS = The Sphere
UVK = Uli von Kapff
VB = Vanessa Burger
VF = Vanity Fair
WC = Wikipedia Commons
WCA = Western Cape Archives and Record Service
WK = Walter Knirr
WM = whitemay
WY = wynnter

Cover: tl NVDH, tm NVDH, tr JH/CMMF, m WC, bl NVDH, br RDLH/AI; **Back cover**: tl JH/CMMF, tr ABWM, mr ABWM, b ABWM; **Spine**: t JH/CMMF, c WC; **Half-title page**: CC; **Title page** RDLH/AI; **Contents page** SU, bl BHTC; **14** SU; **15** both WC; **16** t NVDH, b MA; **17** t WCA, b CC; **18** t CC, b RDLH/IOA; **19** t CC, b SU; **20** t WCA, b NLSA; **21** t SU, b WK/IOA; **24** RDLH/AI, map and tl JH/CMMF; **26** LHMD, **TL**: tl IS/DC, bl IS/JJ, m IS/HR, r IS/WY; **27** both BS; **28** NZAV; **29** VB/IOA **TL**: t WC, b MA; **30** t MA, b DB/VM; **31** LHMD; **32** SU, **TL**: m RHS, b IS/DNY; **33** t PJ, b NVDH; **34** t HHS, b PJ; **35** HHS, **TL**: both WC; **36** t PJ, b NLSA; **37** t HHS, m JH/CMMF; **38** JDP, **TL**: l IS/MI, m WC, r WC; **39** t CW vol. 1, b RDLH/AI; **40** t WC, b NLSA; **41** PJ, **TL**: NVDH; **42** MA; **43** t NVDH, b WCA; **44** NVDH, **TL**: WC; **45** both NVDH; **46** GTZW; **47** m PJ, b NVDH; **48** t JDP, b MA; **49** LC, **TL**: SU; **50** t DB/VM, r SU; **51** t NVDH, b NLSA; **52** UVK, **TL**: t LCW/RHS, b SU; **53** t NVDH, b NLSA; **54** PJ, **TL**: WCA; **56** NVDH; **57 TL**: NLSA; **58** KM, **TL**: all WC; **60** t NVDH, b CW vol. 4; **61** both PJ, **TL**: t WCA, b ABWM; **62** t BB, m and b WC; **63** PJ; **65** both PJ; **66** NVDH; **67** t CDA, b PJ, **TL**: WC; **68** t WC, b PJ; **69** t NVDH; b PJ; **70** NVDH, **TL**: t VF/WC, b BB; **71** t RDLH/AI, m NLSA; **72** t PJ, b ABWM; **73** ABWM; **74** t PJ, m NVDH; **75** t PJ, b ABWM; **76** t PJ, b ABWM; **77** ABWM; **79** tl RDLH/AI, tr CDA, br ABWM; **80** both NVDH; **81** RDLH/AI, **TL**: both ABWM; **82** t JH/CMMF, b NLSA; **83** t NVDH, b RDLH/AI; **84** t PJ, m and b ABWM; **85** CDA; **86** NASA; **87** t PJ, b ABWM; **88** t PJ, b ABWM; **89** WC; **91** NVDH; **92** NVDH; **93** t CDA, b WCA, **TL**: WCA; **94** DMC; **95** ABWM; **97** NVDH; **98** CW vol. 4; **99** CW vol. 3, **TL**: ABWM; **100** t ABWM, b PJ; **101** t ABWM, m JH/CMMF; **102** ABWM; **103** t PJ, b ABWM;
105 both PJ; **106** PJ; **107** RDLH/AI, **TL**: CC; **108** JH/CMMF; **109** ABWM; **111** NVDH; **112** NVDH; **113** RDLH/AI, **TL**: ABWM; **114** NVDH; **115** NDVH; **117** t RDLH/AI, b CDA; **118** both CDA; **119** AEP, **TL**: t WC, b JH/CMMF/TG; **120** t NVDH, b PJ; **121** NVDH, **TL**: t WC, b NVDH; **122** PJ; **123** t WCA, b PJ; **125** tl PJ, tr JH/CMMF; **126** t PJ, b ABWM; **127** ABWM, **TL**: ABWM; **128** PJ; **129** t NVDH, b PJ; **130** PJ, **TL**: t WCA, b NVDH; **131** t PJ, b ABWM; **132** NVDH; **133 TL**: both WC; **134** PJ; **135** ILN, **TL**: t NLSA, m NVDH; **136** CC; **137** RDLH/AI; **138** t SH, b CC; **139** RHS; **140** l RDLH/AI; r IS/RX, b NVDH; **141** t NVDH, b RDLH/AI; **143** RDLH/AI; **144** PJ; **145** both PJ, **TL**: TG; **146** t RDLH/AI, b PJ; **147** t CC, b WC; **149** NVDH; **150** t NVDH, b NLSA; **151** RDLH/AI, **TL**: both WC; **152** t WC, m NLSA; **153** t NVDH, b JH/CMMF; **154** JH/CMMF/TS, **TL**: t IS/AX, b PJ; **155** t CH, b RDLH/AI; **156** DMC; **157** RDLH/AI; **159** l JDP, r NVDH; **160** t ABWM, b NVDH; **161** CDA; **162** DB/VM; **163** LC, **TL**: IS/AV; **164** t RDLH/AI, b MC/CMMF; **165** PJ; **166** NVDH, **TL**: both WC; **167** t NVDH, m ABWM; **168** PJ, **TL**: t CW vol. 2, b GH/WC; **169** SH; **170** VF/WC; **171** t SH, b NVDH; **172** l NLSA, r JH/CMMF; **173** PJ; **174** t CC, PJ, **TL**: t ILN/WC, m MA, b WCA; **175** CC; **177** l PJ, r SH, b PJ; **178** t CC, b ABWM; **179** ABWM, **TL**: MA; **180** CDA, **TL**: both WC; **181** CDA; **182** t CW vol. 6, b CC; **183** JH/CMMF **TL**: NVDH; **184** t ILN, b SH; **185** t CDA, b JH/CMMF; **186** CDA, **TL**: JH/CMMF; **187** RT; **188 TL**: ABWM; **189** t NDVH, b SH; **190** ILN/WC, **TL**: ILN/WC; **191** t SH, b NVDH; **192** t SH, b IS/DC; **193** ABWM; **195** l SH, r ILN/WC; **196** both NVDH; **197** t CW vol. 3, b ABWM, **TL**: ILN/JH/CMMF; **198** t both CDA, b NVDH; **199** t CDA, b ABWM; **200** JDP, tl JH/CMMF; **202** WCA,

TL: both WC; **203** MA; **204** t HVH/IOA, b SU; **205** both PJ; **206** PJ, **TL**: t NVDH, b ABWM; **207** t ABWM, b PJ; **208** CW vol. 7; **209** NVDH; **210** NVDH; **211** both PJ, **TL**: WC; **212** t PJ, b CC; **213** JH/CMMF/TG, **TL**: IS/BD; **214** PJ; **215** t JH/CMMF/TS, b PJ; **216** PJ, **TL**: ABWM; **217** PJ; **218** t ABWM, b PJ; **219** NVDH; **220** t MA, b CW vol. 2; **221** CW vol. 5, **TL**: t WCA, m NVDH, b ABWM; **222** ABWM; **223** t JH/CMMF, b NVDH; **224** ABWM, **TL**: both ABWM; **225** both NVDH; **226** ABWM; **227** NVDH, **TL**: t WC, b WCA; **228** t WCA, m CW vol. 6; **229** t JH/CMMF, b DMC, **TL**: PG/WC; **230** ABWM; **231** both NVDH; **232** IS/BT, **TL**: CDB/WC; **233** t NVDH, bl WC, br IS/FB; **234** JDP, tl JH/CMMF; **236** NVDH, **TL**: l WC, m WC, r WC; **238** both ABWM; **239** t PJ, m ABWM, b PJ; **240** t NLSA b CW vol. 5; **241** ABWM, **TL**: WC; **242** t NDVH, b WCA; **243** DS, **TL**: both WC; **244** LCW/RHS; **245** NVDH; **246** NVDH, **TL**: PJ; **248** CW vol. 5; **249** NVDH; **250** WCA, **TL**: IS/AY; **251** t NVDH, b PJ; **252** JH/CMMF, **TL**: t JH/CMMF, m IS/RL; **253** NVDH; **254** t NVDH, b PJ; **255** ABWM, **TL**: WC; **256** t ABWM, b PJ; **257** t PJ, b ABWM; **258** both JH/CMMF; **259** CW vol. 4, **TL**: WCA; **260** t JH/CMMF, b NVDH; **261** JH/CMMF, **TL**: t CW vol. 2, b JH/CMMF; **262** m PJ, b WCA; **263** t PJ, b ABWM; **264** t PJ, b WCA; **265** NVDH; **267** both PJ; **268** t PJ, b NVDH; **269** JH/CMMF, **TL**: t JH/CMMF, b /RDLH/IOA; **270** t WC, b PJ; **271** t PJ, b NVDH; **273** WCA; **274** t PJ, m JH/CMMF, b CW vol. 3; **275** ABWM, **TL**: t WC, m DMC; **276** m WCA, b PJ; **277** t JH/CMMF, b ABWM; **278** SU, **TL**: JH/CMMF; **279** t DMC, b WC; **280** NVDH; **281** CW vol. 2, **TL**: ABWM; **282** PJ; **283** ABWM, **TL**: WC; **284** both PJ; **285** PJ, **TL**: PJ; **286** MA, **TL**: all WC; **288** t LP, b WCA; **289** PJ, **TL**: WCA; **290** WCA; **291** t BHTC, b NLSA; **292** WCA, **TL**: WC; **293** MA; **294** t NVDH, b WCA; **295** t CS, b SU; **296** NZAV; **297** NVDH, **TL**: t NVDH, b HJ/CMMF; **298** t NVDH, b CW vol. 4; **299** t NVDH, **TL**: JH/CMMF; **300** JH/CMMF; **301** PJ; **302** PJ, **TL**: t CW vol. 3, b WC; **303** t PJ, b NZAV; **304** t WCA, b CW vol. 3; **305** CH; **306 TL**: CW vol. 3; **307** PJ; **308** both ABWM; **309** ABWM; **310** both PJ; **311** t ABWM, b PJ; **312** RDLH/AI, tl JH/CMMF; **314** RDLH/AI, **TL**: both WC; **315 TL**: l LOC/WC, r WC; **316** ABWM; **317** PJ; **318** PJ, **TL**: WCA; **319** t SU, b JH/CMMF; **320** WCA, **TL**: WCA; **321** WCA; **322** WK/IOA, tl JH/CMMF, map NLSA; **324** SU, **TL**: l IS/NC, m IS/D39, r IS/JZ; **326** t SU, b WCA; **327** WCA, **TL**: both WC; **328** t RT, b WCA; **329** t WC, b LM; **330** t MA, m JH/CMMF; **331** t MA, b JH/CMMF, **TL**: WC; **332** t WCA, b MA; **333** t LM, b WCA

Every effort has been made to trace copyright holders. The publisher apologises for any inadvertent omissions and would be grateful if notified of any corrections, which shall be included in future reprints and editions of the book.

Index

Page numbers in *italics* point to illustrations. Page numbers in **bold** indicate towns on the way or near to battle sites.

1st Anglo-Boer War 18–19
   Bronkhorstspruit 212–214
   Ingogo 182–184
   Laing's Nek 187–188
   Majuba Hill 189–195
2nd Anglo-Boer War 19–20
   Alleman Nek 196–199
   Armoured train disaster and Churchill's capture 66–68
   artillery 160–161
   Bakenlaagte 208–209
   Belmont 280–281
   Bergendal 205–207
   Biddulphsberg 240–241
   Blood River Poort 165–166
   Boshof 258–259
   Botha's Pass 185–186
   Colenso 69–79
   Diamond Hill 215–217
   Doornkop 220–222
   Doornkraal 226–227
   Driefontein 249–250
   Elandslaagte 120–125
   Fabersput 282–283
   Graspan 277–279
   Groenkop 129–131
   Holkrans 178–179
   Koedoesberg Drift 274–275
   Labuschagne's Nek (4 March 1900) 306–307
   Labuschagne's Nek (30 December 1899) 305–306
   Ladysmith 112–117
   Magersfontein 260–267
   Modder River 268–273
   Modderspruit 113, 116–117
   Nicholson's Nek 114–115, 116–117
   Paardeberg 254–257
   Pink Hill 296–297
   Platrand 106–111
   Poplar Grove 251–253
   Rhenosterkop 210–211
   Rietfontein 118–119
   Roodewal 223–224
   Rooiwal 228–230
   Sannaspos 245–248
   Scheeper's Nek 167–168
   Spioenkop 80–91
   Stormberg 301–304
   Surrender Hill 126–128
   Talana Hill 153–159
   Tugela Heights 98–105
   Vaalkrans 92–97
   West Australia Hill 298–300
   Willowgrange 60–65

A

abaQulusi 169–172
Abrahamskraal *see* Driefontein
agterryers 95
Alleman Nek 196–198
Allemansnek
   see Alleman Nek
Almond's Nek
   see Alleman Nek
abaQulusi 178–179
Anglo-Zulu War 17–18
Gingindlovu 43–45
Hlobane 169–172
Isandlwana 134–143
Khambula 173–177
Nyezane 44
Prince Imperial of France, death of 150–152
Rorke's Drift 144–149
ultimatum *15*, 46–47
Ulundi 53–55
armoured train *261*
armoured train disaster and Churchill's capture 66–68
artillery during the 2nd Anglo-Boer War 160–161
British 4.7-inch naval gun *83*
British 5-inch Armstrong fortress gun *130*
British long 12-pounder naval gun *93*
Krupp gun *279*
Long Cecil 276
Australia and the 2nd Anglo-Boer War 299

B

Baird, Major General David (Blaauwberg) 330–333
Bakenlaagte 208–209
Bambatha, Chief (Mome Gorge) 34–37
battle categories 14–21
Bellairs, Lieutenant Colonel William (Bronkhorstspruit) 212–214
Belmont 280–281

344   FIELD GUIDE TO THE BATTLEFIELDS OF SOUTH AFRICA

Benson, Lieutenant Colonel
  George (Bakenlaagte)
  208–209
Benson, Major George
  (Magersfontein) 262–267
Beresford, Lord William 55
Bergendal 205–207
Bergville **66**, **80**
Bethlehem **126**, **129**, **240**
Bethune, Lieutenant
  Colonel E. C. (Scheeper's
  Nek) 167–168
Biddulphsberg 240–241
Blaauwberg 330–333
blockhouses 225, *302*
Bloemfontein **242**, **245**,
  251, **254**, **258**, **296**
Bloemfontein & Kimberley
  regions
  Belmont 280–281
  Berea 242–244
  Biddulphsberg 240–241
  Boshof 258–259
  Driefontein 249–250
  Fabersput 282–283
  Graspan 277–279
  Koedoesberg Drift
    274–275
  Lattakoo 284–285
  Magersfontein 260–267
  Modder River 268–273
  overview 236–237
  Paardeberg 254–257
  Poplar Grove 251–253
  Sannaspos 245–248
Blood River 162–164
Blood River Poort 165–166
Bloukrans Massacre 29–30
Boomplaats 288–290
Boshof **258**, 258–259
Botha, General Christiaan
  (Botha's Pass) 185–186
Botha, General Louis

Bakenlaagte 208–209
Bergendal 205–207
Blood River Poort
  165–166
Colenso 70–73, 78–79
Diamond Hill 215–217
Modderspruit 112–117
Spioenkop 80–91
Tugela Heights 99–105
Vaalkrans 94–97
Willowgrange 60–65
Botha, Sophie 152
Botha's Pass 185–186
Bothaville **226**
Bothaville (battle)
  see Doornkraal
Brabant, General Edward
  (Labuschagne's Nek,
  4 March 1900) 306–307
Broadwood, Brigadier
  General Robert
  (Sannaspos) 245–248
Bromhead, Lieutenant
  Gonvill (Rorke's Drift)
  144–149
Bronkhorstspruit **210**, **212**,
  212–214
Buller, Sir Redvers 74–75
  Alleman Nek 196–199
  Bergendal 205–207
  Botha's Pass 185–186
  Colenso 70–73
  Hlobane 170–171
  Khambula 173–177
  Spioenkop 80–91
  'supply before strategy'
    81
  Tugela Heights 99–105
  Vaalkrans 92–97
Burger, General Schalk
  Spioenkop 89
  Vaalkrans *93*
Burgersdorp **301**

C

Cape Colony
  Blaauwberg 330–333
  Boer invasion 280, 289,
    294, 296
  boundaries 31, 314–315
  diamond fields
    dispute 236
  Grahamstown 319–321
  Lattakoo 284–285
  Muizenberg 326–328
  Slagtersnek 317–318
Cape rebels 282–283, 303
Cape rebels (Labuschagne's
  Nek, 30 December 1899)
  305–306
Cape Town region
  Blaauwberg 330–333
  Muizenberg 326–328
  overview 324–325
Carey, Lieutenant J. B.
  (Death of Prince Imperial
  of France) 150–152
Carleton, Lieutenant
  Colonel F. R. C.
  (Nicholson's Nek)
  114–115
categories of battle
  see battle categories
Cathcart, Major General
  George (Berea) 242–244
Cetshwayo, King *39*, 40, 42
  Gingindlovu 43–45
  ultimatum from British to
    46–47
  Ulundi 53–55
Chapman, Frick 61
Chard, Lieutenant John
  (Rorke's Drift) 144–149
Charlesville **288**
Chelmsford, Lord *147*
  advance into Zululand 47
  Gingindlovu 43–45

Isandlwana 134–139,
142–143
Ulundi 53–55
Chieveley **66**
Churchill, Winston,
capture 66–68
Cilliers, Sarel (Vegkop)
231–233
Clarens **126**
Clements, Major General
Ralph (Pink Hill) 296–297
Coghill, Lieutenant
Neville 141
Colenso 66, **69**, 69–79,
92, **98**, **106**
Colesberg **288**, **291**,
296, **298**
Colesberg region
Boomplaats 288–290
Brit versus Boer
engagements 294–295
Labuschagne's Nek
(4 March 1900)
306–307
Labuschagne's Nek
(30 December 1899)
305–306
overview 286–287
Pink Hill 296–297
Stormberg 301–304
Swartkoppies 291–293
West Australia Hill
298–300
Colley, General Sir
George Pomeroy
Ingogo 182–184
Laing's Nek 187–188
Majuba Hill 189–195
colonial and frontier
conflicts 14–15
Berea 242–244
Blaauwberg 330–333
Boomplaats 288–290

Durban 31–33
Grahamstown 319–321
Mome Gorge 34–37
Muizenberg 326–328
Slagtersnek Rebellion
317–318
Swartkoppies 291–293
Tugela 29
concentration camps
238–239
Congella *see* Durban
Cookhouse **317**
cosmos flowers 128
Craig, Major General James
(Muizenberg) 326–328
Cronjé, General Piet
Magersfontein 262–267
Paardeberg 254–257
Crow's Nest Hill *see*
Doornkop
Cullinan **215**

D

Dalmanutha *see* Bergendal
Dalton, Assistant
Commissary James
(Rorke's Drift) 145–146
Dambusa (Italeni) *16*, 48–50
Day of the Vow 164
Dealesville **258**
Delareyville **223**
De la Rey, General Koos
Colesberg engagements
294–295
Doornkop 220–222
Graspan 277–279
Koedoesberg Drift 275
Magersfontein 260–267,
263
Modder River 268–273
Pink Hill 296–297
West Australia Hill
298–300

Delmas **212**
De Montmorency, Captain
Raymond (Labuschagne's
Nek, 30 December 1899)
305–306
De Villebois-Mareuil, Comte
Combat General (Boshof)
258–259
De Villiers, General
Abraham (Biddulphsberg)
240–241
De Villiers, General P. J.
(Fabersput) 282–283
De Wet, General
Christiaan *131*
Doornkraal 226–227
Groenkop 129–131
Paardeberg 256–257
Poplar Grove 251–253
Rooiwal 228–230
Sannaspos 245–248
Diamond Hill 215–217
Dingane, King 28–30,
48, 49
Dingiswayo 52
Dinuzulu, Chief 35, *36*, 37
Tshaneni 56–57
Dithakong **284**
dogs
Patch 192
Plumbe, Major J. H.'s 279
Donkerhoek *see* Diamond
Hill
Doornkop 220–222
Doornkraal 226–227
Dordrecht **305**
Doringkop *see* Doornkop
Douglas **282**
Driefontein **118**, **249**,
249–250
Dundee **120**, **144**, **150**,
153, **162**, **165**
Dundee region

Blood River 162–164
Blood River Poort
　165–166
Hlobane 169–172
Holkrans 178–179
Isandlwana 134–143
Khambula 173–177
overview 132–133
Prince Imperial of France,
　death of 150–152
Rorke's Drift 144–149
Scheeper's Nek 167–168
Talana Hill 153–159
Dunne, Bugler John
　Francis 77
Dunn, John 41, 42, 46
Du Plooy, Commandant
　Floris (Koedoesberg Drift)
　274–275
Durban **31**, 31–33, **66**, **80**
Durban & Pietermaritzburg
　region *see* Pietermaritzburg
　& Durban region
Durnford, Colonel Anthony
　(Isandlwana) 136–138

E

Eastern Cape *see*
　Grahamstown region
Eddy, Major George
　(Pink Hill) 297
Elandslaagte **120**, 120–125
Elphinstone, Vice Admiral
　George (Muizenberg)
　326–328
eMakhazeni (Belfast) **205**
eMalahleni (Witbank) **208**
eMkhando (Piet Retief) **173**
Erasmus, General 'Maroela'
　(Talana Hill) 155
Eshowe, siege **34**, **43**
Eshowe, siege 45
Estcourt **28**, **60**, **66**

F

Fabersput 282–283
fire-and-manoeuvre
　technique 88
Fish Hoek **326**
Fitzpatrick, Trooper
　George 61
fodder supply 128
Fourie, General Joachim
　(Alleman Nek) 196–199
Fouriesburg **126**
Frankfort **231**
Free State & Northern
　Cape *see* Bloemfontein
　& Kimberley, Colesberg
　regions
French, General John
　Colesberg engagements
　294–295
　Diamond Hill 215–217
　Doornkop 220–222
　Driefontein 249–250
　Elandslaagte 121–125
　Poplar Grove 251–253
Frere **66**
frontier wars 15, 289, 315,
　318, 319–321
Fynn, Henry Francis 32

G

Ga-Nala (Kriel) **208**
Gandhi, Mahatma 81, 84
Gatacre, General William
　(Stormberg) 301–304
Gauteng & surrounds *see*
　Pretoria, Johannesburg &
　surrounding regions
Ghost Mountain *see*
　Tshaneni
Gingindlovu 43–45
Goff, Captain W. E. D
　(Scheeper's Nek) 167–168
Gordon, Colonel Robert 329

Muizenberg 326–328
Gough, Colonel Hubert
　(Blood River Poort)
　165–166
Gqokli Hill 51–52
Grahamstown **319**
Grahamstown region
　Grahamstown 319–321
　overview 314–315
　Slagtersnek Rebellion
　317–318
Grant, Captain A. G. W.
　(Rooiwal) 228–230
Graspan 277–279
Great Trek *see* Voortrekker
　battles; Voortrekkers
Grimwood, Colonel
　Geoffrey (Modderspruit)
　113
Griqua 236, 288–290,
　291–293
Groblersdal **210**
Groenkop 129–131

H

Hamilton, Ian 192
Hamu, Chief 170, *175*
Harrismith **126**, **129**
Hannay, Colonel Ormelie
　(Paardeberg) 256
Hart, Major General Fitzroy
　Colenso 71–73
　Tugela Heights 100–102
Hart's Hill 101–102
Heilbron **231**
heliograph 85
Helpmekaar **112**
Hildyard, Major General
　(Willowgrange) 60–65
Hlangwane **69**
Hlobane 169–172
Hobkirk's Farm *see* Pink Hill
Holkrans 178–179

INDEX　**347**

horns-of-the-buffalo
formation 139
Hunter, Lieutenant General
Archibald (Surrender Hill)
126–128

I

Imperial Yeomanry
(Boshof) 259
Indian stretcher bearers **81**,
84
indigenous conflicts
Gqokli Hill 51–52
Lattakoo 284–285
Ndondakasuka 40–42
Tshaneni 56–57
Ingogo 182–184
Irish pro-Boers 77, 112
Irish regiments
Colenso 71–73, 76–77
Tugela Heights 100–102
Isandlwana 134–143
Italeni 48–50

J

Jagersfontein **288**, **291**
Janssens, General Jan
(Blaauwberg) 330–333
Johannesburg **80**, **92**, **196**
Johannesburg
see Doornkop; Pretoria,
Johannesburg &
surrounding regions
Johannesburg Police
206–207, 211, 268–273
Joubert, Commandant
Frans (Bronkhorstspruit)
212–214
Joubert, General Piet
Laing's Nek 187–188
Modderspruit 113
Platrand 106–111
Rietfontein 118–119

K

Kambula *see* Khambula
Kemp, General Jan
(Roodewal) 223–224
Kestell **126**, **129**
Khambula 173–177
Khoikhoi 317–318, 320,
321, 325
Kimberley **249**, **251**, **254**,
258, **260**, **268**, **274**,
277, **280**
Kimberley & Bloemfontein
regions *see* Bloemfontein
& Kimberley regions
Kimberley, siege 276
King, Dick 32–33
Kinross 208
Kitchener, Lord General
Horatio 255, *264*
Paardeberg 256
Roodewal 223–224
Klipriviersberg *see* Doornkop
Koedoesberg Drift 274–276
Kok, Adam lll
Boomplaats 288
Swartkoppies 291–293
Koornspruit *see* Sannaspos
Koppies **228**
Krismis Kop *see* Groenkop
Kruger, President Paul *18*,
218–219
Krupp gun *279*
Kuruman **284**
KwaDukuza (Stanger) **40**, **43**
KwaGingindlovu **40**, **43**
KwaZulu-Natal *see* Dundee,
Ladysmith, Newcastle,
Pietermaritzburg &
Durban, Ulundi regions

L

Labuschagne's Nek (30
December 1899) 305–306

Ladysmith **69**, **92**, **98**, **106**,
112, **118**, **120**, **126**
Ladysmith region 112–117
armoured train disaster
and Churchill's capture
66–68
Colenso 69–79
Elandslaagte 120–125
Groenkop 129–131
Ladysmith 112–117
Modderspruit 113,
116–117
Nicholson's Nek 114–115
overview 58–59
Platrand 106–111
Rietfontein 118–119
Spioenkop 80–91
Surrender Hill 126–128
Tugela Heights 98–105
Vaalkrans 92–97
Willowgrange 60–65
Laing's Nek 187–188
Lattakoo 284–285
Lee-Metford ammunition,
Boers' secret store 230
Le Gallais, Colonel Philip
(Doornkraal) 226–227
Liebenberg girls 232
Lindley **240**
Lloyd, Colonel George 211
logistical challenges of war
199 *see also* fodder supply
Long Cecil 276
Louwsburg **169**
Lykso **284**
Lyttelton, Major General
Neville 82, 87–88

M

Magersfontein 260–267
Majuba Hill 189–195
Makana *see* Nxele
Mandini **40**

348 FIELD GUIDE TO THE BATTLEFIELDS OF SOUTH AFRICA

Maritz, Gert (Zaailaager) 29–30
Maseru **242**
Matabele *see* Ndebele people
Matshana, Chief (Isandlwana) 135–136
Mauser rifle 62
Mavumengwana, Chief (Isandlwana) 134–139, 142–143
Maxim Nordenfeldt gun *241*
Maxwell, Lieutenant Frank 247
Mbuyazi, Prince (Ndondakasuka) 40–42
McDonald, General Hector (Koedoesberg Drift) 274–275
McKenzie, Colonel Duncan (Mome Gorge) 34–37
Melmoth **134**
Melvill, Lieutenant Teignmouth 140–141
Methuen, General Lord Paul
  Belmont 280–281
  Graspan 277–279
  Modder River 268–273
Methuen, General Paul
  Boshof 258–259
  Magersfontein 260–267
Meyer, General Lucas (Tugela Heights) 99–105
Middelburg **205**, **215**, **301**
military attachés, abandoned 253
mKalipi (Vegkop) 231–233
Mkuze **56**
Molteno **301**
Modder River 268–273
Modderspruit 113, 116–117
Mooi River **60**, **66**
Mome Gorge 34–37

Moore, Major Hatherley (West Australia Hill) 299–300
Moshoeshoe (Berea) 242, 244
Mothibi, Chief (Lattakoo) 284–285
Mpande, King 40
Mthethwa army 51–52
Muizenberg **326**, 326–328

N

Napier, Lieutenant George (Berea) 243–244
Napier, Sir George 291–293
Napoleon, Prince Imperial Louis, death of 150–152
Natal Colony 32–33, 34–37, 80
naval guns, British *83*, *93*
Ndebele people (Vegkop) 231–233
Ndlambe, regent (Grahamstown) 319–321
Ndlela (Italeni) 48–50
Ndondakasuka 40–42
Ndwandwe army 51–52
Newcastle **98**, **112**, **118**, **120**, **182**, **185**, **187**, **189**
Newcastle region
  Alleman Nek 196–199
  Botha's Pass 185–186
  Ingogo 182–184
  Laing's Nek 187–188
  Majuba Hill 189–195
  overview 180–181
Ngqika, Prince (Grahamstown) 319–321
Nicholson's Nek 114–115
Nkandla **34**
Nomahlanjana (Gqokli Hill) 51–52
Nondweni **150**

Northern Cape & Free State *see* Colesberg, Kimberley & Bloemfontein regions;
Norvalspoort **298**
Nqutu **134**, **144**, **150**, **162**
nTuli, Ndhlela (Blood River) 162–164
Nxele (Grahamstown) 319–321
Nyezane 44

O

Olivier, General J. H.
  Labuschagne's Nek, (4 March 1900) 306–307
  Stormberg 301–304
Ondini 53
Oosthuizen, Marthinus 30
Opperman, Commandant Koot (Scheeper's Nek) 167–168
O'Toole, Sergeant 55

P

Paardeberg 256
Paget, Major General Arthur (Rhenosterkop) 210–211
Patch (dog) 192
Paulpietersburg **173**, **178**
Pearson, Colonel Charles (Nyezane) 44
Penn Symons, Major General William (Talana Hill) 154–156
Petrusburg **251**
Philip, Dr John 291
Pietermaritzburg **173**, **178**
Pietermaritzburg & Durban region
  Durban 31–33
  Mome Gorge 34–37
  overview 26–27

Richmond, refusal to pay
poll tax 36
Tugela 29
Zaailaager 28–30
Pink Hill 297
Pitts, James 109
Platrand 106–111
Popham, Commodore
Sir Home (Blaauwberg)
330–333
Poplar Grove 251–253
Potgieter, Field Cornet Jan
(Holkrans) 178–179
Potgieter, Hendrik 48–49
Italeni 48–50
Swartkoppies 291–293
Vegkop 231–233
Pretoria 315
Pretoria, Johannesburg and
surrounding regions
Bakenlaagte 208–209
Bergendal 205–207
Bronkhorstspruit 212–214
Diamond Hill 215–217
Doornkop 220–222
Doornkraal 226–227
overview 202–204
Renosterkop 210–211
Roodewal 223–224
Rooiwal 228–230
Vegkop 231–233
Pretorius, Andries 162–164
Boomplaats 288–290
Durban 31–33
Prince Imperial of France,
death of 150–152
princes *see* Ndondakasuka
Prinsloo, Chief
Commandant Jacobus
Belmont 280–281
Graspan 277–279
Prinsloo, General Marthinus
126–128

Q

Queen's Colour, attempt to
save 140–141

R

Randfontein **220**
Reitz **129**
Retief, Piet *17*, 28
Rhenosterkop 210–211
Richmond, refusal to pay
poll tax 36
Rietfontein 118–119
Ritchie **274**
Roberts, Lord General
Frederick
Bergendal 205–207
Diamond Hill 215–217
Paardeberg 254–257
Poplar Grove 251–253
Roberts, Lieutenant Freddy
75–76
Roodepoort **220**
Roodewal 223–224
Rooiwal 228–230 *see* Roodewal
Rorke's Drift 144–149
Rundle, Lieutenant
General Leslie
Biddulphsberg 240–241
Groenkop 130, 131

S

Sannaspos 245–248
Sasolburg **228**
Scheepers, General Gideon
316
Scheeper's Nek 167–168
Schmidtsdrift **282**
Scott, Robert 109
Senekal **240**
Shaka, King (Gqokli Hill)
51–52
Shepstone, Sir Theophilus
203

Shezi, Chief Sigananda
(Mome Gorge) 34–37
Sikhobobo, Chief (Holkrans)
178–179
Skuinshoogte *see* Ingogo
Slagtersnek Rebellion
317–318
Slingersfontein *see* West
Australia Hill
Sluysken, Governor
Abraham (Muizenberg)
326–328
Smit, General Nicolaas
Ingogo 182–184
Majuba Hill 189–195
Smith, Major Thomas
(Durban) 31–33
Smith, Sir Harry
(Boomplaats) 288–290
Smit, Susanna 33
Smuts, General Jan
Christiaan 308–311
Somerset East **317**
Soweto **220**
Spioenkop 80–91
Staatsartillerie 269, 220–221
St James **326**
Stormberg 301–304
Steynsburg **301**
stretcher bearers, Indian 84
Surrender Hill 126–128
Swartkoppies 291–293

T

Talana Hill 153–159
Thaba Bosiu 242
Theron, Scout Danie
(Paardeberg) *256*
Thorneycroft, Colonel
Alexander (Spioenkop)
83–85, 86, 87
Tinta Nyoni *see* Rietfontein
Transorangia 288–290

transport *see* logistical challenges of war
trekboers (Swartkoppies) 291–293, 314
Treves, Sir Frederick 82
Trompsburg **288**, **291**
Tshaneni *16*, 56–57
Tshingwayo, Chief (Isandlwana) 134–139, 142–143
Tugela 29
Tugela Heights 98–105
Tweefontein *see* Groenkop
Twee Riviere *see* Modder River

U

Ulundi 39, **51**, **53**
Ulundi region
    Gingindlovu 43–45
    Gqokli Hill 51–52
    Italeni 48–50
    Nyezane 44
    overview 38–39
    Tshaneni 56–57
    ultimatum that led to war in Zululand 46–47
    ultimatum tree *15*
    Ulundi 53–55
Utrecht **165**
Uys, Piet and Dirkie (Italeni) 48–50

V

Vaalkrans 92–97
Van Aardspos **317**
Van Rensburg family 30
Vanrhynsdorp **310**, **311**
Vegkop *16*, 231–233
Vereeniging **228**
Viljoen, Commandant Ben (Vaalkrans) 94, 95
Viljoen, General Ben (Rhenosterkop) 210–211
Viljoenspos **165**
Vlug Kommando *see* Italeni
Voortrekker battles 16–17
    Blood River 162–164
    Italeni 48–50
    Vegkop 231–233
    Zaailaager 28–30
Voortrekkers 26–27, 58
Vryheid **134**, **153**, **162**, **165**, **167**, **169**, **173**, **178**

W

Wagon Hill *see* Platrand
Walmsley's daughter 41
Warren, General Sir Charles
    Faberspur 282–283
    Spioenkop 81–91
    Tugela Heights 99–105
Waterboer, Andries (Lattakoo) 285
weapons of Zulu army *52*
Weilbach, Commandant Johan (Driefontein) 249–250
West Australia Hill 298–300
Western Cape *see* Cape Town region
White, General Sir George
    Ladysmith 112–117
    Platrand 107–111
    Rietfontein 118–119
Williams, Major General George (Groenkop) 129–131
Willowgrange 60–65
Willshire, Lieutenant Colonel Thomas (Grahamstown) 319–321
Winterton **69**
Wood, Colonel Evelyn (Hlobane) 169–172
Wood, General Evelyn (Khambula) 173–177
Wynberg **326**

X

Xhosa 289, 314–315, 319–321

Z

Zaailaager 28–30
Zibhebhu, Chief (Tshaneni) 56–57
Zuid-Arikaansche Republiek Politie (ZARP) 206–207, 268–273 *see also* Johannesburg Police
Zulu army weapons *52*
Zwartkoppies *see* Swartkoppies

Military history titles published by Random House Struik (Zebra Press)

Troepie, From Call-Up to Camps	Cameron Blake	9781770220515
Troepie, Van Blougat tot Bosoupa	Cameron Blake	9781770220546
From Soldier to Civvy: Reflections on National Service	Cameron Blake	9781770221345
Zulu Zulu Golf: Life and Death with Koevoet	Arn Durand	9781770221482
Zulu Zulu Foxtrot: To Hell and Back with Koevoet	Arn Durand	9781770224346
Days of the Generals: The Untold Story of South Africa's Apartheid-era Military Generals	Hilton Hamann	9781868723409
32 Battalion: The Inside Story of South Africa's Elite Fighting Unit	Piet Nortje	9781868729142
The Terrible Ones: A Complete History of 32 Battalion	Piet Nortje	9781770223974
Dingo Firestorm: The Greatest Battle of the Rhodesian Bush War	Ian Pringle	9781770224285
Angels of Mercy: Foreign Women in the Anglo-Boer War	Chris Schoeman	9781770224995
Engele in die Vreemde: Buitelandse Vroue in die Anglo-Boereoorlog	Chris Schoeman	9781770225022
Boer Boy: Memoirs of an Anglo-Boer War Youth	Chris Schoeman	9781770221383
Boerseun: Memoires van 'n Anglo-Boereoorlogseun	Chris Schoeman	9781770221437
Brothers in Arms: Hollanders in the Anglo-Boer War	Chris Schoeman	9781770223400
Broers in die Stryd: Hollanders in die Anglo-Boereoorlog	Chris Schoeman	9781770223417
Churchill's South Africa: Travels During the Anglo-Boer War	Chris Schoeman	9781920545475
An Unpopular War: From Afkak to Bosbefok	J. H. Thompson	9781770073012
Dit Was Oorlog: Van Afkak tot Bosbefok	J. H. Thompson	9781770220096
Memories at Low Altitude: Memoirs of a Mozambican Security Chief	Jacinto Veloso	9781770221505

Join our military history mailing list at
www.randomstruik.co.za/militaryhistory to receive information about new releases, special offers, launches, author events and competitions.